Food Tourism Around the World: Development, Management and Markets

Food Tourism Around the World: Development, Management and Markets

A.R. Chauhan

RANDOM

RANDOM PUBLICATIONS

NEW DELHI (INDIA)

Food Tourism Around the World:
Development, Management and Markets

ISBN 978-93-5111-329-4

Published in 2014 in India by

RANDOM PUBLICATIONS

4376-A/4B, Gali Murari Lal, Ansari Road
New Delhi-110 002
Phone : +91-11-43580356, +91-11-23289044
e-mail: randomexports@gmail.com, sales@randompublications.com, info@randompublications.com

Type Setting by : Keystoneprintads, Delhi-110051
Printed at : Printed at Thomson Press (India) Ltd

Preface

Food is any substance consumed to provide nutritional support for the body. It is usually of plant or animal origin, and contains essential nutrients, such as carbohydrates, fats, proteins, vitamins, or minerals. The substance is ingested by an organism and assimilated by the organism's cells in an effort to produce energy, maintain life, or stimulate growth. Historically, people secured food through two methods: hunting and gathering, and agriculture. Today, most of the food energy consumed by the world population is supplied by the food industry.

Food tourism is experiencing the food of the country, region, or area, and is now considered a vital component of the tourism experience. Dining out is common among tourists and "food is believed to rank alongside climate, accommodation, and scenery" in importance to tourists. Food tourism is defined by the World Food Travel Association (WFTA) as the pursuit of unique and memorable eating and drinking experiences. Food tourism differs from agri-tourism in that food tourism is considered a subset of cultural tourism whereas agritourism is considered a subset of rural tourism, but food tourism and agritourism are inextricably linked, as the seeds of cuisine can be found in agriculture. Food tourism is not limited to gourmet food; the WFTA reports that "gourmet" comprises 8.1% of culinary travelers.

I thank all members of my team who have helped in the preparation of the book. My special thanks go to "Random Publications" who have published the book.

—A.R. Chauhan

Contents

1

The Industry of Food: An Introduction

AN OVERVIEW

The food industry is on a high as Indians continue to have a feast. Fuelled by what can be termed as a perfect ingredient for any industry - large disposable incomes - the food sector has been witnessing a marked change in consumption patterns, especially in terms of food.

CHANGE IN CONSUMPTION PATTERNS

Increasing incomes are always accompanied by a change in the food basket, says an ICRA report, which analyses food expenditure patterns over the last three decades in India. The report observes that the proportionate expenditure on cereals, pulses, edible oil, sugar, salt and spices declines as households climb the expenditure classes in urban India while the opposite happens in the case of milk and milk products, meat, egg and fish, fruits and beverages. For instance, the proportionate expenditure on staples (cereals, grams, pulses) declined from 45 per cent to 44 per cent in rural India while the figure settled at 32 per cent of the total expenditure on food in urban India. A large part of this shift in consumption is driven by the processed food market, which accounts for 32 per cent of the total food market. It accounts for US$ 29.4 billion, in a total estimated market of US$ 91.66 billion.

The food processing industry is one of the largest industries in India — it is ranked fifth in terms of production, consumption, export and expected growth. The Confederation of Indian Industry (CII) has estimated that the food processing sector has the potential of attracting US$ 33 billion of investment in 10 years and generate employment of 9 million person-days.

Policy Initiatives

The Government has formulated and implemented several schemes to provide financial assistance for setting up and modernising of food processing units, creation of infrastructure, support for research and development and human resource development in addition to other promotional measures to encourage the growth of the processed food sector.

- The Centre has permitted under the Income Tax Act a deduction of 100 per cent of profit for five years and 25 per cent of profit in the next five years in case of new agro processing industries set up to package and preserve fruits and vegetables.
- Excise Duty of 16 per cent on dairy machinery has been fully waived off and excise duty on meat, poultry and fish products has been reduced from 16 per cent to 8 per cent.
- Most of the processed food items have been exempted from the purview of licensing under the Industries (Development and regulation) Act, 1951, except items reserved for small-scale sector and alcoholic beverages.
- Food processing industries were included in the list of priority sector for bank lending in 1999.
- Automatic approval for foreign equity up to 100 per cent is available for most of the processed food items except alcohol, beer and those reserved for small-scale sector subject to certain conditions.

Foreign Direct Investment

- Foreign direct investment (FDI) in the country's food sector is poised to hit the US$ 3-billion mark. In the last one year alone, FDI approvals in food processing have doubled.
- The cumulative FDI inflow in food processing reached US$ 2,804 million in March '06. In '05-06, the sector received approvals worth US$ 41 million. This figure is almost double the US$ 22 million approved in '04-05.

Ready-to-eat food

The popularity of ready-to-eat packs and the bottomlines of eateries have a story to tell. Eating out no longer marks a special occasion. Not only does the traditional eat-at-home type prefer to eat out, he is very demanding too. He wants value for his money in terms of quality and variety. No wonder, multi-cuisine restaurants are mushrooming even in small towns. Italian, Mexican, Lebanese, Japanese, Cajun – the list is growing.

Corroborating this trend, Euromonitor International, a market research company, says the amount of money Indians spend on meals outside the home has more than doubled in the past decade, to about US$ 5 billion a year and is expected to double again in about half that time. The industry is estimated to grow at 9-12 per cent, on the basis of an estimated GDP growth rate of 6-8 per cent, during the tenth five-year plan period.

Value addition of food products is expected to increase from the current 8 per cent to 35 per cent by the end of 2025. Fruit and vegetable processing, which is currently around 2 per cent of total production will increase to 10 per cent by 2010 and to 25 per cent by 2025. The popularity of food and agro products is not surprising when the sector is now offering a growth of more than 150 per cent in sales. With such promise in the sector, a number of foreign companies have joined the fray. While US brands such as McDonald's, Pizza Hut and Kentucky Fried Chicken have become household names, more are on their way. The new wave in the food industry is not only about foreign companies arriving here attracted by the prospective size of the market.

It is also about the migration of the Made in India tag on food products travelling abroad. Indian food brands and fast moving consumer goods (FMCGs) are now increasingly finding prime shelf-space in the retail chains of the US and Europe. These include Cobra Beer, Bikanervala Foods, MTR Foods' ready-to-eat food stuff, ITC's Kitchen of India and Satnam Overseas' Basmati rice.

FOOD SCIENCE

Food science is a discipline concerned with all technical aspects of food, beginning with harvesting or slaughtering, and ending with its cooking and consumption. It is considered one of the agricultural sciences, and is usually considered distinct from the field of nutrition. Examples of the activities of food scientists include the development of new food products, design of processes to produce these foods, choice of packaging materials, shelf-life studies, sensory evaluation of the product with trained expert panels or potential consumers, as well as microbiological and chemical testing.

Food scientists at universities may study more fundamental phenomena that are directly linked to the production of particular food product and its properties. In the U.S., food science is typically studied at land-grant universities. Food science is a highly interdisciplinary applied science. It incorporates concepts from many different fields including microbiology, chemical engineering, biochemistry, and many others.

FOOD PRESERVATION

Food preservation is the process of treating and handling food in such a way as to stop or greatly slow down spoilage to prevent foodborne illness while maintaining nutritional value, texture and flavour.

Preservation Processes

Preservation usually involves preventing the growth of bacteria, fungi and other micro-organisms, as well as retarding the oxidation of fats which cause rancidity. It also includes processes to inhibit natural aging and discolouration that can occur during food preparation such as the polyphenoloxidase reaction in apples which causes browning when apples are cut. Some preservation methods require the food to be sealed after treatment to prevent re-contamination with microbes; others, such as drying, allow food to be stored without any special containment for long periods.

- Preservation processes include:
- Heating to kill or denature organisms (e.g. boiling)

- Oxidation (e.g. use of sulphur dioxide)
- Toxic inhibition (e.g. smoking, use of carbon dioxide, vinegar, alcohol etc.)
- Dehydration (drying)

Osmotic Inhibition (e.g. use of Syrups)

Low temperature inactivation (e.g. freezing)

Many Combinations of these Methods

- *Chelation:* Common methods of applying these processes include drying, freeze drying, freezing, vacuum-packing, canning, preserving in syrup, sugar crystalisation, food irradiation, adding preservatives or inert gases such as carbon dioxide. Other methods that not only help to preserve food, but also add flavour, include pickling, salting, smoking, preserving in syrup or alcohol, sugar crystalisation and curing.
- *Drying:* One of the oldest methods of food preservation is by drying, which reduces water activity sufficient to delay or prevent bacterial growth. Most types of meat can be dried and this is especially valuable in the case of pig meat since this is difficult to keep without preservation. Many fruits can also be dried and the process is often applied to apples, pears, bananas, mangos, papaya, coconut etc. Currants, sultanas and raisins are all forms of dried Grapes. Drying is also the normal means of preservation for cereal grains such as wheat, maize, oats, barley, rice, millet and rye.
- *Freezing:* Probably as old as drying, many Arctic communities would preserve food in holes or larders dug into the ice. There is a tradition in Scandinavia of preserving fish and especially herrings in this way.
- Freezing is also one of the most commonly used processes commercially and domestically for preserving a very wide range of food stuffs including prepared food stuffs which would not have required freezing in their unprepared state. For example, potato waffles are stored in the freezer, but potatoes themselves require only a cool dark place to ensure many months' storage. Cold stores provide large volume, long-term storage for strategic food stocks held in case of national emergency in many countries.
- *Vacuum Packing:* Vacuum-packing stores food in a vacuum environment, usually in an air-tight bag or bottle. The vacuum environment strips bacteria of oxygen needed for survival, hence preventing the food from spoiling. Vacuum-packing is commonly used for storing nuts.
- *Curing:* Curing draws moisture from the meat through a process of osmosis. Meat is cured with salt or sugar, or a combination of the two. Nitrates and nitrites are also often used to cure meat.

- *Sugar:* Sugar is used to preserve fruits, either in syrup with fruit such as apples, pears, peaches, apricots, plums or in crystalised form where the preserved material is cooked in sugar to the point of crystralisation and the resultant product is then stored dry. This method is used for the skins of citrus fruit (candied peel), angelica and ginger. A modification of this process produces glacé fruit such as glacé cherries where the fruit is preserved in sugar but is then extracted from the syrup and sold, the preservation being maintained by the sugar content of the fruit and the superficial coating of syrup. The use of sugar is often combined with alcohol for preservation of luxury products such as fruit in brandy or other spirits. These should not be confused with fruit flavoured spirits such as Cherry Brandy or Sloe gin

PICKLING

Pickling is a method of preserving food by placing it or cooking it in a substance that inhibits or kills bacteria and other micro-organisms, This material must also be fit for human consumption. Typical pickling agents include brine (high in salt), vinegar, ethanol, and vegetable oil, especially olive oil but also many other oils. Most pickling processes also involve heating or boiling so that the food being preserved becomes saturated with the pickling agent.

Frequently pickled items include vegetables such as cabbage (to make sauerkraut and curtido), peppers, and some animal products such as corned beef and eggs. A less-common form of pickling uses sodium hydroxide (lye) to make the food too alkaline for bacterial growth. Lye will saponify fats in the food, which will change its flavour and texture. Lutefisk and hominy use lye in their preparation, as do some olive recipes.

Canning

Canning is a method of preserving food by first heating it to a temperature that destroys contaminating microorganisms, and then sealing it in air-tight jars, cans or pouches. Because of the danger of botulism and other pathogens, the only safe method of canning most foods is under conditions of both high heat and pressure, normally at temperatures of 240-250°F (116-121°C).

Foods that must be pressure canned include most vegetables, meats, seafood, poultry, and dairy products. The only foods that may be safely canned in a boiling water bath (without high pressure) are highly acidic foods with a pH below 4.6, such as fruits, pickled vegetables, or other foods to which acid has been added.

Bottling

During the early Revolutionary Wars, the notable French newspaper *Monde,* prompted by the government, offered a hefty cash award of 12,000 Francs to any inventor who could come up with a cheap and effective method of preserving large amounts of food. The massive armies of the period required regular supplies of quality food, and so preservation became a necessity. In 1809, the French confectioner Nicolas François Appert developed a method of vacuum-sealing food inside glass jars. However, glass containers were unsuitable for transportation.

Tinning

Glass jars were replaced with cylindrical tin or steel cans. Tin-openers were not to be invented for another thirty years — at first, soldiers had to cut the cans open with bayonets. The French Army began experimenting with issuing tinned foods to its soldiers, but the slow process of tinning foods and the even slower development stage prevented the army from shipping large amounts around the Empire, and the war ended before the process could be perfected. Unfortunately for Appert, the factory which he had built with his prize money was burned down in 1814 by Allied soldiers invading France. Following the end of the Napoleonic Wars, the process was gradually put into practice in other European countries and in the United States.

Based on Appert's methods of food preservation the packaging of food in sealed airtight tin-plated wrought-iron cans was first patented by an Englishman, Peter Durand, in 1810. Initially, the canning process was slow and labour-intensive, making the tinned food too expensive for ordinary people to buy.

However, increasing mechanisation of the process, coupled with a huge increase in urban populations across Europe, resulted in a rising demand for tinned food. Early methods employed poisonous lead solder for sealing the tins, which had disastrous consequences for the 1845 Franklin expedition to the Arctic ocean.

A number of inventions and improvements followed, and by the 1860s, the time to process food in a can reduced from six hours to 30 minutes. Thomas Kensett established the first U.S. cannery for oysters, meats, fruits and vegetables in New York in 1812 and also patented an improved tin canister method. Urban populations in Victorian era Britain demanded ever-increasing quantities of cheap, varied, good-quality food that they could keep on the shelves at home without having to go to the shops every day for fresh produce. In response, companies such as Nestlé, Heinz, and others emerged to provide shops with good-quality tinned food for sale to ordinary working class city-dwellers.

Demand for tinned food skyrocketed during the First World War, as military commanders searched for cheap, high-calorie food which could be transported safely, would survive trench conditions, and which would not spoil in between the factory and the front lines. Complete meals in a tin appeared in 1916, but throughout the war soldiers generally subsisted on very low-quality tinned foodstuffs, such as the British "Bully Beef" (cheap corned beef) and Pork and Beans produced by the MacConnaughy Corporation.

Shortages of tinned food in the British Army in 1917 led to the government issuing soldiers with cigarettes and even amphetamines to suppress their appetites. After the war, companies that had supplied tinned food to national militaries improved the quality of their goods for sale on the civilian market. Canned foods were soon commonplace, and today tin-coated steel is the material most commonly used. Some food firms are currently dabbling with self-heating cans. Laminate vacuum pouches are also now used for canning, such as those found in an MRE.

JELLYING

Food may be preserved by cooking in a material that solidifies to form a gel. Such materials include gelatine, agar, maize flour and arrowroot flour. Some foods naturally form a protein gel when cooked such as eels and elvers, and sipunculid worms which are a delicacy in the town of Xiamen in Fujian province of China. Jellied eels are a delicacy in the East End of London where they are eaten with mashed potatoes. Potted meats in aspic, (the gel made from arrowroot flour) were a common way of serving meat off-cuts in the UK until the 1950s

Irradiation

A 1950s issue of Popular Mechanics details the impending arrival of "food irradiation". But the implications of irradiation are not fully understood, and the use of the technology is limited. Irradiation of potatoes, strawberries, and meat is common in many countries where refrigerated facilities and trucks are not. In 2002, the FDA permitted irradiation of meat and poultry to reduce the spread of E. coli and salmonella.

In the US and most of Europe, irradiation of spices is common, as the only alternative (treatment with gas) is potentially carcinogenic. The process is called "cold pasteurization" because it is feared that the label "irradiation" would hurt sales. Foods may also carry labels saying "Picowaved For Your Protection" as food processors may not want to openly label their foods as being irradiated.

MODIFIED ATMOSPHERE

Modified atmosphere is a way to preserve food operating on the atmosphere around it. Salad crops which are notoriously difficult to preserve are now being packaged in sealed bags with an atmosphere modified to reduce the oxygen concentration and increase the carbon dioxide concentration. There is concern that although salad vegetables retain their appearance and texture in such conditions, this method of preservation may not retain nutrients, especially vitamins.

Grains may be preserved using carbon dioxide. A block of dry ice is placed in the bottom and the can is filled with grain. The can is then "burped" of excess gas. The carbon dioxide from the sublimation of the dry ice prevents insects, mold, and oxidation from damaging the grain. Grain stored in this way can remain edible for five years.

CLAMPS

Many root vegetables are very resistant to spoilage and require no other preservation other than storage in cool dark conditions, usually in field clamps. Some foods, such as many traditional cheeses, will keep for a long time without use of any special procedures. The preservation occurs because of the presence in very high numbers of beneficial bacteria or fungi which use their own biological defences to prevent other organisms gaining a foot-hold.

FOOD PARKS

In a bid to boost the food sector, the Government is working on agrizones and the concept of mega food parks. Twenty such mega parks will come up across the country in various cities to attract Foreign Direct Investment (FDI) in the food processing sector.

The Government has released a total assistance of US$ 23 million to implement the Food Parks Scheme. It has so far approved 50 food parks for assistance across the country. The Centre also plans US$ 22 billion subsidy for mega food processing parks.

FOOD PRESERVATION TECHNIQUE

Preserving food to extend its shelf-life, whilst ensuring its safety and quality, is a central preoccupation of the food industry. As a result, there has been a steady stream of new 'minimal' preservation techniques. At the same time, the development of the hurdle concept has led to renewed interest in the use of more traditional preservation methods and the ways they can be combined with newer technologies. With its distinguished editors and international team of contributors, Food preservation techniques provides an authoritative review of these developments and the ways they can be combined to preserve particular foods.

- *Part 1:* begins by looking at the emergence of a new generation of natural preservatives in response to consumer concerns about synthetic additives. There are chapters on natural antimicrobials, bacteriocins, natural antimicrobials, antimicrobial enzymes and edible coatings, together with a discussion of how natural antimicrobial systems can be combined with other technologies.
- *Part 2:* considers current research on the application of traditional preservation techniques. There are chapters on the control of pH and water activity to prevent microbial growth, and developments in heat treatment and freezing. These are complemented by discussion of how these techniques can be combined with each other and newer technologies to extend shelf-life without compromising safety or quality.

- *Part 3:* covers these newer technologies. It includes chapters on the use of biotechnology, developments in membrane filtration, high intensity light, ultrasound, modified atmosphere packaging, pulsed electric fields and high hydrostatic pressure.
- *Part 4:* considers the challenges in combining these techniques in a way that preserves sensory quality without compromising product safety. There are chapters on key issues such as modelling spoilage and the effectiveness of preservation techniques, the increasingly important problem of microbial resistance to the use of milder preservation methods, and setting safety criteria to account for such problems.

Food preservation techniques will be a standard reference in helping food processors extend shelf-life whilst maximising food safety and quality.

FOOD AND LIVESTOCK TREACHEBILITY

Recent devastating outbreaks such as foot and mouth disease, mad cow disease and avian flu plus contamination recalls and bioterrorism are driving strict new legislation on food traceability. In addition, consumers are also demanding more information about the food they consume (as do the police and customs).

This report analyses the need for RFID, DNA and other technologies to enable food traceability. Ten year forecasts, case studies and technology evaluations provide a complete analysis on the topic in this 250 page market intelligence report researched globally by our experts.

Traceability has become a buzzword in the food industry. Consumer demands for higher-quality foods and more variety have never been greater. Spurred on by recent food scares around the world, such as mad cow disease and bioterrorism fears, governments are forcing the adoption of food traceability systems. Everyone from producer to retailer will be affected by food traceability. This state-of-the-art review deals with the key topics of traceability - technology, law, forecasts and case studies. A must read for anyone involved in the food industry.

Although tens of millions of RFID tags have been applied to livestock and food and millions of biometric procedures have been carried out, there is no analysis of the global situation and the lessons of success and failure. The potential for RFID tagging of livestock is billions yearly and the potential for radio tagging of food is in trillions a year, but what are the forecasts for such tagging at animal, pallet/case and item level for the next ten years? Which countries are in the lead and where will the next wave of technologies, laws and mandates be applied? These and other vital questions are answered for the first time in this major new report.

This industry is on the move in a major way. It includes market pull, with McDonald's the world's largest outlet for cooked meat recently mandating full traceability from suppliers and Wal-Mart, the world's largest retailer, mandating RFID on all incoming pallets and cases. This is a prelude to tagging everything. It has legal push with the new European Union legislation in 2005 demanding "one up one down" traceability and the US Homeland Security legislation demanding unprecedented levels of traceability. China and Japan are also in the lead, and they have their own concerns. For example, Japan is convicting criminals that pass off inferior foreign fish as coming from Japanese waters.

Billion dollar businesses will be created as a consequence - much the same as happened with barcodes years ago. We believe that by 2015 900 billion food items could be RFID tagged, and 824 million livestock will have more sophisticated, more expensive tags on or in them. However, new technologies, now being developed, will be needed for the food items. The livestock figure could easily be doubled if chickens are tagged, something of vital interest to the Government of Thailand, which ships 400 million chicken carcasses yearly and could have its whole industry wiped out by the new, virulent avian flu. The safety of poultry meat and eggs continues to be a major concern for consumers. As a result, there has been a wealth of research on identifying and controlling hazards at all stages in the supply chain. "Food Safety Control in the Poultry Industry" summarises this research and its implications for all those involved in supplying and marketing poultry products. With its distinguished editor and international team of contributors, "Food Safety Control in the Poultry Industry" will be a standard reference for both academics and food companies.

RUSSIAN FOOD PRODUCTION

Russia's food production is forecast to grow across the board over the next couple of years thanks to better buying power and import regulations, according to a government report. The Russian Ministry of Economic Development predicted domestic food production will have more than doubled by 2008, compared with levels in 2004.

Russia's food industry is already the country's biggest sector outside of heavy industry, including energy and steel. Some of the fastest development is expected in the dairy industry, thanks to the government's predicted rise in raw milk stocks and both domestic and foreign investment in cheese. Cheese market growth, currently around eight per cent per year, is forecast to slow to around five per cent by 2008. Imports should remain strong in the premium segment for the time being, the government said.

Meat and animal fat production are other areas forecast for good growth. The government expects there to be double-digit rises in meat production annually up to 2008, while manufacture of fish products, including fish preservatives, is expected to double. Sceptics argue that Russia has been playing with protectionism via import bans. It has banned various food products, including most recently fresh fish from Norway and dairy and meat from Ukraine, on food safety grounds.

The Russian government has said it wants average meat consumption to reach 70kg per person in Russia, and is actively promoting domestic producers to help achieve this. Current consumption is around 50-55kg. One of Russia's biggest meat import firms, Euroservice, will begin building ten new meat processing factories for Russian meat this year to help satisfy consumers' growing demand for meat, and especially sausage. The short-term results of Russia's import bans may be price increases on the market, however.

The United States Department of Agriculture's Foreign Agricultural Service said between January and October 2005 Russia imported €165m worth of fresh salmon from Norway. Russian fish processors, it claimed, now feared chilled salmon would quickly disappear from the shelves, causing a potential increase in frozen fish prices of 20-30 per cent.

UK FOOD REGULATOR

Food fraud can result in processors receiving illegally sourced meat that may be of low quality or even unfit for human consumption, posing a health risk for consumers and a business problem for manufacturers. Such trade cuts into the sales of legitimate food producers by placing cheaper products on the market.

Adulterated butter, buffalo meat declared as beef, tigernuts imported as flower bulbs are some of the products that have been stopped at the EU's borders.

A task force on the issue was set up by the Food Standards Agency (FSA) board in April 2006 to initially concentrate on red and white meat fraud, but it will consider other food sector problems later in the process of making recommendations for action. The group of experts were also asked to propose sufficient legal deterrents to make it less attractive for individuals and companies to engage in food fraud.

The food fraud task force (FFTF) was launched in the wake of the FSA investigation into Euro Freeze, a Northern Ireland cold store operation that allegedly was involved in the illicit repackaging, re-labelling and distribution of meat throughout the EU. In August this year, a UK court condemned the meat from Euro Freeze as having illegal health labelling and ordered the destruction of 254 pallets.

In the first of three planned reports to the board, to be presented at the meeting on 7 December, the task force said it has not discovered to date any issues that need early action and at this time it has no recommendations.

- "At this stage in their deliberations, the Food Fraud Task Force are of the opinion that the current measures for tackling food fraud are largely adequate but may be augmented by recommendations taking into account the findings contained within this chapter," the report stated.

And as the Euro-Freeze case is still before the courts, the task force has not had the full details for detailed consideration.

- " However it is hoped that before the final report of the FFTF is made in October 2007, the details will be accessible and any lessons learned from this event can be considered and commented on," the unit's first report stated as released ahead of the board meeting.

However members have identified some areas for further consideration by the board, including the problem of the possible re-use of health markings.

The FFTF says its recognises that the movement of meat and poultry no longer intended for human consumption may occur in the same premises as those used for foods. Such a situation may occur when products materials become outdated.

- "In order to prevent any possible confusion and the possibility of food moving back to human food areas, it is suggested that once moved into animal by-product areas, all food containers should have their identification marks defaced or destroyed in order to prevent any re-use of the material or containers for human food," the report stated.

In an update for an FSA board meeting on 12 October, the task force recommended that current legislation and traceability procedures need to be reviewed. The task force has also said it would consider the current controls in place to deal with food fraud and their, suitability to control and deter food fraud. The review includes a review of health marking requirements. The task force will also review inspection and audit arrangements for meat plants particularly cold stores.

It will also consider whether inspections should be made more frequent so as to assess food fraud risk. It will also review of the roles and effectiveness of the Illegal Meat Task Force, the food fraud data base and the FSA's local authorities. Laws relating to the prosecution and penalties will also be reviewed to see whether they act as a sufficient deterrent to food fraud. The members of the task force include those representing regulators, government agencies, the British Retail Consortium, the British Poultry Council, the Food and Drink Federation, consumer group Which?, and the Dungannon Meats Group.

EU laws on traceability that entered into force on 1 January 2005. The laws harmonises the bloc's requirements on the traceability of food products, the withdrawal of dangerous products from the market, operator responsibilities and requirements applicable to imports and exports. The new mandatory traceability requirement applies to all food, animal feed, food-producing animals and all types of food chain operators from the farming sector to processing, transport, storage, distribution and retail to the consumer.

All information on the name, address of producer, nature of products and date of transaction must be systematically registered within each operator's traceability system. The law requires the information to be kept for a period of five years and on request, it must immediately be made available to regulators. EU customs seized around 75 million counterfeit articles in 2005. Growth in seizures of fakes dangerous to health and safety also continued. For the first time, the number counterfeit foodstuff, drinks and alcohol products seized at the borders surpassed the five million market.

FOOD IN AMERICA

It was not the last time cannibalism would be resorted to in America. Later Virginians wanted to grow a profitable crop; they tried sugar but the climate was too cold. They settled on tobacco. Soon tobacco was bringing in so much money that people planted it on any available land—they ripped up their gardens, even grew it between graves. But who would hoe and harvest these thousands of acres of tobacco? The Native Americans who didn't die of Old World diseases refused to do it. African slaves were too expensive, although some arrived in 1619. England had the perfect Labour force: a surplus of poor, desperate young men in their late teens and early twenties. They signed an indenture— a contract—giving them a free trip to America and free room and board in exchange for four to six years of work.

Then they were supposed to get their freedom, tools, corn, and land of their own—something they had zero chance of getting in England. The person who hired the indentured servant and paid for his trip received free Labour and fifty acres of land. It was a sweetheart deal all around. Most of these young men didn't live four years after they got to America. They died from dysentery, typhoid, malaria. The ones who did live found that there was only one woman for every six men. And soon the best land was in huge plantations owned by a few wealthy men who also had all the political power.

In 1676, when former indentured servants couldn't get land, women, or the vote, they went on a rampage. Bacon's Rebellion ended with Jamestown burned and more than 20 former indentured servants hanged. Planters wanted a Labour force they could control, not these Englishmen who used violence to get their rights. In 1698, when England ended the Royal African Company's monopoly on the slave trade, anyone with a ship could get into the slave trade. With competition, the price of slaves dropped. Now it was affordable to own Africans and profitable to sell them.

THE CAROLINAS AND RICE

At about the same time, the English established a colony south of Virginia—Carolina, named after King Charles II. Many of the settlers were from Barbados. They intended to grow food for the Caribbean sugar plantations and to export more expensive items, but after failing at wine, olive oil, and silk, they decided on rice as their staple crop. Rice requires skilled Labour; Africans had this skill. They were also immune to malaria, and weren't Christian, so according to the Christian world at that time, they could be enslaved for the rest of their lives. The settlers also imported the Barbados slave code, with punishments that escalated from whipping to facial mutilation and sometimes death, which the code said was the slave's fault for forcing his master to discipline him. Charleston, South Carolina, became the primary port through which slaves entered the United States. By 1710, black slaves outnumbered white settlers in the coastal regions of the area that became South Carolina.

In spite of the conditions under which the slaves were brought to America, some of their African cuisine and culture survived. This influenced how cooking developed in the American South, since they were the cooks. Along with their knowledge of rice cultivation, cooking, and storage, they brought yams, okra, watermelon, and their love of fried food. They also brought back foodstuffs that had been taken from the New World to Africa, like the chile pepper and the peanut, and their word for it—*goober.*

They brought the banjo and the drum and the music that would become jazz. New England:" Almost Beyond Believing" In 1620, Pilgrims—Protestants who wanted to be allowed to worship without being persecuted—landed at Plymouth, Massachusetts. Before they went ashore, the men on the ship entered into an agreement. The Mayflower Compact was the first constitution in America. Only one paragraph long, it sets forth an important principle: that all would be equal and work together as a community. The Pilgrims, and the Puritans who settled the Massachusetts Bay Colony in Boston ten years later, had their work cut out for them.

These were people used to living in towns. They didn't know how to hunt or fish or farm. But they didn't like many of the strange plants and animals in North America anyway—those huge quahog clams, the slimy steamers. And the codfish and lobsters were bigger than they were, sometimes six feet long. They wouldn't eat them at first, even after the Indians showed them how. But with the help of the native tribes, the Pilgrims survived their first year and had a celebration. Thanksgiving Foods "The turkey is certainly one of the most delightful presents which the New World has made to the Old." Most of the foods Americans eat at Thanks giving dinner now are native to the Americas: turkey, cranberry sauce, mashed potatoes, sweet potatoes, corn-bread stuffing, pumpkin pie. In French the word for turkey is *dinde,* short for *poulet d'inde,* which means "chicken from India," because the French, like other Europeans, thought the turkey was from the Indies. Geese, ducks, and other wild fowl were abundant only during certain seasons in the New World, but turkeys don't migrate, so they were available all year. And they had an instinct that helped humans: when one turkey was shot, the others froze in place. It was easy to kill a dozen turkeys in a morning. Nobody ever called anybody a turkey and meant it as a compliment.

Cranberries and blueberries, both members of the heather family and both native to New England, were more than food in sauce and pies. Mashed and mixed with sour milk, they were used as paint. That is why the colours most often associated with colonial American buildings are muted cranberry and milky purple-gray. Although pumpkin was widely used in the colonies, recipes for pumpkin pie didn't appear in print until the first American cookbook, written by Amelia Simmons in 1796. She called it "pompkin" and gave two different versions. Both had pumpkin, ginger, and eggs, but one used cream and sugar, the other milk and molasses. One used the Old World spices mace and nutmeg, the other New World allspice.

THE CODFISH

The staple "crop" in the Massachusetts Bay Colony was the codfish, *Gadus morhua.* What sugar was to the Caribbean and tobacco was to the FOOD FABLE c SQUANTO AND FISH FERTILIZERC Contrary to what American myth has long held, it is quite unlikely that alewives or other fish were uses as fertilizer in Indian fields, notwithstanding the legendary role of the Pilgrims' friend Squanto in teaching colonists this practice. Squanto probably learned the technique while being held captive in Europe, and if any Indians used it in New England, they did so in an extremely limited area. Having no easy way to transport large amounts of fish from river to field, and preferring quite sensibly to avoid such back-breaking work, Indians simply abandoned their fields when the soil lost its fertility. Fertilizing fields with fish, as the English eventually did, seemed to Indians a wholly unnecessary labour.

CHESAPEAKE, COD WAS TO MASSACHUSETTS

There were millions off the coast, north to Newfoundland and Labrador. Once it was salted and dried, cod was stiff as a board and could be stacked and shipped like lumber. It was also almost 80 per cent protein. In this form it made its way to Europe: *bacalà* in Italy, *bacalao* in Spain, *bacalhau* in Portugal. According to historian Mark Kurlansky, by the middle of the 16th century, "60 per cent of all fish eaten in Europe was cod." It was the perfect food for Lent. The best grade was sent to Spain; the worst fed the slaves in the West Indies. It could also be bartered for slaves in Africa. Shipbuilders got rich because of cod, too. The cod was so important to the economy of Massachusetts that a large carved wooden cod hangs in the statehouse in Boston. Fifty-one Pilgrim men, women, and children hosted ninety men of the Wampanoag tribe and their chief, Massasoit. It was in the fall, to celebrate the good harvest of corn (wheat and barley weren't as successful).

The celebration lasted three days. There were "wild fowl" and five deer. The idea of a national day of thanks was raised in the late 1700s with the first president, George Washington, who proposed November 26 as the date. Nothing came of it until the 1850s, when magazine journalist Sarah Josepha Hale rallied the women of America to pressure the president for a national holiday. In 1863, the third year of the Civil War, President Lincoln declared that the last Thursday in November should be a day of giving thanks. It was the same year that Lincoln issued the Emancipation Proclamation freeing the slaves, and made his speech at the battlefield in Gettysburg, Pennsylvania, in which he said these famous words: "that government of the people, by the people, for the people, shall not perish from the earth."

In 1939, President Franklin D. Roosevelt wanted to extend the Christmas shopping season to give the economy a boost and help it recover from the depression. He moved Thanksgiving one week earlier. Congress objected. The president and Congress did a tug-of-war over the date until 1941, when it was settled: Thanksgiving is the fourth Thursday in November. In 1970, Wampanoag leader Wampsutta (Anglo name: Frank James) was invited to speak at the Thanksgiving celebration at Plymouth, Massachusetts. When word got out that his speech was about the oppression of Native Americans, the invitation was revoked. He gave his speech anyway, in front of the statue of Massasoit, overlooking the replica of the *Mayflower*. That was the first Native American National Day of Mourning for the culture, the religion, and the lives and lands of their ancestors. Maple Syrup: Tapping the Sap of the Sugar Tree "Maple Moon" was what Native Americans called the time in the spring when the sap started to flow in the sugar maple tree, *Acer saccharum*.

Just as the grapevine was a symbol of resurrection for the ancient Greeks, so the maple was for Native Americans. Flowing sap meant the end of winter and the rebirth of nature. The Iroquois performed a religious ritual, a maple dance, to pray for warm weather and plenty of sap. According to legend, an Iroquois chief pulled his tomahawk out of a tree where he had thrown it the night before and went off to hunt. In the meantime, the weather turned warm and sap oozed into a container left by accident at the base of the tree.

On her way to get water for cooking, his wife saw the container of liquid and used that instead; everyone agreed it was much better than water. Seventeenth-century European writers give Native Americans full credit for knowing how to make maple syrup and sugar, but in the 18th century, Europeans started to claim that they taught the Indians. As historians Helen and Scott Nearing have pointed out, language is on the side of the tribes. All their words for maple syrup translate as "drawn from wood," "sap flows fast," "our own tree," while they called white sugar "French snow"—a clear indication of its origin.

Maple sugar was a primary food in Native American cooking; among some tribes it was the only condiment. It replaced salt, which they did not like, and it was used to season dried cornmeal porridge, mixed with bear fat as a sauce for roasted venison, sprinkled on boiled fish, and eaten with berries or all by itself, a pound a day. It was reconstituted into a sweet drink that was used in ceremonies, along with tobacco smoked in the peace pipe. Women boiled the sap from maple, walnut, hickory, box elder, butternut, birch, and sycamore trees down to sugar crystals, which was difficult because before Europeans came, they had no metal pots.

Their vessels were made of birch bark or gourds which held between one and two gallons and could not be placed directly over fire. Instead, they dropped heated stones into the liquid until it boiled, which involved continuously taking out cool stones and replacing them with hot ones. These small amounts of liquid were then poured into hundred-gallon moose-skin vats.

It is not surprising that the Indians began to trade for metal pots and utensils as soon as the Europeans introduced them. Another way to process the syrup was to let it freeze at night, then scrape the ice off the top. This required several nights until just syrup was left. Maple sugar that was to be used for gifts was poured into molds that one European described as shaped like "bear's paws, flowers, stars, small animals, and other figures, just like our gingerbread-bakers at fairs." The American Culinary Tradition: Pocket Soup and Johnnycake American cooking developed along two parallel lines. In the South, where slave Labour did the kitchen work, cooking could take more time.

Labour-intensive cooking, such as barbecue, could be done by slaves. Barbecue needed a great deal of preparation. Either beef or pork had to be properly butchered and marinated. Then the fire had to reach just the right temperature, and the meat had to be added. The fire had to be carefully watched and the temperature maintained. This required a great deal of Labour. However, pit cooking developed differently in New England, in the form of the clambake. There, a fire was allowed to burn down in a pit; then clams, lobsters, and corn were buried under wet seaweed and left to steam for several hours. No Labour was necessary to prepare the food before or after it was placed in the pit, except to dig it out. American cooking in the North arose from the middle-class necessity of doing a great deal of work as quickly as possible. They invented shortcuts and new ways to preserve foods. Two examples are pocket soup and johnnycake. Travel was not easy in the colonies. Roads were poor or nonexistent, and there was no guarantee that travellers would be able to find food when they needed it. Sailors, too, appreciated a bit of home. Pocket soup, also known as portable soup, was the solution.

This was an early bouillon cube—soup cooked down until it was a condensed gelatinous mass, then cut into small cubes and dried for ten days. Dropped into a cup of water, it reconstituted into soup. Johnnycake or journey cake was a cornmeal cake that would keep without becoming moldy or disintegrating. Another example of New England fast food was hasty pudding, made famous in the song "Yankee Doodle" (and in the name of a Harvard University club).

This was cornmeal—called Indian or "Injun" meal—or rye meal cooked on top of the stove, not baked, so it was ready in half an hour. This is a long time by today's microwave standards, but the baking times for regular cornmeal pudding recipes in *American Cookery* range from one and a half hours to two and a half hours. Sara Josepha Hale's recipes for cornmeal pudding require three to four hours of cooking, even those that are boiled. What makes hasty pudding hasty is that the meal is soaked first and added a bit at a time, and the pudding is boiled and stirred constantly. In this cooking technique, it resembles polenta. Cobbler, Slump, Grunt, Dumpling, Crumble, and Crisp Just as regional cooking developed according to the kind of produce and

Labour available in each area, different areas had different names for the same food.

For example, in most of the country, a cobbler is chopped, sweetened fruit with a sweet biscuit dough baked on top. The exception is New England, where it is called a slump, with the further exception of Cape Cod, where it is called a grunt. Other combinations of fruit and dough are a dumpling, pieces of fruit or a whole fruit, like an apple, wrapped in a pastry square and baked. A crumble is a mixture of flour, butter, sugar, and seasonings like cinnamon and nutmeg crumbled over chopped fruit and then baked.

A crumble is different from a crisp because a crisp has more butter, which makes the topping crisper. The topping on a crisp sometimes includes oats. Brown Betty, Sally Lunn, and Anadama Women, perhaps cooks, have left their names on various foods but not much other information. Brown Betty is a thrifty New England BUONA FORCHETTA'S ANA DAMA BREAD 1 large or 2 small loaves 2 cups water 11D 2 teaspoons salt 1D 2 cup stone-ground yellow cornmeal 3 tablespoons melted unsalted butter or olive oil 1D 4 cup honey or dark molasses 2 tablespoons active dry yeast 1D 2 cup lukewarm water (85º to 95ºF) 5 to 6 cups unbleached bread flour In a large pot, bring the water and salt to a boil over medium-high heat.

With a wire whisk, slowly stir the cornmeal into the water, making sure it does not lump. When it has thickened, remove it from the heat and stir in oil or butter and honey or molasses. Transfer to a large mixing bowl and let cool completely. Dissolve the yeast in the lukewarm water. Stir into the cornmeal mixture. Stir in the flour, a cup or so at a time, mixing well as you go to incorporate it. This will form a firm dough that should not be too dry. When the dough pulls away from the sides of the bowl, stir well a few more times, rub oil on your hands, and transfer the dough to a clean oiled bowl.

Same-day method: Cover the bowl with plastic wrap and let the dough rise in a warm place until doubled in volume, about 1 hour. Proceed with the shaping instructions. *Overnight method:* Cover the bowl and refrigerate overnight. The dough will rise in the refrigerator and acquire flavour from the slower yeast action. Remove the dough 3 hours before shaping and let stand, covered, in a warm place. Proceed with shaping instructions. *To shape into loaves:* Preheat the oven to 500ºF. Oil one seasoned nonstick, ovenproof 9-inch skillet or two 5-inch skillets. Shape the dough into 1 large or 2 small round loaves. Place the loaf or loaves in the oiled pan or pans and let rise for about 40 minutes or until doubled. Brush the tops of the loaves with olive oil, if desired.

TO BAKE LOAVES

Place the bread in the oven and reduce the oven temperature to 400ºF. Bake for about 40 minutes or until nicely browned and loaf sounds hollow when tapped with your finger. Remove the loaf from a pan and cool on a wire rack dessert that layers leftover bread with fruit, usually apples, and is baked. It isn't a bread pudding because it lacks eggs to make the custard binder. Sally Lunn is a very light, yeast-risen egg bread. Anadama is supposedly named after Anna, who kept cooking only one thing— a cornmeal and molasses bread—until her husband finally burst out, "Anna, damn her!" Suzanne Dunaway's Buona Forchetta Bakery in southern California makes an updated version of this bread.

BEER - A GOOD FAMILY DRINK

As food historian John Hull Brown points out in *Early American Beverages,* men, women, and children in colonial America drank alcoholic beverages. Beer, familiar from England, was the earliest drink in the colonies. Women were the brewers; they made beer from nearly anything that grew. They made vegetable beers from corn, tomatoes, potatoes, turnips, pumpkins, and Jerusalem artichokes. They made tree beers from the bark of birch, spruce, and sassafras, and from maple sap. Fruit-based beers were brewed from persimmons, lemons, and raisins.

There were herb beers using wintergreen, and spice beers made of ginger, allspice, and cinnamon. Even flowers became beer: rose beer. There was molasses beer. They made their ale two barrels at a time, from 8 or 9 bushels of malt, 12 pounds of hops, 5 quarts of yeast, and 72 gallons of water. And, of course, just as in ancient Egypt, once they had beer they had leavening for bread, either from the beer itself or from the "leavins"—the dregs. They also distilled "spirituous waters" and cordials using spices from the Middle East like coriander, cardamom, and anise seed, and the stones of apricots, peaches, and cherries. Wine was made from ginger, currants, and cherries, but sweet wines, sack, and Madeira were imported. Later, the Scots-Irish brewed whiskey from corn, barley, or oats.

Colonial Americans drank hard cider distilled from apples, peachy made from peaches, and perry made from pears. The colonists liked to dress up their alcoholic beverages with cream, sugar, eggs, mace, and nutmeg—like eggnog. "Kill-Devil" Rum, Stonewall, Bogus, and Flip Rum, distilled in New England after 1670, was cheap and available.

It was called by a variety of names—rhum, rumbullion, rumbooze— and used in a variety of mixtures: stonewall, which was cider and rum; bogus, which was unsweetened beer and rum; blackstrap, made with molasses and rum; and flip, a popular drink that appears at least as far back as 1690 in New England. Here's one way to make it. Punch, with its five ingredients of tea, arrack, sugar, lemons, and water, arrived from India via the British East India Company. New Englanders added a sixth ingredient, and rum punch was born. Life was good to New Englanders; they could expect to live ten years longer than if they had stayed in old England. But since they attributed their longer life to drinking alcohol, it became difficult to enforce laws restricting its intake.

Life was longer, but food preparation was still difficult and time consuming. Before the modern stove with a cooktop and an oven was invented in the mid-19th century, most cooking was done with the quadriceps, because it involved long hours of squatting to stir foods in front of the open hearth. A stool or rocking chair could be pulled up next to the fire, but it still involved long hours next to open flames, as the picture on the following page shows. On wealthy southern plantations, meats were hung in a separate smokehouse, as the picture on the following page shows.

THE GOLDEN AGE OF THE NETHERLANDS

Between England's colonies in New England and the Chesapeake was the Dutch colony of New Netherland. The Dutch knew that they would have to entice people from other countries to settle New Netherland, because the Dutch people, prosperous and free to practice the religion of their choice, had no reason to leave their own country. The Dutch settlers who did go to New Netherland found oak trees that grew seventy feet high and made logs that burned hot and bright for hours. As in the Netherlands, bread was a staple in New Nether- land, but it was baked at home.

The Netherlands was urbanized, so commercial bakers made bread, but parts of the colony were very sparsely populated, so it was necessary for people to have their own brick ovens built into the wall next to the fireplace. American ingredients like corn and pumpkin found their way into standard Dutch recipes like pancakes. Bread was more than food in the Dutch colony; it was a trade item so much sought after by the Native Americans— especially white breads and sweet cakes—that by 1649 there were laws against making bread to trade with the Indians.

New Netherland was just a small part of a vast Dutch empire. The Dutch replaced the Italians—the Medicis of Florence and the Venetians—as the international bankers, and the world banking center moved to the Netherlands. The Dutch dominated or controlled the world shipping trade in spices, sugar, coffee, slaves, precious gems, and grain. The Dutch fleet of 10,000 ships also delivered oil, wine, and salt from Portugal, Spain, and France to northern Europe, and gold and silver from New World mines to Old World vaults. One of the reasons the Netherlands rose to power was that it was unique—a unified, religiously tolerant republic.

During the 16th century, while the European monarchies fought with the Church and within their own countries over religion (and in some places killed a greater percentage of the population than the Black Death had), the Netherlands was open for business. Many of the Jews who had been driven out of Spain by the Inquisition went north to the hospitable Protestant Netherlands and contributed their knowledge of banking and business to an already flourishing economy. The stock exchange, called the *bourse* (French for "purse"), was created in Amsterdam in the middle of the 16th century. In 1609, the Bank of Amsterdam opened. It had an international money exchange, it used the system of writing checks invented by the Arabs in the Middle Ages, and the Dutch government guaranteed the safety of deposits—something not available in the United States until 1933. The Dutch florin was accepted as payment all over the world, much as the American dollar is today. "God Made the World, but the Dutch Made Holland" Dutch life was tied to the sea and was a constant battle with it. The Dutch invented windmills to pump water out of the fields and reclaim land from the sea, and dikes, walls to hold back the sea. Much of Dutch food and industry centered around the sea. Twenty-five per cent of the Dutch population was connected to the herring industry, from fishing and selling to preserving by smoking, salting, and pickling.

In a time when the economy of other European countries was suffering, the Dutch were extremely prosperous, with a large middle class and a high standard of living. Dutch virtues were cleanliness and thrift. Every morning, Dutch housewives washed not only their own stoops but also the public sidewalks in front of their houses. They lived and ate well. At fish markets, the Dutch bought only live fish. They threw away dead fish, as well as mackerel and red mullet.

Even workers could afford meat, cheese, and butter, and the urban poor were provided for in poorhouses that had been recycled from monasteries or convents when the Netherlands converted to Protestant from Catholic. Sailors on warships were fed a 4,800-calorie-per-day diet of mutton, beef, pork, smoked ham, bread, beans, peas, and smoked and pickled fish, much of it herring.

They were a country that grew no grain and made no wine, but they controlled trade from the breadbasket of Europe, the countries around the Baltic Sea. "French *haute cuisine* did not appear until a century later and then showed little Italian influence; and there is no evidence that Catherine's cooks had any impact on French cooking in the early 16th century."

Catherine supposedly introduced frozen ices, artichokes, parsley, and the fork to France. Wheaton says further that Catherine didn't have much power at court because she didn't have children for 14 years; because her husband was not supposed to become king, but his brother died; and because her husband's mistress set court fashions.

There was a dramatic shift in French cuisine in the middle of the 17th century. In 1651, a French chef named La Varenne published a cookbook called *Le Cuisinier françois*—The French Cook. As Anne Willan, who has named her cooking school in France after him, pointed out, *Le Cuisinier françois* "is a seminal work; it marks the end of medieval cooking and the beginning of *haute cuisine.*" More fresh fruits and vegetables appear in these recipes, because they are more readily available and because gardening had advanced considerably, especially among the upper classes. However, there were still not many foods from the New World. La Varenne used the foods that were trendy among the French nobility, like peas, lettuce, and artichokes. People *had* to have peas.

Woe to the host who served asparagus instead, although asparagus could be served disguised as peas. *Le Pastissier* is the first thorough pastry cookbook, with precise, clear instructions and definitions of weights and measures, perhaps the influence of the Scientific Revolution that was then taking place in Europe. However, Willan thinks that *Le Pastissier* was probably not written by La Varenne or was written by him and an anonymous Italian pastry chef, because Italian pastry chefs were the best in the world at that time.

Also, cooking and pastry were two separate professions. In any case, it is sophisticated—there are fifteen varieties of marzipan. It also has the first cakelike biscuit recipes.

HYGIENE IN FOOD PROCESSING

A high standard of hygiene is a prerequisite for safe food production, and the foundation on which HACCP and other safety management systems depend. Edited and written by some of the world's leading experts in the field, and drawing on the work of the prestigious European Hygienic Engineering and Design Group (EHEDG), Hygiene in food processing provides an authoritative and comprehensive review of good hygiene practice for the food industry.

- An authoritative and comprehensive review of good hygiene practice for the food industry
- Draws on the work of the prestigious European Hygienic Engineering and Design Group (EHEDG)
- Written and edited by world renowned experts in the field
  - *Part 1:* looks at the regulatory context, with chapters on the international context, regulation in the EU and the USA.
  - *Part 2:* looks at the key issue of hygienic design. After an introductory chapter on sources of contamination, there are chapters on plant design and control of airborne contamination. These are followed by a sequence of chapters on hygienic equipment design, including construction materials, piping systems, designing for cleaning in place and methods for verifying and certifying hygienic design.
  - *Part 3:* then reviews good hygiene practices, including cleaning and disinfection, personal hygiene and the management of foreign bodies and insect pests.

Drawing on a wealth of international experience and expertise, Hygiene in food processing will be a standard work for the food industry in ensuring safe food production.

CHICKENS SHOWS PATHOGEN

While critics from the US Agriculture Department (USDA) have labelled the report "junk science" for not doing a wide enough sampling, the publishing of the survey by an influential consumer organisation is a direct attack on the food safety practices at leading poultry processors.As well, the USDA's own figures show that samples in broilers, ground chicken and ground turkey testing positive for salmonella at US slaughter and processing plants have surged since 2002, indicating that companies might soon be pushed to do more to bring down the levels. Broilers had the highest rates of salmonella, with 16.3 per cent of samples testing positive in 2005, up from 11.5 per cent in 2002, USDA figures released earlier this year showed.

The highest level was reached in 1998, when salmonella was found in 20 per cent of the broilers sampled. Meanwhile the Consumer Reports survey tested 525 chickens – including samples from Perdue, Pilgrim's Pride and Tyson Foods. Campylobacter was present in 81 per cent of the chickens, salmonella in 15 per cent and both bacteria in 13 per cent. Only 17 per cent had neither pathogen. That's the lowest percentage of clean birds in all four of the organisation's tests since 1998, and far less than the 51 per cent of clean birds it found in a 2003 survey, the organisation stated.

- "Leading chicken producers have stabilized the incidence of salmonella, but spiral-shaped campylobacter has wriggled onto more chickens than ever," Consumer Reports stated. "And although the US Department of Agriculture tests chickens for salmonella against a federal standard, it has not set a standard for campylobacter."

Overall, chickens labeled as organic or raised without antibiotics and costing $3 to $5 per pound were more likely to harbor salmonella than were conventionally produced broilers that cost more like $1 per pound, the study found.

Moreover, most of the bacteria we tested from all types of contaminated chicken showed resistance to one or more antibiotics, including some fed to chickens to speed their growth and those prescribed to humans to treat infections. Among all brands, 84 per cent of the salmonella and 67 per cent of the campylobacter organisms showed resistance to one or more antibiotics.

- "The findings suggest that some people who are sickened by chicken might need to try several antibiotics before finding one that works," the organisation concluded.

No major brand fared better than others overall. Foster Farms, Pilgrim's Pride, and Tyson chickens were lower in salmonella incidence than Perdue, but they were higher in campylobacter. There was an exception to the poor showing of most premium chickens. As in its previous tests, Ranger—a no-antibiotics brand sold in the Northwest—was extremely clean. Of the 10 samples the organisation analysed, none had salmonella, while two had campylobacter.

To keep contamination in check, processors follow procedures collectively known as Hazard Analysis and Critical Control Point (HACCP) analysis as a means of reducing the risks. HACCP requires companies to spell out where contamination could be controlled during processing, then build in procedures—such as scalding carcasses—to prevent it. The report cited the example of Bell and Evans, which spent $30 million to modernize its processing plant in 2005. The sum included $9 million for a high-tech air-chill system designed in part to reduce cross-contamination.

The system whisks carcasses on two miles of track through chambers in which they're misted and chilled with air, then submerged in an antimicrobial dip. Tom Stone, the company's marketing director, says the measures helped reduce the rate of salmonella to less than 3 per cent in recent in-house tests of chickens done before packaging. But in Consumer Reports tests of 28 store-bought chickens, five of the Bell and Evans samples had salmonella and 19 had campylobacter, the organisation stated. Other government studies back up the growth trend, while reporting significantly lower levels of the pathogens compared to the Consumer Reports survey. SDA testing shows that Salmonella is found in about 12 per cent of broiler chickens in a sample of 3,242 nationwide in the third quarter of 2006. The industry association also cited a large-scale study by Dr. Norman Stern, an expert with the USDA Agricultural Research Service, which showed that 26 per cent of the chickens sampled had detectable level of Campylobacter.

Stern's study took place over 13 months, in 13 poultry complexes, and included 4,200 samples. This study was published in the Journal of Food Protection earlier this year.

- "As for the suggestion that bacteria that may be found on raw chicken are becoming more resistant to antibiotics, the fact is that Campylobacter is notoriously resistant to some antibiotics regardless of whether they are used in chicken or not," the assocition stated. "We are not aware of any actual human cases in which antibiotics have failed to work because of any usage in live chickens. The use of antibiotics in live chickens has declined sharply in recent years."

Another criticism of the Consumer Reports study came this week, with Reuters news service quoting a spokesman with the USDA as saying the Consumer Reports study was riddled with flaws such as a small sample size and uncertainty over the report's methodology. Steven Cohen, spokesman for the agency, said the report did not go back to all the stores used.

- "There is virtually nothing or any conclusion that anyone could draw from 500 samples," Reuters quotes Cohen as stating. "They're passing along junk science and calling it an investigation."

The federal Centers for Disease Control and Prevention (CDC) this month published USDA figures showing that the presence of Salmonella enterica serotype Enteritidis in broiler chicken carcass rinses collected from 2000 through 2005 increased four-fold over the period. The proportion of establishments with Salmonella Enteritidis–positive rinses increased nearly three fold during the same period.

- "We present US Department of Agriculture (USDA) Food Safety and Inspection Service (FSIS) Salmonella testing programme data collected from 2000 to 2005 that suggest a need for interventions to prevent the emergence of this Salmonella serotype in broiler chickens in the United States," the CDC stated in its study.

Campylobacter and salmonella from all food sources sicken about 3.4 million Americans and kill about 700 annually, according to the latest estimates from the CDC. The CDC said that in 2004, poultry was involved in 24 per cent of infection outbreaks in which a single product was identified, up from 20 per cent in 1998. In 2004, about 53 per cent of campylobacter samples and 18 per cent of salmonella samples were resistant to at least one antibiotic. In July 2006, Food and Water Watch, an environmental health organization, published the names of 106 chicken processing plants that failed federal salmonella standards in at least one test period between 1998 and 2005. In August 2006, the USDA reported that the rate of positive salmonella tests in broilers had jumped to 16.3 per cent in 2005, up from 11.5 per cent in 2002.

THE USE OF THIN WALLED PACKAGING FOR FOOD

In a survey of the segment, Applied Market Information (AMI) says thin-walled packaging has become an increasingly well delineated sub-segment of the rigid plastics market. In total in Europe the segment accounts for about two million tonnes of thermoplastics. The report indicates some of the trends in this plastic packaging segment, as the market responds to higher raw material costs, and changes in demand for particular types of food products. Thin walled packaging is used mainly to display goods for sale, but the format may also incorporate features for extending shelf-life and other functions. Thin walled packaging is defined to include yoghurt pots, butter and margarine containers, meat and fruit trays, blister packaging and similar containers. It excludes CD, DVD and blow moulded packaging.

The largest single application of thin-walled packaging is dairy products, which account for 22 per cent of the market. The fastest growing application is in the chilled ready meals segment, in which demand is growing at about six per cent.

While some of the applications for thin-walled packaging are mature others are evolving rapidly such as meat packaging, which is in the process of shifting from being packed within store to being packed centrally. The fruit and vegetables segment accounts for eight per cent of the demand, meat, fish and poultry another eight per cent, frozen foods eight per cent, delicatessen products for seven per cent, bakery for five per cent, yellow fats for five per cent, chilled meals for four per cent and ambient products two per cent. Disposable products account for another 17 per cent of the demand and non-food products 14 per cent. In terms of composition, PET and PP are gaining market share, while polystyrene (PS) and polyvinyl chloride (PVC) are losing market share. Recently, plant-based and compostable polymers have emerged that offer brand owners exciting new opportunities to align sustainable and natural food propositions — such as organic food — with the packaging itself.

VISION FOR INDIAN POULTRY INDUSTRY

India is the fifth largest producer of eggs and ninth largest producer of poultry meat in the world, producing over 34 billion eggs and about 1,715,000 Metric ton of poultry meat in 2004. In the overall market for poultry products, India was positioned 17 in World Poultry Production. And analysts estimate that the poultry sector in India has been growing at a much faster rate, along with other industries such as BPO and Securities market. Over the past decade the poultry industry in India has contributed approximately US $229million, to the Gross National Product (GNP).

Several breakthroughs in poultry science and technology have led to the development of genetically superior breeds capable of higher production, even under adverse climatic conditions that offer opportunities for overseas entrepreneurs to expand export and import of poultry products on a large scale. The average per capita poultry meat consumption is also estimated to increase from 0.69 to 1.28 kilograms, during the 2000-2004. Overall, analysts studies that the total egg consumption is estimated to increase from 34 billion in 2000 and to 106 billion in 2020, while poultry meat consumption is predicted to increase from 687 million kilograms to 1,674 million kilograms. The market research report "Vision for Indian Poultry Industry: Current Scenario and Future Prospects" predicts a relatively strong growth for the egg and poultry meat industry, in both the urban and rural areas, in the next two decades. It has been found that egg consumption has grown at a much faster pace, than the consumption of poultry meat. With the continual rise in income, it is estimated to nearly triple by 2020. The report also examines the consumption pattern of egg and poultry meat for 2010 by taking into account urbanization and differences in consumption patterns across various income groups, both in urban and rural areas. The report deals in detail with the market structure, as well as highlights the production, consumption, import/export statistics etc., of the Indian poultry market, including broilers and processed poultry.

Report Highlights

- Assesses recent trends in Indian poultry production and consumption.
- Growth in India's poultry sector relative to other countries.
- Economic factors affecting food demand, including population, income, and urbanization.
- Consumption shares of poultry products.
- Gains in real per capita incomes and changes in poultry prices.
- Religion and regional preferences for poultry products.
- Structure and costs of production in the Indian poultry meat industry from region to region.
- Poultry production practices by geographic regions like facilities and equipment, breeding and feeding practices.

- Foreign direct investment inflow (FDI) in poultry inputs.
- Policies affecting market integration and feed trade, key to future growth.
- Performance indicators and variable costs for poultry in India, according to region.
- Marketing practices in Indian poultry industry.
- Regional variations in retail prices and margins.
- Tariff levels, regulatory barriers, and import potentials in the Indian poultry sector.
- Trends in supply and demand for key broiler feeds, corn, and soy meal.
- Key factors behind the recent growth of the Indian poultry sector.
- Impact of increase in income, integration, and corn free trade on the Indian poultry sector.

Report Features

This report assesses the supply/demand structure, and policy factors affecting the growth of the Indian poultry industry. The objectives of the report are twofold: to gain a better understanding of the prospects for the poultry industry, in one of the world's largest and fastest growing developing economies, and to take advantage of the information developed on India's diverse sector, to arrive at the implications for growth prospects in the poultry sectors, in other developing countries. To help meet these objectives, this report analyses the impacts of alternate economic, technical, and policy assumptions on poultry supply and demand prospects and the implications for the feed trade.

FOOD AND BEVERAGES

While U.S. hotels have enjoyed a strong increase in room revenue during the current recovery period, growth in hotel food and beverage sales, while improving, lacked the same kind of sizzle, according to an recent study by a leading hospitality consultant. Fortunately, tight cost controls by management have enabled food and beverage profitability to keep pace with the profit growth of other operating departments. In 2004, hotel food and beverage (F&B) revenues grew 6.7 per cent, the result of a 6.9 per cent increase in food sales and a 5.5 per cent bump in beverage sales. The 6.7 per cent growth rate is certainly very healthy, but it does fall short of the 8.6 per cent growth in rooms revenue, and 7.6 per cent increase in total hotel revenues achieved during the same time period.

Table. Mix of Food and Beverage Revenues 2004

Banquet Food	38.2%
Food Outlets/ In Room	25.0%
Other	15.5%
Beverage Outlets/ In Room	11.1%
Banquet Beverage	6.1%
Banquet Meeting Room Rental	4.1%

"While the magnitude of the increase in food and beverage revenue may have fallen short, the pace of profit growth equaled that of the other operated departments within a hotel. This can be attributed to good expense control practiced by F&B management," Woodworth concluded. In 2004, food and beverage departmental expenses grew 6.2 per cent versus and an average of 6.9 per cent for all other operated departments. The bottom- line was an 8.1 per cent growth in food and beverage profits for 2004. This equals the increase in total Operated Department Income for all hotels.

Food and beverage revenues and expenses are just some of the 200 discrete hotel revenue and expense items captured in 2005 Trends in the Hotel Industry report. The 2005 report marks the 69th annual review of U.S. hotel operations conducted by PKF. This year's sample draws upon year-end 2004 financial statements received from more than 5,000 hotels across the country. Hotel managers use the PKF Trends report to benchmark the performance of their hotel's revenues, expenses, and profits.

Revenue Gains

The growth in food and beverage revenues appears to be driven more by increased guest and customer counts, as opposed to increases in pricing. While food and beverage revenues measured on a per-available-room basis grew 6.7 per cent in 2004, food and beverage revenue measured on a per-occupied-room basis grew 2.3 per cent. "The implication from these two statistics is that the increase in F&B revenue was more attributable to the fact that there were 4.3 per cent more rooms occupied, as opposed to any substantial increase in the F&B expenditures per occupied room. Of course, another reason could be a boost in food and beverage patronage from local residents.

When looking at the sources of food and beverage business for the typical hotel in PKF's sample, revenues from banquet events account for 44.3 per cent of the total sales. This compares to 36.1 per cent of the total sales volume that comes from the restaurants, lounges, and room service. The remaining 19.6 per cent is derived from the rental of meeting and banquet rooms, as well as other miscellaneous sources. When looking at growth by the revenue source, we found sales emanating from restaurants and lounges increased 6.1 per cent in 2004, while banquet and catering related revenues grew 7.0 per cent.

Expense Controls

For hotel food and beverage departments, the "prime costs" are Labour and cost of goods sold. In 2004, the cost of food and liquor purchased for re-sale averaged 25.6 per cent of total food and beverage revenue. Salaries, wages, and employee benefits combined for another 56.1 per cent of the dollars spent in the department. Like most other departments in a hotel, labour costs are the biggest expense item. In 2004, F&B labour costs rose 6.1 per cent. This compares

Favourably to the 6.3 per cent overall growth rate in Labour costs throughout the hotel. It also looks like the chefs and bartenders did a good job in the back-of-the- house limiting food and beverage cost increases to only 4.9 per cent." As a result of the tight cost controls, food and beverage department profit margins improved from 30.4 per cent in 2003 to 31.0 per cent in 2004. While food and beverage sales accounted for 26.2 per cent of total hotel revenues in 2004, F&B department profits were only 11.1 per cent of total Operated Department Income for the year.

Free Food

Since the proliferation of limited-service and all-suite hotels, a growing percentage of travellers have grown accustomed to complimentary breakfast and/or cocktail receptions. These expectations have become so prevalent that an increasing number of full-service, resort, and convention hotels are now offering complimentary food and beverages as part of special packages, preferred guest programmes, or corporate rate contracts. The amount of money U.S. hotels spent on complimentary food and beverage increased 13.1 per cent from 2003 to 2004. For the industry segments that have traditionally offered complimentary breakfast, growing competition and evolving social patterns have resulted in an increase in both the quantity and healthiness of the food offered. "When measured on a dollar per-occupied-room basis, limited-service and all-suite hotels increased their spending on complimentary food and beverage by 5.0 per cent.

Clearly, these segments are making an effort to upgrade the quality and quantity of the food and beverages they offer to their guests. Stale doughnuts just don't cut it anymore," Woodworth said. Food and beverage serving and related workers are the front line of customer service in restaurants, coffee shops, and other food service establishments. These workers greet customers, escort them to seats and hand them menus, take food and drink orders, and serve food and beverages. They also answer questions, explain menu items and specials, and keep tables and dining areas clean and set for new diners. Most work as part of a team, helping coworkers to improve workflow and customer service.

Waiters and waitresses, the largest group of these workers, take customers' orders, serve food and beverages, prepare itemized checks, and sometimes accept payment. Their specific duties vary considerably, depending on the establishment. In coffee shops serving routine, straightforward fare, such as salads, soups, and sandwiches, servers are expected to provide fast, efficient, and courteous service. In fine dining restaurants, where more complicated meals are prepared and often served over several courses, waiters and waitresses provide more formal service emphasizing personal, attentive treatment and a more leisurely pace. They may recommend certain dishes and identify ingredients or explain how various items on the menu are prepared. Some prepare salads, desserts, or other menu items tableside.

Additionally, they may check the identification of patrons to ensure they meet the minimum age requirement for the purchase of alcohol and tobacco products. Waiters and waitresses sometimes perform the duties of other food and beverage service workers. These tasks may include escorting guests to tables, serving customers seated at counters, clearing and setting up tables, or operating a cash register.

However, full-service restaurants frequently hire other staff, such as hosts and hostesses, cashiers, or dining room attendants, to perform these duties. *Bartenders* fill drink orders either taken directly from patrons at the bar or through waiters and waitresses who place drink orders for dining room customers. Bartenders check identification of customers seated at the bar, to ensure they meet the minimum age requirement for the purchase of alcohol and tobacco products. They prepare mixed drinks, serve bottled or drought beer, and pour wine or other beverages. Bartenders must know a wide range of drink recipes and be able to mix drinks accurately, quickly, and without waste. Besides mixing and serving drinks, bartenders stock and prepare garnishes for drinks; maintain an adequate supply of ice, glasses, and other bar supplies; and keep the bar area clean for customers.

They also may collect payment, operate the cash register, wash glassware and utensils, and serve food to customers seated at the bar. Bartenders usually are responsible for ordering and maintaining an inventory of liquor, mixes, and other bar supplies. The majority of bartenders directly serve and interact with patrons. Bartenders should be friendly and enjoy talking with customers. Bartenders at service bars, on the other hand, have less contact with customers. They work in small bars often located off the kitchen in restaurants, hotels, and clubs where only waiters and waitresses place drink orders. Some establishments, especially larger, higher volume ones, use equipment that automatically measures, pours and mixes drinks at the push of a button.

Bartenders who use this equipment, however, still must work quickly to handle a large volume of drink orders and be familiar with the ingredients for special drink requests. Much of a bartender's work still must be done by hand to fill each individual order. *Hosts and hostesses* welcome guests and maintain reservation or waiting lists. They may direct patrons to coatrooms, restrooms, or to a place to wait until their table is ready. Hosts and hostesses assign guests to tables suitable for the size of their group, escort patrons to their seats, and provide menus.

They also schedule dining reservations, arrange parties, and organize any special services that are required. In some restaurants, they act as cashiers. *Dining room and cafeteria attendants and bartender helpers* assist waiters, waitresses, and bartenders by cleaning tables, removing dirty dishes, and keeping serving areas stocked with supplies. Sometimes called backwaiters or runners, they bring meals out of the kitchen and assist waiters and waitresses by distributing dishes to individual diners. They also replenish the supply of clean linens, dishes, silverware, and glasses in the dining room and keep the bar stocked with glasses, liquor, ice, and drink garnishes. Dining room attendants set tables with clean tablecloths, napkins, silverware, glasses, and dishes and serve ice water, rolls, and butter.

At the conclusion of meals, they remove dirty dishes and soiled linens from tables. Cafeteria attendants stock serving tables with food, trays, dishes, and silverware and may carry trays to dining tables for patrons. *Bartender helpers* keep bar equipment clean and wash glasses. *Dishwashers* clean dishes, cutlery, and kitchen utensils and equipment. *Counter attendants* take orders and serve food in cafeterias, coffee shops, and carryout eateries. In cafeterias, they serve food displayed on steam tables, carve meat, dish out vegetables, ladle sauces and soups, and fill beverage glasses. In lunchrooms and coffee shops, counter attendants take orders from customers seated at the counter, transmit orders to the kitchen, and pick up and serve food.

They also fill cups with coffee, soda, and other beverages and prepare fountain specialties, such as milkshakes and ice cream sundaes. Counter attendants also take carryout orders from diners and wrap or place items in containers. They clean counters, write itemized checks, and sometimes accept payment. Some counter attendants may prepare short-order items, such as sandwiches and salads. Some food and beverage serving workers take orders from customers at counters or drive-through windows at fast-food restaurants. They assemble orders, hand them to customers, and accept payment. Many of these are *combined food preparation and serving workers* who also cook and package food, make coffee, and fill beverage cups using drink-dispensing machines.

2

Food and Beverage Services Management

Food and beverage services are among the most visible locations at ski areas, and a ski area's environmental commitment is often judged by the environmental practices within these establishments. Food and beverage services at ski areas range from fine dining establishments to bars and cafeterias. Numerous programmes exist for the food and beverage service industry that help restaurants and their customers minimize environmental impacts.

These programmes have established systematic approaches to help restaurants reduce their environmental impacts. Involvement in environmental programmes is a good way for a restaurant to learn more about environmental best practice opportunities.

Food and beverage serving and related workers are the front line of customer service in restaurants, coffee shops, and other food service establishments. These workers greet customers, escort them to seats and hand them menus, take food and drink orders, and serve food and beverages. They also answer questions, explain menu items and specials, and keep tables and dining areas clean and set for new diners. Most work as part of a team, helping coworkers to improve workflow and customer service.

Waiters and waitresses, the largest group of these workers, take customers' orders, serve food and beverages, prepare itemized checks, and sometimes accept payment. Their specific duties vary considerably, depending on the establishment. In coffee shops serving routine, straightforward fare, such as salads, soups, and sandwiches, servers are expected to provide fast, efficient, and courteous service. In fine dining restaurants, where more complicated meals are prepared and often served over several courses, waiters and waitresses provide more formal service emphasizing personal, attentive treatment and a more leisurely pace.

They may recommend certain dishes and identify ingredients or explain how various items on the menu are prepared. Some prepare salads, desserts, or other menu items tableside. Additionally, they may check the identification of patrons to ensure they meet the minimum age requirement for the purchase of alcohol and tobacco products.

Waiters and waitresses sometimes perform the duties of other food and beverage service workers. These tasks may include escorting guests to tables, serving customers seated at counters, clearing and setting up tables, or operating a cash register. However, full-service restaurants frequently hire other staff, such as hosts and hostesses, cashiers, or dining room attendants, to perform these duties.

Bartenders fill drink orders either taken directly from patrons at the bar or through waiters and waitresses who place drink orders for dining room customers. Bartenders check identification of customers seated at the bar, to ensure they meet the minimum age requirement for the purchase of alcohol and tobacco products. They prepare mixed drinks, serve bottled or drought beer, and pour wine or other beverages. Bartenders must know a wide range of drink recipes and be able to mix drinks accurately, quickly, and without waste. Besides mixing and serving drinks, bartenders stock and prepare garnishes for drinks; maintain an adequate supply of ice, glasses, and other bar supplies; and keep the bar area clean for customers. They also may collect payment, operate the cash register, wash glassware and utensils, and serve food to customers seated at the bar. Bartenders usually are responsible for ordering and maintaining an inventory of liquor, mixes, and other bar supplies.

The majorities of bartenders directly serves and interact with patrons. Bartenders should be friendly and enjoy talking with customers. Bartenders at service bars, on the other hand, have less contact with customers. They work in small bars often located off the kitchen in restaurants, hotels, and clubs where only waiters and waitresses place drink orders. Some establishments, especially larger, higher volume ones, use equipment that automatically measures, pours and mixes drinks at the push of a button. Bartenders who use this equipment, however, still must work quickly to handle a large volume of drink orders and be familiar with the ingredients for special drink requests. Much of a bartender's work still must be done by hand to fill each individual order.

Hosts and hostesses welcome guests and maintain reservation or waiting lists. They may direct patrons to coatrooms, restrooms, or to a place to wait until their table is ready. Hosts and hostesses assign guests to tables suitable for the size of their group, escort patrons to their seats, and provide menus. They also schedule dining reservations, arrange parties, and organize any special services that are required. In some restaurants, they act as cashiers.

Dining room and cafeteria attendants and bartender helpers assist waiters, waitresses, and bartenders by cleaning tables, removing dirty dishes, and keeping serving areas stocked with supplies. Sometimes called backwaiters or runners, they bring meals out of the kitchen and assist waiters and waitresses by distributing dishes to individual diners. They also replenish the supply of clean linens, dishes, silverware, and glasses in the dining room and keep the bar stocked with glasses, liquor, ice, and drink garnishes.

Dining room attendants set tables with clean tablecloths, napkins, silverware, glasses, and dishes and serve ice water, rolls, and butter. At the conclusion of meals, they remove dirty dishes and soiled linens from tables. Cafeteria attendants stock serving tables with food, trays, dishes, and silverware and may carry trays to dining tables for patrons. Bartender helpers keep bar equipment clean and wash glasses. *Dishwashers* clean dishes, cutlery, and kitchen utensils and equipment.

Counter attendants take orders and serve food in cafeterias, coffee shops, and carryout eateries. In cafeterias, they serve food displayed on steam tables, carve meat, dish out vegetables, ladle sauces and soups, and fill beverage glasses. In lunchrooms and coffee shops, counter attendants take orders from customers seated at the counter, transmit orders to the kitchen, and pick up and serve food. They also fill cups with coffee, soda, and other beverages and prepare fountain specialties, such as milkshakes and ice cream sundaes. Counter attendants also take carryout orders from diners and wrap or place items in containers. They clean counters, write itemized checks, and sometimes accept payment. Some counter attendants may prepare short-order items, such as sandwiches and salads.

Some food and beverage serving workers take orders from customers at counters or drive-through windows at fast-food restaurants. They assemble orders, hand them to customers, and accept payment. Many of these are combined food preparation and serving workers who also cook and package food, make coffee, and fill beverage cups using drink-dispensing machines.

Other workers serve food to patrons outside of a restaurant environment, such as in hotels, hospital rooms, or cars. Food and beverage service workers are on their feet most of the time and often carry heavy trays of food, dishes, and glassware. During busy dining periods, they are under pressure to serve customers quickly and efficiently. The work is relatively safe, but care must be taken to avoid slips, falls, and burns.

Part-time work is more common among food and beverage serving and related workers than among workers in almost any other occupation. In 2004, those on part-time schedules included half of all waiters and waitresses, and 40 per cent of all bartenders.

Food service and drinking establishments typically maintain long dining hours and offer flexible and varied work opportunities. Many food and beverage serving and related workers work evenings, weekends, and holidays. Many students and teenagers seek part time or seasonal work as food and beverage serving and related workers as a first job to gain work experience or to earn spending money while in school. Around one-fourth of food and beverage serving and related workers were 16 to 19 years old—about six times the proportion for all workers.

There are no specific educational requirements for food and beverage service jobs. Many employers prefer to hire high school graduates for waiter and waitress, bartender, and host and hostess positions, but completion of high school usually is not required for fast-food workers, counter attendants, dishwashers, and dining room attendants and bartender helpers. For many people a job as a food and beverage service worker serves as a source of immediate income, rather than a career. Many entrants to these jobs are in their late teens or early twenties and have a high school education or less. Usually, they have little or no work experience. Many are full-time students or homemakers. Food and beverage service jobs are a major source of part-time employment for high school and college students.

Restaurants rely on good food and quality customer service to retain loyal customers and succeed in a competitive industry. Food and beverage serving and related workers who exhibit excellent personal qualities—such as a neat clean appearance, a well-spoken manner, an ability to work as a member of team, and a pleasant way with patrons—will be highly sought after.

Waiters and waitresses need a good memory to avoid confusing customers' orders and to recall faces, names, and preferences of frequent patrons. These workers also should be comfortable using computers to place orders and generate customers' bills. Some may need to be quick at arithmetic so they can total bills manually. Knowledge of a foreign language is helpful to communicate with a diverse clientele and staff. Prior experience waiting on tables is preferred by restaurants and hotels that have rigid table service standards.

Jobs at these establishments often offer higher wages and have greater income potential from tips, but they may also have stiffer employment requirements than other establishments, such as prior table service experience or higher education. Usually, bartenders must be at least 21 years of age, but employers prefer to hire people who are 25 or older. Bartenders should be familiar with State and local laws concerning the sale of alcoholic beverages.

Most food and beverage serving and related workers pick up their skills on the job by observing and working with more experienced workers. Some full-service restaurants also provide new dining room employees with some form of classroom-type training that alternates with periods of actual on-the-job work experience. These training programmes communicate the operating philosophy of the restaurant, help establish a personal rapport with other staff and instill a desire to work as a team.

They also provide an opportunity to discuss customer service situations and the proper ways of handling unpleasant circumstances or unruly patrons with new employees. Additionally, managers, chefs and servers may meet before each shift to discuss the menu and any new items or specials, review ingredients for any potential food allergies, or talk about any food safety concerns, coordination between the kitchen and the dining room, or any customer service issues from the previous day or shift.

Some employers, particularly those in fast-food restaurants, use self-instruction or on-line programmes with audiovisual presentations and instructional booklets to teach new employees food preparation and service skills. Some public and private vocational schools, restaurant associations, and large restaurant chains provide classroom training in a generalized food service curriculum. All employees receive training on safe food handling procedures and sanitation practices.

Some bartenders acquire their skills by attending a bartending or vocational and technical school. These programmes often include instruction on State and local laws and regulations, cocktail recipes, proper attire and conduct, and stocking a bar. Some of these schools help their graduates find jobs. Although few employers require any minimum level of educational attainment, some specialized training is usually needed in food handling and legal issues surrounding serving alcoholic beverages and tobacco. Employers are more likely to hire and promote based on people skills and personal qualities rather than education.

Due to the relatively small size of most food-serving establishments, opportunities for promotion are limited. After gaining experience, some dining room and cafeteria attendants and bartender helpers advance to waiter, waitress, or bartender jobs. For waiters, waitresses, and bartenders, advancement usually is limited to finding a job in a busier or more expensive restaurant or bar where prospects for tip earnings are better. Some bartenders, hosts and hostesses and waiters and waitresses advance to supervisory jobs, such as dining room supervisor, maitre d'hotel, assistant manager, or restaurant general manager. A few bartenders open their own businesses. In larger restaurant chains, food and beverage service workers who excel at their work often are invited to enter the company's formal management training programme.

EMPLOYMENT

Food and beverage serving and related workers held 6.8 million jobs in 2004. The overwhelming majority of jobs for food and beverage serving and related workers were found in food services and drinking places, such as restaurants, coffee shops, and bars. Other jobs were found primarily in traveller accommodation (hotels); amusement, gambling, and recreation industries; educational services; grocery stores; nursing care facilities; civic and social organizations; and hospitals.

Jobs are located throughout the country but are typically plentiful in large cities and tourist areas. Vacation resorts offer seasonal employment, and some workers alternate between summer and winter resorts, instead of remaining in one area the entire year.

Job Outlook

Job openings are expected to be abundant for food and beverage serving and related workers. Overall employment of these workers is expected to increase as fast as the average over the 2004-14 period as population, personal incomes, and employment expand. While employment growth will create many new jobs, the overwhelming majority of openings will arise from the need to replace the high proportion of workers who leave the occupations each year. There is substantial movement into and out of these occupations because education and training requirements are minimal and the predominance of part-time jobs are attractive to people seeking a short-term source of income rather than a career. However, keen competition is expected for bartender, waiter and waitress, and other food and beverage service jobs in popular restaurants and fine dining establishments, where potential earnings from tips are greatest.

Projected employment growth between 2004 and 2014 varies somewhat by type of job; however, average employment growth is expected for almost all food and beverage serving and related occupations. Employment of combined food preparation and serving workers, which includes fast-food workers, is expected to increase as fast as the average in response to the continuing fast-paced lifestyle of many Americans and the addition of healthier foods at many fast-food restaurants.

Average employment growth is expected for waiters and waitresses and hosts and hostesses because increases in the number of families and the more affluent, 55-and-older population will result in more restaurants that offer table service and more varied menus. Employment of bartenders, dining room attendants, and dishwashers will grow more slowly than other food and beverage serving and related workers because diners increasingly are eating at more casual dining spots, such as coffee bars and sandwich shops, rather than at the full-service restaurants and drinking places that employ more of these workers.

Earning

Food and beverage serving and related workers derive their earnings from a combination of hourly wages and customer tips. Earnings vary greatly, depending on the type of job and establishment. For example, fast-food workers and hosts and hostesses usually do not receive tips, so their wage rates may be higher than those of waiters and waitresses and bartenders in full-service restaurants, who typically earn more from tips than from wages. In some restaurants, workers contribute all or a portion of their tips to a tip pool, which is distributed among qualifying workers. Tip pools allow workers who don't usually receive tips directly from customers, such as dining room attendants, to feel a part of a team and to share in the rewards of good service.

In May 2004, median hourly earnings (including tips) of waiters and waitresses were $6.75. The middle 50 per cent earned between $6.04 and $8.34. The lowest 10 per cent earned less than $5.60, and the highest 10 per cent earned more than $11.27 an hour. For most waiters and waitresses, higher earnings are primarily the result of receiving more in tips rather than higher hourly wages. Tips usually average between 10 and 20 per cent of guests' checks; waiters and waitresses working in busy, expensive restaurants earn the most.

Bartenders had median hourly earnings (including tips) of $7.42 in May 2004. The middle 50 per cent earned between $6.34 and $9.26. The lowest 10 per cent earned less than $5.72, and the highest 10 per cent earned more than $12.47 an hour. Like waiters and waitresses, bartenders employed in public bars may receive more than half of their earnings as tips. Service bartenders often are paid higher hourly wages to offset their lower tip earnings.

Median hourly earnings (including tips) of dining room and cafeteria attendants and bartender helpers were $7.10 in May 2004. The middle 50 per cent earned between $6.24 and $8.25. The lowest 10 per cent earned less than $5.68, and the highest 10 per cent earned more than $9.88 an hour. Most received over half of their earnings as wages; the rest of their income was a share of the proceeds from tip pools.

Median hourly earnings of hosts and hostesses were $7.52 in May 2004. The middle 50 per cent earned between $6.48 and $8.63. The lowest 10 per cent earned less than $5.77, and the highest 10 per cent earned more than $10.49 an hour. Wages comprised the majority of their earnings. In some cases, wages were supplemented by proceeds from tip pools.

Median hourly earnings of combined food preparation and serving workers, including fast food, were $7.06 in May 2004. The middle 50 per cent earned between $6.18 and $8.25. The lowest 10 per cent earned less than $5.65, and the highest 10 per cent earned more than $9.85 an hour. Although some combined food preparation and serving workers receive a part of their earnings as tips, fast-food workers usually do not.

Median hourly earnings of counter attendants in cafeterias, food concessions, and coffee shops (including tips) were $7.53 in May 2004. The middle 50 per cent earned between $6.50 and $8.59 an hour. The lowest 10 per cent earned less than $5.80, and the highest 10 per cent earned more than $10.38 an hour.

Median hourly earnings of dishwashers were $7.35 in May 2004. The middle 50 per cent earned between $6.41 and $8.37. The lowest 10 per cent earned less than $5.76, and the highest 10 per cent earned more than $9.81 an hour.

Median hourly earnings of nonrestaurant food servers were $7.95 in May 2004. The middle 50 per cent earned between $6.64 and $9.98. The lowest 10 per cent earned less than $5.86, and the highest 10 per cent earned more than $12.53 an hour.

Many beginning or inexperienced workers start earning the Federal minimum wage of $5.15 an hour. However, a few States set minimum wages higher than the Federal minimum. Also, various minimum wage exceptions apply under specific circumstances to disabled workers, full-time students, youth under age 20 in their first 90 days of employment, tipped employees, and student-learners.

Tipped employees are those who customarily and regularly receive more than $30 a month in tips. The employer may consider tips as part of wages, but the employer must pay at least $2.13 an hour in direct wages. Employers also are permitted to deduct from wages the cost, or fair value, of any meals or lodging provided. Many employers, however, provide free meals and furnish uniforms. Food and beverage service workers who work full time often receive typical benefits, while part-time workers usually do not.

In some large restaurants and hotels, food and beverage serving and related workers belong to unions—principally the Hotel Employees and Restaurant Employees International Union and the Service Employees International Union.

FOOD AND BEVERAGE COST

This portion presents the professional techniques and methods used to effectively purchase, receive, and store food products. It teaches the formulas used to compute the true cost of the food you provide your guests, as well as a process for estimating the value of food you have used on a daily or weekly basis, by applying the food cost percentage method, which is the standard in the hospitality industry.

The U.S. Bureau of Labour Statistics consumer expenditure surveys reported that sales of food consumed away from home grew an average of 5% per year in the 1990s, with annual increases expected to be even higher in the 2000s. According to the National Restaurant Association's current forecasts, continued economic growth, gains in consumers' real disposable income, and changes in the lifestyles of today's busy American families are all spurring the sustained rise in the number of meals served away from home. This is good news for your career as a hospitality manager.

All this growth, activity, and consumer demand, however, will also create challenges for you. Consider the situation you would encounter if you used sales histories to project 300 guests for lunch today at the restaurant you manage. Your restaurant serves only three entrée items: roast chicken, roast pork, and roast beef. The question you would face is this, "How many servings of each item should we produce so that we do not run out of any one item?" If you were to run out of one of your three menu items, guests who wanted that item would undoubtedly become upset. Producing too much of any one item would, on the other hand, cause costs to rise to unacceptable levels unless these items could be sold for their full price at a later time.

Clearly, in this situation, it would be unwise to produce 300 portions of each item. While you would never run out of any one item, that is, each of your 300 estimated guests could order the same item and you would still have enough, you would also have 600 left overs at the end of your lunch period. What you would like to do, of course, is instruct your staff to make the "right" amount of each menu item. The right amount would be the number of servings that minimize your chances of running out of an item before lunch is over, while also minimizing your chance of having excessive leftovers. The answer to the question of how many servings of roast chicken, pork, and beef you should prepare lies in accurate menu forecasting. Let us return to the example cited previously. This time, however, assume that you were wise enough to have recorded last week's menu item sales on a form.

An estimate of 300 guests for next Monday makes sense because the weekly sales total last week of 1,500 guests served averages 300 guests per day (1,500/5 days _ 300/day). You also know that, on an average day, you sold 73 roast chicken (365 sold/5 days _ 73/day), 115 roast pork (573 sold/5 days _ 115/day), and 112 roast beef (562 sold/5 days _ 112/day).

Once you know the average number of people selecting a given menu item, and you know the total number of guests who made the selections, you can compute the popularity index, which is defined as the percentage of total guests choosing a given menu item from a list of alternatives. In this example, you can improve your "guess" about the quantity of each item to prepare if you use the sales history to help guide your decision. If you assume that future guests will select menu items much as past guests have done, given that the list of menu items remains the same, that information can be used to improve your predictions.

If we know, even in a general way, what we can expect our guests to select, we are better prepared to make good decisions about the quantity of each item that should be produced. In this example, your best guess of what your 300 guests are likely to order when they arrive. The basic formula for individual menu item forecasting, based on an item's individual sales history. The predicted number to be sold is simply the quantity of a specific menu item likely to be sold given an estimate of the total number of guests expected. Once you know what your guests are likely to select, you can determine how many of each menu item your production staff should be instructed to prepare. It is important to note that foodservice managers face a great deal of uncertainty when attempting to estimate the number of guests who will arrive on a given day because a variety of factors influence that number.

These, as well as other factors that affect sales volume, makes accurate guest count prediction very difficult. In addition, remember that sales histories track only the general trends of an operation. They are not able to estimate *precisely* the number of guests who may arrive on any given day. Sales histories, then, are a guide to what can be expected. In our example, last week's guest counts range from a low of 280 (Monday) to a high of 320 (Tuesday). In addition, the percentage of people selecting each menu item changes somewhat on a daily basis. As a professional foodservice manager, you must take into account possible increases or decreases in guest count and possible fluctuations in your predicted number to be sold computations when planning how many of each menu item you should prepare.

Forecasting can involve estimating the number of guests you expect, the dollar amount of sales you expect, or even what those guests may want to purchase. This forecasting is crucial if you are to effectively manage your food expenses. In addition, consistency in food production and guest service will greatly influence your overall success.

FOOD ACTION RESEARCH IN HOTEL

Interactive social science research may be regarded as a pragmatic, utilitarian, or user-oriented approach to research and incorporates a value-base that is committed to promoting change through research. It is democratic and participatory by nature and is in sharp contrast to the positivistic 'top-down' approach which has been accused of 'lifting decisions from the village square' and placing them with 'experts or outside agencies' (Bryant, 2001). The practice goes by many names: community-based research, participatory research, collaborative research, and others, but rests on two main principles: democratization of the knowledge process, and social change.

Action research forms part of this genre, and is associated with attempts to bring about emancipation and social justice based on the desires and direct involvement of ordinary people. Its roots may be traced to writers such as Marx, Engels, Gramsci and Freire, and has been used to promote the empowerment of disadvantaged and oppressed groups through the development of common knowledge and critical awareness which are suppressed by the dominant knowledge in a society. Action research is now used within a range of settings and has developed by drawing from pragmatic philosophy, critical thinking, and humanistic and transpersonal psychology, constructionist theory, systems thinking and complexity theory.

An important element of action research is participation by 'informants' who engage in 'collective, self-reflective enquiry…in social situations in order improve the rationality and justice of their own social practices'. A key feature is empowerment through participation. This may, for example, involve the researcher identifying the user group, working in close collaboration with the users, and getting them involved in identifying their needs, setting up research questions, and using the research findings. The practice involves people reflecting on issues and processes during the research, participants as co-researchers, and entails an element of risk given that the process and outcomes are in a state of on-going change. It is transformed by emergent findings, which, in turn, impact upon the process itself, and subsequent outcomes. As the focus becomes redirected, outcomes may not be readily predicted and, for this reason alone, power holders may not be fully at ease with what they are not in control of: the 'knowledge' it produces, the thinking it stimulates, or the action it promotes.

Action research has now found its way into a diverse range of areas, including the experiential learning movement, community development, action learning, humanistic psychology, popular education, organization development, and feminist thinking. Each field has shaped and redefined 'action research' according to its particular requirements. For example, interactive research has been closely associated with the environmental movement, democratic evaluation has links with education, and empowerment evaluation aims to 'help others to help themselves' in areas that include substance abuse prevention, HIV/AIDS prevention, and adult probation.

When commissioning research, an organisation may perceive that subsequent outcomes will take place within specified parameters that will help to further its overall aims, including the need to develop or maintain working relations with other bodies (eg Tackling Drugs to Build a Better Britain, 1998). What they may not realise, however, is that action research has the potential to instigate certain forms of action which undermine the 'collaborative' framework that they seek. Unlike more professionally-directed models of research, action research can be difficult to 'manage' once underway.

In the area of drugs prevention, action research has been used in tandem with an approach that stresses the role of community development and community involvement. As a philosophy, 'community drugs prevention' entails residents gaining access to a range of social, political and economic resources. In this respect, drugs prevention is concerned with wider quality of life issues that residents define as important and will serve to reduce the demand for drug use. Action research has been used to mobilise communities in order to achieve these objectives.

The research used as a case study for the purpose of this chapter took place in a locality exhibiting the usual indices of long-term social and economic decline, including widescale drugs-related difficulties. Initially, the commissioning agency (administered by the Home Office) was committed to devising a community-led drugs prevention strategy. Its original intention was that through operationalising action research, community concerns about drug misuse would be elicited alongside residents' perceptions of what 'drugs prevention' should involve, and residents would be encouraged to get involved in setting up projects and lobbying policy makers for relevant change. The commissioning agency perceived that the local urban regeneration agency would be a key funder for any future projects that may result from the research.

Initially, in-depth individual and group interviews became central to the research process. Later, a series of small-scale public meetings occurred, and community newsletters were produced. At the meetings the earlier findings were fed back to residents who, in turn, commented on them and suggested future directions that the project should take. Residents' participation took various forms. Apart from acting as 'informants' during the interviews, they produced articles that appeared in the newsletters, were actively involved in developing and conducting interviews with other residents, initiated and developed an on-going community forum which discussed the issues emerging from the research, and began lobbying local agencies to take part in various working groups in order that their concerns may be addressed.

Although the initial research agenda had been more or less professionally-led, as time progressed, residents were changing the agenda and were leading the process through their actions.

The research had stimulated community awareness around 'drugs prevention' issues, had succeeded in producing an action plan for prevention, and a community forum had emerged comprising of local residents and representatives from local agencies. The regeneration agency (which had not become directly involved in the research process) became critical of the agency that had commissioned the research, the researcher, and the 'biased' outlook of residents that was being put forward in the newsletters published by the forum, and through the emerging research findings published in a working paper which was widely distributed within the locality.

According to its view, the research was merely serving to stir-up and magnify unjustified hostility toward its role in the area. The consequence was that other key agencies in the area (and involved with the forum) became reluctant to continue to support the activities of the local residents for fear of producing tensions between themselves and the powerful regeneration agency. Consequently, as the forum lacked backing from certain key voluntary and statutory sector agencies, the regeneration agency felt justified in not providing funding for projects outlined in the action plan. Funding for the action research and for the researcher expired after a six month period and residents were either unable or unwilling to continue their activities through the forum.

In some ways the action research ignited a powder keg that had been waiting to go off. Simmering tensions between sections of the community and the regeneration agency had frequently boiled over during a long period of time prior to the research. The locality traditionally had a strong and vocal community sector, and was predominantly staunchly left-wing in political outlook. They possessed little faith in the overall aims and objectives of the regeneration agency from not long after its inception - perceiving it to be an imposition from central government whose outlook was regarded as having changed little from those of previous Conservative administrations. The action research became part of the local political process and arguably politicized those residents who were previously not very vocal within the area.

At the outset, the commissioning body expressed a commitment toward 'community involvement' in drugs prevention, but it is doubtful whether it fully appreciated the potential implications of the action research. Based on a model used elsewhere, the agency perceived that the research would primarily involve a consultation exercise culminating in greater levels of community representation in existing and potential new projects. The agency perceived that the research would contribute toward an integrated approach for prevention, bringing organisations and residents together.

Residents expressed a strong commitment to the action research, given the emancipatory and participatory background of the paradigm, and viewed it as a welcome change from previous professionally controlled research that they had regarded as having been an end in itself: a mechanism for integrating residents and community groups into government and prevailing structures thereby giving programmes a degree of credibility and legitimacy, but not bringing about the changes for communities and residents that they desire (Todhunter, 2001). However, action research may appear to offer a potential for change, but just how much change may be expected given the wider interests of agencies and organisations that may be juxtaposed to proposed change?

Agencies may (unconsciously) seek to define residents' needs according to their specific remit, and attempt to set a research agenda accordingly - even though they may label it as 'action' research. In the case outlined here, the commissioning body appeared to put into operation their own limited notion of 'action research'. However, through the research residents emphasised a desire for exerting more direct power in order to facilitate their identity and rights as citizens. They were calling for equal participation on the partnership board of the regeneration agency which they felt was slanted against the interests of local people in favour of statutory sector and business interests. In effect, they were challenging the prevailing power structures by questioning the legitimacy of key agencies. Subsequently, the agency that commissioned the research was not able to respond fully to the needs or views of residents once unpacked.

In the shorter term, action research may produce a 'feel good' factor among participants - consciousness raising, 'participation' and mobilisation may instill a self-belief in ordinary people's capacity to bring about change. In the longer term, real and radical change may indeed come about. To do this however, commitment to change must be forthcoming among all local agencies and interest groups. Otherwise, action research may leave a bitter taste in the mouths of residents, whose expectations are raised, and subsequent programmes for change may have to cope with the damage done by previous projects that failed to deliver. Any good faith which may have been present among residents may have drained away leaving an embittered community that is hostile or cynical toward future programmes which come along.

In many respects the pitfalls that emerged in the case study presented here have been somewhat reminiscent of those surrounding the Community Development Projects of the 1970s. Workers in many of the projects came to reject the analysis and strategies of the original project proposals. They sought to organise and research around larger questions of inequality and deindustrialisation Workers who entered the field in the late 1960s and early 1970s exhibited a readiness to take up oppositional positions. By 1974 the Home Office had largely given up on the projects and they were wound up in 1976.

Commissioning bodies need to be fully aware of the potential pitfalls of undertaking action research. They must understand what 'action research' implies, and that it does not sit easily with conventional and easily manageable 'consultation' exercises - thus making it a high risk strategy. By committing to a process of action research, agencies are legitimizing residents' voices and actions, and their participation in social policy. In some respects they will embarking upon a programme that bucks a wider cultural and social trend encouraging 'involvement' which seeks to guarantee consensus and integration rather than change, and may find themselves in uncomfortable situations.

Action research is a tool that research commissioners must not take lightly, and not undertake impulsively. The groundwork has to be prepared thoroughly, given the potential impact. Agencies must give due thought about imposing a standard model of action research applied elsewhere to a different area, as in the study outlined here. They have to decide how feasible action research and change may be, given wider trends and local political situations, and must also prepare the groundwork effectively prior to committing to the research, bringing on board key players who may find themselves bearing the brunt of residents' frustrations and providing them with a chance to negotiate the shifting research agenda in tandem with residents.

For at least seventy years, some researchers around the world have been identifying what they do using terms like 'action research', or 'participatory research', or a combination of these. Some have stressed the action component,1 while others have focused more on the participatory process. Still others have come from the field of social science and have identified it as a means of inquiry or research per se. This chapter came about in response to requests to speak about some of the collective wisdom that has been generated over many decades by people who have identified what they do using the term 'participatory action research'. It is the way I tell the story.

Throughout this account participatory action research is contrasted with formulations of conventional research science. For me, participatory action research is not a different and separate matter from science at all, but constitutes a formulation of how I understand all science in the wake of the wave of thinking that is popularly being called the 'new physics'. This 'new physics' or 'new paradigm science' in the natural physical world seems to me to match a 'new paradigm science' in the social world. I identify 'participatory action research' not as an optional variant or specialist technique, but as one of the more inclusive descriptions of this new understanding of social science.

This short paper sets out to identify some of the main characteristics of participatory action research for me, and to try and show why I have come to the following two conclusions:

- 'Participatory action research' is a description of social research per se (albeit social research which is more conscious of its underlying assumptions, and collectivist nature, its action consequences and its driving values).

- It faces numerous barriers to its practice which mean that, even when we think we might be doing 'it', we often have our doubts! I have come to conclude that pretty much all of the research we are involved in, is more or less an approximation in the direction of 'it'. That is, every piece of research is more or less participatory. It more or less enables action as part of the process. And it all involves more or less critical reflexive, skeptical and imaginative inquiry.

What do we typically do when we 'do a piece of research'? Let's take a couple of everyday examples.

We are going about our business and a piece of equipment fails to work. We are pulled up in our tracks as we experience a discrepancy between our practice and our expectations. Out of our need for it to 'work', a question arises: 'Why is it so?'. We have a look at the piece of equipment: perhaps involving a little piece of hands-on 'participant observation' fieldwork! Perhaps we employ also some 'secondary analysis' as we consult the maker's manual for their theories and advice! We may develop a hunch (hypothesis) and draw some conclusions.

Then we try it out in a form of a naturalistic experiment and we 'give it a go'. Again we go about our business. The equipment works and we carry on. Or, it fails to work again and we again stop in our tracks and raise our question again, and try further fieldwork to develop yet another theory and try yet another tack, and so on.

We are looking for our daughter's shoes in the early morning scramble. We review previous 'historical data' (memories of earlier experiences!) as part of planning our 'research design'. We generate several hypotheses and move quickly into the 'field' to involve other participants and gather new data to test them! We use some observational anthropology.

Two brief interviews with daughter and sibling result in reports of failed hunches! (they weren't in their cupboards or on the back verandah!); we engage in further open-ended interviews with the entire household population.

Then secondary analysis of the previous day's timetable generates a further hunch (Sports Day!: shoes replaced with runners) and an additional round of observation reveals: shoes in school bag!

These trivial microcosms contain a structure which reliably:

- commences - ironically - with stopping. That is, we do not begin to inquire until we actually suspend our current action because of the:
- Raising of a question; which then provokes us to go about:
- Planning ways to get answers - ways which will involve identifying and involving 'questioners', 'the questioned' and an idea of for who or for what we desire answers;
- Engaging in fieldwork about new, current or past action in order to get answers and improve our experiential understanding of the problematic situation;

- Generating from the 'answers' an imaginative idea of what to do to change and improve our actions;
- The putting into practice of the new actions (followed by further stopping, reflecting and possible 'problematisation').

This is precisely the cycle of action, reflection, raising of questions, planning of 'fieldwork' to review current (and past) actions - its conduct, analysis of experiences encountered, the drawing of conclusions, and the planning of new and transformed actions - that characterizes all research endeavor. If we are to distinguish this cycle in any ways from what we 'do all the time', we find the important distinctions are in degree rather than kind. That is, in participatory action research we are:

- More conscious of 'problematising' an existing action or practice and more conscious of who is problematising it and why we are problematising it;
- More explicit about 'naming' the problem, and more self-conscious about raising an unanswered question and focusing an effort to answer it;
- More planned and deliberate about commencing a process of inquiry and involving others who could or should be involved in that inquiry;
- More systematic and rigorous in our efforts to get answers;
- More carefully documenting and recording action and what people think about it and in more detail and in ways which are accessible to other relevant parties;
- More intensive and comprehensive in our study, waiting much longer before we 'jump' to a conclusion;
- More self-sceptical in checking our hunches;
- Attempting to develop deeper understandings and more useful and more powerful theory about the matters we are researching, in order to produce new knowledge which can inform improved action or practice; 6 and
- Changing our actions as part of the research process, and then further researching these changed actions.

One of the ways this understanding of research differs from conceptions of conventional research or 'old paradigm science' is revealed in the diagrams below. Conventional research often sees itself as proceeding from point A to point B along a straight line - commencing with a hypothesis and proceeding to a conclusion which may then be published in a journal. However new paradigm social science (or participatory action research) considers it critical to the success of the inquiry that the hypothesis is relevant and useful and thus asks: Where did the hunches or hypotheses come from? Are they just any old hypotheses? Or have they been carefully constructed and well-grounded, over time, from deep and engaged involvement in the field being studied? Are they plausible? Are they relevant? Are they already well-evidenced and thus already substantiate new action? (rather than having to spend time re-discovering or re-confirming the already-established).

Furthermore, new paradigm science asks: Have they been checked in practice? Findings, 'discoveries' or new ideas are not accepted until tested in action - otherwise they remain merely 'interesting ideas' or 'just academic'.

Instead of a linear model, participatory action research thus proceeds through cycles, 'starting' with reflection on action, and proceeding round to new action which is then further researched. The new actions differ from the old actions - they are literally in different places.

Interestingly, all science seems to me to follow this logic. However many 'old paradigm' scientists are unaware of their implication in this. There is always new action resulting - even if it is just the same as the old (which we might describe as reproducing the 'status quo'). Inquiry inevitably leads somewhere - even if it isn't far from where it started, or only a small number of people are consciously aware of it.

Once inquirers are aware of the implications of inquiring, they are faced with a choice. They can ignore it (or treat it as peripheral or of nuisance value), or they can resolve to work with it as a positive feature of their research environment. Action researchers, it seems to me, are really just researchers who have come to understand the practical and ethical implications of the inevitability of the value-driven and action-effects of their inquiry, that is:

- The effects of raising some questions and not others,
- The effects of involving some people in the process (or even apparently only one) and not others,
- The effects of observing some phenomena and not others,
- The effects of making this sense of it and not alternative senses, and
- The effects of deciding to take this action (or 'no' action) as a result of it rather than any other action and so on.

All research involves these kinds of decisions. Participatory action research attempts to make these decisions more consciously and in relation to more clearly-worked out purposes, and using more appropriate designs and techniques for exploring them.

The Action Element

All research seems to me to be implicated in action. Not only is research itself an action in and on existing situations, but it also always has consequences. Things inevitably change as a result of research - the mere act of asking questions is an intervention in a situation, and giving and hearing answers and making sense of them inevitably brings about changes in those involved. Whether people then choose to continue as before or to change course means that the new situation will either be different from that before, or it will be the same. To 'not change' is nevertheless action: some might call it inaction!

Participatory action research is aware of its inevitable intervention in the social situations within which it operates and seeks to turn these to consciously-applied effect. Most participatory action research sets out to explicitly study something in order to change and improve it. It most often arises from an unsatisfactory situation that those most affected wish to alter for the better (although it can also arise from the experience of something which works well, which provokes the desire to reproduce or expand it).

The moving to new and improved action involves a creative 'moment' of transformation. 7 This involves an imaginative leap from a world of 'as it is' to a glimpse of a world 'as it could be'. Where existing situations benefit or promote some but disadvantage or subordinate others, then creative change may be construed as 'political'. As well, participatory action research does not conceptualise this as the development of predictive cause-effect theory ('if this, then that'). Instead, as in the slogan: 'the future is made, not predicted', it is more like 'what if we..., then maybe'. Possibility theory rather than predictive theory. That is, human actors are both wilful and capable of thwarting research prediction, and wilful and capable of selecting and implementing theories or probabilities they want to see manifested! Conventional science sees this as undesirable 'contamination' and 'bias'. Participatory action research sees this as a goal, and the stuff of which 'real life' is made or enacted.

Action research, like the discovery phase of any science, knows it is coming from somewhere and going to somewhere, even though it does not know in advance where precisely it is going to end up or what the new state will look like. Participatory action research, unlike conventional science, does not consider this to be an embarrassment! However it can be difficult for researchers (and research funders) accustomed primarily to a formal experimental approach (the verificationist phase of science), since all that can be stated at the outset is that certain parties have noticed certain problematic matters and have planned certain participatory processes in order to try and 'crack it' for a new way to approach the matter. It may be that funders need to fund iterative or emergent research in connecting stages of 'seeding', 'sapling' and 'tree' phases (and not with up to a year's time lapse in between, as at present). As there is an infinity of 'could be' worlds, then the action phase is crucially guided by the depth and quality of theorising achieved by the research participants. Superficial or trivial research will result in superficial and trivial ideas for practice.

The major challenge for all participatory action researchers (and indeed all researchers) is to design a process which can result in maximum creativity and imagination. Some of the most spectacular ideas have come about because researchers (or self-researchers) were able to draw on unusual sources for ideas, and then submit them to their critical reference group 10 to see if they 'resonated'. If such creative and imaginative efforts have been well-driven by a critical reference group perspective and well-grounded in an understanding of the critical reference group and their context or environment (including the effects of others and of 'structural' matters or opportunities impinging), then they stand a much better chance of 'getting it right' and ideas 'taking off'. Pretty much every initiative we now see around us as A Good Thing happened in this way: as a product of people who 'knew their turf', knew who they were doing it for, and had the imagination to collectively envision a desirable new state and attract others who shared that vision.

In participatory action research, while there is a conceptual difference between the 'participation' 'action' and 'research' elements, in its most developed state these differences begin to dissolve in practice. That is, there is not participation followed by research and then hopefully action. Instead there are countless tiny cycles of participatory reflection on action, learning about action and then new informed action which is in turn the subject of further reflection.

Every minute of every hour may see participants absorbing new ways of seeing or thinking in the light of their experience, leading to new related actions being taken on the spot. Often these will pass unnoticed and unrecorded, but with practice these too become the subject of further reflection and group self-understanding. Change does not happen at 'the end' - it happens throughout. A hallmark of a genuine participatory action research process is that it may change shape and focus over time (and sometimes quite unexpectedly) as participants focus and refocus their understandings about what is 'really' happening and what is really important to them.

It is not possible to do any social research without the participation of other human beings. In typical research there might be one or more 'researchers', there might be people who are 'researched', and there might be people who are 'researched for' - such as those who are to be informed or influenced by findings, or, at a more fundamental level, those who have a problem on which the research is to cast light. However even the research that seems to involve 'no-one', such as the most lone and unobtrusive academic researcher, examining written historical records of people long dead, who seems to be isolated from 'real world practice', and is relatively unknown to peers, still exists in a social world peopled by family, friends, fellow academics, academic administrators, tax-payers and politicians, funding bodies, editors of journals or thesis-examiners, as well as by the written representations of the researched (and there may also be some living representatives) which nevertheless must 'speak' and be 'heard' and understood by the researcher. These all impinge on, and 'construct' the research environment and it's findings, regardless of their apparent invisibility.

More usually there are known groups of researchers, people who commission the research, and live populations of 'researched' and 'researched for', many of whom may know of the research and want to have a say about its conduct or contribute a view about its subject-matter.

Various parties to research 'participate', but the questions become 'Who is treated as participants?', 'How much do they participate?', 'In what ways do they participate?', and 'How is their participation taken into account or not taken into account?'.

Indeed the reason why many of us have felt compelled to add the "p" for participation to the "ar" for action research has been because we have noticed that many have taken existing levels of conventional 'participation' for granted. More importantly there may have been a complacency about the adequacy of current input. Here is a chicken and egg. How do existing participants know the limits of their own perceptions without new participants being there to illuminate the relativism of the existing participants' perceptions - and how would the new participants get to be involved, invited (or tolerated) if their value is not known?

It is worth drawing out the differences between the parties to research in more detail to examine the new possibilities for participation.

In a conventional piece of research there may be less apparent participation. For example, management (group iv), is puzzled or uneasy about some existing matter, or under pressure from another group (iii) or (iv) to Do Something. They might typically employ an independent researcher, (i), to go and study some of the people-with-a-problem, (iii) and perhaps also have some informal discussions with staff, (iv). They may limit their involvement to an initial briefing, the receipt of progress reports, attendance at a steering committee, and receipt of a final report. The researcher may be an academic or a private consultant with some other interests in the matter themselves, (i) and (iv).

They are constrained to appear to be neutral or perhaps mildly on everyone's side. They may also be on a short term, highly paid contract with high performance expectations. They expect to get into the field, get the data, get out cleanly, write it up, add some recommendations that seem feasible and then move on to the next demanding job.

The people-with-a-problem: 'clients', 'patients', 'students', or other group of disadvantaged people, (iii), may be directly hurt or disadvantaged by the existing problematic matter, and may or may not have questioned whether there might be a reason for it, and/or a better way. This group is frequently part of 'the researched', although sometimes they may not know it. If they do, they may typically find themselves on the receiving end of a questionnaire or an interview. One of their number may be invited to sit on an Advisory Committee.

Some other 'stakeholders': staff, carers, providers, (iv), may be indirectly involved. In conventional research, they may also be questionnaire or interviewed about the group-with-the-problem, or about their service to them or care of them, and perhaps even asked what they think should be changed; and they might also be on the Committee. All then await the researchers' announcement of their 'findings'.

What can typically plague the whole process of such conventional research are the consequences of non participation:

- In the first place there can be confusion or lack of agreement regarding the direction and purpose of the inquiry (for whom and for what).
- There is subsequent disagreement about the form the study should take (how, where, when, who should be involved).
- Alternatively the wrong direction is taken and dissent suppressed or ignored. The wrong questions are asked. The data is then irrelevant. And the conclusions useless.
- There can be misunderstandings about participants' perceptions (about the situation being studied).
- There can be conflict over interpretations and analyses (the 'why' and 'how').
- And there can be disagreement about what these imply for change in action (what next).
- And there can be shooting of the messenger! Or of the manager. Or mutinous troops. And critical reference groups' situations left unchanged.

There is an important point to be made here. Over many years I have observed that where the parties (i), (ii), (iii) and (iv) are more distant from each other and from involvement in the process of inquiry, trouble ensues.

Once in the past a place might have been seen for participation by the various parties at the outset on a committee, or at the end as recipients of a report. Increasingly instead they might become contributors to all stages of the research cycle - as designers, selectors of methods, contributors of 'data', 'analysers' and 'concluders', and then 'takers (or monitors) of new actions', and so on. All parties begin to operate much more as both co-researchers and co-subjects.

In participatory action research, the four conceptual categories of participants may thus in practice become much more overlapping depending on the purposes of the research, and who is 'driving' it. For example, there may be more participation, where a self help group (iii), self-researches (i) its own experiences (ii) and those of others (iv), for itself or for others (i or iv).

The arguments for there being more rather than less participation by all four parties are as follows:

- Those commissioning or carrying out the research These usually already participate the most since they choose the questions, decide how they will be answered, interpret the answers and decide what has been 'discovered'. Yet frequently even they feel constrained to disguise, restrict or eliminate their ideas and values, or refrain from putting in their experiences or their views or opinions, on the grounds the research should be 'objective' and 'unbiased', and 'value-free'. In this way, other participants may never be properly informed about the nature and purposes of the research, and the research design may begin way back 'behind the eight ball' instead of where there is a genuine unanswered question. This may truly bias or distort the research. Feminist 13 and other critical theory 14 research as well as so-called fourth generation evaluation 15 has begun to show a way for researchers (and those commissioning the research) to be more genuine and honest participants in and contributors to their own research.

These approaches have shown also how there can be more of a dissolution of the distinction between researcher/s and 'researched for' (the critical reference group).

- Thus, for example, a more participating researcher would be more clear about why they are interested in the research - perhaps describing their own personal experiences that have led to the questions they are wanting to ask. This clarifies the purposes for other participants, and helps each participant know where the other is 'coming from'. Further, the participating researcher/s, having identified the interests they wish to pursue, can see (and be seen in) their relationship to the critical reference group, and pursue more consciously and sceptically, alternative formulations of the situation.
- The critical reference group: This group conventionally participates least since professional and academic research largely researches on and about and speaks for the disadvantaged, or groups with unmet needs the research is meant to benefit. Laura Nader has called this approach 'studying down' (1972). The identification and involvement of the critical reference group, or even broad relevant critical reference 'arenas' or critical reference 'publics' however, I have noticed leads to:
  - Improved relevance of the inquiry to those who share in the problem;
  - Sharper focusing of the research questions;
  - Enhanced relevance of the inquiry to those whose jobs are to do something about the problem (whether as a service provider, a carer, an administrator, a funder, etc.);
  - Increased effectiveness of the research design (what is asked, by whom, of whom, when, where and how);
  - Improved meaningfulness of the information thus gained (the researched especially have a say in whether any inquiry 'got it right' in regard to the meaning of what they said or did);
  - The power and accuracy of the theory developed to understand the problem;

— The relevance, creativity and effectiveness of the new actions decided-on;
— And the commitment to observing the new actions and acting on and researching of them further.

The difficulties in involving critical reference groups and them remaining involved are numerous. The discussion of how to achieve these conditions of mutual involvement, participation and collaboration are very similar to the discussions about how to achieve 'community development'. For example, the more disempowered you are, the less hope you may have about either the value of participating or even the chances of something good coming out of it. If you are radically disempowered you may not even be able to envisage something better, when even a vague or indistinct vision is a prerequisite for pursuing one at all.

Nevertheless, members of critical reference groups who have problematised a situation are in the most strategic position to work on its improvement. Participatory action research, in its most-developed form, works to assist critical reference groups - and those who share their perspective - pursue their inquiries, by themselves and for themselves, as a community-of-interest. The role of 'outsiders' or those who are not members of critical reference groups changes radically. Rather than operating as the independent expert determiner of the truth-of-the-situation (with critical reference groups assisting the researcher in their pursuit of The Truth), the 'researcher' becomes a facilitator of or an assistant to the critical reference group's own pursuit of their truth (or truths).

- Stakeholders other than the researcher/s and the critical reference group (and whether interested or hostile)
  These typically participate only at the outset: perhaps to convene a Committee or allocate a research brief or contribute funds, or just at the end: to receive a research report or hear of its findings. The pitfalls and wastage that can be associated with this level of participation are numerous. A few possible results include:
  — Manipulation of the research process 'off stage' (by powerful parties who never participated in a democratic process around a table with all other parties), and possible ultimate resistance by other parties when their participation proves to be pointless;
  — Rejection of a report by some or all because they simply never went through the same learning process as did the researcher/s and the critical reference group and never reached the same conclusions;
  — Frustration with a process that does not reflect their realities;
  — Inability to see what are the practical consequences of a set of findings or recommendations.

Service providers can specially benefit from full participation so that the link between their 'theory' (why they do what they do) is in closer connection with their 'practice' (what they actually do). Indeed, in much action research in Western countries, the primary participants are service-providers who work in small circles, examining their practice and trying out alternative ways of working. For the value of this to be maximised, participation needs to be organised around the interests of the critical reference group or driven by a critical reference group perspective, or else the research can risk becoming sidetracked.

- The researched: This may typically be the critical reference group, along with some service-providers or their representatives. However, again I have found that the more there is active participation the greater the chances of maximising both the accuracy and meaningfulness of all contributions, and also the sharing of perceptions and of emerging understandings about the value of what new actions should next be taken.

Research which involves the collaboration of people, rarely is sustained without a shared purpose, and this 'shared purpose' stems from what understandings people have together developed about what is of value. If understanding is not for 'its own sake', but directed towards understanding something 'in order to...', then the point of purposeful inquiry is action. As pointed out before, where the categories 'the researched' and 'the researchers' and 'the researched for' begin to become less distinct, this collaboration can become more cohesive.

What kind of action is for the parties to decide - focused by the perspective of the critical reference group. As pointed out earlier, that new action might be the reproduction of the same old action as was taken previously if it involves researchers who believe they neither are contributing (nor want to contribute) to change. This is research which may carefully reproduce the status quo. Other research, which is self-conscious about why it asked the questions it does, wishes instead to head towards a different and improved state of affairs.

Participatory action research is a term that brings together a set of assumptions underlying 'new paradigm' science and in contrast to those of traditional or 'old paradigm' science. These new assumptions underline the importance of social and collective processes in reaching conclusions about 'what is the case', and what the implications are for change which is deemed useful by those whose problematic situation led to the research in the first place.

In 'real life', actual researchers often straddle (more or less uncomfortably) the two paradigms, but the paradigms themselves are coherent bodies of thought that are not theoretically commensurable. But a paradigm addresses the unsolved problems of the previous paradigm. So while positivism arose to bring certainty and verifiability to a world construed as 'irrational', post positivism addresses the inability to handle enormous complexity in large, cybernetic, self-changing human systems. If conventional science wanted to give a group of people the power to determine 'truth' for and on behalf of others, the new science arose from a world of multiple and competing versions of truth and reality as a way of assisting people both come to the truth of their own reality, and also to embrace that of others.

The urgency of such mutual understanding is to be found in the topics selected by PAR practitioners - mostly concerned with difficult situations of social change, the loss of ways to meet human needs, the rise of anxieties and fears as we become strangers to each other, and the threat of dissolution into violence and alienation.

On such big fronts, participatory action research proceeds modestly, but it does proceed! For all these reasons participatory action research is not just research which we hope will be followed by action! It is action which is researched, changed and re-researched, within the research process by participants. Nor is it simply an exotic variant of consultation. Instead, it aims to be active co-research, by and for those to be helped. Nor can it be used by one group of people to get another group of people to do what is thought best for them - whether that is to implement a central policy or an organisational or service change. Instead it tries to be a genuinely democratic or non-coercive process whereby those to be helped, determine the purposes and outcomes of their own inquiry. Paradoxically it is quite close to a common-sense way of 'learning by doing'. But at the same time it is very hard to achieve the ideal conditions for putting it fully into practice.

Essentially participatory action research is research which involves all relevant parties in actively examining together current action (which they experience as problematic) in order to change and improve it. They do this by critically reflecting on the historical, political, cultural, economic, geographic and other contexts which make sense of it.

'Current problematic action' may range from the trivial to the life-threatening. Much participatory action research lies between these ends of the scale, and typically involves yourself; those who share your concerns, experiences and interests; others suffering from the problematic situation; others trying to assist it to change; and those who oversee the material resources needed to underpin the change effort (such as funds, people, salaries, services, office resources, etc.). Bringing these parties together, and absorbing new ones as the action research effort proceeds to unfold and implicate parties further afield, is not merely a side issue of 'entry to the field' but a central focus for achieving understanding and change. As well, action research is not research which sees these as 'contaminating' processes which 'bias' the scientific effort, nor does it have a problem with the 'researcher/s' identifying with 'the researched' and the 'researched for', - seeing this rather as essential to the gaining of engaged understanding.

What 'drives' participatory action research, like any research, is our 'need to know' in order to bring about desired change. We often shorthand term this our 'values' - which are our precious images of valued states or ways of being. Rather than seeing this holding-of-values as subjective and potentially a source of bias, the strength of the values we hold will determine the power and direction of our research efforts. Two key additional factors which will shape what we do is the strength of our imaginations (to theorise more creatively, deeply and imaginatively) and our scepticism (to keep our theory closely in relationship to the practices we are observing). Like any other research, the critical moment is that of 'discovery' or rather: 'invention' of a different and better way of seeing and understanding our realities. The old adage about science being 5% inspiration and 95% perspiration may hold true enough! The hard sweat and toil comprises the long hours of talking and thinking and sharing the results of our 'fieldwork' with one another. The moment of inspired thinking is when collective values are expressed in a new way of connecting ideas or a new way of 'naming' the world, that advances the collective situation of participants.

The field of action research deriving from education (particularly school room practice) and third world development more often have stressed the necessity of moving relatively quickly towards new action.

The post-war British field of action research, drawing on theory about group psychology or group dynamics, stressed the area of process, sometimes involving very diverse interests from the outset.

They include the classical social anthropology-trained sociologist William Foote Whyte who has moved to action research from what he now calls 'participatory research' (eg. his classic 1943 ethnographic study of an inner city immigrant American-Italian community). Another prominent American sociologist Shulamit Reinharz tells her story of moving from disembodied researching 'on' people to humanistic, qualitative and experiential researching 'with' people (1979). I, myself (Yoland Wadsworth), a Monash-trained sociologist have told of a similar trajectory (1985), moving from using standard large-scale random sample surveys analysed by the obligatory SPSS, to embracing interpretivist phhenomonology to working increasingly with and for critical reference groups using a critical constructivist methodology.

Old paradigm social science is often popularly termed 'positivist'. This refers to a school of philosophical thought which saw the world as having a single 'reality' which existed independently of the observer, and which could only be discovered by an objective and uninvolved scientist through acts of pure perception, ideally in a laboratory setting where all variables could be controlled and manipulated, and exact causation determined. This account has been difficult to sustain in practice - as with Newtonian science - given the limitations of such an uninvolved science. Far more engaged research - literally 'going native' - yields far better understanding. As well, when the social world is encountered, it takes as many forms as there are people. That is, understanding the social world depends on the exchange and communication of interpretations about what is going on. These are multiple and may be conflicting. As with post-Einsteinian physics, the 'observed' is importantly constructed by 'the observer' - and in the social world, is then further reconstructed by the observed (sometimes in the light of the observer's observations!).

For old paradigm science this is all so much unwanted 'bias' and 'contamination'. For new paradigm science it is the nature of the 'beast', and all so much more material for illuminating inquiry. New paradigm science also grasps the value-driven nature of inquiry and is in a position to focus its research in the interests of those who might problematise their existing undesirable situations. This offers a better chance of 'driving' theory towards better contributing to practice, and also avoiding the unethical and totalitarian consequences of a science which sees itself as 'value free'.

More formal language which is used to describe 'participatory action research' as a particular philosophy of knowledge (theory of how we know, or the grounds for knowledge, i.e. epistemology) also includes 'critical constructivist', 'post positivist' or 'critical interpretive' methodology.

Ironically, conventional experimental science can have its own problems and 'fail' when an ungrounded (irrelevant and wide of the mark) hypothesis is elaborately and expensively tested, only to discover that it was a poor proposition in the first place.

Alternatively, in social science, such poor propositions can survive in the literature and even make their researchers famous (and lead to high status positions!) in the absence of participatory processes or testing in practice which would supply the necessary feedback about their faulty or narrow character. The spectacular failure of European sociologists to predict the bringing down of the Berlin Wall testifies in the same way as the failure of meteorologists to predict the weather accurately.

Mostly both sociologists and meteorologists (as well as ordinary people who are observant and shrewd, and who can tap their barometers and feel the aches in their bones) pretty much get it right. Newtonian science mainly works. The break downs occur when matters are enormously complex and defy 'control of variables'. Unfortunately these may be precisely the critical times in messy complex changing human societies.

As well, some academic researchers claim with pride that there are no known beneficiaries of research (and not even an arena of potential beneficiaries). This is what they might call 'pure' research, or 'curiosity-driven' research 'for its own sake'.

It is very important that there be time and space for curiosity and speculative forays out into unknown waters and apparently 'irrelevant' matters. However even 'idle' curiosity is always historically and socially located (eg. Fleming's noticing of the penicillin mould) and thus shaped by the social world in which the 'idle curious' have grown up, learned language, learned values, and learned to notice some things and not others. 80% of all scientists, 'pure' and 'applied' alike, just happen to be curious in ways helpful to defence establishments all around the world. On the other hand even the most apparently esoteric inquirer frequently has quite well-formed views about the relevance of their line of inquiry (for example the relationship between Jacobin clothing styles and early capitalist modes of economy, and its relevance to late twentieth century post modernity). Where researchers themselves have no insight, someone else might well be able to carry out a little 'archaeology' and suggest something. For most research in the human services area, the critical reference group is very much more readily identified as service users.

Feminist research utilises (more or less sucessfully) a participatory action research methodology and additionally works in a topic area determined by a particular critical reference group: that of women. The kind of feminist theory used will reflect and in turn determine what kind of use is made of the research, and by whom.

Critical theory is a school of social science which developed firstly in Frankfurt and then in the United States of America after its members went into exile before and during the second world war. It has attempted to bring together the insights of Freudian (and now post Freudian) psychology and Marxian economics, in order to understand how the personal and the structural come together into ideological forms from which some benefit at the expense of others. Its better-known theorists include Adorno, Horkheimer, Habermas and Marcuse. It is now used as a term to describe a range of approaches which raise critical questions about the conditions which sustain existing forms of social life that are experienced as problematic by particular groups of people.

Fourth generation evaluation is a term coined by the Americans Egon Guba and Yvonna Lincoln to describe the application of constructivist methodology to evaluation (in the wake of three previous generations of evaluation which they have criticised on the grounds of over-adherence to a positivist epistemology and to managerialist dominance). They argued for the admission of all relevant parties to the process, and re-cast the evaluator as a facilitator of an essentially self-evaluation process.

For example school-based action research where parents and students may be involved, however the primary questions identified are those of the teachers. See also hospital projects which similarly stem from nurses' concerns in the absence of patients. Or welfare research about youth suicide or single mothers without any representation of these groups in the research team or committee. Where the questions are not necessarily those of the critical reference group, the research relies on disembodied critical theory to illuminate the assumptions behind things and thus reveal new choices of more relevant topics.

For example, say psychiatric nurses want to research how to protect themselves from patient violence. They could recommend regular time off for themselves to recover from their stress. The asking of critical question, such as 'what would be also good for patients?' might lead to this particular solution being problematised however, and set in train a further search for a different solution which does not meet the needs of one group at the expense of another. If patients participate in the research, they might give their perceptions of why the violence arises, leading to a different solution which also might not compound patients' existing problems of loss of staff continuity.

STANDARDIZED RECIPES

While it is the menu that determines what is to be sold and at what price, the standardized recipe controls both the quantity and the quality of what your kitchen will produce. A standardized recipe consists of the procedures to be used in preparing and serving each of your menu items. The standardized recipe ensures that each time a guest orders an item from your menu, he or she receives exactly what you intended the guest to receive.

Critical factors in a standardized recipe, such as cooking times and serving size, must remain constant so the menu items produced are always consistent. Guests expect to get what they pay for. The standardized recipe helps you make sure that they do. Inconsistency is the enemy of any quality foodservice operation.

It will make little difference to the unhappy guest, for instance, if you tell him or her that while the menu item he or she purchased today is not up to your normal standard, it will be tomorrow, or that it was the last time the guest visited your operation. Interestingly, despite their tremendous advantages, many managers refuse to take the time to develop standardized recipes. Of the preceding arguments, only the last one, staff's inability to read English, has any validity.

The effective operator should have the standardized recipes printed in the language of his or her production employees. Standardized recipes have far more advantages than disadvantages.

Reasons for incorporating a system of standardized recipes include:

- Accurate purchasing is impossible without the existence and use of standardized recipes.
- Dietary concerns require some foodservice operators to know exactly the kinds of ingredients and the correct amount of nutrients in each serving of a menu item.
- Accuracy in menu laws require that foodservice operators be able to tell guests about the type and amount of ingredients in their recipes.
- Accurate recipe costing and menu pricing is impossible without standardized recipes.
- Matching food used to cash sales is impossible to do without standardized recipes.

- New employees can be better trained with standardized recipes.
- The computerization of a foodservice operation is impossible unless the elements of standardized recipes are in place; thus, the advantages of advanced technological tools available to the operation are restricted or even eliminated.

In fact, standardized recipes are so important that they are the cornerstones of any serious effort to produce consistent, high-quality food products at an established cost. Without them, cost control efforts become nothing more than raising selling prices, reducing portion sizes, or lessening quality. This is not effective cost management. It is hardly management at all. Without established standardized recipes, however, this happens all too frequently.

Any recipe can be standardized. The process can sometimes be complicated, however, especially in the areas of baking and sauce production. It is always best to begin with a recipe of proven quality. Frequently, you may have a recipe designed to serve 10 guests, but you want to expand it to serve 100 people.

In cases like this, it may not be possible to simply multiply each ingredient used by 10. A great deal has been written regarding various techniques used to expand recipes. Computer software designed for that purpose is now on the market. As a general rule, however, any item that can be produced in quantity can be standardized in recipe form and can be adjusted, up or down, in quantity.

When adjusting recipes, it is important that measurement standards be consistent. Weighing with a pound or an ounce scale is the most accurate method of measuring any ingredients. The food item to be measured must be recipe ready. That is, it must be cleaned, trimmed, cooked, and generally completed, save for its addition to the recipe. For liquid items, measurement of volume (i.e., cup, quart, or gallon, etc.) may be preferred. Some operators like to weigh all ingredients, even liquids, for improved accuracy.

PERCENTAGE METHOD

The percentage method deals with recipe weight, rather than with a conversion factor. It is sometimes more accurate than using a conversion factor alone. Essentially, the percentage method involves weighing all ingredients and then computing the percentage weight of each recipe ingredient in relation to the total weight of all ingredients. To facilitate the computation, many operators convert pounds to ounces prior to making their percentage calculations.

These are converted back to standard pounds and ounces when the conversion is completed. To illustrate the use of the percentage method, let us assume that you have a recipe with a total weight of 10 pounds and 8 ounces, or 168 ounces. If the portion size is 4 ounces, the total recipe yield would be 168/4, or 42, servings. If you want your kitchen to prepare 75 servings, you would need to supply it with a standardized recipe consisting of the following total recipe weight: When adjusting recipes for quantity (total yield), two general methods may be employed.

They are:

- Factor method
- Percentage technique

FACTOR METHOD

When using the factor method, you must use the following formula to arrive at a recipe conversion factor: You now have all the information necessary to use the percentage method of recipe conversion. Note that% of total is computed as ingredient weight/total recipe weight. The proper conversion of weights and measures is important in recipe expansion or reduction.

The judgment of the recipe writer is critical, however, since such factors as cooking time, temperature, and utensil selection may vary as recipe sizes are increased or decreased. In addition, some recipe ingredients, such as spices or flavorings, may not respond well to mathematical conversions. In the final analysis, it is your assessment of product taste that should ultimately determine ingredient ratios in standardized recipes. All recipes should be standardized and used as written. It is your responsibility to see that this is done.

INVENTORY CONTROL

With a knowledge of what is likely to be purchased by your guests (sales forecast) and a firm idea of the ingredients necessary to produce these items (standardized recipes), you must make decisions about desired inventory levels.

A desired inventory level is simply the answer to the question, "How much of each needed ingredient should I have on hand at any one time?" It is clear that this question can only be properly answered if your sales forecast is of good quality and your standardized recipes are in place so you do not "forget" to stock a necessary recipe ingredient.

Inventory management seeks to provide appropriate working stock, which is the amount of an ingredient you anticipate using before purchasing that item again, and a minimal safety stock, the extra amount of that ingredient you decide to keep on hand to meet higher than anticipated demand.

Demand for a given menu item can fluctuate greatly between deliveries periods, even when the delivery occurs daily. With too little inventory, you may run out of products and therefore reduce guest satisfaction. With too much inventory, waste, theft, and spoilage can become excessive. The ability to effectively manage the inventory process is one of the best skills a foodservice manager can acquire.

DETERMINING INVENTORY LEVELS

Inventory levels are determined by a variety of factors. Some of the most important ones are as follows:

- Storage capacity
- Item perishability
- Vendor delivery schedule
- Potential savings from increased purchase size
- Operating calendar
- Relative importance of stock outages
- Value of inventory dollars to the operator

Storage Capacity: Inventory items must be purchased in quantities that can be adequately stored and secured. Many times, kitchens lack adequate storage facilities. This may mean more frequent deliveries and holding less of each product on hand than would otherwise be desired. When storage space is too great, however, the tendency by some managers is to fill the space. It is important that this not be done, as increased inventory of items generally leads to greater spoilage and loss due to theft. Moreover, large quantities of goods on the shelf tend to send a message to employees that there is "plenty" of everything. This may result in the careless use of valuable and expensive products. It is also unwise to overload refrigerators or freezers. This not only can result in difficulty in finding items quickly, but also may cause carry overs (those items produced for a meal period but not sold) to be "lost" in the storage process.

Item Perishability: If all food products had the same shelf life, that is, the amount of time a food item retains its maximum freshness, flavour, and quality while in storage, you would have less difficulty in determining the quantity of each item you should keep on hand. Unfortunately, the shelf life of food products varies greatly. Because food items have varying shelf lives, you must balance the need for a particular product with the optimal shelf life of that product.

Serving items that are "too old" is a sure way to develop guest complaints. In fact, one of the quickest ways to determine the overall effectiveness of a foodservice manager is to "walk the boxes." This means to take a tour of a facility's storage area. If many products, particularly in the refrigerated area, are moldy, soft, overripe, or rotten, it is a good indication of a foodservice operation that does not have a feel for proper inventory levels based on the shelf lives of the items kept in inventory. It is also a sign that sales forecasting methods either are not in place or are not working well.

VENDOR DELIVERY SCHEDULE

It is the fortunate foodservice operator who lives in a large city with many vendors, some of whom may offer the same service and all of whom would like to have the operator's business. In many cases, however, you will not have the luxury of daily delivery. Your operation may be too small to warrant such frequent stops by a vendor, or the operation may be in such a remote location that daily delivery is simply not possible. Consider, for a moment, the difficulty you would face if you were the manager of a foodservice operation located on an offshore oil rig.

Clearly, in a case like that, a vendor willing to provide daily dough nut delivery is going to be hard to find! In all cases, it is important to remember that the cost to the vendor for frequent deliveries will be reflected in the cost of the goods to you. Vendors will readily let you know what their delivery schedule to a certain area or location can be. It is up to you to use this information to make good decisions regarding the quantity of that vendor's product you must buy to have both working stock and safety stock.

POTENTIAL SAVINGS FROM INCREASED PURCHASE SIZE

Sometimes, you will find that you can realise substantial savings by purchasing needed items in large quantities. This certainly makes sense if the total savings actually outweigh the added costs of receiving and storing the larger quantity. For the large foodservice operator, who once a year buys canned green beans by the railroad car, the savings are real. For the smaller operator, who hopes to reduce costs by ordering two cases of green beans rather than one, the savings may be negligible. Generally, however, reduced packaging and shipping costs result in lower per unit costs when larger bags, boxes, or cartons of ingredients are purchased.

Remember, too, that there are costs associated with extraordinarily large purchases. These may include storage costs, spoilage, deterioration, insect or rodent infestation, or theft. As a general rule, you should determine your ideal product inventory levels and then maintain your stock within that need range. Only when the advantages of placing an extraordinarily large order are very clear should such a purchase be undertaken.

Operating Calendar

When an operation is involved in serving meals seven days a week to a relatively stable number of guests, the operating calendar makes little difference to inventory level decision making. If, however, the operation opens on Monday and closes on Friday for two days, as is the case in many school foodservice accounts, the operating calendar plays a large part in determining desired inventory levels. In general, it can be said that an operator who is closing down either for a weekend (as in school foodservice or a corporate dining situation) or for a season (as in the operation of a summer camp or seasonal hotel) should attempt to reduce overall inventory levels as the closing period approaches.

This is expecially true when it comes to perishable items. Many operators actually plan menus to steer clear of highly perishable items near their closing periods. They prefer to work highly perishable items, such as fresh seafood and some meat items, into the early or middle part of their operating calendar. This allows them to minimize the amount of perishable product that must be carried through the close-down period.

RELATIVE IMPORTANCE OF STOCK OUTAGES

In many foodservice operations, not having enough of a single food ingredient or menu item is simply not that important. In other operations, the shortage of even one menu item might spell disaster. While it may be all right for the local French restaurant to run out of one of the specials on Saturday night, it is not difficult to imagine the problem of the McDonald's restaurant manager who runs out of French fried potatoes on that same Saturday night! For the small operator, a mistake in the inventory level of a minor ingredient that results in an outage can often be corrected by a quick run to the grocery store.

For the larger facility, such an outage may well represent a substantial loss of sales or guest goodwill. Whether the operator is large or small, being out of a key ingredient or menu item is to be avoided, and planning inventory levels properly helps prevent it. In the restaurant industry, when an item is no longer available on the menu, you "86" the item, a reference to restaurant slang originating in the early 1920s (86 rhymed with "nix," a Cockney term meaning "to eliminate").

If you, as a manager, "86" too many items on any given night, the reputation of your restaurant as well as your ability to manage it will suffer. A strong awareness and knowledge of how critical this outage factor is help determine the appropriate inventory level. A word of caution is, however, necessary. The foodservice operator who is determined never to run out of anything must be careful not to set inventory levels so high as to actually end up costing the operation more than if realistic levels were maintained.

VALUE OF INVENTORY DOLLARS TO THE OPERATOR

In some cases, operators elect to remove dollars from their bank accounts and convert them to product inventory. When this is done, the operator is making the decision to value product more than dollars. When it is expected that the value of the inventory will rise faster than the value of the banked dollar, this is a good strategy. All too often, however, operators overbuy or "stockpile" inventory, causing too many dollars to be tied up in non-interest-bearing food products.

When this is done, managers incur opportunity costs. An opportunity cost is the cost of foregoing the next best alternative when making a decision. For example, suppose you have two choices, A and B, both having potential benefits or returns for you. If you choose A, then you lose the potential benefits from choosing B (opportunity cost). In other words, you could choose to use your money to buy food inventory that will sit in your storeroom until it is sold, or you could choose not to stockpile food inventory and invest the money. If you stockpile the inventory, then the opportunity cost is the amount of money you would have made if you had invested rather than holding the excess inventory.

If the dollars used to purchase inventory must be borrowed from the bank, rather than being available from operating revenue, an even greater cost to carry the inventory is incurred since interest must be paid on the borrowed funds.

In addition, a foodservice company of many units that invests too much of its money in inventory may find that funds for acquisition, renovation, or marketing are not readily available. In contrast, a state institution that is given its entire annual budget at the start of its fiscal year (a year that is 12 months long but may not follow the calendar year) may find it advantageous to use its purchasing power to acquire large amounts of inventory at the beginning of the year and at very low prices.

SETTING THE PURCHASE POINT

A purchase point, as it relates to inventory levels, is that point in time when an item should be reordered.

This point is typically designated by one of two methods:

1. As needed (just in time)
2. Par level

As Needed When you elect to use the as-needed, or just-in-time, method of determining inventory level, you are basically purchasing food based on your prediction of unit sales and the sum of the ingredients (from standardized recipes) necessary to produce those sales. Then, no more than the absolute minimum of needed inventory level is secured from the vendor. When this system is used, the buyer compiles a list of needed ingredients and submits it to management for approval to purchase. For example, in a hotel foodservice operation, the demand for 500 servings of a raspberries and cream torte dessert, to be served to a group in the hotel next week, would cause the responsible person to check the standardized recipe for this item and, thus, determine the amount of raspberries that should be ordered. Then that amount, and no more, would be ordered from the vendor.

Par Level

Foodservice operators may set predetermined purchase points, called par levels, for some items. In the case of the raspberries and cream torte dessert referred to previously, it is likely that the torte will require vanilla extract. It does not make sense, however, to expect your food production manager to order vanilla extract by the tablespoon! In fact, you are likely to find that you are restricted in the quantity you could buy due to the vendor's delivery minimum, namely, bottle or case, or the manufacturer's packaging methods. In cases such as this, or when demand for a product is relatively constant, you may decide to set needed inventory levels for some items by determining purchase points based on appropriate par levels. When determining par levels, you must establish both minimum and maximum amounts required. Many foodservice managers establish a minimum par level by computing working stock, then adding 25 to 50% more for safety stock.

Then, an appropriate purchase point, or point at which additional stock is purchased, is determined. If, for example, you have decided that the inventory level for coffee should be based on a par system, the decision may be made that the minimum (given your usage) amount that should be on hand at all times is four cases. This would be the minimum par level. Assume that you set the maximum par level at ten cases. While the inventory level in this situation would vary from a low of four cases to a high of ten cases, you would be assured that you would never have too little or too much of this particular menu item.

If cases of coffee were to be ordered under this system, you would always attempt to keep the number of cases between the minimum par level (four cases) and the maximum par level (ten cases). The purchase point in this example might be six cases; that is, when your operation had six cases of coffee on hand, an order would be placed with the coffee vendor. The intention would be to get the total stock up to ten cases before your supply got below four cases. Since delivery might take one or two days, six cases might be an appropriate purchase point. Whether we use the as-needed or the par level method, or, as in the case of most operators, a combination of the two, each ingredient or menu item should have a management-designated inventory level. As a rule, highly perishable items should be ordered on an as-needed basis, while items with a longer shelf life can often have their inventory levels set using a par level system. The answer to the question "How much of each ingredient should I have on hand at any point in time?" must come from you. Many factors will impact this decision. The decision, however, must be made and compliance monitored on a regular basis.

PURCHASING

Regardless of the method used to determine inventory levels, once the quantity needed on hand has been determined, you must then turn your attention to the extremely important area of purchasing.

Purchasing is essentially a matter of determining the following:

- What should be purchased?
- What is the best price to pay?
- How can a steady supply be assured?

What Should Be Purchased?

Just as it is not possible to determine inventory levels or items to be purchased without standardized recipes, it is not possible to manage costs where purchasing is concerned without the use of product specifications, or "specs." A product spec is simply a detailed description of an ingredient or menu item. A spec is a way for you to communicate in a very precise way with a vendor so that your operation receives the *exact* item requested every time.

A foodservice specification generally consists of the following information:

- Product name or specification number
- Pricing unit
- Standard or grade
- Weight range/size
- Processing and/or packaging
- Container size
- Intended use
- Other information such as product yield

It is very important to note that the product specification determines neither the "best" product nor the product that costs the least. It is the product that you have determined to be the *most appropriate* product for its intended use in terms of both quality and cost. A product specification that is written too loosely can be a problem because the needed level of item quality may not be delivered. On the other hand, if your product specifications are too tight, that is, if they are overly and unnecessarily specific, too few vendors may be able to supply the product, resulting in your paying excessively high costs for that item. The necessity of specifications will become clear if we listen in on a telephone call made by Louie, a manager who is about to place an order for bread with a new vendor, Sam's Uptown Bakery:

Louie:	*"Sam, I need bread for sandwiches."*
Sam:	*"Louie, you know I have the best bread in town!"*
Louie:	*"Well, send me 50 loaves as soon as possible."*
Sam:	*"No problem, Louie. We will deliver this afternoon!"*

Little does Louie know that Sam's definition of bread for sandwiches is *quite* different from his own. Louie is expecting 1pound, white, split, thin-sliced, 45-slices-to-the-bag bread. From Sam's exotic shop, however, he may well receive a 2-pound, thick-sliced, sesame seed–topped Italian loaf. Thus, even for a product as common as bread, a specification must be developed. Fortunately, the process is relatively simple because it depends mainly on your own view of appropriate product quality. Each menu item or ingredient should have its own spec. In fact, management should make it a habit to ensure that only telephone conversations such as the following take place:

Louie:	*"Sam, I need 50 loaves of my spec #617 as soon as possible."*
Sam:	*"Spec #617? Let's see, I've got it right here. That's your* white bread for sandwiches spec, right?"
Louie:	*"That's right, Sam."*
Sam:	*"No problem, Louie. We will deliver this afternoon!"*

Product Name

This may seem self-explanatory, but, in reality, it is not. Mangos are a fruit to those in the southwestern United States, but the word may mean a bell pepper to those in the Midwest. Bell peppers do not come only in green, their most common colour, but can also be purchased in yellow and red forms. Thus, the product name must be specific enough to clearly and precisely identify the item you wish to buy. Many canned hams are pear shaped, but a Pullman canned ham is square. You may be requesting 100% maple syrup when you place a syrup order, but your vendor could assume maple-"flavored" syrup is the item you desire.

Purchasing food becomes even more difficult when you realise that, especially in the area of meats and seafood, different regions in the country may have different names for the same product. When developing the product specification, you may find it helpful to assign a number to the item as well as its name. This can be useful when, for example, many forms of the same ingredient or menu item may be purchased.

A deli-restaurant may use 10 to 20 different types of bread, depending on the intended use of the bread; thus, in our product specification example, bacon, which this operation uses in many forms, has both a name and a number assigned to the specification. The same may be true with a number of items such as cheese, which may come in a brick, sliced, shredded, or a variety of other forms, as well as several types.

PRICING UNIT

A pricing unit may be established in terms of pounds, quarts, gallons, cases, or any other commonly used unit. Parsley, for example, is typically sold in the United States by the bunch. Thus, it is also priced by the bunch. How much is a bunch? You must know. Grapes are sold by the "lug." Unless you are familiar with the term, you may not be able to buy that product in an effective way. Again, knowledge of the pricing unit, whether it is a gallon, pound, case, bunch, or lug, is critical when developing a product specification. You should insist that your vendor supply you with definitions of each pricing unit upon which that vendor bases his or her selling price.

Standard or Grade

Many food items are sold with varying degrees of quality or desirability. Because that is true, the U.S. Department of Agriculture, Bureau of Fisheries, and the Food and Drug Administration have developed standards for many food items. In addition, grading programmes are in place for many commonly used foodservice items. Trade groups such as the National Association of Meat Purveyors publish item descriptions for many of these products. Consumers also are aware of many of these distinctions. Prime beef, in the consumer's mind, may be superior to choice beef. In a similar manner, you may wish to purchase and serve Coca-Cola rather than a lower cost generic fountain soda.

When developing a specification, a specific brand name or product source (A-1 Steak Sauce, Maine lobster) may be included in this section. You should be cautious, however, about specifying a brand name unless it is actually critical to your operation. Unless several vendors are able to supply you with a product you need, the price you may pay to the vendor who does have the item may be too high.

Weight Range/Size

Weight range or size is important when referring to meats, fish, poultry, and some vegetables. In our standardized recipe example of roast chicken, the quarters were to have come from chickens in the 3- to 3_ pound range. This will make them very different than if they came from chickens in the 4- to 4_pound range. In the case of products requiring specific trim or maximum fat covering, that should be designated also, such as 10-ounce strip steak, maximum tail 1 inch, fat covering half inch.

Four-ounce hamburger patties, 16-ounce T-bones, and one by fourth pound hot dogs are additional examples of items of the type that require, not a weight range, but an exact size. It is important to note that while the operator may specify such a specific weight, it is likely that he or she will pay a premium for such accuracy, especially in items such as steaks, where the supplier's ability to perfectly control product weight is somewhat limited.

Count, in the hospitality industry, is a term that is used to designate size. For example, 16- to 20-count shrimp refers to the fact that, for this size shrimp, 16 to 20 of the individual shrimp would be required to make 1 pound. In a like manner, 30- to 40-count shrimp means that it takes 30 to 40 of this size shrimp to make a pound. Many fruits and vegetables are also sold by count. For example, a 48-count avocado means that 48 individual avocados will fit in a standard case. In general, the larger the count, the smaller the size of the individual food items.

PROCESSING AND/OR PACKAGING

Processing and packaging refers to the product's state when you buy it. Apples, for example, may be purchased fresh, canned, or frozen. Each form will carry a price appropriate for its processed or packaged state. It is important to note that the term "fresh" is one with varying degrees of meaning. Fish that has been frozen and then thawed should be identified as such. Packaging is also extremely important when determining product yield. For example, 3 pounds of canned corn will not yield the same number of 3-ounce servings as 3 pounds of fresh ear corn. Fresh fruits and vegetables may be of excellent quality and low in cost per pound, but the effective food service operator must consider actual usable product when computing the price per pound. Also, the Labour cost of washing, trimming, and otherwise preparing fresh products must be considered when comparing their price to that of a canned or frozen product.

The U.S. food supply is one of great variety and quality. Food can come packed in a large number of forms and styles, including slab packed, layered cell packed, fiberboard divided, shrink packed, individually wrapped, and bulk packed. While it is beyond the scope of this text to detail all of the many varieties of food processing and packing styles, it is important for you to know about them. Your vendors will be pleased to help explain to you all the types of item processing and packaging they offer.

Container Size

This term refers to the can size, number of cans per case, or weight of the container in which the product is delivered. Most operators know that a 50-pound bag of flour should contain 50 pounds. Some may not be sure, however, what the appropriate weight for a "lug" of tomatoes would be.

Intended Use

Different types of the same item are often used in the same foodservice operation, but in a variety of ways. Consider, for example, the operator who uses strawberries in a variety of ways. Obviously, perfect, large berries are best for chocolate-dipped strawberries served on a buffet table. Less-than-perfect berries, however, may cost less and be a perfectly acceptable form for sliced strawberries on strawberry shortcake. Frozen berries may make a good choice for a baked strawberry pie and would be much more cost effective. Breads, milk products, apples, and other fruits are additional examples of foods that come in a variety of forms; this requires you to know that the "best" form of a food product is not necessarily the most expensive.

Other Information Such as Product Yield

Additional information may be included in a specification if it helps the vendor understand exactly what you have in mind when your order is placed. An example is product yield. Product yield is simply the amount of product that you will have remaining after cooking, trimming, portioning, or cleaning. Product yield will help you and your vendor determine how much product you will have to purchase in order to have the desired product quantity after waste is removed.

WHAT IS THE BEST PRICE TO PAY?

Once purchase specifications have been developed and quantities to be purchased have been established, your next step is to determine how to buy these items at the best price. Some would say that determining the best price should be a simple matter of finding who has the lowest cost product and placing an order with that person. In fact, that is almost always a sure sign of a manager who lacks understanding of the way vendors operate. The best price, in fact, is more accurately stated as the lowest price that meets the long-term goals of both the foodservice operation and its vendor.

When you have a choice of vendors, each supplying the same product (your specification), it is possible to engage in comparison shopping. The vehicle used to do this is called the bid sheet. The bid sheet includes vendor information, buyer information, and item description, unit of bid, bid price, salesperson's signature, and date. It also includes the dates that the bid prices will be "fixed," which means the dates that the supplier agrees to keep the bid price in effect. The bid sheet would be sent to all meat vendors each week on Friday to be returned Monday for the weekly bid prices. Then you would compare the item prices to see which vendor you would buy. After you have received bids from your suppliers, you can compare those bids on a price comparison sheet. A price comparison sheet typically has a place to list the category being bid on, namely, produce, dairy products, meats, and so on, the name of the vendors available to bid, bid date, item description, unit of purchase, best bid price, best company quote, and last price paid. This information may then be used to select a vendor, based on the best price. Once the best price is determined for each item, then a purchase order using the best prices can be developed for each vendor.

Bid sheets and price comparison sheets may be used to determine the specific vendor who can supply the *lowest* price, but they do not give enough information to determine the *best* price. This makes sense when you realise that your own guests do not necessarily go to the lowest-priced restaurants for all of their meals. If they did, there would be no hope of success for the operator who tried to provide a better food product, in a better environment, with better service. In fact, most foodservice operators would resent guests who came into their operation and claimed they could get the exact same item for a lower price down the street.

It is a truism that any product can be sold a little cheaper if quality is allowed to vary. Even with the use of product specifications, vendor dependability, quality of vendor service, and accuracy in delivery can be determining factors when attempting to determine the "best price." Bill's Produce may be the preferred vendor for these items if price alone is the issue. If, however, Bill's Produce is frequently late in delivery, has questionable sanitary habits, and frequently is short or unable to deliver the promised product, the lower price may be no bargain. Davis Foods, on the other hand, may have a reputation for quality products and service that make it the vendor of choice. Any foodservice operator who uses price as the only criterion when shopping will find it very difficult to develop any meaningful relationship with a supplier.

For the smaller operation, the manager may be interested in comparing the *total* price from each supplier, rather than the price of individual items. That is, each ordering day, the manager would multiply the quantity of an item needed by the best price. An approach such as this is used when buying strictly from the price comparison sheet may result in orders too small to meet a supplier's minimum order requirement, that is, the smallest order that can be placed with a vendor who delivers.

If the minimum order requirement cannot be met using the lowest prices, then the manager may have to choose the supplier with the next highest price to fill a complete order. In some cases, the vendor to be used by the foodservice operator has been determined in advance.

This is often true in a large corporate organization or in a franchise situation. Contracts to provide goods may be established by the central purchasing department of these organizations. When that happens, the designated vendor may have a national or a long-term contract to supply, at a predetermined price, items that meet the operation's specifications.

HOW CAN A STEADY SUPPLY BE ASSURED?

Unfortunately, very little has been written in the field of foodservice about managing costs through cooperation with vendors. Your food salesperson can be one of your most important allies in controlling costs. Operators who determine their supplier only on the basis of cost will find that they receive only the product they have purchased, whereas their competitors are buying more than just food! Or, as one food salesperson said when asked why he should be selected as the primary food vendor, "With my products, you also get me!" And so it is; just as good foodservice operators know that guests respond to both products and personal service levels, so, too, do effective food suppliers.

Assuring a steady supply of quality products at a fair price is extremely important to the long-term success of a foodservice operator, yet many operators treat their suppliers as if they were the enemy. In fact, suppliers can be of immense value in assuring a steady supply of quality products at a fair price if you remember the following points.

Suppliers Have Many Prices, Not Just One

Unlike the restaurant business, which tends to hold its prices steady between menu reprints and generally charges the same price to all who come in the door, suppliers have a variety of prices based on the customer to whom they are quoting them. Therefore, when an operator gets a quote on a case of lettuce, the telephone conversation may sound like this:

Foodservice manager:	*"Hello, is this Ready Boy Produce?"*
Ready boy:	*"Yes, how can I help you?"*
Foodservice operator:	*"What is your price on lettuce today?"*
Ready boy:	*"$28.50 per case."*
This conversation should really be interpreted, as follows:	
Foodservice operator:	*"Hello, is this Ready Boy Produce?"*
Ready boy:	*"Yes, how can I help you?"*
Foodservice operator:	*"What is my price on lettuce today?"*
Ready boy:	*"Based on our relationship, it is $28.50 per case."*

Suppliers Reward Volume Customers

It is simply in the best interest of a supplier to give a better price to a high-volume customer. The cost of delivering a $1,000 order is not that much different from the cost of delivering a $100 order. It still takes one truck and one driver. Those operators who decide to concentrate their business in the hands of fewer suppliers will, as a general rule, pay a lower price.Of course, the volume of products you must buy from a vendor to meet his or her minimum delivery requirement will vary. In addition, larger foodservice units certainly have a greater degree of flexibility in selecting multiple vendors because managers of these large units can more easily meet supplier requirements while still minimizing overall costs.

Cherry Pickers Are Serviced Last

Cherry pickers is the term used by suppliers to describe the customer who gets bids from multiple vendors, then buys only those items each vendor has "on sale" or for the lowest price. If an operator buys only a vendor's low-end item, the vendor will usually respond by providing limited service. It is a natural reaction to the foodservice operator's failure to take into account varying service levels, long-term relationships, dependability, or any other vendor characteristic, except cheapest price.

It is important to remember, however, that a foodservice manager who meets minimum delivery requirements and buys regularly from the same vendor is not seen as a cherry picker just because he or she buys each item from the vendor with the lowest price. The key concept here is to develop a history of regular buying and cooperation with your vendor.

Slow Pay Means High Pay

Those operators who do not pay their bills in a timely manner would be surprised to know what their competitors are paying for similar products. In most cases, operators who are slow to pay will find that the vendor has decided to add the extra cost of carrying their account to the price the operator pays for his or her products.

Vendors Can Help Reduce Costs

Vendors have a knowledge of the products they sell that exceeds that of the average foodservice operator. This skill can be used to help the competition, or it can be harnessed for your own good use. Vendors can be a great source of information related to new products, cooking techniques, trends, and alternative product usage.

ONE VENDOR VERSUS MANY VENDORS

Every operator is faced with the decision of whether to buy from one vendor or many vendors. In general, the more vendors there are, the more time must be spent in ordering, receiving, and paying invoices. Many operators, however, fear that if they give all their business to one supplier, their costs may rise because of a lack of competition. In reality, the likelihood of this occurring is extremely small. Just as foodservice operators are unlikely to take advantage of their best guests (and, in fact, would tend to offer additional services not available to the occasional guest), so, too, does the vendor tend to behave in a manner that is preferential to the operator who does most of his or her buying from that vendor.

In fact, it makes good business sense for the vendor to do so. It is never advisable, however, to be at the mercy of a particular vendor. A good business relationship can only occur among equals; thus, many operators strive to maintain both a primary and a secondary supplier of most products. Using one or two vendors tends to bring the average delivery size up and should result in a lower per item price.

On the other hand, giving one vendor all of the operation's business can be dangerous and costly if the items to be purchased vary widely in quality and price. Staples and nonperishables are best purchased in bulk from one vendor. Orders for meats, produce, and some bakery products are best split among several vendors, perhaps with a primary and a secondary vendor in each category so that you have a second alternative should the need arise. If you are using bid buying as a purchasing method, having three vendors is advisable so that you have an adequate choice of prices and services.

Purchasing Ethics

Purchasing food products is an area that can test the ethics of even the most conscientious manager. Ethics have been defined as the choices of proper conduct made by an individual in his or her relationships with others. Ethics come into play in purchasing products because of the tendency for some suppliers to seek an unfair advantage over the competition by providing "personal" Favours to the buyer.

These Favours can range from small holiday gifts given in appreciation for another year's partnership to outright offers of cash "bribes"/kickbacks to the buyer in exchange for volume purchases. Some suppliers have been known to offer buyers computers, monthly cash payments, trips to Hawaii, and other such "big ticket" items to guarantee business.

Although you, as a buyer, might personally benefit from these items, the foodservice operation, your employer, will ultimately "pay" for these kickbacks through higher product prices. Should you get caught accepting these items, it is possible that you will be fired. It is the wise manager who knows the boundaries of appropriate behaviour with suppliers. Some large foodservice organizations have formal codes of conduct for their buyers. When these are in place, they should, of course, be carefully reviewed and followed. If your organization does not have a formal set of ethical guidelines for buying, the following self-tests can be helpful in determining whether a considered course of action with your supplier is indeed ethical.

Ethical Guidelines

- Is it legal?
  - Any course of action that violates written law or company policy and procedure is wrong.
- Does it hurt anyone?
  - Are benefits accruing to the buyer that rightfully belong to the owner of the business? Discounts, rebates, and free products are the property of the business, not the buyer.
- Am I being honest?
  - Is the activity one that you can comfortably say reflects well on your integrity as a professional, or will the activity actually diminish your reputation with other suppliers?
- Would I care if it happened to me?
  - If you owned the business, would you be in Favour of your buyer behaving in the manner you are considering? If you owned multiple units, would it be good for the business if all of your buyers followed the considered course of action?
- Would I publicize my action?
  - A quick way to review the ethical merit of a situation is to consider whom you would tell about it. If you are comfortable telling your boss and your other suppliers about the considered course of action, it is likely ethical. If you would prefer that your actions go undetected, you are probably on shaky ethical ground.

DAILY INVENTORY SHEET

Before you can place an order, you will need to find out what you need! The process is much like going through your house and making a shopping list of all items before you go to the store. Some managers say that they intuitively "know" what they need without looking at their storage areas. If you have ever gone grocery shopping without a list, however, you know that you will inevitably miss a few items. We have all been in a situation in which we went to the store, purchased what we thought we needed, only to find that we forgot an important item!

You, as a foodservice manager, will want to have a detailed look at your inventory before you place an order. A good way to make sure that you have checked all your items in your storage areas is to use a daily inventory sheet. A daily inventory sheet will have the items listed in your storage areas, the unit of purchase, and the par value preprinted on the sheet. In addition, the form will have the following columns: on hand, special order, and order amount.

A preprinted list of all your items in storage and unit of purchase is important so that you will not have to write down the items every time you check the inventory. The list should be in the same order that you store the items so that you can quickly and easily locate your products. The par value is listed so that you know how much inventory you should have in storage at any given time. You may also want to list the purchase point, if appropriate. To use the daily inventory sheet, you would physically walk through your storage areas to determine what items (and amounts) you should order for the following day. Under the "On Hand" column, you would list how many of each item you have on hand, that is, sitting on the shelf. You also need to list any "Special Order" amounts needed above the par level. An example of this would be extra cases of perishables, such as strawberries, ordered for a banquet.

PREPARING THE PURCHASE ORDER

Some items will be purchased daily, others weekly, and some, perhaps, monthly. In addition, you may be able to choose from a variety of ways to communicate with your supplier. Of course, much purchasing is done face-to-face, but the technology available for placing orders today is significant and includes the fax machine, telephone keypad, e-mail, and direct access to the vendor's order system via modem on software supplied to you by that vendor.

Some vendors will also come to your business and place orders for you on their laptop computers and then transfer your order electronically. In addition, more and more vendors are posting current prices on their Web pages, thus ensuring a rapid transfer of information to their customers.

Regardless of your communication method, however, it is critical that you prepare a written purchase order, or record of what you have decided to buy. The purchase order (PO) should be made out in triplicate (three copies). One copy goes to the receiving area for use by the receiving clerk. One copy is retained by management for the bookkeeping area. The original is, of course, sent to the vendor. If the purchase order is developed by telephone, management retains the original copy, with a notation in the Comments section, stating that the vendor has not seen the PO. In all cases, however, it is important to place all orders using a purchase order form. If this is not done, the receiving clerk will have no record of what is coming in on the delivery. Purchase order preparation can be simple or complex, but, in all cases, the written purchase order form should contain space for the following information:

Purchase Order Information

- Item name
- Spec number, if appropriate
- Quantity ordered
- Quoted price
- Extension price

- Total price of order
- Vendor information
- Purchase order number
- Date ordered
- Delivery date
- Ordered by
- Received by
- Delivery instructions
- Comments

Each order you place should result in the preparation of a PO. This is true even if the vendor is delivering a standing order on a daily basis.

The advantages of a written purchase order are many and include the following:

- Written verification of quoted price
- Written verification of quantity ordered
- Written verification of the receipt of all goods ordered
- Written and special instructions to the receiving clerk, as needed
- Written verification of conformance to product specification
- Written authorization to prepare vendor invoice for payment

The chef has used a sales forecast to determine the quantity of products needed for next Thursday's delivery. A check of the produce walk-in lets the chef know what is on hand and the quantity of each product required. This information allows for the accurate preparation of the PO. In this case, the order is then faxed to Scooter's Produce. The receiving clerk at the Ardmoor is now prepared with the information necessary to effectively receive the product from Scooter's.

RECEIVING

Once the PO has been prepared by the purchasing agent, it is time to prepare for the acceptance or receiving of the goods. This function is performed by the receiving clerk in a large operation or may be performed in a smaller operation by you, as the manager, or by a staff member you designate. In all cases, however, it is wise for you to establish the purchasing and receiving functions so that one individual places the order, while another individual is responsible for verifying delivery and acceptance of the product.

When this is not done, the potential for fraud or theft is substantial. Auditors, those individuals responsible for reviewing and evaluating proper operational procedures, have frequently found that the purchasing agent in an operation ordered a product, signed for its acceptance, and thus authorized invoice payment when, in fact, no product was ever delivered! In this case, the purchasing agent could be getting cash payment from the purveyor or supplier without the manager's knowledge. This could happen unless there are additional individuals in the purchasing chain.

If it is not possible to have more than one person involved in the buying process, the work of the purchasing agent/receiving clerk must be carefully monitored by management to prevent fraud. There is probably no area of the foodservice establishment more ignored than the area in which receiving takes place. This is truly unfortunate, since this is the area where we are ensuring we receive the quality of products we ordered.

Proper receiving includes all of the following features:

- Proper location
- Proper tools and equipment
- Proper delivery schedules
- Proper training

PROPER LOCATION

The "back door," which is usually reserved for receiving, is often no more than that—just an entrance to the kitchen. In fact, the receiving area must be adequate to handle the job of receiving, or product loss and inconsistency will result. First, the receiving area must be large enough to allow for checking products delivered against both the invoice, which is the supplier's record of products delivered and price charged, and the PO, which is the operation's record of the same thing. In addition to space required to allow for counting and weighing, accessibility to equipment required to move products to their proper storage area and to dispose of excess packaging is important.

A location near refrigerated areas is helpful in maintaining refrigerated and frozen products at their desired temperatures. You should make sure the area stays free of trash and clutter, as these make it too easy to hide delivered food items that may be taken home at the end of the dishonest employee's shift. It is important to remember that the delivery person is also a potential thief. While most suppliers are extremely careful to screen their delivery personnel for honesty, it is a fact that a delivery person has access to products and has a truck available to *remove* as well as deliver goods. For this reason, it is important that the receiving clerk work in an area that has a clear view of both delivery personnel and their vehicles.

The receiving area should be kept extremely clean, since you do not want to contaminate incoming food, or provide a carrying vehicle for pests. Often, suppliers themselves are responsible for delivering goods that can harbor roach eggs or other insects. A clean receiving area makes it easier to both prevent and detect this type of problem. The area should be well lit and properly ventilated. Excessive heat in the receiving area can quickly damage delivered goods, especially if they are either refrigerated or frozen products. Too little light may cause product defects to go unnoticed; therefore, the receiving area should be well lit. Flooring should be light in colour and of a type that is easily cleaned. In colder climates, it is important that the receiving area be warm enough to allow the receiving clerk to carefully inspect products. The outside dock area in February, if the temperature is below freezing, is no place for an employee to conduct a thorough inspection of incoming products!

PROPER TOOLS AND EQUIPMENT

While the tools and equipment needed for effective receiving vary by type and size of operation, some items are standard in any receiving operation. These include the following:

Scales

Scales should be of two types: those accurate to the fraction of a pound (for large items) and those accurate to the fraction of an ounce (for smaller items and pre-portioned meats). Scales should be calibrated regularly to ensure accuracy.

Wheeled Equipment

These items, whether hand trucks or carts, should be available so that goods can be moved quickly and efficiently to their proper storage areas.

Box Cutter

This item, properly maintained and used, allows the receiving clerk to quickly remove excess packaging and thus accurately verify the quality of delivered products. Of course, care must be taken when using this tool, so proper training is essential.

Thermometer

Foods must be delivered at their proper storage temperatures. You must establish the range of temperatures you deem acceptable for product delivery. For many operators, those temperatures would be the following:

Item Acceptable Temperature Range

- °F °C
- Frozen Foods 10°F or less _12°C or less
- Refrigerated Foods 30–45°F _1–7°C

Calculator

Vendor calculations should always be checked, especially when the invoice has been prepared by hand. It is especially useful if the calculator has a physical tape that can be used by the receiving clerk when needed. The calculator should also be available in case the original invoice is either increased or decreased in amount due to incorrect vendor pricing or because of items that were listed on the invoice but not delivered. In addition, invoice totals will change when all or a portion of the delivery was rejected because the items were of substandard quality.

Records Area

This area should, in the best of cases, include a desk, telephone, computer/fax, copy machine, file cabinet, and ample office supplies such as pens, pencils, and a stapler. Obviously, larger operations are more likely to have such an area. In a smaller operation, however, the need for basic equipment still exists. In all cases, the records area should include a copy of all product specifications so there is no confusion about whether a delivered food or supply item meets the spec and, thus, should be accepted or rejected.

PROPER DELIVERY SCHEDULES

In an ideal world, you would accept delivery of products only during designated hours. These times would be scheduled during your slow periods, when there would be plenty of time for a thorough checking of the products delivered. In fact, some operators are able to demand that deliveries be made only at certain times, say between 9:00 A.M. and 10:30 A.M. These are called acceptance hours. In a case such as this, the operation may refuse to accept delivery at any other time.

Some large operations prefer to establish times in which they will *not* accept deliveries, say between 11:00 A.M. and 1:00 P.M. These are called refusal hours.

Since a busy lunchtime may make it inconvenient to accept deliveries at this time, some operators will simply not take deliveries then. In both cases, however, the assumption is that the operator is either a large enough or a good enough customer to make demands such as these.

You may find yourself in a situation, however, where the supplier will determine when goods are delivered. While this may seem inconvenient (and often is), remember that all foodservice units would like to have their deliveries made during the slow periods, between peak meal times. In many cases, it is simply not possible for the supplier to stop his or her trucks for several hours to wait for a good delivery time. In fact, in a remote location, some foodservice operators will be told only the day a delivery will be made, not a specific time! The key to establishing a successful delivery schedule with suppliers is, quite simply, to work with them.

If an operator is seen as especially difficult or costly to do business with, the supplier will pass those costs on, in the form of higher prices. On the other hand, the foodservice operator must make the supplier understand that there are certain times of the day when it is just not possible to accept delivery. While every relationship between operator and supplier is somewhat different, both sides, working together, can generally come to an acceptable solution on delivery hours. If you do decide to post either acceptance hours or refusal hours, these should be equally enforced with all vendors.

PROPER TRAINING

Receiving clerks should be properly trained to verify the following product characteristics:

- Weight
- Quantity

- Quality
- Price

Weight

One of the most important items to verify when receiving food products is, of course, their weight. It is simply true that 14 pounds of ground beef in a box looks exactly like 15 pounds. There is no way to tell the difference without putting the product on the scale. Receiving clerks should be required to weigh all meat, fish, and poultry delivered.

The only exception to this rule would be unopened Cryovac (sealed) packages containing items such as hot dogs, bacon, and the like. In this situation, the entire case should be weighed to detect shortages in content. Often, meat deliveries consist of several items, all of which are packaged together.

When the receiving clerk or supplier is very busy, the temptation exists to weigh all of the products together. The following example shows why it is important to weigh each item rather than the entire group of items as a whole.

Assume that you ordered 40 pounds of product from Bruno's Meats. When the Bruno's delivery person arrived, all three items were in one box and the deliverer was in a hurry. He, therefore, suggested that your receiving clerk simply weigh the entire box. Your receiving clerk did just that and found that the contents weighed 40_1 2 _ pounds. Since the box itself weighed about _1 2 _ pound, she signed for delivery.

If you called the supplier to complain about the overcharge ($248.50 total price _ $232.75 actual value _ $15.75 overcharge), you would likely be told that the misdelivery was simply a mistake caused by human error. It may well have been, but the lesson here is to always instruct your receiving personnel to weigh delivered items individually, even if they are in a hurry. When an item is ordered by weight, its delivery should be verified by weight. It is up to the operator to train the receiving clerk to *always* verify that the operation is charged only for the product weight delivered. Excess packaging, ice, or water in the case of produce can all serve to increase the delivered weight. The effective receiving clerk must be aware of and be on guard against deceptive delivery practices as far as the delivery of the agreed-upon product is concerned.

Quantity

The counting of products is as important as weighing them. It is a fact that suppliers make more mistakes in not delivering products than they do in excessive delivery. Products delivered but not charged for cost the supplier money. Products *not* delivered but charged for cost you money. If you order five cases of green beans, then, of course, you want to receive and pay for five cases. This is important for two reasons. First, you only want to pay for products that have been delivered. Second and just as important, if you have prepared your purchase order correctly, you truly need five cases of green beans.

If only three are delivered, you may not be able to prepare the menu items that are necessary to service your guests. If this means you will run out of an item or have to make a substitute, you may be forced to deal with unhappy diners. Shorting is the term used in the industry to indicate that an ordered item has not been delivered as promised. When a vendor shorts the delivery of an item you ordered, that item may or may not appear on the invoice. If it does not appear, note must be taken so that management knows that the item is missing and appropriate action can be taken.

If the item is listed on the invoice, the delivery driver should sign a credit memo. The credit memo should be filled out in triplicate (three copies). One copy goes to the receiving area to be filed. One copy is retained by management for the bookkeeping area. The original is, of course, sent to the vendor. Note that the credit memo has a place for the signature of a representative from your operation, as well as that of the vendor. It must be signed by both.

The credit memo is simply a formal way of notifying the vendor that an item listed on the original invoice is missing, and, thus, the value of that item should be deducted from the invoice total. If a supplier consistently shorts your operation, that supplier is suspect in terms of both honesty and lack of concern for your operation's long-term success.

The counting of boxes, cases, sacks, barrels, and the like must be routine behaviour for the receiving clerk. Counting items, such as the number of lemons or oranges in a box, should be done on a periodic basis, but the value of counting items such as these on a regular basis is questionable. While an unscrupulous supplier might be able to remove one or two lemons from each box delivered, the time it would take for an employee to detect such behaviour is hardly worth the effort expended.

It is preferable to do a periodic check and to work with reputable vendors. The direct delivery of products to a foodservice operator's storeroom or holding area is another cause for concern. The delivery person may deliver some items, such as bread, milk, and soda, directly to the storage area, thus bypassing the receiving clerk.

This should not be allowed. After such an activity, it simply may be impossible to verify the accurate quantity of items delivered. If this process must be used, product dates on each item can help assure that all products listed on the invoice were indeed delivered.

Quality

No area of your operation should be of greater concern to you than that of the appropriate quality of product delivered. If you go to the trouble of developing product specifications, but then accept delivery of products that do not match these specifications, you are simply wasting time and effort.

Without product specifications, verification of quality is difficult because management itself is unsure of the quality level that is desired. Some foodservice operators think that all food items are basically alike.

Nothing could be further from the truth. Suppliers know their products. They also know their customers. Some customers will accept only those items they have specified. Others will accept anything that comes in the back door because they do not take the time to verify a product's quality when it is delivered. If you were a supplier and you had a sack of onions that was getting a bit old, which customer would you deliver it to?

Unscrupulous suppliers can cost your operation guests because of both overcharging and shortchanging. Imagine, for example, a restaurant manager who requests a ¼-inch fat cover on all New York strip steaks ordered. Instead, the meat company delivers steaks with a ½-inch fat cover.

The operation will, of course, pay too much for the product, since steaks with a ¼-inch fat covering sell at a higher price per pound than those with a ½-inch covering. Guests, however, will hold the operator responsible for steaks that suddenly seem to be a little "fatter" than they used to be.

Coincidentally, the guests who eat the fatter steaks may tend to be a bit fatter themselves in the future! Checking for quality means checking the entire shipment for conformance to specifications. If only the top row of tomatoes in the box conforms to spec, it is up to the receiving clerk or manager to point that out to the vendor. If the balance of the box does not meet the specification, it should be refused. The credit memo can then be used to reduce the total on the invoice to the proper amount.

Sometimes, quality deficiencies are not discovered until after a delivery driver has left your establishment. When that is the case, you should notify the vendor that a thorough inspection has uncovered substandard product. The vendor is then instructed to pick up the nonconforming items. Many managers use the same "Additional Information" section of the credit memo to record this requested pickup. When the product is picked up, the pickup information is recorded.

Alternatively, a separate memo to the vendor requesting a product pickup could be produced. It is best, however, to keep the number of cost control forms to a minimum whenever possible, especially when minor modifications of one form will allow that form to serve two purposes.

Vendors are sometimes out of a product, just as you may sometimes run out of a menu item. In cases such as these, the receiving clerk must know whether it is management's preference to accept a product of higher quality, lower quality, or no product at all, as a substitute. If this information is not known, one can expect that suppliers will be able to downgrade quality simply by saying that they were "out" of the requested product and did not want the operator to be "shorted" on the delivery.

Training your receiving clerk to assess and evaluate quality products is a continuous process. The effective receiving clerk should develop a keen eye for quality. This is done not merely to protect the operation and ensure that it gets what it pays for, but also to ensure that guests get what they pay for.

The receiving clerk might accept a lower quality. Your guests, however, may not. In fact, accepting a lower-quality substitute merely because it costs less is almost always a sure sign that management is unclear about the concept of establishing quality standards and sticking to them.

Price

In the area of training for price, two major concerns are to be addressed. *They are*:

1. Matching PO unit price to invoice unit price
2. Verifying price extensions and total

Matching Purchase O3rder Unit Price to Invoice Unit Price

When the person responsible for purchasing food for the operation places an order, the confirmed quoted price should be written on the purchase order because it is never safe to assume that the delivered price will match the price on the purchase order. While most suppliers are honest, it is amazing how often the price quoted on the telephone or in person ends up being lower than the price the operation is charged at delivery time. Often, this variation is said to be "computer error" or a "clerical mistake."

It is interesting to note, however, that the errors most often result in the foodservice operator being overcharged and rarely result in an undercharge. As an ethical manager, you should not be happy with either an overcharge or an undercharge for a purchased product. Just as you would hope that a guest would inform you if a waiter forgot to add the price of a bottle of wine to the dinner check, a good receiving clerk works with the supplier to ensure that the operation is fairly charged for all items delivered.

The proper acceptance of products puts the integrity of both supplier and operator on the line. Honesty and fair play must govern the actions of both parties. If the receiving clerk has a copy of the purchase order, it is a simple matter to verify the quoted price and the delivered price. If these two do not match, management should be notified immediately. If management notification is not possible, both the driver and the receiving clerk should initial the "Comments" section of the purchase order, showing the difference in the two prices, and a credit memo should be prepared. Obviously, if the receiving clerk has no record of the quoted price, from either a purchase order or an equivalent document, price verification of this type is not possible. An inability to verify the quoted price and the delivered price *at the time of delivery* is a sure indication that all is not well in the food cost control system.

Some operators deal with suppliers in such a way that a contract price is established. A contract price is simply an agreement between buyer and seller to hold the price of a product constant over a defined period of time. For example, Bernardo uses Dairy O Milk. Dairy O agrees to supply Bernardo with milk at the price of $2.55 per gallon for three months from January 1 through March 31. Bernardo is free to buy as much or as little as he needs.

The milk will always be billed at $2.55 per gallon; $2.55, then, is the contract price. The advantage to Bernardo is that he knows exactly what his per-gallon milk cost will be for the three-month period. The advantage to Dairy O is that it can offer a lower price in the hope of securing all of Bernardo's milk business. Even in the case of a contract price, however, the receiving clerk must verify the invoice delivery price against the established contract price.

Verifying Price Extensions and Total

Price extension is just as important for you to monitor as is the ordered/delivered price. Price extension is the process by which you compute extended price. Extended price is simply the unit price multiplied by the number of units delivered. Extended price verification is extremely important. It is critical that the receiving clerk verify: Unit prices Number of units delivered Extended price computations (unit price _ number of units delivered) Invoice totals There seem to be two major reasons why operators do not always insist that the receiving clerk verify the extended prices and invoice totals. The most common reason is the belief that there is not enough time to do so. The driver may be in a hurry and the operation may be very busy. If that is the case, the process of verifying the extended price can be moved to a slower time. Why? Because there is a written record provided by the vendor of both the unit price and the number of units delivered. Remember that verification of price extensions is a part of the receiving verification process that need not be done at the time of delivery.

Extension errors are vendor errors, in the vendor's own handwriting! Or, more accurately, today they are in the vendor's own computer. The second reason operators sometimes ignore price extensions is related to these same computers. Some operators believe that if an invoice is computer generated, the mathematics of price extension must be correct. Nothing could be further from the truth.

Anyone familiar with the process of using computers knows that there are many possible entry errors that can result in extension errors. Once all extensions have been verified, it is always a good idea to check the invoice total against the sum of the individual, correct price extensions. Managers must ensure that delivery clerks verify both extension prices and invoice totals. If this cannot be done at the time of delivery, it must be done as soon thereafter as possible. Errors are made, and they can cost your operation greatly if they go undetected.

RECEIVING RECORD OR DAILY RECEIVING SHEET

Some large operations use a receiving record when receiving food. This method, while taking administrative time both to prepare and to monitor, does have some advantages.

A receiving record generally contains the following information:

- Name of supplier
- Invoice number
- Item description
- Unit price
- Number of units delivered
- Total cost
- Storage area (unit distribution)
- Date of activity

Note that some items are placed directly into production areas (direct use), while others may be used in specific units or sent to the storeroom. Sundry items, such as paper products, ashtrays, matches, and cleaning supplies, may be stored in specific nonfood areas. Note also that subtotals for storage areas can be determined in terms of both units or dollars, as the operator prefers.

In all cases, the sums for each distribution area should equal the total for all items received during the day. Receiving reports can be useful to management if it is important to record where items are to be delivered or where they have been delivered. While some foodservice operators will find the receiving report useful, many will not, since most of the information it contains is also included in the receiving clerk's copy of the purchase order.

STORAGE

The ideal situation for you and your operation would be for you to store only the food you will use between the time of a vendor's delivery and the time of that vendor's next delivery. This is true because storage costs money, both in terms of providing the storage space for inventory items and in terms of money that is tied up in inventory items and, thus, unavailable for use elsewhere. It is always best, whenever possible, to order only the products that are absolutely needed by the operation. In that way, the vendor's storeroom actually becomes your storeroom.

The vendor then absorbs the costs of storing your needed products. In all cases, however, you must have an adequate supply of products on hand to service your guests. They are your main concern. If you are doing your job well, you will have many guests and will need many items in storage! Once the receiving clerk has properly accepted the food products you have purchased, the next step in the control of food costs is that of storing those items.

The storage process, in most foodservice establishments, consists of essentially four main parts:

- Placing products in storage
- Maintaining product quality and safety

- Maintaining product security
- Determining inventory value

PLACING PRODUCTS IN STORAGE

Food products are highly perishable items. As such, they must be moved quickly from your receiving area to the area selected for storage. This is especially true for refrigerated and frozen items. An item such as ice cream, for example, can deteriorate substantially if it is at room temperature for only a few minutes.

Most often, in foodservice, this high perishability dictates that the same individual responsible for receiving the items is the individual responsible for their storage. Consider the situation of Kathryn, the receiving clerk at the Fairview Estates, an extended care facility with 400 residents. She has just taken delivery of seven loaves of bread. They were delivered in accordance with the purchase order and now must be put away. While Kathryn stores these items, she must know whether management requires her to use the LIFO (last in, first out) or FIFO (first in, first out) method of product rotation.

LIFO System

When using the LIFO storage system, the storeroom operator intends to use the most recently delivered product (last in) before he or she uses any part of that same product previously on hand. If Kathryn decides, for example, to use the new bread first, she would be using the LIFO system. In all cases, you must strive to maintain a consistent product standard. In the case of *some* bread, pastry, dairy, fruit, and vegetable items, the storeroom clerk could practice the LIFO system, if these items have been designed as LIFO items by management. With LIFO, you will need to take great care to order only the quantity of product needed between deliveries. If too much product is ordered, loss rates will be very high. Costs can rise dramatically when LIFO items must eventually be discarded or used in a way that reduces their revenue-producing ability. For most items you will buy, the best storage system to use is the FIFO system.

FIFO System

First in, first out (FIFO) means that you intend to rotate your stock in such a way that product already on hand is sold prior to the sale of more recently delivered product. If this is the case, the storeroom clerk must take great care to place new stock behind or at the bottom of old stock. It is the tendency of employees not to do this. Consider, for example, the storeroom clerk who must put away six cases of tomato sauce. The cases weigh about 40 pounds. The FIFO method dictates that these six cases be placed *under* the five cases already in the storeroom. Will the clerk place the six newly delivered cases underneath the five older cases? In many instances, the answer is no.

Unless management strictly enforces the FIFO rule, employees may be tempted to take the easy way out.

FIFO is the preferred storage technique for most perishable and nonperishable items. This is because it is generally a good idea to sell the oldest stock first. Failure to implement a FIFO system of storage management can result in excessive product loss due to spoilage, shrinkage, and deterioration of quality. All of these must be avoided if you are to effectively manage food expenses. Decisions about storing food items according to the LIFO or FIFO method are your decisions. Once these decisions have been made, they should be communicated to the storeroom clerk and monitored on a regular basis to ensure compliance. To ensure that this is so, some foodservice managers require the storeroom clerk to mark or tag each delivered item with the date of delivery.

These markings provide a visual aid in determining which product should be used first. This is especially critical in the area of highly perishable and greater-cost items such as fresh meats and seafood. Special meat and seafood date tags will be available from your vendor. These tags contain a space for writing in the item name, quantity, and delivery date. The use of these tags or an alternative date tracking system is strongly recommended. If the supplier has computerized his or her delivery, the box or case may already bear a strip identifying both the product and the delivery date. When this is not the case, however, the storeroom clerk should assume this function.

Storage Areas

The food and related products you buy will generally be placed in one of the following three major storage areas within your facility:

1. Dry storage
2. Refrigerated storage
3. Frozen storage

Dry Storage

Dry-storage areas should generally be maintained at a temperature ranging between 65°F (18°C) and 75°F (24°C). Temperatures lower than those recommended can be harmful to food products. More often, however, dry-storage temperatures can get very high, exceeding by far the upper limit of temperature acceptability. This is because storage areas are frequently in poorly ventilated closed-in areas of the building. Excessive temperatures damage dry-storage products. Many dry-storage areas are not air conditioned, so it may be necessary to monitor the temperature of these areas with a thermometer.

Shelving in dry-storage areas must be easily cleaned and sturdy enough to hold the weight of dry products. Local health codes can vary, but shelving should generally be placed at least 6 inches above the ground to allow for proper cleaning beneath the shelving and to ensure proper ventilation.

Dry-goods products should never be stored directly on the ground, and it is a violation of all local health codes to do so. Slotted shelving is generally preferred over solid shelving when storing food, because slotted shelving allows better air circulation around the product. Can labels should face out for easy identification.

For those bulk items stored in bins or large containers, wheels on these containers should be used whenever possible so that heavy lifting and resulting employee injuries can be avoided. Most important, dry-storage space must be sufficient in size to handle your operation's needs. Cramped and cluttered dry-storage areas tend to increase costs because inventory cannot be easily rotated, maintained, and counted. Theft can go undetected, and you may find yourself accidentally using the FIST (first in, still there!) method of inventory storage because products get "lost" in the storeroom.

Refrigerated Storage

Refrigerator temperatures should generally be maintained between 32°F (0°C) and 36°F (2°C). In fact, the refrigerator itself will vary as much as four degrees (F) between its coldest spot (near the bottom) and its warmest spot. The bottom tends to be coldest in a refrigerator because warm air rises and cold air falls. Refrigerators actually work by removing heat from the contents, rather than "making" food cold.

This is an important point to remember when refrigerating food. Foods that are boiling hot should be precooled to 160°F (71°C) before placing them in the refrigerator. This results in lower operating costs for the refrigerator, but is still well above the potentially hazardous food danger zone, which most food experts place at 40°F to 140°F (4°C to 60°C).

Refrigerators should have easily cleaned shelving units that are at least 6 inches off the floor and are slotted to allow for good air circulation. They should be properly cleaned on a regular basis and should be opened and closed quickly, both to lower operational costs and to ensure that the items in the refrigerator stay at their peak of freshness. Carryover items should be properly labeled, wrapped, and rotated so that items can be found easily, resulting in both greater employee efficiency and reduced energy costs because refrigerator doors will be opened for shorter periods of time. Many managers find that requiring foods to be stored in clear plastic containers also helps in this regard.

Freezer Storage

Freezer temperatures should be maintained between 0°F and _10°F (_18°C and _23°C). What is usually called a freezer, however, is more properly a "frozen-food storage unit." The distinction is an important one. To be frozen at its peak of freshness, a food item must be frozen very quickly. This involves temperatures of _20°F (_29°C) or lower. Freezer units in a foodservice operation do not generally operate at these temperatures; thus, they really are best at "holding" foods that are already frozen, rather than freezing food. Frozen foods comprise an increasingly large portion of the foods you are likely to buy. Therefore, the conversion of dry or refrigerated space to frozen-food storage is highly recommended. Most foodservice operators also find that their carryover items will, in many cases, have a longer shelf life when held frozen rather than in refrigeration. Frozen foods should be wrapped securely to reduce moisture loss, and newly delivered products should be carefully checked with a thermometer when received to ensure that they are at the proper temperature. In addition, these items should be carefully inspected to ensure that they have not been thawed and refrozen.

Frozen-food holding units must be regularly maintained, a process that includes cleaning inside and out and constant temperature monitoring to detect possible improper operation. A thermometer permanently placed in the unit or read from outside the unit, as is the case with digital displays, is required in most areas. It is also a good idea to periodically check that gaskets on freezers, as well as refrigerators, tightly seal the food cabinet. This will not only reduce operating costs, but will also maintain food quality for a longer period of time.

STORAGE BASICS

Regardless of the storage type, food and related products should be stored neatly in some logical order. This makes them easier to find and to count when the need arises. You may decide, for example, to arrange your stored products on the basis of how often your staff uses them. That is, frequently used items are placed near the front of the storage area. When a few items constitute a majority of the sales volume in your unit, this can be an effective storage technique. No matter what type of storage system you choose, make sure your inventory sheet matches the physical order of items in storage. This saves time in taking inventory, and it results in fewer errors. It is also important to note that the objective of a neat storage area is both to maximize storage space and to minimize the time it takes to locate the item in storage. When possible, the storage area should be in close proximity to the area in which the product will be used. This reduces unnecessary time lost in traveling to remote storage areas to secure needed products.

In this regard, proper storage techniques, while assisting in lowering the cost of food products, also help in reducing costs associated with Labour. It is sometimes amazing how long it can take an employee to go to the storeroom for a can of beans! In an improperly maintained storage area, employees can claim that it took a long time to "find" the desired product. When a storage area is well located, properly labeled, kept clean, and monitored regularly, problems such as this will not occur.

MAINTAINING PRODUCT QUALITY AND SAFETY

It is a fact that food product quality rarely improves with increased storage time. In most cases, the quality of ingredients you buy is at its peak when the product you ordered is delivered to you. From then on, the products can only decline in freshness, quality, and nutrition. The only exception to this might be the gourmet restaurant that elects to age some of its own products. The general case, however, is that your storeroom clerk must make every effort to maintain food quality in all of your storage areas, since food quality tends to diminish during the storage process. The primary method for ensuring product quality while in storage is through proper product rotation and high standards of storeroom sanitation. Storage areas are excellent breeding grounds for insects, some bacteria, and also rodents.

To protect against these potentially damaging hazards, you should insist on a regular cleaning of all storage areas. Compressor units on refrigerators and frozen-food holding units should be checked regularly for the buildup of dust and dirt. Interior storage racks should be kept free of spills and soil. Refrigerators and frozen-food holding units remove significant amounts of stored product moisture, causing shrinkage in meats and produce and freezer burn in poorly wrapped or stored items kept at freezing temperatures.

Unless they are built in, refrigerators and frozen-food holding units should be high enough off the ground to allow for easy cleaning around and under them to prevent cockroaches and other insects from living beneath them. Both refrigerators and frozen-food holding units should be kept 6 to 10 inches from walls to allow for the free circulation of air around, and efficient operation of, the units.

Drainage systems in refrigerators should be checked at least weekly. Ideally, frozen-food holding units and refrigerators should have *externally visible* internal thermometers, whether they are read as a digital display or in the more traditional temperature scale. In larger storage areas, hallways should be kept clear and empty of storage materials or boxes. This helps both in finding items in the storage area and in reducing the number of hiding places for insects and rodents.

Maintaining Product Security

Food products are the same as money to you. In fact, you should think of food inventory items in exactly that way. The apple in a produce walk-in is not just an apple. It represents, at a selling price of $2.00, that amount in revenue to the airport foodservice director, who hopes to sell a crisp, fresh apple to a weary traveller. If the apple disappears, revenue of $2.00 will disappear also. When you think of inventory items in terms of their sales value, it becomes clear why product security is of the utmost importance. As such, systems must be in place to reduce employee, vendor, and guest theft to the lowest possible level.

All foodservice establishments will experience some amount of theft, in its strictest sense. The reason is very simple. Some employee theft is impossible to detect. Even the most sophisticated, computerized control system is not able to determine if an employee or vendor's employee walked into the produce walk-in and ate one green grape. Similarly, an employee who takes home two sugar packets per night will likely go undetected for a great length of time. In neither of these cases, however, is the amount of loss significant, and certainly not enough to install security cameras in the walk-in or to frisk your employees as they leave for home at the end of their shifts.

What you do want to do, however, is to make it difficult to remove significant amounts of food from storage without authorization, so that you can know when that food has been removed. Good cost control systems must be in place if you are to achieve this goal. It is amazing how large the impact of theft can be on profitability. Consider the following example. Jesse is the receiving clerk at the Irish Voice sports bar. On a daily basis, Jesse takes home $2.00 worth of food products. How much, then, does Jesse cost the bar in one year?

The answer is a surprising $14,600 in sales revenue! If Jesse steals $2.00 per day for 365 days, the total theft amount is $730 (365 days _ $2.00 per day _ $730). If the bar makes an after-tax profit of 5% on each dollar of food products sold, the operation must sell _ $730 _ $14,600 to recover the lost $730.

In order to recover the dollar amount of Jesse's theft, the sports bar must sell $14,600 of food per year and make 5 cents per dollar sold on these sales. In the case of a smaller bar, $14,600 may well represent several days' sales revenue. Clearly, small thefts can add up to large dollar losses! Most foodservice operators attempt to control access to the location of stored products. This may be done, in some areas, by a process as simple as keeping the dry-storage area locked and requiring employees to "get the keys" from the manager or supervisor. In other situations, cameras may be mounted in both storage areas and employee exit areas.

While the physical layout of the foodservice operation may prevent management from being able to effectively lock and secure all storage areas, too much traffic is sure to cause theft problems. This is not because employees are basically dishonest. Most are not. Theft problems develop because of the few employees who either feel that management will not miss a few of whatever is being stolen or feel that they "deserve" to take a few things because they work so hard and are paid so little! It is your responsibility to see to it that the storeroom clerk maintains good habits in securing product inventory. As a general rule, if storerooms are to be locked, only one individual should have the key during any shift.

The temptation sometimes exists for management to hang the key by the door, that is, to have the storeroom locked, but give the key to any employee who says that he or she needs it. This obviously defeats the purpose of the locked system. In reality, it is simply not possible to keep all inventory items under lock and key. Some items must be received and immediately sent to the kitchen for processing or use. Also, what would happen if you or another designated "key holder" were gone from the operation for a few minutes?

Most operators find that it is impossible to operate under a system where all food products are locked away from the employees.

Storage areas should, however, not be accessible to guests or vendor employees. Unlocked storage areas near exits are extremely tempting to the dishonest individual. If proper control procedures are in place, employees will know that you can determine if theft has occurred. Without such control, employees are aware that theft can go undetected. This must, and can, be avoided.

Determining Inventory Value

The inventory you have on hand should be maintained in a way that makes it easy to issue (place into production), as well as to count and to determine its monetary value. This is because you must be able to answer this fundamental question: "What is the value of the products I currently have on hand?"

The answer to this question is critical because it is simply not possible to know your actual food expense without an accurate inventory. In fact, the mathematical formula used to determine the cost of food sold (food expense) is driven primarily by knowing the dollar value of all food products in inventory. The process of determining inventory value is quite simple, even if the actual task can be very time consuming. Valuing, or establishing a dollar value for your entire inventory, is done by using the following inventory valuation formula:

Item Amount _ Item Value _ Item Inventory Value

Item Amount

Item amount may be determined by counting the item, as in the case of cans, or by weighing items, as in the case of meats. Volume, that is, gallons, quarts, and the like, is another method of establishing product amounts. If an item is purchased by the pound, it is generally weighed to determine item amount. If it is purchased by the piece or case, the appropriate unit to determine the item amount may be either pieces or cases. If, for example, canned pears are purchased by the case, with six cans per case, management might decide to consider the item either as case or as can.

That is, three cases of the canned pears might be considered as three items (by the case) or as 18 items (by the can). Any method you use to accurately establish the amount of product you have on hand is acceptable. If product is undercounted, your expenses will appear higher than they actually are. If, on the other hand, you erroneously (or on purpose) compute overstated, or padded inventory, costs will appear artificially low until the proper inventory values are determined.

Item Value

An item's actual value can be more complicated to determine than its amount. This is because the price you pay for an item may vary slightly each time you buy it. Assume, for example, that you bought curly endive for $2.20 per pound on Monday, but the same item was $2.50 per pound on Wednesday. On Friday, you see that you have one pound of the curly endive in your refrigerated walk-in. Is the value of the item $2.20 or $2.50? Item value is, generally speaking, determined by using either the LIFO or the FIFO method. When the LIFO method is in use, the item's value is said to be the price paid for the least recent (oldest) addition to item amount.

If the FIFO method is in use, the item value is said to be the price paid for the most recent (newest) product on hand. In the hospitality industry, most operators value inventory at its most recently known value; thus, FIFO is the more common method. A simple illustration may help. Peggy purchased grapes on Monday and paid $30.00 per lug. On Friday, she again purchased grapes, but paid $40.00 per lug. On Saturday morning, she took inventory and found that she had 1_1 2 _ lugs of grapes.

What is their inventory value? The LIFO system says that Peggy's grapes have an inventory value of $45.00 ($30.00 LIFO price _ 1.5 lugs _ $45.00). The FIFO method places a value of $60.00 on the grapes ($40.00 FIFO price _ 1.5 lugs _ $60.00). Because it is closest to the actual replacement cost of the inventory item, choosing to value inventory at the most recently paid price (FIFO) is the best method for establishing item value for the majority of hospitality operators. This inventory valuation sheet has a place for all inventory items, the quantity on hand, and the unit value of each item.

There is also a place for the date the inventory was taken, a spot for the name of the person who counted the product, and another space for the person who extended or established the value of the inventory. It is recommended that these two be different individuals to reduce the risk of inventory valuation fraud.

The inventory valuation sheet should be completed each time the inventory is counted. It can be preprinted from a computerized list of items, a process that saves much in the way of staff time and effort. Regardless of the form used, the item's inventory value is determined as described earlier.

Thus, if we have five cases of fresh beets in our inventory, and each case has a value of $20.00, the inventory value of our beets is value of the item by the number of units on hand.

The process becomes more difficult when one realises that the average foodservice operation has hundreds of items in inventory. Thus, "taking the inventory" can be a very time-consuming task. A physical inventory, one in which the food products are actually counted, must, however, be taken to determine your actual food usage. Some operators take this inventory monthly, others weekly or even daily! Some, unfortunately, feel that there is no need to ever take inventory. These operators cannot effectively control their costs because they do not know what their costs are.

DETERMINING ACTUAL FOOD EXPENSE

Assume that you own and manage a small ice cream store that makes its own products. You have reviewed your records for the past month and found the following: You have determined your revenue figure from the sales history you maintained. You have determined your food expense by adding the dollar value of all the properly corrected delivery invoices that you accumulated for the month. That is, you totaled the value of all food purchased and delivered between the first day of the month and the last.

Would it be correct to say that your food expense for the month of January is $39,000? The answer is No. Why not? Because you may have more, or less, of the food products required to make your ice cream in inventory on the last day of January than you had on the first day. If you have more food products in inventory on January 31 than you had on January 1, your food expense is less than $39,000. If you have fewer products in inventory on January 31 than you had on January 1, your food expense is higher than $39,000. To understand why this is so, you must understand the formula for computing your actual food expense.

BEGINNING INVENTORY

Beginning inventory is the dollar value of all food on hand at the beginning of the accounting period. It is determined by completing an actual count and valuation of the products on hand.

Purchases

Purchases are the sum cost of all food purchased during the accounting period. It is determined by adding all properly tabulated invoices for the accounting period.

Goods Available for Sale

Goods available for sale is the sum of the beginning inventory and purchases. It represents the value of all food that was available for sale during the accounting period.

Ending Inventory

Ending inventory refers to the dollar value of all food on hand at the end of the accounting period. It also is determined by completing a physical inventory.

Cost of Food Consumed

The cost of food consumed is the actual dollar value of all food used, or consumed, by the operation. Again, it is important to note that this is not merely the value of all food sold, but rather the value of all food no longer in the establishment and includes the value of any meals eaten by employees.

Employee Meals

Employee meal cost is a Labour-related, not food-related cost. Free or reduced-cost employee meals are a benefit much in the same manner as medical insurance or paid vacation. Therefore, the value of this benefit, if provided, should be transferred and charged not as a cost of food but as a cost of employee benefits. The dollar value of food eaten by employees is subtracted from the cost of food consumed to yield the cost of food sold.

Cost of Food Sold

As stated earlier, the cost of food sold is the actual dollar value of all food expense incurred by the operation except for those related to employee meals. It is not possible to determine this number unless a beginning inventory has been taken at the start of the month, followed by another inventory taken at the end of the month. Without these two numbers, it is impossible to accurately determine the cost of food sold. In the ice cream store example, had you completed such a form, you would have known your actual cost of food sold. Every manager should, on a regular basis, compute the actual cost of food sold because it is not possible to improve your cost picture unless you first know what your costs are.

VARIATIONS ON THE BASIC COST OF FOOD SOLD FORMULA

Unit to Another

This is the case when, for example, an operator seeks to compute one cost of food sold figure for a bar and another for the bar's companion restaurant. In this situation, it is likely that fruits, juices, vegetables, and similar items are taken from the kitchen for use in the bar, while wine, sherry, and similar items may be taken from the bar for use in the kitchen. The formula for cost of food sold in this situation would be as follows:

Cost of Food Sold		
Accounting Period: to ______		
Unit Name: ______		
Beginning Inventory	$ ______	
Plus		
Purchases	$ ______	
Goods Available for Sale		$ ______
Less		
Ending Inventory		$ ______
Cost of Food Consumed		$ ______
Less		
Employee Meals		$ ______
Cost of Food Sold		$ ______

It is important for you to know exactly which formula or variation is in use when analyzing cost of food sold. The variations, while slight, can make big differences in the interpretation of your cost information. In all cases, it is critical that accurate beginning and ending inventory figures be maintained if accurate cost data are to be computed. In the following example, both beginning inventory and ending inventory figures are known, thus enabling you to determine your actual cost of food sold.

It is important to note that ending inventory for one accounting period becomes the beginning inventory figure for the next period. For example, in the case of your ice cream store, the January 31 ending inventory figure of $27,500 will become the February 1 beginning inventory figure. In this manner, it is clear that physical inventory need only be taken one time per accounting period, not twice.

Again, while the physical inventory process can be time consuming, it must be performed in order to determine actual food expense. While there is no reliable method for replacing the actual counting of inventory items on hand, there are many computer programmes on the market programmed to allow an individual to scan the bar codes on products using a handheld scanning device and, thus, perform both the counting and the price extension process necessary to develop actual inventory valuations. Using technology in this manner can make a time-consuming task much less tedious and more efficient.

FOOD COST PERCENTAGE

Food expense is often expressed as a percentage of total revenue or sales. Since you can now determine your actual cost of food sold, you can also learn to compute and evaluate your operation's food cost percentage. Again, this is both the traditional way of looking at food expense and generally the method used by most operators when preparing the profit and loss statement. Food cost% represents that portion of food sales that was spent on food expenses. In the case of the ice cream store discussed previously, you know that the cost of food sold equals $33,275.

Estimating Daily Cost of Food Sold

Many operators would like to know their food usage on a much more regular basis than once per month. When this is the case, the physical inventory may be taken as often as desired. Again, however, physical inventories are time consuming. It would be convenient if you could have a close estimate of your food usage on a weekly or daily basis without the effort of a daily inventory count. Fortunately, such an approximation exists. One of them is to estimate food cost% on a daily or weekly basis. As an example, assume that you own an Italian restaurant that serves no liquor and caters to a family-oriented clientele. You would like to monitor your food cost percentage on a more regular basis than once a month, which is your regular accounting period.

You have decided to use a sixcolumn form to estimate your food cost percentage. Since you keep track of both daily sales and purchases, you can easily do so. In the space above the first two columns, write the word Sales. Above the middle two columns, write Purchases, and above the last two columns, enter the term Cost%. You then proceed each day to enter your daily sales revenue in the column labeled Sales Today. Your invoices for food deliveries are totaled daily and entered in the column titled Purchases Today. Dividing the Purchases Today column by the Sales Today column yields the figure that is placed in the Cost% Today column.

Purchases to Date (the cumulative purchases amount) is divided by Sales to Date (the cumulative sales amount) to yield the Cost% to Date figure. You buy most of your food at the beginning of the week, while sales are strongest in the later part of the week. This is a common occurrence at many foodservice establishments. As can also be seen, your daily cost percentage ranges from a high of 130% (Monday) to a low of 0% (Sunday), when no deliveries are made. In the Cost% to Date column, however, the range is only from a high of 130% (Monday) to a low of 39.20% (Sunday). What is your best estimate about what your food cost% actually is as of Sunday? The answer is that it will be slightly less than 39.20%. Why? Let us go back to the formula for cost of food sold.

Before we do, we must make one important assumption: "For any time period we are evaluating, the beginning inventory and ending inventory amounts are the same." In other words, over any given time period, you will have approximately the same amount of food on hand at all times. If this assumption is correct, the six-column food cost estimate is, in fact, a good indicator of your food usage. The reason is very simple. The formula for cost of food sold asks you to add beginning inventory and then later subtract ending inventory. If these two numbers are assumed to be the same, they can be ignored, since adding and subtracting the same number to any other number will result in no effect at all. For example, if we start with $10, add $50, and subtract $10, we are left with $50. In terms of the cost of food sold formula, when beginning inventory and ending inventory are assumed to be the same figure, it is the mathematical equivalent of adding a zero and subtracting a zero. To continue our example, if we start with $0, add $50, and subtract $0, we are left, again, with $50.

Therefore, as stated earlier, if you assume that your inventory is constant, your cost of food sold for the one-week period is a little less than $4,034.21, or 39.20% of sales. Why a little less? Because we must still subtract the value of employee meals, if any are provided, since they are an employee benefit and not a food expense. How accurate is the six-column form?

For most operators, it is quite accurate and has the following advantages:

- It is very simple to compute, requiring 10 minutes or less per day for most operations.
- It records both sales history and purchasing patterns.
- It identifies problems before the end of the monthly accounting period.

- By the ninth or tenth day, the degree of accuracy in the To Date column is very high.
- It is a daily reminder to both management and employees that there is a very definite relationship between sales and expenses. The use of a six-column food cost estimator is highly recommended for the operator who elects to conduct a physical inventory less often than every two weeks.

The control of food expense is critical to all foodservice operations. From the purchase of the raw ingredient to its receiving and storage, the effective foodservice operator strives to have the proper quality and quantity of product on hand at all times. Food represents a large part of your overall expense budget. Protecting this product and accounting for its usage are extremely important in helping to manage overall costs.

3

Globalisation and Food Consumption in Tourism

The hospitality industry, particularly its food-service component, is an important sector of many nations' economies. Developing nations should take steps to encourage development of hotels and restaurants. Those steps include improving training, offering tax incentives, and clearing up questions about land ownership. By the same token, restaurant and hotel operators should seek to make the best possible use of local resources, for example, by serving locally produced foods when possible. By setting up a five-year plan for tourism development, national governments can gain the advantages of international tourism. One source of development will undoubtedly be United States-based food-service chains, which are now expanding internationally. As an example, the food-service industry is an important part of the U.S. economy and with proper assistance can become vital to other nations' economies.

Tourism as Industry

Like other industrial projects, tourism projects too involve professional management, capital investment, special skills and training. The Government of India and a number of other states have declared tourism as an industry. Gujarat State which is at the forefront of the industrial development will also declare tourism as an industry. This will enable the tourism projects to be reliable to get benefits contained in the paras 5.1.2 and 5.1.3 below.

Availability of land is a primary requirement of any project. The process of grant of land will be facilitated in urban areas for the projects concerning setting up of hotels, restaurants and apartment hotels etc. Existing arrangements for grant of government waste land to industrial units will be made applicable to various tourism projects. Arrangements will be made to acquire private land under Land Acquisition Act for various tourism projects by companies registered under the Companies Act. The existing commercial rates of NA assessment applicable to land involving tourism projects would be reviewed and rates of NA assessment for industrial purposes will be made applicable to them. As one of the sets of infrastructural institutions, the State Financial Institutions have made an important contribution in creating conductive environment for industrial entrepreneurs. They will be called upon to do the same for tourism entrepreneurs in terms of making available adequate finance.

Food Industry and Hospitality

The food industry is the complex, global collective of diverse businesses that together supply much of the food energy consumed by the world population. Only subsistence farmers, those who survive on what they grow, can be considered outside of the scope of the modern food industry.

The food industry includes:

- *Regulation*: local, regional, national and international rules and regulations for food production and sale, including food quality and food safety, and industry lobbying activities
- *Education*: academic, vocational, consultancy
- *Research and development*: food technology
- *Manufacturing*: agrichemicals, seed, farm machinery and supplies, agricultural construction, etc.
- *Agriculture*: raising of crops and livestock, seafood
- *Food processing*: preparation of fresh products for market, manufacture of prepared food products
- *Marketing*: promotion of generic products (e.g. milk board), new products, public opinion, through advertising, packaging, public relations, etc
- *Wholesale and distribution*: warehousing, transpor-tation, logistics
- *Retail*: supermarket chains and independent food stores, direct-to-consumer, restaurant, food services

Overview

Essentially, the food industry involves the commercial movement of food from field to fork. The modern food industry is the result of technological and cultural changes that have occurred over the last 150 years. Traditionally, over thousands of years, food production was centered around two activities:

1. Labour-intensive agricultural activities, the farming of grain, produce and livestock;
2. Personal food preparation, where individuals and families acquire raw and minimally processed ingredients, and prepare them for their own consumption.

A significant per centage of the population was directly involved in farming, and in the process, many people actually fed themselves, from field to table. By contrast, the modern food industry relies far more on technology, particularly on mechanization and biochemistry, than on human and animal labour. In this way, food is raised, manipulated, preserved and moved around, resulting in a food industry that is to a great degree global in nature, with food and related resources travelling great distances.

For example, farm machinery and parts from Europe and agrichemicals from the US may routinely travel to farms in South America, where farm products are raised and shipped to North America for fresh market consumption, or for use in processed foods which may then travel to further points around the world. The point at which foods are gathered and prepared has also become fragmented: much of what we eat has already been assembled for consumption.

This modern food system relies heavily on technology, transportation, management and logistics for physical fulfillment, and on marketing and government regulation for maintaining an efficient consumer market. An incredibly wide range of businesses and individuals are employed by and profit from all aspects of this huge and complex system. A tremendous amount of governmental regulation and administration is also involved in this continual flow of materials, food products, and related information.

Definitions

Food industry is not a formally defined term, however, it is usually used in a broadly inclusive way to cover all aspects of food production and sale. The Food Standards Agency, a government body in the UK, describes it thus:

> "...the whole food industry – from farming and food production, packaging and distribution, to retail and catering."

The Economic Research Service of the USDA uses the term food system to describe the same thing:

"The U.S. food system is a complex network of farmers and the industries that link to them. Those links include makers of farm equipment and chemicals as well as firms that provide services to agribusinesses, such as providers of transportation and financial services. The system also includes the food marketing industries that link farms to consumers, and which include food and fiber processors, wholesalers, retailers, and foodservice establishments."

A comfortable room, good food, and a helpful staff can make being away from home an enjoyable experience for both vacationing families and business travellers. While most lodging managers work in traditional hotels and motels, some work in other lodging establishments, such as camps, inns, boardinghouses, dude ranches, and recreational resorts. In full-service hotels, lodging managers help their guests have a pleasant stay by providing many of the comforts of home, including cable television, fitness equipment, and voice mail, as well as specialized services such as health spas. For business travelers, lodging managers often schedule available meeting rooms and electronic equipment, including slide projectors and fax machines.

Lodging managers are responsible for keeping their establishments efficient and profitable. In a small establishment with a limited staff, the manager may oversee all aspects of operations. However, large hotels may employ hundreds of workers, and the general manager usually is aided by a number of assistant managers assigned to the various departments of the operation. In hotels of every size, managerial duties vary significantly by job title.

General managers have overall responsibility for the operation of the hotel. Within guidelines established by the owners of the hotel or executives of the hotel chain, the general manager sets room rates, allocates funds to departments, approves expenditures, and ensures expected standards for guest service, decor, housekeeping, food quality, and banquet operations. Managers who work for chains also may organize and staff a newly built hotel, refurbish an older hotel, or reorganize a hotel or motel that is not operating successfully. In order to fill entry-level service and clerical jobs in hotels, some managers attend career fairs.

Resident or hotel managers are responsible for the day-to-day operations of the property. In larger properties, more than one of these managers may assist the general manager, frequently dividing responsibilities between the food and beverage operations and the rooms or lodging services. At least one manager, either the general manager or a hotel manager, is on call 24 hours a day to resolve problems or emergencies.

Assistant managers help run the day-to-day operations of the hotel. In large hotels, they may be responsible for activities such as personnel, accounting, office administration, marketing and sales, purchasing, security, maintenance, and pool, spa, or recreational facilities. In smaller hotels, these duties may be combined into one position. Assistant managers may adjust charges on a hotel guest's bill when a manager is unavailable.

An Executive Committee made up of a hotel's senior managers advises the general manager, assists in setting hotel policy, coordinates services that cross departmental boundaries, and collaborates on efforts to ensure consistent and efficient guest services throughout the hotel. The Committee may be comprised of the department heads for housekeeping, front office, food and beverage, security, sales and public relations, meetings and conventions, engineering and building maintenance, and human resources. Executive committee members bring a different perspective of guest service to the total management objective reflecting the unique expertise and training of their positions.

Executive housekeepers ensure that guest rooms, meeting and banquet rooms, and public areas are clean, orderly, and well maintained. They also train, schedule, and supervise the work of housekeepers, inspect rooms, and order cleaning supplies.

Front office managers coordinate reservations and room assignments, as well as train and direct the hotel's front desk staff. They ensure that guests are treated courteously, complaints and problems are resolved, and requests for special services are carried out. Front office managers may adjust charges posted on a customer's bill.

Convention services managers coordinate the activities of various departments in larger hotels to accommodate meetings, conventions, and special events. They meet with representatives of groups or organizations to plan the number of rooms to reserve, the desired configuration of the meeting space, and banquet services. During the meeting or event, they resolve unexpected problems and monitor activities to ensure that hotel operations conform to the expectations of the group.

Food and beverage managers oversee all food service operations maintained by the hotel. They coordinate menus with the Executive Chef for the hotel's restaurants, lounges, and room service operations. They supervise the ordering of food and supplies, direct service and maintenance contracts within the kitchens and dining areas, and manage food service budgets.

Catering managers arrange for food service in a hotel's meeting and convention rooms. They coordinate menus and costs for banquets, parties, and events with meeting and convention planners or individual clients. They coordinate staffing needs and arrange schedules with kitchen personnel to ensure appropriate food service.

Sales or marketing directors and public relations directors oversee the advertising and promotion of hotel operations and functions, including lodging and dining specials and special events, such as holiday or seasonal specials. They direct the efforts of their staff to purchase advertising and market their property to organizations or groups seeking a venue for conferences, conventions, business meetings, trade shows, and special events. They also coordinate media relations and answer questions from the press.

Human resources directors manage the personnel functions of a hotel, ensuring that all accounting, payroll, and employee relations matters are handled in compliance with hotel policy and applicable laws. They also oversee hiring practices and standards and ensure that training and promotion Programme reflect appropriate employee development guidelines.

Finance (or revenue) directors monitor room sales and reservations. In addition to overseeing accounting and cash-flow matters at the hotel, they also project occupancy levels, decide which rooms to discount and when to offer rate specials.

Computers are used extensively by lodging managers and their assistants to keep track of guests' bills, reservations, room assignments, meetings, and special events. In addition, computers are used to order food, beverages, and supplies, as well as to prepare reports for hotel owners and top-level managers. Managers work with computer specialists to ensure that the hotel's computer system functions properly. Should the hotel's computer system fail, managers must continue to meet the needs of hotel guests and staff.

Industry size

Processed food sales worldwide are approximately US$3.2 trillion (2004). In the U.S., consumers spend approximately US$1 trillion annually for food, or nearly 10 per cent of the Gross Domestic Product (GDP). Over 16.5 million people are employed in the food industry.

Agriculture is the process of producing food, feed, fiber and other desired products by the cultivation of certain plants and the raising of domesticated animals (livestock). The practice of agriculture is also known as "farming", while scientists, inventors and others devoted to improving farming methods and implements are also said to be engaged in agriculture. More people in the world are involved in agriculture as their primary economic activity than in any other, yet it only accounts for four per cent of the world's GDP.

A vast global transportation network is required by the food industry in order to connect its numerous parts. These include suppliers, manufacturers, warehousing, retailers and the end consumers.

With populations around the world concentrating in urban areas, food buying is increasingly removed from all aspects food production. This is a relatively recent development, taking place mainly over the last 50 years. The supermarket is a defining retail element of the food industry, where tens of thousands of products are gathered in one location, in continuous, year-round supply.

Food preparation is another area where change in recent decades has been dramatic. Today, two food industry sectors are in apparent competition for the retail food dollar. The grocery industry sell fresh and largely raw products for consumers to use as ingredients in home cooking. The food service industry offers prepared food, either as finished products, or as partially prepared components for final "assembly".

Food Industry Technologies

Sophisticated technologies define modern food production. They include many areas. Agricultural machinery, originally led by the tractor, has practically eliminated human labour in many areas of production. Biotechnology is driving much change, in areas as diverse as agrichemicals, plant breeding and food processing. Many other areas of technology are also involved, to the point where it is hard to find an area that does not have a direct impact on the food industry. Computer technology is also a central force, with computer networks and specialized software providing the support infrastructure to allow global movement of the myriad components involved.

Marketing

As consumers grow increasingly removed from food production, the role of product creation, advertising, publicity become the primary vehicles for information about food. With processed food as the dominant category, marketers have almost infinite possibilities in product creation. The smooth flow of international trade is critical to the functioning of the modern food industry. Government regulations have to be synchronized to some greater degree to allow this.

Labour and Education

Until the last 100 years, agriculture was labour intensive. Farming was a common occupation. Food production flowed from millions of farms. Farmers, largely trained from generation to generation, carried on the family business. That situation has changed dramatically. In North America, over 50 per cent of the population were farm families only a few decades ago; now, that figure is around 1-2 per cent, and some 80 per cent of the population lives in cities. The food industry as a complex whole requires an incredibly wide range of skills. Several hundred occupation types exist within the food industry.

Research and Development

Research in agricultural and food processing technologies happens in great part in university research environments. Projects are often funded by companies from the food industry. There is therefore a direct relationship between the academic and commercial sectors, as far as scientific research.

Prominent Food Companies

Monsanto is a leading producer of pesticide, seeds, and other farming products. Both Archer Daniels Midland and Cargill process grain into animal feed and a diverse group of products. ADM also provides agricultural storage and transportation services, while Cargill operates a finance wing.

Bunge is a global soybean exporter and is also involved in food processing, grain trading, and fertilizer. Dole Food Company is the world's largest fruit company. Chiquita Brands International, another US based fruit company, is the leading distributor of bananas in the United States. Sunkist Growers, Incorporated is a U.S. based grower's cooperative. Tyson Foods is the world's largest processor and marketer of chicken and the largest beef exporter from the United States. Smithfield is the world's largest pork processor and hog producer.

Nestlé is the world's largest food and beverage company. The Altria Group owns 88.1 per cent of Kraft Foods, the largest U.S. based food and beverage company. Unilever is an Anglo-Dutch company that owns many of the world's consumer product brands in foods and beverages.

Cuisine in Indian Hotels

The finest of India's cuisines is as rich and diverse as it's civilization. It is an art form that has been passed on through generations purely by word of mouth, from guru teacher to vidhyarthi (pupil) or from mother to daughter. The range assumes astonishing proportions when one takes into account regional variations. Very often the taste, colour, texture and appearance of the same delicacy changes from state to state. The hospitality of the Indians is legendary. In Sanskrit Literature the three famous words 'Atithi Devo Bhava' or 'the guest is truly your god' are a dictum of hospitality in India. Indians believe that they are honoured if they share their mealtimes with guests. Even the poorest look forward to guests and are willing to share this meager food with guest. And of particular importance is the Indian woman's pride that she will not let a guest go away unfed or unhappy from her home. Indians are known for their incredible ability to serve food to their guests invited or uninvited. Food customarily forms the crowning part of most festivities and celebrations. Whatever the occasion Indians eat with great gusto and are adept at finding reasons to feast and make merry. At traditional and festive meals, the thali (plate) or banana leaf is decorated with rangoli.

Kashmiri

Kashmiri cuisine is essentially meat-based. Lamb, goat's meat and chicken form the basis of many a famous dish. It is flavored delicately with saffron and kashmiri chillies which are not too spicy but impart a rich red colour to the food. The abundance of dry fruit like walnuts, dried dates, and apricots also inspire the Kashmiri connoisseur to use them lavishly in puddings, curries and snacks. Cottage cheese or chaman as it is called, is also a popular accompaniment to many meats and vegetables. Fresh water fish like trout found in the numerous fresh water streams flowing down from the Himalayas is also a delicacy. Food is generally followed by a generous serving of fresh fruits like strawberries, plums, cherries and apples which grow here and not all over India due to the cool climate.

Punjabi

Punjabi people are robust people with robust appetites and their food is like the Punjabis themselves, simple, sizeable and hearty with no unnecessary frills or exotic accompaniments. The Punjabi tandoori cooking is celebrated as one of the most popular cuisines throughout the world. Huge earthen ovens are half buried in the ground and heated with a coal fire lit below it. Marinated meat, chicken, fish, paneer, rotis and naans of many types are cooked in this novel oven and the results are absolutely scrumptious.

Punjab has imbibed some aspects of its cuisine from external influences. Connoisseurs of the cuisine say that the gravy component of Punjabi cuisine came from the Mughals. The most popular example is the murg makhani. It served the state well to combine this influence in its cooking since it had a lot of pure ghee and butter. Murg makhani also provided a balance to tandoori chicken, which was dry because it was charcoal cooked.

Nans and parathas, rotis made of maize flour are typical Punjabi breads. Of course, over the years the roti has been modified to add more variety, so there is the rumali roti, the naan and the laccha parathas, all cooked in the tandoor. Winter, in Punjab, brings in the season of the famous makki ki roti(maize flour bread) and sarson ka saag(mustard leaf gravy). No meal is complete without a serving of lassi(sweet or salted drink made with curd) or fresh curd and white butter which is consumed in large quantities. The other popular dishes, which belong exclusively to Punjab, are ma ki dal, rajma (kidney beans) and stuffed parathas.

Mughlai

Having reigned over India for so long, the Moghuls left a deep and long lasting influence on Delhi's cuisine. The Mughlai cuisine is literally 'fit for royalty'. With it's rich sauces, butter-based curries, ginger flavoured roast meats, and mind-blowing sweets, it has captured the fancy of food lovers all over the world. From a tangy shorba or soup to the rose petal strewn kulfi, Mughlai food offers a rich fare that is irresistible. Although available throughout the country, the best place to try this royal cuisine is in Delhi.

Bengali

Bengal's greatest contribution to the food heritage of India is a magnificent spectrum of sweets made from burnt milk and curd. 'Rasogullas', 'gulab jamuns', 'cham cham', 'malai sandwich', 'chena murki', 'anarkali', 'rajbhog' - the list of mouth-watering delicacies is endless. 'Mishti dhoi' or yoghurt sweetened with jaggery is a must in every Bengali home. Guests are always welcomed with 'sandesh' or sweets made from burnt milk and 'singadas' or crisp samosas.

Besides sweets, the Bengalis eat fish with great relish and most of the popular Bengali dishes are made from fish. A variety of styles are adopted to cook fish. They are at times marinated in spices, at other times cooked in curd. The cuisine of West Bengal differs from that of Bangladesh in that the use of coconut in this cuisine is much lesser and mustard oil is cooking medium instead of coconut oil. The spices differ from those used in the heartland of India, but are similar to those used in the interiors of the East Coast. The specialty of Bengali cooking is the use of panchphoron i.e. five basic spices which include zeera, kalaunji, saunf, fenugreek and mustard seeds. Generally, Bengali food is a mixture of sweet and spicy flavors and dining with these gentle people is a definate treat.

Maharashtrian

Maharashtrians are by and large, meat eaters. The cuisine includes subtly flavoured vegetarian delicacies and hot, aromatic meat and fish curries. Their crunchy, crisp sweets are made mostly from rice and jaggery. The exotic 'Konkani' and 'Malwani' cuisines also have their origins in the coastal parts of this region and are sea-food based. As in most of the other states of India, rice is the staple food grain in Maharashtra too. Like the other coastal states, there is an enormous variety of vegetables in the regular diet and lots of fish and coconuts are used. Grated coconuts spice many kinds of dishes, but coconut oil is not very widely used as a cooking medium. Peanuts and cashewnuts are widely used in vegetables and peanut oil is the main cooking medium.

Another feature is the use of kokum, a deep purple berry that has a pleasing sweet and sour taste. Kokum, most commonly used in an appetizer-digestive called the sol kadhi, is served chilled. All non-vegetarian and vegetarian dishes are eaten with boiled rice or with bhakris, which are soft rotis made of rice flour. Special rice puris called vada and amboli, which is a pancake made of fermented rice, urad dal, and semolina, are also eaten as a part of the main meal.

The most popular dessert of Maharashtra is the puran poli, which is roti stuffed with a sweet mixture of jaggery and gram flour and is made at the time of the Maharashtrian New Year. Other popular sweets are the ukdiche modak (these are served during the Ganesh festival), the panpole ras, and the shreekhand. Shreekhand, a sort of thick yogurt sweet dish, is a great Favourite at weddings and the Dussehra festival. Flavored with cardamom powder and saffron, this aromatic dish is served with piping hot puris.

Goan

Famous for it's distinctive cuisine, Goa can boast of delicacies like the tangy pork 'vindaloo', spicy 'sorpotel' and the ever popular Goan fish curry with rice. Goa's luscious coconut and fish based dishes draw in people from all over the world. Goans often accompany their meal with one of their innumerable local wines or the local liqueur called 'Feni'. Goan food is simple but one has to bear in mind that most, though not all, of it is chili hot, spicy, and pungent. Rice, fish, and coconut are the basic components of the typical Goan food platter. Delicacies made from these three items can be expected in nearly every Goan meal. Besotted with seafood, the Goans find truly world-class prawns, lobsters, crabs, and jumbo pomfrets along the coastline and use them to make a variety of soups, salads, pickles, curries, and fries.

An essential ingredient in Goan cooking is coconut milk made by grating the white flesh of a coconut and soaking it in a cup of warm water. Equally important is the 'kokum', a sour, deep red coloured fruit that gives it a sharp and sour flavor. The famous red Goan chilies are also a must for most dishes, as is tamarind. Goans make their own version of vinegar from toddy. Then there are innumerable chutneys that are typical of the state.

Goa is not particularly known for its vegetarian dishes. While Hindus like lamb and chicken, Christians prefer pork. However, both prefer fish and seafood to any other meat. Pork is a must for any festive occasion in Goa and the most famous preparation is the vindaloo. It is a spicy concoction, lots of red chilies, garlic, cooked with chunks of pork, Goa vinegar, and hard palm jaggery and is best enjoyed with plain boiled rice. Another mouth-watering delicacy made of pork is the sarpotel. A curry with a thick gravy to the layman, this exotic concoction comprises boneless pork, liver, heart, kidneys, red chilies, cinnamon, cloves bathed in tangy toddy vinegar, which is needed to balance the strong taste of pig's blood: another traditional ingredient of this revered dish.

For those with a sweet tooth, Goan cuisine offers the famous bebinca. The extract of coconut milk is added to flour, sugar, and other delectable ingredients are used to make this delicacy. Each scrumptious layer has to be baked before the next one is added, though not many people nowadays have the time to make the traditional 16 layers. Even so, a good bebinca is a mouth-melting dream.

Other sweets include a soft jaggery flavored fudge called dodol made from finger-licking palm-sap jaggery, rice flour and coconut; the crispy delicate rose-a-coque that are flower-like waffles and can be eaten alone or drenched with cream or honey; the curled and sugared kulkuls spiraled around the tines of forks and deep-fried as Christmas goodies and Easter eggs known as ovos da pascoa. Similarly, during the Hindu festival of Ganesh Chaturthi, cone-shaped dumplings called modaks are a favourite fare.

Gujarati

Gujaratis have truly perfected the art of vegetarian cooking. From the simplest lentils and vegetables, they create a mouth-watering variety of food. Gujarat is known as the land of milk and butter. Predictably so, yoghurt and buttermilk are a part of the Gujarati's daily diet. While in Gujarat, a 'thali' dinner - literally meaning a meal served on a silver platter- is a delight you must not miss. An endless procession of fresh vegetables cooked in aromatic spices, a variety of crisp, fried snacks and an array of delectable confections typically appear in the 'thali'.

In Gujarat, during winter when green vegetables are available in plenty, a delicious vegetable concoction called undhyoo is made using potato, brinjal, and green beans amongst several other vegetables. The main dish of gujarati cuisine is the khichdi, a simple lentil and rice mixture. It is eaten with kadhi, a savory curry made with yogurt using bay leaves, ginger, chilies and finely chopped vegetables as garnishing, onions and pickle.

Using the same lentils and rice, Kutchi kitchens produce delectable items like the khaman dhokla, a salty steamed cake made from chickpea flour; doodha pak, sweet, thickened milk confectioned with nuts, and srikhand, a dessert made of yogurt, flavored with saffron, cardamom, nuts and candied fruit which is eaten with hot, fluffy pooris. These three delicacies have made their way into the Favourites list of the rest of India too and can be found in restaurants all over the country.

Rajasthani

The ancient princely state of Rajasthan gave rise to a royal cuisine. The Rajas who went on hunting expeditions ate the meat or the fowl that they brought back. Even today, Rajasthani princely feasts flaunt meat delicacies that are incomparable. In contrast are the vegetarian Rajasthanis. Their food cooked in pure ghee is famous for it's mouth- watering aroma. Rajasthani cooking was also influenced by both the war-like lifestyles of its inhabitants and the availability of ingredients in the desert region. Food that could last for several days and could be eaten without heating was preferred, more out of necessity than choice. Scarcity of water and lack of fresh green vegetables also had their effect on Rajasthani cooking.

Dried lentils and beans from indigenous plants like sangri, ker etc. are staples of the Rajasthani diet, as wheat and rice do not grow very well in the desert land. Gram flour is an integral cooking ingredient and is used to make delicacies and so are powdered lentils. Bajra and corn are used all over the state for making rotis and other varieties of bread. In Rajasthan, bajre ki roti (millet bread) and lahsun ki chutney (hot garlic paste) combined with spring onions are the staple diet of the locals as these are believed to be safeguards against the hot winds. In the desert belt of Jaisalmer, Barmer and Bikaner, cooks still use very little water and instead use milk, buttermilk and clarified butter as alternatives.

The balance to using these milk products is provided by the appropriate use of digestives, especially asafetida, black rock salt, ginger and ajwain. The Favoured spices are fenugreek seeds, kasuri methi (dried fenugreek leaves) and aniseed. A distinct feature of the Maheshwari cooking is the use of mango powder, a suitable substitute for tomatoes, scarce in the desert, and asafetida, to enhance the taste in the absence of garlic and onions.

Hyderabadi

The cuisine of Andhra Pradesh is reputedly the spiciest and hottest of all Indian cuisine. The cuisine includes both the original Andhra cooking and the Hyderabadi cuisine with its Mughlai influence. It is the former which is red hot. The vegetables and greens are prepared with various different masalas giving the same vegetable different flavours. Traditional Andhra cuisine also has many non-vegetarian dishes which are also spicy and unique in taste. Hyderabadi cuisine is rich and aromatic with a liberal use of exotic spices and ghee, not to speak of nuts and dry fruits. Lamb is the most widely used meat in the non-vegetarian dishes. The biryanis (flavoured rice with meat or vegetables) is one of the most distinct Hyderabadi food.

Food based Tourism

In a recent survey of tourist perceptions of the UK food industry, two-thirds of Britons said that food and drink influenced their holiday choice. The West Country, Wales and Scotland occupied the top three destinations. For no longer is British food synonymous with fish, chips and roast dinners (except, of course, for Jacques Chirac, who has complained that only the Finns have worse cuisine).

During the 20th Century, industrialisation began to threaten artisan producers and many abandoned their traditional techniques. But in the past two decades, there's been a resurgence in demand for quality products made by time-honoured methods. The appetite is growing for regional produce, such as Somerset cider, Caerphilly cheese and Cromer crabs. Food tourism has become big business, worth nearly £4bn a year.

Since the Malt Whisky Trail was set up around Scottish distilleries several decades ago, the number of food and drink trails has multiplied. New additions include a wine trail around the South-East, sausage trails in the Midlands and the North-West, and a Lake District afternoon tea trail. Alexia Robinson, the organiser of British Food Fortnight, says food adds to a visitor's experience of a place. "Taste is one of our senses. We usually experience a place visually, such as on a castle or cathedral tour, so why not add to that through our taste buds?"

Even once-sleepy backwaters such as Bray in Berkshire, Padstow in Cornwall and Shropshire's Ludlow have become gastronomic hotspots thanks to star chefs Heston Blumenthal, Rick Stein and Shaun Hill (who has since closed the Michelin-starred Merchant House, which in 2003 ranked among the world's top 20 eateries). And the latest series of BBC Two's Full on Food - pitched firmly at the growing foodie market - catered for the interest in regional produce by dispatching a chef to find the tastiest local treats, be it ice cream, wild salmon or real ale.

Taste of Home

For Alexia Robinson, the variety of local specialities reflects the UK's diverse geography. Many regional dishes have evolved over centuries using ingredients best suited to the conditions and lifestyles of that area.

Cheese varieties are one such example, as is the Cornish pasty, devised to provide a filling lunch for the county's lead miners. And niche habitats such as salt marshes in Wales give lamb from the area a distinctive taste. What producers and caterers find is that the more local a food seems, the better the sales pitch. Hence detailed menus which name-check the farm which supplies the meat or the allotment where they grow their own asparagus.

For provenance sells, says Ms Robinson. "People want to know where their food comes from. I've even seen a wonderful menu entry for apple and blackberry pie, 'all blackberries picked from our local hedgerows'." She says that holidaymakers want foods which emphasise the heritage and culture of a place. "If you stay in a Gloucestershire BandB, for example, you'll probably be served sausages made from Gloucester Old Spot pigs. In the north of England, tourists seek out potted shrimps, and apple pie is popular in Kent." And who, at the seaside, hasn't been lured into an establishment famed for serving the best fish 'n' chips on that stretch of coast?

Food miles

Nor do we need to travel to track down regional delights. Delicatessens now stock British goodies as well as the more usual olives and Italian meats. Farmers' markets typically draw crowds, with London's Borough Market recently voted the capital's top tourist attraction. With producers and fine food stockists going online, tasty treats from around the UK can be delivered to your door.

Food also holds a key place in the "think globally, act locally" debate. Some buyers are keen to support local businesses, or protect the environment by avoiding foods which have been transported long distances. Environmentalists and tourism bosses alike must be heartened that two-thirds of Britons say they would consider holidaying at home, rather than jet off somewhere sunny, because of the food and drink on offer. Bon appetit indeed.

Food Tourism on the Boil

It could be the colourful sight of a giant rustic paella in a Spanish seaside town or the smell of a warm bagel on a New York street. But whatever the dish, it seems food is something an increasing number of us remember from our travels. Like never before, holiday makers are choosing where they go by what they can put in their stomachs - and catering for them is now top of the menu for tour operators and destinations. Fiona Jeffery, Group Exhibition Director of World Travel Market, who undertook the independent research with 2000 people throughout the UK of all ages and socio economic groups, said: "Food tourism today is where eco-tourism was 20 years ago; people are starting to take an interest.

"Although the research was carried out on behalf of World Travel Market was in the UK, we believe it is representative of a new and growing phenomenon within the international industry. "The industry needs to take note and use the opportunity to its advantage. Holidaymakers want a hands-on experience and food is a manifestation of a destination's culture. "You can open a different door with every meal." "The last five years has seen an incredible shift in the way holidays are marketed and it's all because people are demanding authentic experiences, said Erik Wolf, president of the International Culinary Tourism Association, a non-profit group representing more than 500 tourism businesses in 19 countries."

For the first time, the true extent of food tourism has been measured in the UK by World Travel Market, the premier business event for the international travel and tourism industry, with research revealing more than half (53per cent) ranked eating traditional dishes as a 'very important' or 'important' part of their holiday. Meanwhile, a staggering 86per cent of Brits quizzed said they enjoyed local foods when abroad. The trend is not just limited to those on specialist tailor-made breaks either, with 83per cent of people who typically go on half- or full-board holidays admitting they willingly miss meals in their hotel or resort to try out local restaurants.

International chef Gary Rhodes, whose TV Programmes has helped open up the world's traditional dishes and ingredients to a hungry audience, has recently opened a Rhodes restaurant in Calabash, on the Caribbean island of Grenada and onboard PandO Cruises' new liner Arcadia. He said: "The potential for tourism through dining is enormous and what better way to learn about a country than at the table! My experience is that travellers are becoming both more sophisticated and daring about what they eat."

Changes in Weekly Shop

Supermarkets have played a major part in the shift in attitudes, making foreign foods more available. One supermarket chain, Waitrose, for example, recently unveiled a range of tapas and Greek dishes that customers might have tried on their holiday. "The world is becoming a smaller place and we are seeing our customers' tastes change to reflect this. Dishes from all corners of the globe are becoming mainstream additions to the British dinner table," said Waitrose communications manager Gill Smith. "Flavours people have sampled on holiday are becoming more popular.

As they travel to further a field, customers are more willing to experiment with new flavours. Our oriental range now extends beyond Chinese dishes to Japanese, Malaysian and Thai foods. "We're also finding that as people travel more, they are more knowledgeable about regional trends within countries. Instead of simply wanting Indian foods, we're finding that customers are aware of Goan and Keralan food and want to buy these dishes at their local supermarket." In the research, the growing trend to change what they put in their supermarket trolley because of holiday experiences is evident. A total of 42per cent said this affected their weekly shop choices. Wolf said that some tourist offices are beginning to highlight food as a way of promoting their country to foreign visitors. This trend though must grow still further.

Chicago Led the Way

Chicago led the way eight years ago when it appointed former chef Judith Hines as director of culinary arts and events. She oversees 275 annual food-related events, including its summer-long Stirring Things Up festival (May 1-Oct 31), which features culinary tours, food festivals, farmers' markets and concerts. Special hotel rates are available to visitors during the period.

Although it's impossible to know how many visitors are drawn by food alone, Hines said millions come for the festivals, including the 11-day Taste of Chicago in July, where 3.5 million people consumed 70,000 pounds of ribs and 250,000 slices of pizza last year. That helped boost hotel occupancy to 90per cent last summer. "Food certainly helps boost tourism. While cultural events like theatre might be a good hook for tourists, it won't appeal to all; the attraction of food is universal" said Hines. "The misperception is that it has to be all five-star fine dining. We have 76 different ethnic neighbourhoods and promote them all. Having really authentic food is part of the attraction."

Chicago's focus on food includes a food concierge in one of the city's largest tourist offices adjacent to a large theatre booking agency. "It's a great tie-up. We explain the food scene to people who are looking for somewhere to eat on their night out." Hines also offers city tours with a difference, with a bus stopping at four local restaurants with diners having a course in each.

"It's a fun way to find out about the city's culture and heritage," she explained.

Operators claim the last five years has seen a significant change in the eating habits of Brits abroad, with clients shunning the 'chips with everything' restaurants and seeking out more local flavours. This is borne out by World Travel Market's independent research which indicated that 62 per cent of those questioned shunned "glamorous" foreign restaurants and wanted to eat in rustic surroundings with the locals. Only 7 per cent said they would prefer to eat in glamorous surroundings when overseas. Only 15 per cent of those questioned would plump for international cuisine rather than food typical of the area in which they were staying.

Demand for Authentic Experience

"People want an authentic experience," claimed Chris Orme, general manager of Far East specialist Travel Indochina. "We are talking much more about food to people when they book and make it a central part of the holiday, going to local restaurants and experimenting. The availability of Chinese, Thai and Vietnamese food in the UK means clients want to try the authentic stuff much more. "People have booked particular holidays with us on the strength of the food. We're certainly not an operator that deals with food tours, but eating has certainly become a big interest for our clients."

Long Travel, a specialist in rural Italy and Sicily, claimed around 85 per cent of its clients now asked specifically for food advice when booking. Contracts manager Laura Bell said: "Customers have very high expectations of the food in Italy because it receives so much good press and is always featured in cookery Programmes. "Getting back to nature and trying out dishes in a traditional setting is a must for our clients. Even the larger hotels we use grow many of their own vegetables and produce wine now."

Restaurant Concierge Service

Mercedes Fehler, marketing manager at upmarket specialist Harlequin Worldwide said demand for local cuisine was so high among its customers the operator had introduced a 'restaurant concierge' service. Customers can contact the operator before departure and the concierge will recommend and make reservations at restaurants around the globe.

"The concierge contacts the hotel the customer is staying in to get advice about the places to eat nearby and will make bookings. It's a very popular service in long-haul destinations," said Fehler. "Short haul, people tend to get out and look themselves. Hunting around for a place to eat in Europe is something people are more comfortable with."

Meanwhile, Caribbean specialist Carib Tours runs a 'food evening' each year for regular clients to showcase the best local restaurants. "People in the UK have access to some of the best restaurants in the world and so they won't settle for poor food when they're away," said Carib Tours managing director

Paul Cleary. "The four aspects of a holiday that are important to our clients are weather, beach, luxury and food. "The trend in the Caribbean has been for 'big name' European restaurants and chefs to open in the last few years. Clients want to eat in them, maybe as a special occasion. They also want to get out and eat locally. In Barbados, the Oistin's Fish Fry is a great example, but then it also has The Cliff, one of the world's best restaurants."

The DIY trend has even started to spread long-haul, according the Martin Grass, sales and marketing director of Rex Hotels., which has nine properties in the Caribbean and two in Kenya. "The Caribbean ahs been dominated by the big all-inclusives in the past and people had no need to go out to eat. While that is still very popular with the US market, people from the UK are a bit more adventurous, especially to the eastern Caribbean. Islands such as Barbados and Antigua have fantastic local restaurants and are seen as safe to venture out at night. The vast majority of our business from the UK is now room-only, because people want to sample the food and it is comparatively cheap to eat out."

But food has become a central part of the overseas marketing for nations around the world. Earlier this year, Portugal teamed up with Harrods to promote its national dishes through the up market stores famous food hall. For the European destination, the message aims to attract not only those on traditional packages, but also the major villa holiday market predominantly served by the low-cost carriers, since these people eat out more.

Portuguese National Tourist Office director José António Preto da Silva said: "Our cuisine is now one of the key attractions for UK visitors, with each region of Portugal offering unique cooking style as well as local specialities. "Mealtimes are highly valued by the Portuguese, providing a leisurely opportunity to indulge in good food and good wine while catching up with family and friends, and this is a tradition we encourage visitors to join in to capture the true essence of our country and people."

The Rise of Food Festivals

Similarly, Singapore hosts an annual food festival each July celebrating a different aspect of its culture. This year (it's 14th) marks the 40th anniversary of the country's independence, majoring on what it is perhaps best known for by foreign visitors andendash; its hawker (street) food. Tee Yen Chew, Singapore Tourism Board's Area Director for Northern and Western Europe said:

"Singaporeans are passionate about food and eating. In almost every corner of the island, you will find an endless variety of food served hot or cold at any hour of the day or night. Singapore's cultural diversity is very much reflected in the variety of local food it has to offer and endash; Chinese, Malay, Indian, Peranakan and Eurasian. It is very important to communicate this to people thinking about visiting Singapore. It's not just a fusion of east and west, it the country's unique cultural tapestry."

Closer to home, VisitScotland has begun to promote food alongside its mainstay messages such as golf and outdoor pursuits. The country has also introduced a national quality assurance scheme, Eat Scotland, aimed at raising standards and educating hoteliers and restaurant owners about the important part food plays for visitors.

Key Driver in Scotland

Sector development manager for Visit Scotland Ewan Fair weather said: "Food is a key driver in the holidaymaking decision. We want those in the industry to shout about their food, be proud and enthusiastic. That will enrich the visiting experience." Las Vegas, meanwhile, is a good example of how destinations have changed the emphasis of their food product as tourism has changed. Food has always been part of the gambling city's attraction from the opening of the first all-you-can-eat buffet andendash; the $1 Midnight Chuck Wagon at the El Rancho hotel. But it was quantity over quality promoted to its original domestic clientele.

Very often, food and drink was considered a loss-leader by the casinos, with establishments giving it away to attract gamblers. The arrival of high-rolling punters, overseas tourists and large business travel contingent means it now boasts some the best restaurants in the US. Today, Las Vegas is home to three restaurants that have earned the AAA Five Diamond rating: the Bellagio's Le Cirque and Picasso and The Mirage's Renoir.

"Dining in Las Vegas has evolved significantly from the days of the all you can eat buffets," said Melanie Jones, of the Las Vegas Convention and Visitors Bureau in the UK. "Las Vegas has now become synonymous with gourmet cuisine and most of the top chefs have now opened restaurants in the city from Wolfgang Puck to Alain du Casse. Even Guy Savoy who allegedly vowed, in the past, that he would not consider opening a restaurant in the US."

Wine and Food Tourism

Wine, Food, and Tourism Marketing is an overview of contemporary practices and trends in food and wine tourism marketing. Local and regional food holds great potential to contribute to sustainable competitiveness in a destination. An analysis of the literature and promotional material of South African and key international destinations, however, indicate that the contribution of food to sustainable tourism and the marketing of destinations has received very little attention globally, as well as in South Africa.

A framework and guidelines for developing and implementing food tourism could enable destination marketers and entrepreneurs to optimise the tourism potential of local and regional food. To this end a food tourism destination-marketing framework was conceptualised, which was based on the findings of a South African situation analysis and international trends and best practices.

The South African situation analysis entailed an empirical investigation among regional and provincial destination marketing organisations to determine the current status and future potential and food tourism initiatives as a key component of destination marketing in South Africa. To support the food tourism destination marketing framework, two key tools were developed, namely TOURPAT (a tourism and culinary atlas linked to a geospatial database) and PAT (a product potential and attractiveness tool).

The framework and tools were tested in a South African destination and provided the stakeholders with mechanisms to develop and implement food tourism. This chapter outlines the key components and an evaluation of the framework and tools that have been developed. Guidelines and recommendations for the development, packaging and marketing of local and regional foods are postulated. Proposals for future research are also outlined.

Tasmanian Wine and Food Tourism Strategy

The Tasmanian Wine and Food Tourism Strategy provides an understanding of where Tasmania is positioned in a national context and identifies ways to create new and maximise existing opportunities to enhance the Tasmanian wine and food tourism experience. Research has provided an insight into the industry segment both nationally and in Tasmania, highlighting two key visitor groups who are Tasters and Epicureans.

The key findings give rise to a range of development strategies and action plans at both the state and regional level. The Wine and Food Tourism Strategy is sector specific and underpins the broader Tasmanian Experience Strategy that addresses how Tasmania's three core appeals of nature, cultural heritage and wine and food in combination give the State a sustainable competitive advantage. The Tasmanian Experience Strategy will complement and build on the Wine and Food Tourism Strategy in the context of the delivery of the broader visitor experience. Wine and food tourism can make a significant contribution to the broader tourism growth targets set under the joint industry-State Government strategic plan, Tourism 21. The targets are $1 billion in visitor expenditure and 26,000 tourism jobs, both by 2007.

In June 2000, it was estimated that visitors to Tasmania spent $69 million on food and wine. A primary objective of this strategy is to increase this expenditure while building on the sector's growing potential to attract higher-yielding visitors to Tasmania. Compared to other states, Tasmanian wine and food tourism is in the early stages of industry development. The Tasmanian Wine and Food Tourism Strategy has been developed as a framework to drive growth, quality of experiences and the ability to value-add within the sector.

A wine and food tourism experience has all three elements present – neither wine, food nor tourism alone comprise a wine and food tourism experience. While the intrastate market will continue to be important for the sector's sustainability, studies conducted as part of the strategy show that the growth potential lies with interstate and international visitors. In addition, market research emphasises that Tasmania's competitive advantage – and its point of differentiation from other visitor destinations – lies in its mix of wine and food with the appeal of natural beauty and history. This strategy has been developed by Tourism Tasmania in consultation with sector operators, industry organisations, the Tourism Council Tasmania and other State Government agencies.

Growth potential

The two main customer groups identified as wine and food purchasers are Tasters (48 per cent including Epicureans 2 per cent) and Non-Tasters (52 per cent), who have little or no interest in wine and food experiences. Studies indicate that the profile of the Tasters group is similar to the overall leisure market, showing that people do not come to Tasmania just for a wine and food experience but are attracted by the interplay of nature and heritage with wine and food.

Research shows the short break market has a particularly high level of interest in food and wine related activities. Tasters represent the majority of holiday visitors and consume wine and food as part of their broader holiday experience, therefore wine and food products are unlikely to attract additional visitor numbers. Along with other states and territories Tasmania achieves a relatively similar market share of Tasters to its market share in overall national visitation. However, a greater number and range of offerings are most likely to increase the spend and yield per visitor during their stay. Wine and food is a key trigger for the Epicurean segment. These visitors make their holiday travel decisions specifically to participate in wine and food activities and have a higher holiday spend.

The segment currently comprises about 7000 interstate and 1300 international visitors to Tasmania annually. Victoria (41 per cent of market share), South Australia (30.1 per cent) and Western Australia (20.9 per cent) dominate the Epicurean market nationally due to the establishment of recognised wine regions. Victoria has at least 10 regions attractive to Epicureans and South Australia has also adopted a multiple region approach. Western Australia has achieved its success using a single wine and food destination with the hub in the Margaret River region, a geographic location not close to an urban centre. Epicureans perceive that there is little on the ground in Tasmania to attract them to the State, which is why only a small number holiday here.

It is apparent that clear action is critical for development of the wine and food sector. While the existing focus on food and wine as an integral part of the Tasmanian holiday experience should continue, a greater number and variety of experiences need to be developed to improve the total spend and yield per visitor for the Tasters.

An even more radical shift in both product and human infrastructure is needed to get onto the "hot list" for Epicureans, including developing more high quality wine and food experiences, events and activities, and adopting a multi-regional approach – with more touring options between Tasmania's wine regions – to encourage longer stays and increased spend. In this context, external pressures that can impact on the capacity of boutique operators to deliver wine and food experiences (i.e. Wine Equalisation Tax) need to be addressed by the industry at large.

Tasmanian Development Strategies

Research shows that wine and food is not a stand alone tourism trigger but one of three interdependent sets of core values of Tasmania's brand alongside wilderness/nature and history/heritage. It is the combination of these values that is most likely to trigger wine and food tourism. Market demand is driven by available product, so if the product is not readily available then the customer will not purchase it, therefore the key to driving demand is supply.

The key research outcomes highlight that: i) wine and food tourism is supply-led; ii) it occurs in identifiable regions; and iii) metropolitan wine and food tourism precincts rely more on local customers rather than visitors. It also identifies a distinct supply-led development sequence for wine and food tourism regions.

The three-stage sequence is:

1. Wine production, dictated by volume and reputation;
2. Food industry development to complement the rise in profile of an area and the character of its wines; and
3. Tourism growth that occurs with the increasing quality and quantity of wine and food and improved branding and reputation of the regions.

Six development strategies have significant potential to lift overall tourism yield and visitor numbers:

1. Continue to ensure that wine and food tourism is integrated with wilderness and nature, as well as history and heritage;
2. Encourage infrastructure development based on the three-stage development pattern;
3. Target the Tasters segment to achieve yield objectives and visitor numbers, while basing the positioning of wine and food tourism in Tasmania on the Epicureans;
4. *Adopt a regional approach* – Tamar Valley, South East and Freycinet;
5. Manage each region as it progresses through product development stages to ensure that its distinctiveness is developed as well as regional strategies; and
6. *Promote the cluster* – The region's range of tourism experiences that encourage visitors to stay longer in an area – as the experience and the destination.

Regional Overview

While nationally Tasmania as a whole is considered to be a food and wine destination, the three emerging sub-regions offer distinct product differentiation. The Product Life Cycle concept reflects the product evolution and industry development stages. Product evolution has five stages:

1. Market development, when a product is small-scale and at the early stages of development;
2. Rapid growth, when demand is driving growth and there is scale-up and diversification;
3. Competitive turbulence, during which there are high rates of new development and a greater scale achieved;
4. Saturation/maturity, the stage of over-supply leading to gradual stagnation of product; and
5. Decline, of product and revenues.

Tasmania's wine regions are each in a different phase of industry development within the Market Development Stage. Tamar Valley has experienced significant investment by the larger wineries. The emerging cluster relies heavily on its hub of Launceston for related food and tourism infrastructure. It is considered to be in the latter phases of this Market Development Stage. While there has been significant investment by some of the larger wineries in the South East region, it is not on the same scale and the industry is still stand-alone, production focused, with Hobart as the hub. It is most likely in the early to mid-phase of the Market Development Stage.

The Freycinet industry is stand-alone, small, with limited product and while on the touring route does not benefit from proximity to a major hub. It is considered to be at the beginning of the Market Development Stage. Because each region is at a different stage of evolution and there is a need to develop its distinctiveness, each requires its own development Action Agenda to achieve growth. Common to each region is the need to address four key attributes that are critical to product evolution:

1. The number and quality of wineries within a region or cluster;
2. The number and quality of restaurants in a region or cluster and their use of local produce and integration with the character of wines of the region;
3. Related tourism infrastructure, including accommodation and the type and quality of activities within the area; and
4. The level and sophistication of customer service standards, which help create the character and brand of product and experience.

The strategy also identifies 16 industry development triggers required for the Freycinet cluster to move from the very early Market Development Stage of the product cycle to the late Market Development Stage. They include: bundling product with other tourism brand values, such as promoting regional wine and food experiences with natural attractions like Freycinet National

Park; adopting the Freycinet Region as the region's name; integrating the region's three national parks into the regional marketing strategy; developing Coles Bay-Swansea-Bicheno as the region to replace a single hub; and increasing direct customer purchase opportunities through actions such as wine-based direct mailing lists.

Food and Restaurant Managers

Fast food restaurant managers are responsible for the provision of standardised food and customer service in outlets based in the high street, motor service areas, stations, airports or multiplexes. Drawing on all the operational functions of a business, the work involves applying financial, marketing and operational know-how, and supervising and training staff.

Managers plan, organise, and co-ordinate all resources and activities in a store. The work involves: setting targets, planning budgets, and controlling stock; recruiting, training and inspiring restaurant teams; creating and driving marketing campaigns; and building bridges with the local community. Ultimately, it is the manager's ideas, initiative and personality that shape the restaurant.

Tasks typically involve:

- Organising the store in terms of products, equipment and people;
- Planning and checking work schedules;
- Carrying out audits to check health safety, food safety and quality f service in the restaurant;
- Making sure the fast-track audit is completed daily to check the safety of equipment and that food is properly cooked, only in-date stock is used, and all other products are discarded;
- Carrying out work outside the restaurant, including 'mystery shopping' at other restaurants within the chain;
- Attending weekly meetings with senior managers;
- Dealing with problems, queries, complaints, staff and customers in the store;
- Monitoring and maintaining high standards of food, service and hygiene;
- Ensuring the company's required standards of customer care are met;
- Administering payrolls;
- Checking and securing cash receipts;
- Budgeting to ensure maximum profitability;
- Achieving set profit and loss targets;
- Maintaining and securing equipment and buildings and all company assets contained within the unit;
- Publicising and marketing restaurants in the locality;
- Motivating restaurant teams;

- Recruiting, selecting and training new staff and fully inducting the restaurant team in accordance with company policy;
- Developing all team members to their fullest potential using the performance management/review system and identifying individual training needs;
- Ensuring the implementation and maintenance of legislation, company standards and procedures;
- Recognising new trends and implementing action plans accordingly;
- Acting as a communication link between senior teams and the restaurant team;
- Leading by example, acting as a role model for the restaurant team.

A successful manager will strike the right balance between creating both a good service for restaurant customers and a fun work environment for members of staff.

Catering Manager

Catering managers plan, organise and manage the food and beverage services of organisations and businesses, both inside and outside the hospitality industry, with the aim of achieving good quality at low cost and maintaining high standards of hygiene and customer satisfaction.

There is a range of jobs in catering management, along with a number of different routes into the industry. Roles include: managing restaurants, bars and other outlets in hotels, resorts or liners; providing catering services at events; and running catering operations at hospitals, schools and other organisations.

With ongoing growth in the service industry, opportunities in this demanding but rewarding area continue to grow.

Typical Work Activities

The role varies according to the size and nature of the establishment: in a small operation, the catering manager has more of a 'hands on' role and will be involved in the day-to-day running of the operation; in contract catering, the catering manager will spend time negotiating with the client organisation, assessing its requirements and ensuring that it is satisfied with the service delivered.

Typical tasks will include:

- Recruiting and training permanent and casual staff;
- Organising, leading and motivating the catering team;
- Planning menus in consultation with chefs;
- Ensuring health and safety regulations are strictly observed;
- Budgeting and establishing financial targets;
- Monitoring the quality of the product and service provided;
- Keeping financial and administrative records;
- Managing the payroll and monitoring spending levels;

- Maintaining stock levels and ordering new supplies as required;
- Interacting with customers if involved with 'front of house' work;
- Liaising with suppliers and clients;
- Negotiating contracts with customers (in contract catering).

In more senior posts, principal tasks will involve:

- Setting and agreeing budgets;
- Monitoring quality standards;
- Overseeing the management of the facilities, for example checking events bookings and the allocation of resources and staff;
- Planning new promotions and initiatives, and contributing to business development;
- Dealing with staffing and client issues, as they arise.

Tourism and Economics

Tourism's economic benefits are touted by the industry for a variety of reasons. Claims of tourism's economic significance give the industry greater respect among the business community, public officials, and the public in general. This often translates into decisions or public policies that are Favourable to tourism. Community support is important for tourism, as it is an activity that affects the entire community. Tourism businesses depend extensively on each other as well as on other businesses, government and residents of the local community.

Economic benefits and costs of tourism reach virtually everyone in the region in one way or another. Economic impact analyses provide tangible estimates of these economic interdependencies and a better understanding of the role and importance of tourism in a region's economy. Businesses and public organizations are increasingly interested in the economic impacts of tourism at national, state, and local levels. One regularly hears claims that tourism supports X jobs in an area or that a festival or special event generated Y million dollars in sales or income in a community. "Multiplier effects" are often cited to capture secondary effects of tourism spending and show the wide range of sectors in a community that may benefit from tourism.

Tourism activity also involves economic costs, including the direct costs incurred by tourism businesses, government costs for infrastructure to better serve tourists, as well as congestion and related costs borne by individuals in the community. Community decisions over tourism often involve debates between industry proponents touting tourism's economic impacts (benefits) and detractors emphasizing tourism's costs.

Sound decisions rest on a balanced and objective assessment of both benefits and costs and an understanding of who benefits from tourism and who pays for it. Tourism's economic impacts are therefore an important consideration in state, regional and community planning and economic development. Economic impacts are also important factors in marketing and management decisions. Communities therefore need to understand the relative importance of tourism to their region, including tourism's contribution to economic activity in the area.

A variety of methods, ranging from pure guesswork to complex mathematical models, are used to estimate tourism's economic impacts. Studies vary extensively in quality and accuracy, as well as which aspects of tourism are included. Technical reports often are filled with economic terms and methods that non-economists do not understand. On the other hand, media coverage of these studies tend to oversimplify and frequently misinterpret the results, leaving decision makers and the general public with a sometimes distorted and incomplete understanding of tourism's economic effects.

How can the average person understand these studies sufficiently to separate good studies from bad ones and make informed choices? The purpose of this bulletin is to present a systematic introduction to economic impact concepts and methods. The presentation is written for tourism industry analysts and public officials, who would like to better understand, evaluate, or possibly conduct an economic impact assessment. The bulletin is organized around ten basic questions that either are asked or should be asked about the economic impacts of tourism.

An Economic Impact Analysis

A variety of economic analyses are carried out to support tourism decisions. As these different kinds of economic analysis are frequently confused, let's begin by positioning economic impact studies within the broader set of economic problems and techniques relevant to tourism. These same techniques may be applied to any policy or action, but we will define them here in the context of tourism. Each type of analysis is identified by the basic question(s) it answers and the types of methods and models that are appropriate.

Benefit cost analysis and economic impact analysis are frequently confused as both discuss economic "benefits". There are two clear distinctions between the two techniques. B/C analysis addresses the benefits from economic efficiency while economic impact analysis focuses on the regional distribution of economic activity. The income received from tourism by a destination region is largely off-set by corresponding losses in the origin regions, yielding only modest contributions to net social welfare and efficiency. B/C analysis includes market and non-market values (consumer surplus), while economic impact analysis is restricted to actual flows of money from market transactions.

While each type of economic analysis is somewhat distinct, a given problem often calls for several different kinds of economic analysis. An economic impact study will frequently involve a demand analysis to project levels of tourism activity. In other cases demand is treated as exogenous and the analysis simply estimates impacts if a given number of visitors are attracted to the area. A comprehensive impact assessment will also examine fiscal impacts, as well as social and environmental impacts.

Be aware that an economic impact analysis, by itself, provides a rather narrow and often one-sided perspective on the impacts of tourism. Studies of the economic impacts of tourism tend to emphasize the positive benefits of tourism. On the other hand environmental, social, cultural and fiscal impact studies tend to focus more on negative impacts of tourism. This is in spite of the fact that there are negative economic impacts of tourism (e.g., seasonality and lower wage jobs) and in many cases positive environmental and social impacts (e.g., protection of natural and cultural resources in the area and education of both tourists and local residents).

An economic impact assessment (EIA) traces changes in economic activity resulting from some action. An EIA will identify which economic sectors benefit from tourism and estimate resulting changes in income and employment in the region. Economic impact assessment procedures do not assess economic efficiency and also do not generally produce estimates of the fiscal costs of an action. For many problems economic impact analysis will be part of a broader analysis. Environmental, social, and fiscal impacts are often equally important concerns in a balanced assessment of impacts.

Tourism Economic Impact Study

An economic impact analysis will assess the contribution of tourism activity to a region's economy. An economic impact analysis also reveals the interrelationships among economic sectors and provides estimates of the changes that take place in an economy due to some existing or proposed action. The most common applications of economic impact analysis to tourism are:

- To evaluate the economic impacts of changes in the supply of recreation and tourism opportunities. Supply changes may involve a change in quantity, such as the opening of new facilities, closing of existing ones, or expansions and contraction in capacity. Supply changes may also involve changes in quality, including changes in (a) the quality of the environment, (b) the local infrastructure and public services to support tourism, or (c) the nature of the tourism products and services that are provided in an area.
- To evaluate the economic impacts of changes in tourism demand. Population changes, changes in the competitive position of the region, marketing activity or changing consumer tastes and preferences can alter levels of tourism activity, spending, and associated economic activity. An economic impact study can estimate the magnitude and nature of these impacts.
- To evaluate the effects of policies and actions which affect tourism activity either directly or indirectly. Tourism depends on many factors at both origins and destinations that are frequently outside

the direct control of the tourism industry itself. Economic impact studies provide information to help decision makers better understand the consequences of various actions on the tourism industry as well as on other sectors of the economy. For example, increased air pollution standards have been opposed in some regions due to the predicted economic consequences of the closing of plants that cannot meet the new standards. Tourism interests counter these arguments with estimates of the potential gains in income and jobs in tourism industries that depend on good air quality and visibility.

- To understand the economic structure and interdependencies of different sectors of the economy. Economic studies help us better understand the size and structure of the tourism industry in a given region and its linkages to other sectors of the economy. Such understandings are helpful in identifying potential partners for the tourism industry as well as in targeting industries as part of regional economic development strategies. Issues such as economic growth, stability, and seasonality may be addressed as part of these studies.
- To argue for Favourable treatment in allocation of resources or local tax, zoning or other policy decisions..By showing that tourism has significant economic impacts, tourism interests can often convince decision-makers to allocate more resources for tourism or to establish policies that encourage tourism. Tax abatements and other incentives frequently given to manufacturing firms have also been granted to hotels, marinas and other tourism businesses based on demonstrated economic impacts in the local area.
- To compare the economic impacts of alternative resource allocation, policy, management or development proposals. Economic impact analyses are commonly used to assess the relative merits of distinct alternatives. The economic contribution of expanded tourism offerings may be compared for example with alternatives such as resource extraction activities (mining, timber harvesting) or manufacturing. Impacts of alternative tourism development proposals may also be evaluated, e.g., tourism strategies that emphasize outdoor recreation, camping development, a convention facility, or a factory outlet mall.

Direct, Indirect and Induced Effects

A standard economic impact analysis traces flows of money from tourism spending, first to businesses and government agencies where tourists spend their money and then to:

1. *Other businesses* — Supplying goods and services to tourist businesses,

2. *Households* - Earning income by working in tourism or supporting industries, and
3. *Government.*— Through various taxes and charges on tourists, businesses and households

Formally, regional economists distinguish direct, indirect, and induced economic effects. Indirect and induced effects are sometimes collectively called secondary effects. The total economic impact of tourism is the sum of direct, indirect, and induced effects within a region. Any of these impacts may be measured as gross output or sales, income, employment, or value added. Direct effects are production changes associated with the immediate effects of changes in tourism expenditures. For example, an increase in the number of tourists staying overnight in hotels would directly yield increased sales in the hotel sector. The additional hotel sales and associated changes in hotel payments for wages and salaries, taxes, and supplies and services are direct effects of the tourist spending.

Indirect effects are the production changes resulting from various rounds of re-spending of the hotel industry's receipts in other backward-linked industries (i.e., industries supplying products and services to hotels). Changes in sales, jobs, and income in the linen supply industry, for example, represent indirect effects of changes in hotel sales. Businesses supplying products and services to the linen supply industry represent another round of indirect effects, eventually linking hotels to varying degrees to many other economic sectors in the region.

Induced effects are the changes in economic activity resulting from household spending of income earned directly or indirectly as a result of tourism spending..For example, hotel and linen supply employees supported directly or indirectly by tourism,.spend their income in the local region for housing, food, transportation, and the usual array of household product and service needs. The sales, income, and jobs that result from household spending of added wage, salary, or proprietor's income are induced effects.

By means of indirect and induced effects, changes in tourist spending can impact virtually every sector of the economy in one way or another.

The magnitude of secondary effects depends on the propensity of businesses and households in the region to purchase goods and services from local suppliers. Induced effects are particularly noticed when a large employer in a region closes a plant. Not only are supporting industries (indirect effects) hurt, but the entire local economy suffers due to the reduction in household income within the region. Retail stores close and leakages of money from the region increase as consumers go outside the region for more and more goods and services. Similar effects in the opposite direction are observed when there is a significant increase in jobs and household income.

Final demand is the term used by economists for sales to the final consumers of goods and services. In almost all cases, the final consumers of tourism goods and services are households. Government spending is also considered as final demand. The same methods for estimating impacts of visitor spending can be applied to estimate the economic impacts of government spending, for example, to operate and maintain a park or visitor Centre.

Regional Economic Models

An input-output model (I-O model) is a mathematical model that describes the flows of money between sectors within a region's economy. Flows are predicted by knowing what each industry must buy from every other industry to produce a dollar's worth of output. Using each industry's production function, I-O models also determine the proportions of sales that go to wage and salary income, proprietor's income, and taxes. Multipliers can be estimated from input-output models based on the estimated re-circulation of spending within the region. Exports and imports are determined based upon estimates of the propensity of households and firms within the region to purchase goods and services from local sources (often called RPC's or regional purchase coefficients). The more a region is self-sufficient and purchases goods and services from within the region, the higher the multipliers for the region.

Multipliers and Multiplier Effects of Tourism

Multipliers capture the secondary economic effects (indirect and induced) of tourism activity. Multipliers have been frequently misused and misinterpreted in tourism studies (Archer 1984) and are a considerable source of confusion among non-economists. Multipliers represent the economic interdependencies between sectors within a particular region's economy. They vary considerably from region to region and sector to sector. There are many different kinds of multipliers reflecting which secondary effects are included and which measure of economic activity is used (sales, income, or employment).

For example,

The Type I sales multiplier = direct sales + indirect sales direct sales.

The Type II or III sales multiplier[1] = direct sales + indirect sales + induced sales direct sales.

Multiplying a Type I sales multiplier times the direct sales gives direct plus indirect sales. Multiplying a Type II or III sales multiplier times the direct sales gives total sales impacts including direct, indirect and induced effects. The multipliers defined above are called ratio type multipliers as they measure the ratio of a total impact measure to the corresponding direct impact. Comparable income and employment ratio type multipliers may be defined by replacing sales with measures of income or employment in the above equations. Ratio multipliers should be used with caution.

A common error is to multiply a sales multiplier times tourist spending to get total sales effects. This will generate an inflated estimate of tourism impacts. The problem is that tourism spending or sales is not exactly the same as the "direct effects", appearing in the multiplier formula. Tourist purchases of goods (vs. services) are the primary source of the problem.

To properly apply tourist purchases of goods to an input-output model (or corresponding multipliers), various margins (retail, wholesale and transportation) must be deducted from the "purchaser price" of the good to separate out the "producer price". In an I-O model, retail margins accrue to the retail trade sector, wholesale margins to wholesale trade, transportation margins to transportation sectors (trucking, rail, air etc.) and the producer prices of goods are assigned to the sector that produces the good. In most cases the factory that produces the good bought by a tourist lies outside of the local region, creating an immediate "leakage" in the first round of spending and therefore no local impact from production of the good.

Before applying a multiplier to tourist spending, one must first deduct the producer prices of all imported goods that tourists buy (i.e. only include the local retail margins and possibly wholesale and transportation margins if these firms lie within the region). Generally, only 60 to 70 per cent of tourist spending appears as final demand in a local region. While all tourist purchases of services will accrue to the local region as final demand, only the margins on goods purchased at retail stores should be counted as local final demand. The ratio of local final demand to tourist spending is called the capture rate.

Capture rate = local final demand./ tourism spending in local area

Capture rates, like multipliers, will vary with the size and nature of the region as well as the kind of tourist spending included. One must therefore be cautious in taking a multiplier or capture rate cited in one study and using it in another.

Another way of calculating a multiplier (generally the preferred approach among economists) is as a ratio of income or employment to sales. This kind of multiplier is sometimes called a Keynesian multiplier or response coefficient.

Type III Income multiplier = Total direct, indirect, and induced income.direct sales

Type III Employment multiplier = Total direct, indirect, and induced employment.direct sales

This income (employment) multiplier produces total income (employment) impacts when multiplied by the direct sales. One must still be careful in distinguishing between tourism spending/sales and direct sales effects. Some studies may embed the capture rate in the multiplier, expressing the ratio in terms of tourism spending rather than direct sales.

The Typical Approaches for an Economic impact Assessment

At the simple, "quick and dirty" end of the spectrum are highly aggregate approaches that rely mostly on judgement to determine tourism activity, spending and multipliers. Such estimates can be completed in a couple hours at little cost and rest largely on the expertise and judgement of the analyst. At the other extreme are studies that gather primary data from visitor spending studies and apply the spending estimates to formal regional economic models for the area in question. In between are a wide range of options that employ varying degrees of judgement, secondary data, primary data, and formal models.

Different levels of detail and corresponding expense (time and money) and accuracy are possible for each of the three steps — estimating tourist volume, spending, and multiplier effects. Four typical approaches illustrate the levels of detail that are possible and the associated methods to sales estimates. With sound judgement in choosing the parameters, the MGM model can yield reasonable ballpark estimates of economic impacts at minimal cost. This approach, however, provides little detail on spending categories or which sectors of the economy benefit from either direct or secondary effects. The aggregate nature of the approach also makes it difficult to adjust recommended spending rates or multipliers to different applications (USDI, National Park Service 1990.).

- The Bureau of Economic Analysis's (BEA) RIMS II user handbook illustrates how to apply published multipliers to estimate economic impacts. This approach starts with visitor spending (from survey or secondary sources) divided into a number of spending categories and makes use of sector specific multipliers to estimate the direct and total sales, income and employment effects. Multipliers from the BEA's RIMS II models are used to estimate secondary effects. Multipliers are reported for 39 sectors for each state in the second edition of their report (USDC 1992). This method uses margins to properly account for retail purchases of goods and makes use of disaggregate sector-specific multipliers for each state. Multipliers for sub-state regions are not as readily available, but can be acquired from BEA or other sources. Secondary effects cannot be disaggregated to individual sectors using the BEA approach. (USDC, BEA 1992).
- The MI-REC/IMPLAN System. Stynes and Propst have developed a fairly complete micro- computer-based system for estimating economic impacts of recreation and tourism. The system combines spreadsheets for estimating spending with the IMPLAN input-output modeling system. IMPLAN uses county level data to estimate 528 sector input-output models for regions down to a.county level. IMPLAN generates a complete set of economic accounts for the region including multipliers and trade flows. MI-REC spreadsheets estimate visitor spending within up to 33 categories based on the number and types of visitors attracted to an area. Spending is then bridged to the IMPLAN model sectors to estimate direct, indirect and induced effects in terms of sales, income

and employment. Users may estimate spending via visitor surveys or use the MI-REC database of spending profiles, compiled from previous studies. The system also includes price indices to easily.update spending data to a current year.

Two other systems for estimating economic impacts of tourism should be noted. The TEIM or Travel Economic Impact Model developed by the U.S. Travel Data Centre (USTDC, 1997) has been widely used to estimate tourism and travel impacts at state and national levels. A more recent development is the satellite accounting approach developed by the World Travel and Tourism Council (WTTC 1996). Both of these systems are primarily designed for estimating the overall economic significance of tourism at national or state levels. They are not readily applied to estimate the impacts of particular policies and actions at the local level. The TEIM relies on national travel surveys to estimate trip volume and spending on a state-by-state basis.

Local estimates of impacts are obtained using simple allocation formulas to distribute statewide impacts to counties and cities within the state. These local estimates do not account very well for the distinct types of tourism activity or spending patterns in different sub-regions of a state. The WTTC effort also focuses on national and statewide accounting of tourism's economic significance. Their satellite tourism account identifies the contribution of travel and tourism to gross national product (GNP) or gross state product (GSP).

Using the standard national system of accounts, they identify the portion of sales, taxes and investment attributable directly to travel and tourism. The WTTC system does not use multipliers or attempt to estimate secondary effects. It does, however, capture a great deal of travel-related economic activity, not covered by visitor trip spending, such as durable goods purchases (boats and RV's), construction and investment in tourism, and government expenditures.

The steps for conducting a tourism economic impact study

An economic impact study involves four basic steps:

Step 1: Define the problem

Step 2: Estimate the change in final demand (tourism spending). Step 3: Estimate the regional economic effects of this change Step 4: Interpret, apply, and communicate the results Procedures for carrying out steps 2 and 3 are outlined under question 6 and illustrated in more detail in the companion report. This bulletin provides background on economic impact concepts and methods to help users of such studies in interpreting and applying the results. We therefore focus on the key elements to consider in defining problems for an economic impact analysis.

The most important part of any study is the first step.— clarifying the nature of the problem being addressed and intended uses of the results. Before launching an economic impact study, be sure this is the kind of study that is needed rather than one or more of the other kinds of economic analyses summarized in question 1. Stynes and Propst (1996) identify seven factors that should be specified as part of defining a problem for an economic impact assessment:

1. Define the action to be evaluated. Begin by clarifying the action or actions involved in the problem. Actions may include construction, government investment, changes in marketing, management, or policies, or changes in the quality or quantity of tourist facilities. If evaluating impacts of existing tourism activity, be sure to define what is to be included as "tourism".
2. Identify the change in the amount and kinds of recreation/tourism activity resulting from the action. The action must be defined precisely enough in step one to be able to estimate the changes in.the number and types of visitors to the area and/or their spending patterns. As a general rule, the analysis should be with vs. without the action rather than simply before vs. after. Thus, if tourism.has been growing by 5 per cent per year and a new promotional Programmes increases this to 10 per cent this year, only half of the 10 per cent growth can likely be attributed to the promotional Programmes. Identifying the net changes in activity that are attributable to an action can be a complex and difficult task. Assessments of economic impact, however, rest firmly on such estimates, so attention to these details is very.important. In situations of some uncertainty, we recommend evaluating impacts using a range of estimates in order to establish rough confidence intervals around your estimates. Evaluating a range of alternatives also helps to evaluate the sensitivity of the results to your initial estimates of changes in activity levels.
3. Identify the kinds of spending to be included. Tourism may impact the local economy through visitor trip spending, durable goods purchases, government spending, or investment and construction. Which to include in a given analysis depends on how the problem is defined, and again, on attributing given spending changes to the proposed action.
4. Identify the study region. Perhaps the most important, yet often neglected part of a recreation and tourism impact assessment is the definition of a study region. The region defines the area for which impacts are desired, as well as the portions of visitor spending that are relevant. An impact assessment evaluates the impacts on households, businesses, and organizations within the given region. Spending that visitors make outside of a study region either at home or enroute are not included in assessing impacts of spending on the designated region. For an economic impact analysis, the study region should be large enough to constitute a viable economic region. Since little economic data exists below the county level, the county

is generally the smallest region one should consider for a tourism impact assessment.

5. Identify key economic sectors and desired sectoral detail. The proposed action and anticipated uses/users of the results should suggest the key sectors that will be impacted. Recreation and tourism activity typically impact the lodging, restaurant, amusements, retail, transportation and government sectors most directly. In the problem definition stage consideration of impacted sectors helps to identify relevant categories of spending. The desired sectoral detail plays an important role in structuring the presentation of results. In some cases only an aggregate measure of impacts may be desired. In other cases, clients may be interested in which particular sectors are most heavily affected and will want estimates of sales and jobs broken down by sector. If formal input-output models are used, impacts may be estimated in considerable sectoral detail. This is not possible if an aggregate spending estimate or multiplier is used.
6. Identify the most important measures of economic activity. Tourism impacts may be reported in terms of visitor spending, business receipts/sales/production, wage and salary income, proprietors income and profits, value added, and employment. The direct effects are the most important and are captured well by estimates of visitor spending. Simple ratios can be used to convert direct spending or sales to the associated income and jobs. Input-output models and multipliers are needed only if one is interested in secondary effects.
7. Identify the tolerable levels of error in the results. Although confidence intervals and estimates of error are rare in economic impact studies, this doesn't mean they are not important. You should have at least a ballpark idea of how much error you can tolerate in the analysis, as this will dictate how much effort and expense you must put into it. The more accuracy you demand, the greater the requirements to gather up-to-date local data on visitation, spending and economic activity. These data allow you to fine tune the spending estimates and input-output models or multipliers. Such fine tuning will require time, knowledge, and money that must be weighed against the benefits of the improved estimates. Estimates of impacts are based on three components: visits, spending, and multipliers. You should try to balance the errors across these components.

An Economic Impact Study Cost

The costs of a tourism economic impact study can range from $500 to $50,000 and more. Costs will depend largely on the size and scope of tourism activity to be covered, the size and complexity of the study region, how much primary data are to be gathered and the level of accuracy and detail desired.

The greatest and perhaps most significant cost will be the technical expertise of the analysts involved. Tourism economic impact studies require considerable technical judgement of specialists and a mix of corresponding skills:

- Knowledge of tourism
- Expertise in conducting tourism surveys, particularly spending studies
- Regional economic modeling skills, including knowledge and access to economic data bases, multipliers and input-output modeling systems
- Communication skills

The cost of conducting economic impact studies has dropped substantially in the past ten years due to improvements in microcomputer Programme for estimating spending and regional economic models. The three principal components of an economic impact estimate (visits, spending, and multipliers) each involve different costs and somewhat different skills. The costs and needed skills will vary considerably depending on whether primary or existing data are to be used.

If levels and types of tourism activity are known and spending averages and multipliers may be taken from secondary sources, a complete economic impact assessment can be conducted in less than a month and in many cases for under $5,000. You are paying primarily for the time, judgement and skills of the analyst. A small visitor spending survey may add another $5,000. For a more complete analysis of secondary effects using a formal input- output model, figure another $2,000- $5,000. Increase the cost estimate if several distinct alternatives are to be evaluated or multiple regions are involved.

There will generally be scale economies in these situations with additional impact analyses costing less than half of the initial one. Costs will increase significantly if the number and types of visitors must be estimated using a general visitor survey or a demand model. Large scale spending surveys and custom input-output models based on primary data will also increase costs considerably.

In many cases, the tourism activity and visitor spending data needed for an economic impact analysis can be gathered in a general visitor survey or market study. Spending averages for particular tourist segments can be estimated by having a portion of the general survey respondents complete an extra page of spending questions. Armed with good estimates of the number and types of visitors and their spending patterns, one can complete an economic impact study at little additional cost.

The principal motivation for a business or region to serve tourists are generally economic. An individual business is interested primarily in its own revenues and costs, while a community or region is concerned with tourism's overall contribution to the economy, as well as its social, fiscal and environmental impacts. A good understanding of tourism's economic impacts is therefore important for the tourism industry, government officials, and the community as a whole.

Tourism economics is unfortunately a technical area, involving concepts, methods, and models that are unfamiliar to most non-economists. In this bulletin I've attempted to define the key concepts and explain the basic methods for estimating the economic impacts of tourism, hopefully in as "non-technical" a way as the subject allows. Understanding the concepts and methods is critical to interpreting, evaluating, and applying economic impact results. This bulletin should be read along with one or more economic impact reports that can be used as examples and opportunities to test your grasp of the issues.

4

Safe Food Handling Guidelines

FOOD SELECTION & STORAGE

FOOD QUALITY & SAFETY

Storage does not improve the quality of any food. The quality of a food will also not decrease significantly during storage as long as the food is stored properly and used within the recommended time frame. Quality is not the same as safety. A poor-quality food may be safe such as stale cereal, overripe fruit or soured pasteurized milk.

An unsafe food may have good quality in terms of appearance and taste, but have a high bacterial count. For example, improperly canned food may contain Clostridium botulinum thus making food unsafe. Or cooked chicken may be placed on a plate that held the raw chicken and become contaminated. The goal of home food storage is to provide both safe and high-quality foods.

Maintaining a food's quality depends on several factors: the quality of the raw product, the procedures used during processing, the way the food is stored and the length of storage. For example, fresh-picked corn will store better than corn that has been in the market for a few days; a tightly folded inside cereal box liner will prevent a ready-to-eat cereal from becoming limp. The recommended storage time takes these factors into consideration. Since bacteria frequently get into food through careless food handling, keep everything — hands, pantry, shelves and storage containers — clean.

SELECTION GUIDELINES

To help assure quality, some products have "open dates" on the package. Product dating is optional on most products. Dates may also be "coded" by the manufacturer and only understood by them.

The most commonly used open dates are:

- *Sell-by Date*: This is the last recommended day of sale. The date allows for home storage and use. You will find the date after the statement "sell by." Breads and baked goods may have "sell-by" dates.

- *Use-by Date*: Tells how long the product will retain top quality after you buy it. You will find this date after statement "Use by." Some packaged goods have "use-by" dates.
- *Expiration Date*: This is the last day the product should be used or eaten. You may find this date after the statement, "Do not use after." Yeast and baking powder have expiration dates.
- *Pack Date*: Canned or packaged foods may have pack dates, which tell you when the product was processed. This does not tell you how long the food will be good.

These are guidelines; if a food is not properly handled, its storage life will be shortened. Follow these tips for purchasing top-quality foods that have been handled safely.

- Look for packages of food that are not torn or broken.
- Canned goods should be free of dents, cracks and bulging lids.
- Refrigerated food should feel cold and frozen food should be frozen solid. Purchase these foods last.
- When shopping, place packaged raw meat, poultry and fish in plastic bags and keep from contact with other foods.
- Take perishable foods home quickly to refrigerate. If travel time will exceed one hour, pack fresh meats in a cooler with ice and keep in the passenger area of the car in warm weather.
- At home, refrigerate perishable food immediately. The "Danger Zone" for most food is 40 to 140 °F. Bacteria grow most rapidly in this range of temperatures, doubling in number in as little as 20 minutes.

STORAGE GUIDELINES

For best results in maintaining product quality practice the rule, First In, First Out. This means you use the oldest products first and the newest products later. A good practice in the home is to place the newly purchased products in back of the same products already on the shelf. It may help to write purchase dates on products without "open dates" on the package. Follow recommended storage times for the refrigerator, freezer and pantry.

Freezer

- Keep freezer temperature at or below 0 °F. A good indication of proper temperature is that ice cream will be frozen solid.
- Use moisture-proof, freezer-weight wrap. Examples are foil, freezer bags and freezer paper. Label and date all packages.
- Food stored beyond the recommended time will be safe to eat, but eating quality and nutritive value will be reduced.
- Keep an inventory of freezer contents.

Refrigerator

- Use a thermometer to check temperature; it must be between 34 °F and 40 °F at all times. Avoid frequently opening the refrigerator door, especially in hot weather.
- Wrapping perishable food prevents the loss of flavor and the mixing of flavor and odors resulting in, for example, onion-flavored milk.
- Raw meat and poultry should be wrapped securely so they do not leak and contaminate other foods. Place the store packages in a plastic bag or place the package on a plate to contain any juices. Clean up leaks with warm soapy water and sanitize with a solution of 1 teaspoon chlorine bleach to 1 quart water.
- Cooked meats and leftovers should be tightly wrapped to prevent leakage and drying out.

Pantry

- Storage cabinets should be cool and dry. Storage areas near oven ranges, hot water pipes or heating ducts should not be used because heat and moisture can cause a food to lose its quality more rapidly.
- High temperature or humidity may reduce storage time considerably.
- Insect infestation can occur in any home. Susceptible foods include cereals, flour, seeds, baking mixes, spices, candy, dried fruits and dry pet foods. Avoid purchasing damaged packages of foods and keep cupboard shelves clean. Storing food in tightly sealed glass, metal or rigid plastic containers may help.
- Pantry foods will probably be safe beyond recommended storage time, but eating quality and nutritive value will be reduced.

SAFE HANDLING OF SEAFOOD

SELECTING THE BEST

Federal regulations require that all parts of the seafood industry implement safe handling practices to keep seafood safe. The regulations require that those handling seafood have a Hazard Analysis and Critical Control Points, or HACCP plan in place in their operation. HACCP is a science-based system that examines each step in processing food, isolates possible hazards and sets limits, or critical control points, within which the food is safe. These regulations help consumers to select safe, quality seafood. In addition, state law mandates the inspection of oyster and clam beds and other waters where seafood is harvested. The bacterial levels of these waters are inspected and are closed to the harvesting of shellfish if the levels are considered too high. Seafood poisoning can occur from eating seafood that has not been handled properly, raw or improperly cooked seafood or fish from tropical water that harbors a toxin. Consumers can protect themselves by purchasing seafood only from certified processors and dealers and by following the suggestions given here for safe handling.

Spotting a Safe Seafood Seller

Always purchase fish from a certified dealer that maintains high quality. *Based on FDA's Food Code, here are some ways of spotting a safe fish dealer:*

- Employees should be in clean clothing and wearing hair coverings.
- Employees should be in clean clothing and wearing hair coverings.
- They should not be smoking, eating or playing with their hair.
- They should not be sick or have any open wounds.
- Employees should be wearing disposable gloves when handling food and change gloves after doing nonfood tasks and after handling raw fish.
- Fish should be displayed on a thick bed of fresh — not melting — ice, preferably in a case or under some type of cover. Fish should be arranged with the bellies down so that the melting ice drains away from the fish, thus reducing the chances of spoilage.

Shrimp

Fresh shrimp have a mild odor and firm-textured meat. The shell or meat is not slippery, and there are no black spots, or patches on the shell or meat. The shell of raw shrimp may be grayish-green, pinkish-tan, or light pink. When cooked, the shell turns red and the meat takes on a reddish tint. Cooked shrimp have firm meat and a mild smell.

Crabs, Lobsters & Crayfish

Live crabs, lobsters, spiny lobsters and crayfish move their legs. The "tail" of a live lobster curls under the body and does not hang down when you pick it up. Frozen spiny or rock lobster tails have clear white meat, no odor and are hard-frozen. Cooked crabs, lobsters and crayfish have bright orange to red shells and are free of any disagreeable odor.

Clams, Oysters & Mussels

Purchase raw shellfish carefully. Buy raw clams, oysters and mussels only from reputable markets. If in doubt, ask the seafood market personnel to show you the certified shipper's tag that accompanies "shell on" products or check the shipper number on shucked oyster containers. Clams, oysters and mussels in the shell are alive, and the shells close tightly when tapped. Gaping shells indicate that the shellfish are dead and not edible. Shucked oysters are plump, and have a mild odor, a natural creamy color, and clear liquid or nectar.

Scallops

Fresh scallops have a sweetish odor and are free of excess liquid when packaged. The meat of the large sea scallop is white, orange or pink. Smaller bay and calico scallops are white, light tan or pinkish.

Frozen Seafood

Flesh is solid, and there is no discoloration or drying on the surface. Odor is not evident or is fresh and mild. Wrapping material is moisture- and vapor-proof, fits closely around the product and is undamaged. Packaging materials do not contain ice crystals or have water stains or other indications that the product had thawed at any point.

Packaged breaded and unbreaded products have a clean and uniform appearance. Individual pieces separate easily. Breading is intact. Packaged frozen seafood may have an expiration date stamped on the label. Use the seafood before the expiration date.

STORAGE

Safe Handling after Purchase

Whether you've purchased seafood that is fresh or frozen, always keep it cold. Never leave perishable items in a hot car unless packed in ice or in a cooler; seafood products must be kept cold to ensure peak quality. It's always a good idea to keep your refrigerator temperature between 32 and 38 °F, and your freezer at 0 °F or colder. Plan to use your seafood purchases within one to two days, or freeze them.

Refrigeration

Place seafood immediately in the refrigerator when you get home from the seafood market. Wrap fresh seafood in cling wrap or store in airtight containers. Store fresh, pasteurized or smoked seafood products at 32 to 38 °F. Refrigerate live clams, oysters, mussels, crabs, lobsters and crayfish in well-ventilated containers. Cover the container with a damp cloth or paper towel. Do not store live shellfish in airtight bags or containers. Storing live shellfish in salt water shortens their shelf life. Storing them in fresh water kills them. Keep live shellfish alive. Do not cook or eat shellfish that have died during storage. Live clams, oysters and mussels have tightly closed shells, or the shells will close when tapped. Live crabs, lobsters and crayfish move their legs. Dead shellfish spoil rapidly and develop off-flavor and off-odors.

Freezing

Store frozen seafood products immediately in the freezer when you get home from the seafood market. Store them in their original moisture- and vapor-proof packages. Frozen seafood packaged in over wrapped trays should be repackaged in moisture- and vapor-proof plastic freezer wrap, freezer paper or foil before you store them in the freezer. Keep frozen seafood products at 0 °F or below until ready to use.

PREPARATION

Cleanliness

Always wash hands thoroughly with hot, soapy water before preparing foods and after handling raw seafood. Don't let raw meat or juices touch ready-to-eat foods either in the refrigerator or during preparation. Don't put cooked foods on the same plate that held raw seafood. Always wash utensils that have touched raw seafood with hot, soapy water before using them for cooked seafood. Wash counters, cutting boards and all surfaces raw seafood has touched.

Thawing

While freezing seafood quickly keeps more cell walls intact, the opposite is true for thawing. Defrost gradually so cells are disturbed less and fewer juices leak out. The best way to thaw is overnight in the refrigerator. Avoid thawing at room temperature. If you must thaw seafood quickly, here are safe options: seal seafood in a plastic bag and immerse in cold water for about an hour OR microwave on the "defrost" setting, stopping when seafood is still icy but pliable.

Marinating

Marinate seafood in the refrigerator, not on the counter. Discard the marinade after use because it contains raw juices, which may harbor bacteria. If you want to use the marinade as a dip or sauce, reserve a portion before adding raw food.

COOKING

Basic Cooking Tips for Shellfish

Shrimp, crabs, scallops, clams, mussels, oysters or lobster become tough and dry when overcooked.

To cook raw shellfish, shucked or in the shell, follow these basic guidelines:

- Raw shrimp turn pink and firm when cooked. Depending on the size, it takes from 3 to 5 minutes to boil or steam 1 pound of medium-sized shrimp in the shell.
- Shucked shellfish become plump and opaque when cooked thoroughly and the edges of the oysters start to curl. The Food and Drug Administration suggests boiling shucked oysters for 3 minutes, frying them in oil at 375 °F for 10 minutes or baking them for 10 minutes at 450 °F.
- Clams, mussels and oysters in the shell will open when cooked. The FDA suggests steaming oysters for 4 to 9 minutes or boiling them for 3 to 5 minutes after they open.

- Scallops turn milky white or opaque and firm. Depending on size, scallops take 3 to 4 minutes to cook thoroughly.
- Place lobster in a pan of boiling water to cover, and return water to boil. Boil a 1-pound lobster for 10 minutes, and allow an extra 3 minutes for each additional pound. If steaming, allow 15 to 18 minutes for a 1½- to 2-pound lobster.

Guidelines for Cooking Fish

Cooked to perfection, fish is at its flavorful best and will be moist, tender and have a delicate flavor. In general, fish is cooked when its meat just begins to flake easily when tested with a fork and it loses its translucent or raw appearance.

Like most foods, fish should be thoroughly cooked. The suggests cooking fish until it reaches an internal temperature of 145 °F. One helpful guideline is the 10-minute rule for cooking fish. Apply it when baking, broiling, grilling, steaming, and poaching fillets, steaks or whole fish. Practice makes perfect and cooking fish properly is all in the timing.

Here's how to use the 10-minute rule:

- Measure the seafood product at its thickest point. If the fish is stuffed or rolled, measure it after stuffing or rolling.
- At 450 °F, cook it 10 minutes per inch thickness of the fish, turning the fish halfway through the cooking time. For example, a 1-inch fish steak should be cooked 5 minutes on each side for a total of 10 minutes. Pieces of fish less than half an inch thick do not have to be turned over.
- Add 5 minutes to the total cooking time if you are cooking the fish in foil or if the fish is cooked in a sauce.
- Double the cooking time for frozen fish that has not been defrosted.

Fish is the original "fast food." It cooks quickly, within minutes, because it lacks the connective tissue of red meats and poultry. Some of the best cooking methods for fish include poaching, broiling, grilling, baking and microwaving because they bring out flavor without adding fat.

SERVING

Basic Tips

Wash hands with soap and water before serving or eating food. Serve cooked products on clean plates with clean utensils and clean hands. Never put cooked foods on a dish that has held raw products unless the dish is washed with soap and hot water.

Hold hot foods above 140 °F and cold foods below 40 °F. Never leave foods, raw or cooked, at room temperature longer than two hours. On a hot day with temperatures at 90 °F or warmer, this decreases to one hour.

LEFTOVERS

Basic Tips

Always use clean utensils and storage containers for safe storage. Divide large amounts of leftovers into small, shallow containers for quick cooling in the refrigerator. For frozen storage, wrap seafood in heavy foil, freezer wrap or place in freezer container. For optimum taste, use seafood within a month. When reheating leftovers, make sure that they have been cooked to 165 °F. If you may have kept the food refrigerated for too long, throw it out. Never taste food that looks or smells strange to see if you can still use it.

Recommended Times for Refrigerator & Freezer Food Storage Food	Refrigerator	Freezer
Fresh Seafood		
Fresh lean fish: cod, flounder, trout, haddock, pollack, perch	1-2 days	4-6 months
Fresh fatty fish: mullet, smelt, salmon, mackerel, bluefish, tuna, and swordfish	1-2 days	2-3 months
Live crabs and lobster	Same day purchased	*
Live mussels and clams	2-3 days	*
Live oysters	7-10 days	*
Shucked mussels and clams	1-2 days	3-4 months
Shucked oysters	5-7 days	3-4 months
Shrimp, crabmeat	2-3 days	4 months
Scallops	2-3 days	3 months
Cooked Seafood		
Crab	1-2 days	3 months
Shrimp	3-4 days	2 months
Fish sticks, commercial	*	18 months
Breaded shrimp, commercial	*	1 year
Cooked fish pieces	3-4 days	3 months

Notes: * Storage by this method is not recommended due to safety or quality issues.

SELECTING & STORING FRUITS & VEGETABLES

SELECTING THE BEST

With satiny yellow skin and a rosy blush, it looks like the perfect peach. But how will it taste once you get it home? Choosing fresh and flavorful produce can sometimes be your greatest challenge in the supermarket. Here are some tips to find great-tasting fruits and vegetables and increase your enjoyment of these healthful foods.

FIND IT FRESH

With modern farming, processing and delivery, many stores are able to put produce out for sale within a day or two after it is picked. Ask your store's produce manager for delivery days so you can get to your favorite fruits and veggies before quality declines.

SELECT WISELY

Vegetables that are characteristic color, shape and size generally have the best taste and texture. However, good produce doesn't have to be picture perfect. Some of the best products don't look very good. Most bananas, for example, have a fuller flavor if they are speckled.

USE YOUR SENSES

Contrary to some consumer practices, thumping or shaking a melon does not indicate ripeness. Instead, authorities recommend feeling a product. In general, produce that's too soft is too ripe; if it's too hard, it's not ripe enough. Try the sniff test, too. With certain fruits, like peaches and melons, a strong scent means they're ripening nicely.

GET THE GRADE

The United States Department of Agriculture (USDA) has established grade standards for most fresh fruits and vegetables. The grades are most often seen on pre-packaged apples, potatoes and onions. "U.S. Fancy" is the top grade, while "U.S. No. 1" is the most common designation. "U.S. No. 2" and "U.S. No. 3" mean lower quality.

LOOK FOR LOCAL PRODUCE

Fruits and vegetables grown by local farmers may be fresher and tastier than those shipped long distances from larger farms. Once again, ask your grocery store's produce manager if any is in stock.

GO TO MARKET

Many communities sponsor weekly farmers' markets to provide a central, in-town site for small farms to sell their produce directly to consumers.

TAKE A STAND

Take a weekend drive into the country to look for roadside stands where farm families sell their produce, usually picked just hours before you buy it. Or visit a farm that allows you to pick your own strawberries, blueberries, peaches and apples. Your local county Extension agent can direct you to such places.

SHOP SEASONALLY

Probably one of the most important tips for finding great-tasting produce is to buy in season, when possible.

Here's a guide to when certain fruits and vegetables are at their peak:

- *Summer*: Apricots, blueberries, cherries, eggplant, fresh herbs, green beans, hot peppers, melon, okra, peaches, plums, sweet corn, sweet peppers, tomatoes, zucchini.
- *Fall:* Apples, broccoli, brussels sprouts, cauliflower, collards, grapes, kale, pears, persimmons, pumpkins, winter squash, yams.
- *Winter:* Beets, cabbage, carrots, citrus fruits, daikon radishes, onions, rutabagas, turnips, winter squash.
- *Spring:* Asparagus, blackberries, green onions, leeks, lettuces, new potatoes, peas, red radishes, rhubarb, spinach, strawberries, watercress.

WAX COATING

Why are wax coatings used on some fruits and vegetables? Are they safe? Many fruits and vegetables make their own natural waxy coating to help retain moisture because most produce is 80 to 95 percent water. After harvest, but before the produce is packed and sent to the supermarket, it is repeatedly washed to clean off dirt and soil. Such extensive washing also removes the natural wax. Therefore, waxes are applied to some produce items at the packing shed to replace the natural ones that are lost.

Waxes are applied in order to:

- Help retain moisture in fruits and vegetables during shipping and marketing;
- Help inhibit mold growth;
- Protect fruits and vegetables from bruising;
- Prevent other physical damage and disease;
- Enhance appearance.

By protecting against moisture loss and contamination, wax coatings help fresh fruits and vegetables maintain wholesomeness and freshness. Waxing does not improve the quality of any inferior fruit or vegetables; rather, waxing - along with proper handling - contributes to maintaining a healthful product. Waxes by themselves do not control decay; rather, they may be combined with some chemicals to prevent the growth of mold. The Food and Drug Administration and the Environmental Protection Agency strictly regulate the safety and use of these substances.

Waxes are also used on candies, pastries and gum and come from natural sources. Wax sources generally are plants, food-grade petroleum products or insects. Some waxes can be made from dairy or animal sources, but we are not aware of any such coatings being used on fruits and vegetables in this country. This is particularly important for people following Kosher or vegetarian diets and who don't want any animal-based wax on their produce. Any commodities that do have this type of coating must be labeled "Coated with animal-based wax." Waxes are used only in tiny amounts. In fact, each piece of waxed fruit only has a drop or two of wax. Waxes may be mixed with water or other wetting agents to ensure they are applied thinly and evenly. The government regulates wax coatings to ensure their safety. Coatings used on fruits and vegetables must meet the food additive regulations of the U.S. Food and Drug Administration. Extensive research by governmental and scientific authorities has shown that approved waxes are safe to eat. Waxes are indigestible, which means they go through the body without breaking down or being absorbed. Produce shippers and supermarkets are required by federal law to label produce items that have been waxed so you will know whether the fruits and vegetables you buy are coated. Consumers will see signs in produce departments that say "Coated with food-grade vegetable-, petroleum-, beeswax-, and/or shellac-based wax or resin, to maintain freshness." None of these coatings are animal-based, and they all come from natural sources. Any consumers who have questions about wax coatings should talk to their grocers. Waxes may turn white on the surface of fruits or vegetables if they have been subjected to excessive heat and/or moisture. This whitening is safe and is similar to that of a candy bar that has been in the freezer. Consumers do have choices. Waxes generally cannot be removed by regular washing. If consumers prefer not to consume waxes - even though the waxes are safe - they can buy unwaxed commodities or can peel the fruit or vegetable, thereby removing any coating. Commodities that may have coatings applied include apples, avocados, bell peppers, cantaloupes, cucumbers, eggplants, grapefruits, lemons, limes, melons, oranges, parsnips, passion fruit, peaches, pineapples, pumpkins, rutabagas, squash, sweet potatoes, tomatoes, turnips and yucca. However, they are not always waxed.

Storage Times for Fruits & Vegetables Food	Refrigerator	Freezer
Fruits:		
Apples	1 month	8-12 months
Apricots	3-5 days	8-12 months
Avocados	3-5 days	8-12 months
Bananas	*	8-12 months
Berries	2-3 days	8-12 months
Cherries	2-3 days	8-12 months
Grapes	3-5 days	8-12 months
Grapefruit	2 weeks	4-6 months
Guavas	1-2 days	8-12 months
Kiwis (Chinese Gooseberry)	3-5 days	4-6 months
Lemons/limes	2 weeks	4-6 months
Mangoes	*	8-12 months
Melons	1 week	8-12 months
Nectarines	3-5 days	8-12 months

Oranges	2 weeks	4-6 months
Papayas	1-2 days	8-12 months
Peaches	3-5 days	8-12 months
Pears	3-5 days	8-12 months
Pineapples	2-3 Days	4-6 months
Plantains	*	8-12 months
Plums	3-5 days	8-12 months
Rhubarb	3-5 days	8-12 months
Fruit Juices:		
Concentrate	*	2 years
Fresh or Reconstituted	5-7 days	8-12 months
Vegetables:		
Artichokes	1 week	*
Asparagus	2-3 days	8-12 months
Beets	2 weeks	8-12 months
Bok Choy	2-3 days	8-12 months
Broccoli	3-5 days	8-12 months
Brussels Sprouts	3-5 days	8-12 months
Cabbage	1-2 weeks	8-12 months
Carrots	2 weeks	8-12 months
Cauliflower	1 week	8-12 months
Celery	1 week	8-12 months
Chilies	1 week	8-12 months
Cilantro	2-3 days	*
Corn	use immediately for best flavor	8-12 months
Green Beans	1 week	8-12 months
Greens (spinach, collards, swiss chard, kale,mustard, etc.)	3-5 days	8-12 months
Jicama	2-3 weeks	8-12 months
Kohlrabi (leaves)	2-3 days	8-12 months
Kohlrabi (stems)	1 week	8-12 months
Lettuce	1 week	*

Table. Storage Times for Fruits & Vegetables

Food	Refrigerator	Freezer
Lima Beans	3-5 days	8-12 months
Mushrooms	1-2 days	8-12 months
Onions, green	3-5 days	*
Okra	1-2 days	8-12 months

Parsley	2-3 days	*
Peas	3-5 days	8-12 months
Peppers	1 week	8-12 months
Radishes	2 weeks	*
Squash, hard	*	8-12 months
Squash, summer	3-5 days	8-12 months
Tomatillos	1 week	8-12 months
Tomatoes	1 week	8-12 months
Yuca (Cassava)	1-2 days	8-12 months
Zucchini	3-5 days	8-12 months

Notes: * Storage by this method is not recommended due to safety or quality issues.

SELECTING & STORING CEREALS & GRAINS

WHEAT FLOUR

Definition

Flour is the product obtained by grinding then sifting wheat kernels, or berries. The kernel consists of three distinct parts: bran, the outer covering of the grain; germ, the embryo contained inside the kernel; and endosperm, the part of the kernel containing the flour. During milling, the three parts are separated and recombined accordingly to achieve different types of flours. There are six different classes of wheat: hard red winter, hard red spring, soft red winter, hard white, soft white and durum. The end products are determined by the wheat's characteristics, especially protein and gluten content. The harder the wheat, the higher the amount of protein in the flour. Soft, low-protein wheats are used in cakes, pastries, cookies, crackers and noodles. Hard, high protein wheats are used in breads and quick breads. Durum is used in pasta and noodles.

Storage

Flour should be stored in airtight containers in a cool, dry place. All-purpose, bread, cake and whole wheat flour will keep for six months at 90 °F, one year at 70 °F, and two years at 40 °F. Store away from foods with strong odors. Before using refrigerated or frozen flour, allow it to warm to room temperature and inspect for rancidity and taste.

Types of Flour

- White flour is the finely ground endosperm of the wheat kernel.
- All-purpose flour is a white flour milled from hard wheats or a blend of hard and soft wheats. It gives the best results for many kinds of products, including some yeast breads, quick breads, cakes, cookies, pastries and noodles. All-purpose flour is enriched and may be bleached or unbleached. Bleaching will not affect nutrient value.

- Bread flour is white flour that is a blend of hard, high-protein wheats and has greater gluten strength and protein content than all-purpose flour. Unbleached, and in some cases conditioned with ascorbic acid, bread flour is milled primarily for commercial bakers, but is available at most grocery stores.
- Cake flour is fine-textured, silky flour milled from soft wheats with a low protein content. It is used to make cakes, cookies, crackers, quick breads and some types of pastry. Cake flour has a greater percentage of starch and less protein, which keeps cakes and pastries tender and delicate.
- Self-rising flour, also referred to as phosphated flour, is a convenience product made by adding salt and leavening to all-purpose flour. It is commonly used in biscuits and quick breads, but is not recommended for yeast breads. One cup of self-rising flour contains 1½ teaspoons of baking powder and ½ teaspoon of salt. Self-rising can be substituted for all-purpose flour by reducing salt and baking powder according to these proportions.
- Pastry flour has properties intermediate between those of all-purpose and cake flours. It is usually milled from soft wheat for pastry making, but can be used for cookies, cakes, crackers and similar products. It differs from hard wheat flour in that it has a finer texture and lighter consistency.
- Semolina is the coarsely ground endosperm of durum, a hard spring wheat with a high-gluten content and golden color. It is hard, granular and resembles sugar. Semolina is enriched and is used to make couscous and pasta products such as spaghetti, vermicelli, macaroni and lasagna noodles. Except for some specialty products, breads are seldom made with semolina.
- Durum flour is finely ground semolina. It is enriched and used to make noodles.
- Whole wheat, stone-ground and graham flour can be used interchangeably; nutrient values differ minimally. They are produced by either grinding the whole-wheat kernel or recombining the white flour, germ and bran that have been separated during milling. Their only differences may be in coarseness and protein content. Insoluble fiber content is higher than in white flours.
- Bran is the outer layer of the wheat kernel that is removed to make white flour. It is sometimes ground into flour or it may come totally unprocessed as "miller's bran."
- Gluten flour is usually milled from spring wheat and has a high protein, low starch content. It is used primarily for diabetic breads, or mixed with other non-wheat or low-protein wheat flours to produce a stronger dough structure. Gluten flour improves baking quality and produces high-protein gluten bread.

- Wheat germ is the heart of the wheat kernel. It comes flaked or in a coarse meal, either raw or toasted. Wheat germ adds a pleasant, nutty flavor to baked goods and increases their protein and mineral content. It is the most oil-rich and therefore the most perishable part of the wheat. At the supermarket, wheat germ is found in vacuum-packed jars that must be refrigerated after opening.

Wheat Flour Terms

The Food and Drug Administration inspects and approves the use of flour treatments and additives that are used to improve the storage, appearance and baking performance of flour. The treatments and additives are in no way harmful.

- Enriched flour is supplemented with iron and three B-vitamins and may also be supplemented with calcium. There is no change in taste, color, texture, baking quality or caloric value of flour.
- Presifted flour is sifted at the mill, making it unnecessary to sift before measuring.
- Bromated flour is largely discontinued in the United States. Ascorbic acid is now being added to strengthen the flour for bread doughs.
- Bleached refers to flour that has been bleached chemically to whiten or improve the baking qualities. No change occurs in the nutritional value of the flour and no harmful chemical residues remain. It is only a process that speeds up the natural lightening and maturing of flour.
- Unbleached flour is aged and bleached naturally by oxygen in the air. It is more golden in color, generally more expensive and does not have the consistency in baking qualities that bleached flour does. Unbleached is preferred for yeast breads because bleaching affects gluten strength.
- Patent flour, bleached or unbleached, is the highest grade of flour. It is lower in ash and protein with good color. Market-wise, it is considered highest in value.
- Organic or chemical-free flour is not standardized, so its definition varies from state to state. It may be grown and stored without the use of synthetic herbicides or insecticides. It may also mean no toxic fumigants were used to kill pests in the grain, and no preservatives were added to the flour, packaging or food product.
- Gluten is a protein formed when water and wheat flours are mixed. Gluten gives bread dough elasticity, strength and gas-retaining properties. Wheat is the only grain with sufficient gluten content to make a raised or leavened loaf of bread.

CORNMEAL

- Cornmeal comes in two types, either ground from yellow corn or from white. They are virtually alike, except that yellow cornmeal contains more vitamin A. Cornmeal is an "enriched" product.

- Water-ground cornmeal still contains the fat-rich germ of the corn kernel and has a fuller flavor than degerminated cornmeal. When buying, avoid packages with a rancid, stale odor.
- Blue cornmeal, from New Mexico, has a bluish-gray tint and a stronger, toastier flavor. It is often used for tortillas and tamales.
- Corn grits are also available in white or yellow. Grits are more coarsley ground than cornmeal.

OTHER FLOUR & GRAIN PRODUCTS

- Barley flour makes a sweet, light-textured loaf of bread. It is usually combined with white flour because it does not have gluten of its own. Barley is sold also as pearl barley to be used mainly as a soup ingredient.
- Buckwheat flour is made from the seed of the fagopyrum, an herb. This flour is suitable for making pancakes. In Russia, it is called kasha. It is popular in Jewish cooking. In Japan and Korea, buckwheat noodles, called soba, are a staple.
- Oatmeal is made by rolling the groats to form flakes. Oat bran is the envelope of the groat, composed of the outer-most pericarp. It is high in soluble fiber.
- Potato flour is sometimes called potato starch and is used in baking and as a thickener. It is made from cooked potatoes that have been dried and ground.
- Quinoa has a nutty flavor, and of all grains, it comes closest to having the "perfect" protein balance.
- Rye flour is the finely ground flour obtained by sifting rye meal. The dark and light varieties are interchangeable in recipes, but the dark does have a stronger flavor. Rye and wheat flours are the only flours containing gluten-forming proteins that are important in baked goods.
- Spelt is a grain that is native to southern Europe and has a subtle, almost hazelnut flavor.
- Soy flour has a strong flavor and must be combined with wheat flour when used in baking. It is ground from whole soybeans and sometimes called soy powder or soya. Breads and cakes made with soy flour will be moist, fine-grained, and very high in iron, calcium and protein. It has none of its own starch or gluten, so it must always be combined with another flour.
- Triticale is a combination of wheat and rye and is used mostly in multigrain flours and in cereal mixes.
- Amaranth is a tall plant similar to corn, with a large shaggy head containing thousands of tiny seeds. The seeds are milled into whole grain flour, or puffed like rice or corn.

PASTA

Definition

"Pasta," an Italian word meaning paste, describes the various shapes and sizes of products made with flour and water. Pasta products may be divided into two types, dried or commercial pasta and fresh or homemade pasta.

They may also be categorized by their shapes:

- *Long Goods*: Like spaghetti
- *Short Goods*: Like macaroni
- *Specialty Products*: Like shells and bow ties
- *Noodles:* Ribbon-like shapes, generally made with eggs. By law, egg noodle products must contain 5.5 percent egg solids by weight.

There are at least 350 shapes available in the United States and possibly 600 shapes worldwide. Pasta shapes can be used interchangeably in recipes. Pasta can be purchased plain or in a variety of colors and flavors such as tomato, spinach, herb and whole wheat, to name a few. Good-quality pasta is a golden color, with a fine, even grain. Pasta that is too white or too gray indicates poor quality flour that will not cook properly and will be limp and sticky. The water will be cloudy after cooking.In the U.S. laws prohibit the use of artificial coloring and most pasta is enriched with iron and four B-vitamins.

Storage

Dry pasta can be stored almost indefinitely if kept in a tightly sealed package or a covered container in a cool, dry place. If cooked pasta is not to be used immediately, drain and rinse thoroughly with cold water. If the pasta is left to sit in water, it will continue to absorb water and become mushy. When the pasta is cool, drain and toss lightly with salad oil to prevent it from sticking and drying out. Cover tightly and refrigerate or freeze. Refrigerate the pasta and sauce separately or the pasta will become soggy. To reheat, put pasta in a colander and immerse in rapidly boiling water just long enough to heat through. Do not allow the pasta to continue to cook. Pasta may also be reheated in a microwave.

Preparation

Bring plenty of water to a rolling boil. Add about one tablespoon of salt per gallon of water, if desired. Add the pasta in small quantities to keep the rolling boil. Stir frequently to prevent sticking. Do not cover the pan. Follow package directions for cooking time.

Do not overcook. Pasta should be "al dente". It should be slightly resistant to the bite, but cooked through. Drain pasta to stop the cooking action. Do not rinse unless the recipe specifically says to do so. For salads, drain and rinse pasta with cold water.

RICE

Most U.S. rice is enriched with iron, niacin, thiamin and folic acid. Rinsing rice, or cooking rice in excess water and draining, results in loss of enrichment and other water-soluble vitamins and minerals, and is not recommended.

Types of rice:

- *Long Grain Rice:* Long, slender kernel, four times longer than it is wide. Cooked grains are separate, light and fluffy.
- *Medium Grain Rice:* Kernel is two to three times longer than it is wide. Cooked grains are moist, tender and slightly clingy.
- *Short Grain Rice*: Kernel is almost round. Cooked grains cling together.
- *Aromatic Rice*: Brown or white rice with a natural aroma and flavor similar to that of roasted nuts or popcorn. The United States grows different kinds of aromatic rice. Some cook dry and separate and some cook moist and tender.
- *Sweet Rice*: An opaque white grain. Cooked grains are very sticky.
- *Rough Rice*: The kernels are still within the hull. Before rice can be prepackaged or cooked, the outer hull or husk must be removed.
- *Brown Rice*: Kernels of rice have had only the hull removed. Brown rice may be eaten as is or milled into regular-milled white rice. Cooked brown rice has a slightly chewy texture and a nut-like flavor. The light brown color of brown rice is caused by the presence of bran layers.
- *Parboiled Rice*: Rough rice that has gone through a steam-pressure process before milling. Parboiled rice is favored by consumers and chefs who desire extra fluffy and separate cooked rice.
- *Precooked Rice*: White or brown rice that has been completely cooked and dehydrated after milling. The process reduces the time required for cooking.
- *Rice Flour*: Ground from either white or brown rice. The white variety has almost no fat; the brown has a considerable amount. A variety of white rice flour called "sweet" rice flour can be used only as a thickener, so read the package label to be sure of what you are getting.

Preparation

For best results, always follow package directions. When no directions are available, use one of these methods for regular white rice.

- *Top-of-the-Range Instructions*: Combine 1 cup regular white rice, 2 cups liquid, 1 teaspoon salt and 1 teaspoon butter or margarine in 2- to 3-quart saucepan. Bring to a boil; stir once or twice. Reduce heat; cover and simmer for 15 to 20 minutes or until rice is tender. If rice is not quite tender or liquid is not absorbed, replace and cook 2 to 4 minutes longer. Fluff with fork.

- *Microwave Oven Instructions*: Combine 1 cup rice, 2 cups liquid, 1 teaspoon salt and 1 teaspoon butter or margarine in 2- to 3-quart deep microwave-proof baking dish. Cover and cook on HIGH for 5 minutes or until boiling. Reduce setting to MEDIUM and cook 15 minutes. Fluff with fork.
- *Rice Cookers*: There are several reliable brands of rice cookers available. Care should be taken to follow individual manufacturer's directions. In general, all ingredients are combined using ¼ to ½ cup less liquid than the top-of-the-range method.
- *Conventional Oven:* Cooking rice in a conventional oven with other foods is an efficient way of saving energy. Use boiling liquid. Combine ingredients in a baking dish or pan; stir. Cover tightly and bake at 350 ºF for 25 to 30 minutes. Fluff with fork.
- *Reheating*: For each cup of cooked rice, add 2 tablespoons liquid. Cover and heat 4 to 5 minutes on top of range or in oven. In microwave oven, cook on HIGH about 1 to 1½ minutes per cup.

Storage

Uncooked rice can be stored on the shelf in a tightly sealed container. The shelf life of brown rice is shorter than that of white rice. The bran layers contain oil that can become rancid. Refrigerator storage is recommended for longer shelf life. Washing rice is not necessary; just measure and cook. Cooked rice can be refrigerated for up to seven days or stored in the freezer for six months.

CEREALS

Corn, wheat, rice, and oats are favorite grains for making cereals. All cereals keep best in airtight containers that keep out moisture, dust and insects. At home, a tightly sealed plastic bag is sufficient protection. Always look for a "use-by" date on the package. Crispness can be restored to ready-to-eat cereal by spreading it in a baking pan and putting it in a 350 °F oven for 5 minutes. Instant hot cereals keep up to one year in their original box, but a tightly covered container is better.

Since whole-grain cereals are rich in natural oils, purchase containers that do not have a rancid odor. Store whole-grain cereals in tightly covered containers or sealed plastic bags in the refrigerator where they should remain fresh for 5 months. When stored at room temperature, they will stay fresh one month.

KEEPING FOODS SAFE AT HOME

Of the millions of cases of food borne illness that occur each year, most can be prevented.

The U. S. Department of Agriculture (USDA) advises using these strategies to keep foods safe at home:

- Buy and use a food thermometer. It's the only way to know if meat, poultry and fish are cooked safely. You can't tell just by looking.
- Use an appliance thermometer in the refrigerator and check to make sure that the temperature is 40 °F or below. In the freezer, make sure the thermometer reads 0 °F or below. Bacteria grow rapidly at temperatures above 40 °F. If the power goes out you will know what temperatures were reached and will be able to make informed decisions about the safety of food in the refrigerator and freezer.
- Do not leave pizza sitting out on the table or a "doggie" bag in the car overnight. Foods should not be left out more than two hours at room temperature or 1 hour if it is over 90 °F. When in doubt, throw it out.
- Do not defrost a turkey in the garage or in the trunk of the car. The only safe way to defrost food is in the refrigerator, in cold water or in the microwave.
- Wash hands and all food preparation surfaces with soap and water before and after touching raw meat, poultry or fish. Bacteria on raw meat, fish or poultry can contaminate other foods such as bread or lettuce that will not be cooked.
- Do not feed "leftovers" or "take-out" food that's no longer fit for people to pets. Animals can also be stricken with food borne illnesses.
- Do not leave "take-out" or "ready-to-eat" food in the refrigerator so long that it's forgotten. You can't tell by looking at or smelling if a food is unsafe. Throw it away after three days and never taste a food when you don't know what it is or how long it has been in the refrigerator!
- Do not lick the spoon or the bowl of homemade cookie dough or cake batter made with raw eggs. Even one taste of raw dough could contain harmful Salmonella bacteria resulting in a very unpleasant and potentially dangerous illness.
- When grilling outdoors, use a clean plate for the cooked hamburgers, hot dogs or other meat or fish. Don't use the same plate that held raw meat! Juices from raw meat, poultry or fish could contaminate your cooked food.
- Separate cooked foods from uncooked foods when preparing a meal, including using separate cutting boards and knives. Cross-contamination could cause harmful bacteria from one food to be transferred to another food.
- Always put an ice pack in a child's lunch box or a lunch bag taken to the office if it includes perishable foods, such as meat, poultry, fish, milk or eggs. Foods in lunch boxes sitting in warm classrooms or offices could result in food borne illnesses. Children under the age of 10 are the most vulnerable.

- Do not "save money" by buying dented cans or cracked jars. Never use food from damaged containers. This applies to containers that are leaking, bulging or badly dented. Do not use food from cracked jars with loose or bulging lids, canned food with a foul odor or any container that spurts liquid when you open it. It's not worth taking a risk to save a few pennies.
- Put meat and poultry packages in plastic bags at the meat counter before putting them in the grocery cart. Leaking packages from meat or poultry could contaminate other foods in the cart, leading to food borne illnesses.

FOOD SAFETY MISTAKES YOU DO NOT WANT TO MAKE

USING DIRTY HANDS TO PREPARE FOODS

We all know we should wash our hands before preparing food. But, did you know that not washing your hands before and during food preparation causes most food borne illnesses? Here is how to properly wash your hands: Wet your hands under warm water. Add hand soap and scrub for 10-15 seconds before rinsing off all soap. Use a clean towel or paper towel to thoroughly dry your hands.

CROSS-CONTAMINATING

Cross-contamination is an important source of food borne illness. Cross-contamination happens when kitchen equipment is used to prepare raw meat, poultry, fish, or eggs, and then is not properly washed before preparing other foods.

Harmful bacteria can transfer from these raw foods to other foods if the surface is not washed properly between uses. To prevent this, thoroughly wash any surfaces, including your hands, which come in contact with raw meat, poultry, fish or eggs.

- Clean all cutting boards, knives, utensils and counter tops with warm, soapy water before food preparation begins.
- Use one cutting board for raw meat, poultry or seafood, and a different cutting board for ready-to-eat foods, such as fresh fruits and vegetables, cheese and bread.
- Sanitize cutting boards that have been in contact with raw meat, poultry or seafood. To sanitize, put the board in a solution of 1 tablespoon liquid chlorine bleach in a gallon of warm water and leave for several minutes. Plastic cutting boards can also be sanitized in a dishwasher using the wash and dry cycle.
- To sanitize kitchen counters, first wash with hot, soapy water. Then use 1 tablespoon unscented chlorine bleach in 1 gallon of water and spread on the counter. Let sit for several minutes and dry with paper towels.

- Sanitize a non-metal kitchen sponge by heating it, while still wet, in a microwave oven for 1 to 1½ minutes. Avoid burns by allowing the sponge to cool before using it.
- Use paper towels to clean up raw meat, poultry and seafood spills on kitchen counters and other surfaces. Wash kitchen cloths and towels, which have been in contact with raw meat juices, in the hot cycle of the washing machine and dry in the dryer before reusing them.

GUESSING FOOD IS DONE

Bacteria can survive on foods that are not properly cooked. Guessing if food is done by looking at changes in the color of meat and poultry is not a good practice. Ground beef can turn brown and look done before it is safely cooked. The best way to know that food is done is to use a food thermometer. A metal-stem, digital thermometer is easy to use and removes the guesswork of when the food is done.

You can buy one at nearly any department store or grocery store:

- Clean the stem and insert into the thickest part of the food to get an accurate reading.
- Use your food thermometer to make sure the foods reach the internal temperatures shown in the chart.

These are minimum temperatures; if preferred, meats may be cooked more well-done.

Table. Minimum Internal Temperatures of Foods

Temperature	Food
145 °F	Fish steaks or fillets. All cuts of beef, lamb, pork and veal. For both safety and quality, allow meat to rest for 4 minutes before carving or eating.
155 °F	Ground, mechanically tenderized or injected meats. Ground fish. Egg dishes.
165 °F	Poultry and wild game. Stuffing and casseroles.

STORING LEFTOVERS UNSAFELY

Bacteria like warm temperatures especially while foods are sitting on the countertop or when they are cooling down in the refrigerator.

Refrigerate leftovers quickly so bacteria will not grow:

- As soon as you finish a meal, refrigerate your leftovers. Make sure your refrigerator is 40 °F or colder.
- Put a piece of tape on the container and write the date on the tape. It is best to use refrigerated leftovers within 4 days. If you won't be eating your leftovers in that time, put them in the freezer where they will keep safely.

- Never put a big pot of hot food in the refrigerator—it will take too long to cool to a safe temperature. Put liquid foods like hot soup or chili in shallow containers, no more than 2 inches deep. Refrigerate or freeze quickly.

BASICS OF SAFE FOOD HANDLING

Bacteria that contaminate food and cause food borne illnesses are everywhere.

Follow these four basic safety tips to keep your food safe:

1. Wash hands and surfaces often.
2. Don't cross-contaminate.
3. Keep foods out of the temperature "Danger Zone."
4. Cook foods thoroughly.

KEEP HANDS & SURFACES CLEAN

Bacteria like Staphylococci are found on hair, skin, mouth, nose and throat. A cough or sneeze can transmit thousands of microorganisms that may cause disease. The best prevention is to keep yourself and your kitchen clean.

Keep your Hands Clean

Wash your hands! Hands become the most potentially dangerous when seemingly innocent acts like scratching the scalp, running fingers through hair, or touching a pimple become the cause for contaminating foods.

Follow the following steps to wash your hands:

- Wet hands thoroughly with warm water.
- Apply soap generously.
- Rub hands for at least 20 seconds.
- Scrub under nails with a clean nailbrush.
- Rinse hands well with warm water.
- Dry hands using a clean paper towel.

Keep Counters & Equipment Clean

Wash counters and equipment with soap and water immediately after use. Sanitize with a chlorine solution of ¾ teaspoon liquid household bleach per quart of water, especially after contact with raw meats. Use a bleach solution to sanitize the kitchen drain and disposal as well. Food particles get trapped and the moist environment is ideal for bacterial growth. Dishes and other utensils should be washed immediately in hot, soapy water and then air-dried, or cleaned in an automatic dishwasher. Bacteria can live in kitchen towels, sponges and cloths.

Wash kitchen towels and cloths regularly and always after using them to clean up raw meat juices, or use paper towels and throw them away. Wash kitchen cloths and towels in the hot cycle of the washing machine and dry them in the dryer before reusing them. Sanitize a non-metal kitchen sponge by heating it, while still wet, in a microwave oven for 1 to 1½ minutes. Avoid burns by allowing the sponge to cool before using it.

Keep Cutting Boards Clean

Whether using a wooden or plastic cutting board, it is important to keep it clean and to prevent cross-contamination after cutting raw meat, poultry and seafood. Non-porous surfaces are easier to clean than wood. It is best to keep one cutting board for fresh produce and bread and a separate one for raw meats. This will prevent bacteria on a cutting board that is used for raw meat, poultry or seafood from contaminating a food that requires no further cooking.

Wash All Cutting Boards Thoroughly

To keep all cutting boards clean wash them with hot, soapy water after each use, then rinse and air-dry or pat dry with fresh paper towels. Non-porous acrylic, plastic or glass boards and solid wood boards can be washed in an automatic dishwasher. Laminated boards may crack and split.

Sanitize Cutting Boards Occasionally

Both wooden and plastic cutting boards can be sanitized with a solution of ¾ teaspoon liquid chlorine bleach per quart of water. Flood the surface with the bleach solution and allow it to stand for several minutes, then rinse and air dry or pat dry with fresh paper towels.

Replace Battered Cutting Boards

Even plastic boards wear out over time. Once cutting boards become excessively worn or develop hard-to-clean grooves, they should be discarded.

PREVENT CROSS-CONTAMINATION

Cross-contamination is the transportation of harmful substances to food by:

- Hands that touch raw foods, such as raw meat, then touch food that will not be cooked, like salad ingredients.
- Surfaces or cleaning cloths that touch raw foods, are not cleaned and sanitized, then touch ready-to-eat food.
- Raw meat, raw poultry and raw seafood that touch or drip fluids on cooked or ready-to-eat foods.

Keep Foods out of the "Danger Zone" Safely Store Perishable Foods

Refrigerate or freeze foods that will spoil at room temperature. Keep your refrigerator between 34 °F and 40 °F and your freezer temperature at or below 0 °F. The "Danger Zone" for most foods is between 40 °F and 140 °F. Bacteria grow most rapidly in this range of temperatures, doubling in number in as little as 20 minutes. Discard any perishable food left out at room temperature for more than two hours.

Safely Thaw Foods

Thaw and marinate foods in the refrigerator, never on the counter.If thawed at room temperature, bacteria can grow in the outer layers of the food before the inside thaws.

Proper thawing is essential to maintaining the safety, taste and texture of frozen foods. It affects the juiciness of meats, the texture and flavor of vegetables and fruits, and moisture level of baked goods.

- Thick meat cuts should be thawed before cooking to retain juiciness. Cuts such as chops, patties and steaks that will be pre- pared by flouring or breading should be thawed before baking.
- Broccoli, cauliflower and greens are more flavorful if partially thawed before cooking.
- Thawing foods should be placed in a shallow pan to catch drippings so that other refrigerated foods will not be contaminated with raw food juices.
- Never thaw foods at or above room temperature. Remember food spoilage bacteria multiply most rapidly at temperatures between 40 °F and 140 °F.
- Thaw frozen fruits, vegetables or meat in the refrigerator overnight, in a sealed freezer container. Foods may be thawed more quickly by immersing the sealed freezer container into cold water and changing the water frequently until food is thawed. Foods may also be thawed in the microwave using the defrost setting.
- If thawed in the microwave or in cold water in the sink, food must be cooked immediately after thawing. Do Not thaw a food and then refrigerate to cook later.
- When you have defrosted food for use, keep in mind that thawed frozen food is more perishable than fresh food.
- Thawed foods that have been at room temperature for over two hours should be discarded.
- Foods thawed in the refrigerator may be refrozen IF they still contain ice crystals. Immediately remove only the amount needed from the freezer container, remove air, reseal and return remaining food to the freezer.
- Thawed meats and poultry kept in the refrigerator should be used within two to three days. Thawed seafood kept in the refrigerator should be used within one to two days.
- Thaw bread and baked goods at room temperature in sealed freezer containers or original wrapping to avoid moisture loss.

Table. Recommended Times for Refrigerator & Freezer Food Storage

Food	Refrigerator	Freezer
Dairy		
Fresh milk	5-7 days	*
Buttermilk	1-2 weeks	*
Canned Milk (opened)	3-5 days	*
Yogurt, cottage cheese	7 days	*
Hard cheese	6-12 weeks	6-12 months
Cheese spreads	3-4 weeks	*
Ice cream	*	2 months
Eggs		
Fresh in shell	3 weeks	*
Hard-cooked	1 week	*
Meats, Fresh		
Beef roasts, steaks	3-5 days	6-12 month
Ground beef or stew	1-2 days	3-4 months
Pork roast, chops	3-5 days	4-6 months
Sausage	1-2 days	1-2 months
Chicken or turkey	1-2 days	9-12 months
Meats, Cooked		
Smoked Sausage, whole ham (fully cooked)	7 days	1-2 months
Ham slices (fully cooked)	3-4 days	1-2 months
Hotdogs, luncheon meats (unopened)	2 weeks	1-2 months
Hotdogs, luncheon meats (opened)	3-7 days	1-2 months
Leftover meat, cooked	3-4 days	2-3 months
Leftover gravy and meat broth	1-2 days	2-3 months
Leftover poultry, cooked	3-4 days	4-6 months
Seafood		
Fresh lean fish: cod, flounder, trout, haddock, halibut, pollack, perch	1-2 days	4-6 months
Fresh fatty fish: mullet, smelt, salmon, mackerel, bluefish, tuna, swordfish	1-2 days	2-3 months
Live crabs and lobster	same day purchased *	*
Live mussels and clams	2-3 days	*
Live oysters	7-10 days	*
Freshly shucked oysters	5-7 days	3-4 months
Scallops, shrimp, shucked mussels and clams	2-3 days	3-4 months

Fruits & Vegetables (Fresh)		
Apples	1 month	8-12 months
Apricots, avocados, grapes, peaches, pears, plums	3-5 days	8-12 months
Berries, cherries	2-3 days	8-12 months
Grapefruit, lemons, limes, oranges	2 weeks	4-6 months
Pineapple	2-3 days	4-6 months
Beets, carrots	2 weeks	8-12 months
Beans, broccoli, greens, peas, summer squash	3-5 days	8-12 months
Celery, cabbage, chilies, lettuce, peppers, tomatoes	1 week	8-12 months
Mushrooms	1-2 days	8-12 months
Pies		
Chiffon pie, pumpkin pie	1-2 days	1 month
Fruit pie	1-2 days	1 year

Notes: * Storage by this method is not recommended due to safety or quality issues.

COOK FOODS THOROUGHLY

Using a thermometer is the only reliable way to ensure safety and to determine the "doneness" of meat and egg dishes. To be safe, these foods must be cooked to an internal temperature high enough to destroy any harmful bacteria that may have been in the food. Color changes in meat are no longer considered reliable proof that all bacteria have been destroyed. Use the following minimum internal temperature chart to determine if foods have been cooked thoroughly.

MINIMUM INTERNAL TEMPERATURES

These temperatures ensure that food borne bacteria have been destroyed. For reasons of personal taste or texture preferences, consumers may choose to cook meat and poultry to higher temperatures.

Table. Minimum Internal Temperatures of Foods

Temperature	Food
145 °F	Fish steaks or fillets. All cuts of beef, lamb, pork and veal. For both safety and quality, allow meat to rest for 4 minutes before carving or eating.
155 °F	Ground, mechanically tenderized or injected meats. Ground fish. Egg dishes.
165 °F	Poultry and wild game. Stuffing and casseroles.

SAFELY HANDLE LEFTOVERS

Divide large amounts of hot leftovers directly into small, shallow containers for quick cooling, and place directly in the refrigerator. Discard food that has been left standing at room temperature for more than two hours. Date leftovers so they can be used within a safe time. Most foods remain safe when refrigerated for three to five days. If you will not be eating the leftovers within that time, freeze them for longer storage. If in doubt, throw it out rather than risk a food borne illness. Never taste food that looks or smells strange to see if you can still use it. Even a small amount of contaminated food can cause illness.

EFFECTS OF TEMPERATURE ON FOOD

BACKGROUND

"Last night I left cooked roast beef on the counter to cool before refrigerating but fell asleep and discovered it this morning. I immediately put it in the refrigerator. Since the meat is cooked, shouldn't it be safe to eat?" The answer to this question is that the roast beef should be thrown out. Why? Because leaving food out too long at room temperature can cause bacteria - such as Staphylococcus aureus, Salmonella enteriditis, Escherichia coli O157: H7, and Campylobacter - to grow to dangerous levels that can cause illness. Bacteria exist everywhere in nature. They are in the soil, air, water and the foods we eat. When the bacteria have nutrients, moisture, time and favorable temperatures, they grow rapidly increasing in numbers to the point where some can cause illness. Therefore, understanding the important role temperature plays in keeping food safe is critical. If we know the temperature at which food has been handled, we can then answer the question, "Is it safe?"

THE DANGER ZONE

Bacteria grow most rapidly in the range of temperatures between 40 and 140 °F, doubling in number in as little as 20 minutes. This range of temperatures is often called the "Danger Zone." That's why perishable foods should never be left out of refrigeration over two hours. If the temperature is above 90 °F, food should not be left out more than one hour.

COOKING

Raw meat and poultry should always be cooked to a safe internal temperature. When roasting meat and poultry, an oven temperature no lower than 325 °F should be used. Use a meat thermometer to assure that meat and poultry have reached a safe internal temperature. Cook beef, lamb, pork and veal steaks, roasts and chops to a safe minimum internal temperature of at least 145 °F, then allow to rest for 4 minutes before carving or eating. Cook longer if you prefer your meat more well-done. Cook ground meats, mechanically tenderized, or injected meats to an internal temperature of 155 °F. All poultry is safe if it reaches a minimum internal temperature of 165 °F throughout the product. For reasons of personal taste preferences, poultry may be cooked longer. If raw meat and poultry have been handled safely, using the above preparation recommendations will make them safe to eat. If raw meats have been mishandled, bacteria may grow and produce toxins, which can cause food borne illness. Cooking does not destroy toxins that are heat-resistant. Therefore, even though cooked, meat and poultry mishandled in the raw state may not be safe to eat even after proper preparation.

STORING LEFTOVERS

One of the most common causes of food borne illness is improper cooling of cooked foods. Bacteria are everywhere, even after food is cooked to a safe internal temperature, and they can be reintroduced to the food and then reproduce. For this reason leftovers must be put in shallow containers for quick cooling, and refrigerated immediately or within two hours of preparation.

REHEATING

Foods should be reheated thoroughly until hot and steaming, and to an internal temperature of 165 °F. In the microwave oven, cover food and rotate so it heats evenly. Follow manufacturer's instructions for stand time for more thorough heating. In the absence of manufacturer's instructions, at least a two-minute stand time should be allowed.

COLD STORAGE TEMPERATURES

Properly handled food stored in a freezer at 0 °F will always be safe. Freezing keeps food safe by slowing the movement of molecules, causing bacteria to enter a dormant stage. Once thawed, these bacteria can again become active and multiply to levels that may lead to food borne illness. Because bacteria on these foods will grow at about the same rate as they would on fresh food, thawed foods should be handled as any other perishable food. A temperature of 34 to 40 °F should be maintained in the refrigerator. In contrast to freezer storage, perishable foods will gradually spoil in the refrigerator. Spoilage bacteria will make themselves known in a variety of ways. The food may develop an uncharacteristic odor, color and/or become sticky or slimy. Molds may also grow and become visible. Bacteria capable of causing food borne illness either don't grow or grow very slowly at refrigerator temperatures. A refrigerator/ freezer thermometer should always be used to verify that the temperature of the unit is correct. Safe food-handling practices are a good defense against food borne illness. Because we know how different temperatures affect the growth of bacteria in our food, we can protect ourselves and our families from food borne illnesses by proper handling and cooking, and by storing foods at safe temperatures.

SAFE HANDLING OF BEEF

SELECTING THE BEST

Fresh is Best

Choose beef that is bright red in color from the fresh meat case. Vacuum packaged beef will be maroon because it has not been exposed to oxygen. Choose beef that is firm to the touch. Look for packages that are cool to the touch, have no wear or punctures, and little or no excess liquid. Always check the "sell-by" date. "Loin" and "rib" are clues that the beef is a more tender cut. "Chuck", "round" and "flank" indicate a less tender cut. Less tender cuts will require marinating or a slower, moist cooking method. Purchase raw meats last. Make sure all meats, whether raw, pre-packaged or from the deli, are refrigerated when purchased. Fresh meats may contaminate other grocery items.

The best way to prevent this cross-contamination is to always keep fresh meats from other items. Put raw meat packages in a plastic bag so juices won't drip onto other foods. Pack raw meats in an ice chest if it will take you more than an hour to get home, and keep the ice chest in the passenger area of the car during warm weather. Take meats straight home to the refrigerator or freezer.

Product Dating

Product dating, applying "sell by" or "use by" dates, is not required by federal regulations. However, many stores and processors may voluntarily choose to date packages of raw beef. Use or freeze products with a "sell by" date within three to five days of purchase. If the manufacturer has determined a "use by" date, observe it. It's always best to buy a product before its date expires. It's not important if a date expires after freezing beef, because all foods stay safe while properly frozen.

Product Inspection

All beef found in retail stores is either USDA inspected for wholesomeness or inspected by state systems which have standards equal to the federal government. Each animal and its internal organs are inspected for signs of disease. The "Passed and Inspected by USDA" seal ensures that the beef is wholesome and free from disease. Although inspection is mandatory, its grading for quality is voluntary, and a plant pays to have its beef graded.

Product Grading

Quality Grade refers to the eating quality of the meat. Grades are determined by the amount of marbling, the texture of the meat and its color and appearance.

USDA grades for beef are as follows:

- *USDA Prime:* The lean is highly marbled and usually very tender and juicy; outside fat may be excessive.
- *USDA Choice*: The lean is average in marbling and usually tender and juicy; outside fat is variable.
- *USDA Select*: The lean contains some marbling; tenderness and juiciness can be extremely variable; usually not much outside fat.
- *USDA Standard:* Little or no marbling; tenderness and juiciness extremely variable; very little outside fat.
- *USDA Commercial, Utility, Cutter and Canner*: Generally applied to older animals. This beef is most often used in processed products and is rarely cut for the freezer.

STORAGE

Refrigeration

Keep beef below 40 °F during storage. Store uncooked beef items together, separate from cooked foods. Refrigerate or freeze fresh beef Immediately after bringing it home. Never leave beef in a hot car or sitting out at room temperature. Packaged whole cuts of fresh beef may be refrigerated in their original wrappings in the coldest part of the refrigerator for three to five days after purchase, while ground beef can be stored in the refrigerator for one to two days. Keep beef refrigerated until you are ready to cook it. When transporting cooked beef to another dining site, place it in an insulated container or ice chest until ready to eat. Cooked whole cuts of beef are best when refrigerated no longer than two to three days. Cooked ground beef is best when refrigerated no longer than one to two days.

Freezing

Freeze whole cuts of fresh beef if you do not plan to cook it within three to five days after purchase. Freeze ground beef if you do not plan to cook it within one to two days after purchase. It is safe to freeze beef in its original packaging or repackage it. However, for long-term freezing, overwrap the porous store plastic with aluminum foil, freezer paper, or place in freezer bags to prevent "freezer burn", which appears as grayish brown leathery spots and is caused by air reaching the surface of food. For best quality, use steaks and roasts within 6 to 12 months, ground beef within 3 to 4 months.

PREPARATION

Cleanliness

Always wash hands thoroughly with hot soapy water before preparing foods and after handling raw beef. Don't let raw meat or juices touch ready-to-go foods, either in the refrigerator or during preparation. Don't put cooked foods on the same plate that held raw beef. Always wash utensils that have touched raw meat with hot, soapy water before using them for cooked meats. Wash counters, cutting boards and other surfaces raw meats have touched. These surfaces may be sanitized by cleaning with a solution of 1 teaspoon chlorine bleach per quart of water.

Thawing

Thaw uncooked beef in the refrigerator or in cold water. Never thaw beef at room temperature. Thawing by refrigeration requires planning ahead and most likely allowing a 24-hour thawing period. To thaw beef in cold water, leave the beef in its original wrapping or place it in a watertight plastic bag. Change the water every 30 minutes. For quick thawing of uncooked or cooked beef, use the microwave, but plan on cooking the meat immediately after thawing because some areas of the food may become warm and begin to cook during microwaving.

Thawing time will vary according to whether you're thawing a whole roast or cuts and the number of parts frozen together. Use the Defrost or Medium-Low setting, according to the manufacturer's directions. Turn the roast and separate parts as they thaw, taking care the meat does not begin to cook. Repeat as needed. Foods defrosted by the cold water method or in the microwave should be cooked before refreezing, because they may have been held at temperatures above 40 °F.

Table. Storage Times for Beef Products

Products	Refrigerator (40 °F)	Freezer (0 °F)
Fresh beef roast, steaks, chops, or ribs	3 to 5 days	6 to 12 months
Fresh beef liver or variety meets	1 to 2 days	3 to 4 months
Home cooked beef, soups, stews or casseroles	3 to 4 days	2 to 3 months
Store-cooked convenience meals	1 to 2 days	2 to 3 months
Cooked beef gravy or beef broth	1 to 2 days	2 to 3 months
Beef hot dogs or lunch meats, sealed in package	2 weeks (or 1 week after a "Use by" date)	1 to 2 months
Beef hot dogs, opened package	7 days	1 to 2 months
Lunch meats, opened package	3 to 5 days	1 to 2 months
TV dinners, frozen casseroles	Keep only in freezer	3 to 4 months
Canned beef products in pantry	2 to 5 years	After opening,

	in pantry; 3 to 4 days after opening	2 to 3 months
Jerky, commercially vacuum packaged	1 year in pantry; 2 to 3 months in refrigerator	Do not freeze

It is safe to cook frozen beef in the oven, on the stove, or grill without defrosting it first, although the cooking time may be about 50% longer. Do not cook frozen beef in a slow cooker.

Marinating

Marinate food in the refrigerator, not on the counter. If you want to use the marinade as a dip or sauce, reserve a portion before adding raw food. Discard uncooked leftover marinade, or bring to a full boil before brushing on cooked beef.

Partial Cooking or Browning

Never brown or partially cook beef, then refrigerate and finish cooking later, because any bacteria present would not have been destroyed. It is safe to partially pre-cook or microwave beef IMMEDIATELY before transferring it to a hot grill or oven to finish cooking.

COOKING

Importance of Kitchen Thermometers

One of the critical factors in controlling bacteria in food is controlling temperature. Pathogenic microorganisms grow very slowly at low temperatures, multiply rapidly in mid-range temperatures, and are killed at high temperatures. Cook foods thoroughly to prevent food borne illness. Using a thermometer is the only reliable way to ensure safety and to determine the "doneness" of beef and most other foods. To be safe, a product must be cooked to an internal temperature high enough to destroy any harmful bacteria that may have been in the food. Many food handlers believe that visible indicators, such as color changes in the food, can be relied on to determine whether foods have been cooked long enough to ensure bacterial destruction. However, recent research has shown that color and texture indicators are not reliable.

Whole Muscle Meats

When cooking whole cuts or parts of beef, the thermometer should be inserted into the thickest part of the meat, away from the bone, fat and gristle. The thermometer may be inserted sideways if necessary. When the food being cooked is irregularly shaped, the temperature should be checked in several places. Steaks and roasts should be cooked to 145 °F followed by a 4 minute rest, 160 °F, or 170 °F.

Ground Beef

Ground beef must be cooked thoroughly to kill harmful bacteria. Unlike whole muscle meat, whose interior meat is sterile, the grinding process exposes the interior meat in ground beef to bacteria, which may be on the surface, in the air, on equipment or on people's hands. To kill these bacteria, food safety experts have one major rule of thumb—cook ground beef to at least 155 °F. This step, while very simple, offers the best protection that consumers can have for serving ground beef products safely.

Microwaving

When microwaving unequally sized pieces of beef, arrange them in a dish or on a rack so thick parts are toward the outside of the dish and thin parts are in the center, and cook on medium-high or medium power. Place a roast in an oven-cooking bag or in a covered pot. Refer to the manufacturer's directions that accompany the microwave oven for suggested cooking times. Remove from microwave and test for doneness in several places with a meat thermometer.

Table. Approximate* Beef Cooking Times

Type of Beef	Size	Cooking Method	Cooking Time	Internal Temperature
Rib roast, bone-in	4 to 6 lbs.	Roast 325 °F	23 to 25 min./lb.	Medium rare 145 °F
Rib roast, boneless rolled	4 to 6 lbs.	Roast 325 °F	Add 5 to 8 min./lb. to times above	Medium rare 145 °F
Chuck roast, brisket	3 to 4 lbs.	**Braise 325 °F	2 to 3 hours	Medium 160 °F
Round or rump roast	2½ to 4 lbs.	Roast 325 °F	30 to 35 min./lb.	Medium rare 145 °F
Tenderloin, whole	4 to 6 lbs.	Roast 425 °F min. total	45 to 60 145 °F	Medium rare
Steaks	¾" thick	Broil/Grill per side	4 to 5 min. 145 °F	Medium rare
Stew or shank cross cuts	1 to 1½" thick	Cover with liquid; simmer	2 to 3 hours	Medium 160 °F
Short ribs	4" long and 2" thick	**Braise 325 °F	1½ to 2½ hours	Medium 160 °F

Notes: *For safety, cook hamburgers and ground beef mixtures such as meat loaf to 155 °F on a meat thermometer. However, whole muscle meats such as steaks and roasts may be cooked to 145 °F (medium rare), if that is followed by a 4 minute rest before carving or eating. The cooking times listed here are approximate for use in meal planning. Use a meat thermometer to check for safe cooking and doneness of beef.

**Braising is roasting or simmering less-tender meats with a small amount liquid in a tightly covered pan.

SAFE HANDLING OF CANNED GOODS

Canning is an important, safe method of food preservation if practiced properly.The canning process involves placing foods in jars or cans and heating them to a temperature that destroys micro-organisms that could be a health hazard or cause the food to spoil. Canning also inactivates enzymes that could cause the food to spoil. Air is driven from the jar or can during heating, and as it cools, a vacuum seal is formed. This vacuum seal prevents air from getting back into the product bringing with it microorganisms to recontaminate the food.

PURCHASING CANNED GOODS

Buy cans and jars that look perfect. Carefully check dented cans and jars for leakage and rust before buying. Cans and jars should be free of dents, cracks or bulging lids, which can indicate a serious food poisoning threat. Dusty cans or torn labels may indicate old stock. Also check for pull dates.

Product Dating

Dates on product packages recommend purchase or "use by" dates. They are not safety dates. Product dating is voluntary and not required by federal regulations. Since product dating is voluntary by federal regulations, a retailer may legally sell foods beyond the date on the package as long as the product is wholesome.

However, it is not legal to alter, change or cover up a date on a product packaged under federal inspection. The product may continue to be offered for sale but the expired date must remain visible to the consumer.

Types of Dates:

- A "sell by" date tells the store how long to display the product for sale. You should buy the product before the date expires to have sufficient time to use it at best quality.
- A "best if used by" date is recommended for best flavor or quality. It is not a purchase or safety date.
- A "use by" date is the last date recommended for the use of the product while at peak quality and has been determined by the manufacturer of the product.
- "Closed or coded dates" are packing numbers for use by the

manufacturer to rotate the stock as well as to locate their products in the event of a recall.

STORAGE OF CANNED GOODS

Storage does not improve the quality of any food. The quality of a food will not decrease significantly if stored properly and if the food is eaten within the recommended time frame. For best results in maintaining product quality, practice the rule, First In, First Out. This means you use the oldest products first. A good practice in the home is to place the newly purchased cans in back of the same products already on the shelf. For best quality, use home canned foods within one year, and commercially processed cans within two years. Storage cabinets should be cool and dry. The best temperature for storing canned foods is between 50 °F and 70 °F. Avoid storing canned foods in a warm place near hot pipes, a range or furnace, or in direct sunlight. Storage time decreases significantly when temperatures are above 75 °F. Keep canned goods dry to prevent cans or metal lids from rusting, which may cause cans to leak and food to spoil.

Recommended Storage for Unopened Canned Foods in a Cool, Dry Pantry:

- *High-Acid Canned Food:* 12 to 18 months Juices, tomatoes, grapefruit, apple products, mixed fruit, berries, pickles, sauerkraut and vinegar-based products.
- *Low-acid Canned Foods:* 2 to 5 years Meat and poultry products, vegetable soups, spaghetti products, potatoes, corn, carrots, beans, beets, peas, pumpkins, etc.
- *Home-Canned Foods:* All types 1 year
- *Opened Canned Foods*: Store tightly covered in a glass or plastic storage container in refrigerator.
  - Baby food: 2 days
  - Meat, seafood, poultry: 2 days
  - Vegetables: 3 days
  - Tomato sauce, fruits: 5 to 7 days
  - Pickles and olives: 1 to 2 months

COOKING OF CANNED GOODS

Commercially canned foods can be safely eaten straight from the can as long as the container is intact. However, Do Not use home canned vegetables unless you have the means to boil them for 10 minutes before eating. Don't taste or use canned foods that show any signs of spoilage! Look closely at all cans before opening them. A bulging lid or leaking can is a sign of spoilage. When you open the can, look for other signs such as spurting liquid, an off odor or mold. Spoiled canned foods should be discarded so they will not be eaten by humans or pets. Remember that once a can is opened, it becomes perishable and should be refrigerator-stored or cooked properly and then stored in the refrigerator if you are not going to eat it right away.

SERVING CANNED GOODS

Serve foods on clean plates, using clean utensils. Keep opened canned foods in the refrigerator until it is time to serve them. Keep cooked canned foods hot, above 140 °F, but not for more than two hours. When outside temperatures are 90 °F or warmer, hold the cooked foods no longer than one hour before reheating, refrigerating or freezing them.

Leftovers

After a meal, refrigerate or freeze uneaten food promptly, but throw it out if the food has been held too long or was a reheated leftover at this meal. Refrigerate or freeze cooked leftovers in small, covered shallow containers within two hours after cooking. Leave airspace around the containers for quick chilling. Date packages of leftovers and use them within a safe period. Cover and reheat leftovers thoroughly before serving them. Bring sauces, soups and gravies to a rolling boil; reheat all other foods to an internal temperature of 165 °F. Reheat only the amount of food needed for one meal. Never reheat a food more than once. Don't taste leftovers to determine if they are safe to eat. If in doubt, throw it out! Discard outdated, unsafe or questionable leftovers. Place them in the garbage disposal or in tightly wrapped packages that cannot be consumed by people or animals.

HANDLING OF CHEESE FOR SAFETY & QUALITY

Cheese comes in many forms ranging from soft to hard and natural to processed. How cheese is handled for safety and best quality is dependent on the type of cheese.

NATURAL CHEESE

Natural cheese can be unripened or ripened. Unripened cheeses include cream cheese and cottage cheese. Cheeses that are ripened by bacteria include cheddar, Swiss and Parmesan. Cheeses that are ripened by mold include Blue, Roquefort and Brie.

Natural cheeses are also categorized by their degree of hardness:

- *Soft:* Brie, Camembert, cottage cheese, cream cheese, ricotta, feta
- *Semi-soft:* Blue, brick, Havarti, Monterey Jack, mozzarella, Muenster, provolone
- *Hard:* Cheddar, Colby, Edam, Gouda, Swiss
- *Very Hard:* Parmesan, Romano

PROCESS CHEESE

Process cheese is a blend of fresh and aged natural cheese that has been melted, pasteurized and mixed with an emulsifier. Process cheese is milder in flavor and softer than the natural cheese from which it was made. It also has very good melting properties.

HOW SHOULD CHEESE BE STORED

Refrigerate all cheese between 35 and 40 °F in its original wrapping until ready to use. It is best to store cheese in a refrigerator drawer so it does not pick up off-flavors from other foods. If cheese is removed from its original packaging, wrap it tightly with plastic film wrap or foil to prevent air pockets. Once cheese is exposed to air, molding and dehydration might occur. To protect cheese from mold it is best to double-wrap cheese and place it in a sealed container after each use. Strong-smelling cheeses, like Limburger, should be well-wrapped and kept in a separate container to prevent odors from transferring to other foods.

HOW LONG IS IT SAFE TO KEEP CHEESE

The "best if used by" date tells you how long the product will keep its best flavor or quality. The term is not a safety date. "Best if used by" dates are general guidelines, as some foods may deteriorate more quickly and other foods may last longer than the times suggested. A number of factors, such as improper handling and inadequate storage, can shorten the shelf-life of a food. Many foods can be eaten after the "best if used by" date if properly stored and handled.

Caution

Throw out soft cheeses that have been at room temperature for more than four hours.

NATURAL CHEESE

As a general rule, the harder the cheese, the longer its shelf-life. But remember, many types of natural cheese will continue to ripen, no matter how carefully they are stored. Hard cheeses will generally keep for several months, whereas softer cheeses will keep from one to three weeks after opening. Large pieces of cheese tend to keep longer than shredded cheese.

PROCESS CHEESE

Unopened packages of process cheese can be used up to six months if refrigerated at 40 °F or below. Opened packages should be tightly rewrapped, refrigerated, and used within three to four weeks.

DOES CHEESE FREEZE WELL

Most hard cheeses and process cheeses can be frozen, but there will be changes in texture. For this reason, thawed cheese is best used crumbled or shredded, in salads or as toppings or in cooked dishes.

Tips for Freezing Cheeses:

- Freeze pieces of a half-pound or less.
- Use moisture-proof and airtight wrapping.

- Freeze quickly and store at 0 °F for two to six months.
- Thaw in refrigerator so cheese won't lose moisture; the slower the cheese is thawed, the better.
- Use as soon as possible after thawing

SHOULD MOLDY CHEESE BE THROWN AWAY

Molds spread through cheese by producing "hyphae," which are root-like structures. In hard cheeses, such as cheddar and many processed cheeses, these mold hyphae do not penetrate very far below the surface. Mold that is not part of the manufacturing process of a cheese should be handled.

Hard Cheese

If the block of cheese is large and molding is not extensive, remove the mold to save the remaining cheese. Remove at least 1-inch around and below the mold spot. Keep the knife out of the mold itself so it will not contaminate other parts of the cheese. Mold requires oxygen to grow, so tightly rewrap the remaining cheese. The old advice to wipe the cheese with a vinegar solution is no longer recommended and is not required to prevent further mold growth.

Semi-Soft & Soft Cheese & All Types of Crumbled, Shredded, & Sliced Cheese

Discard soft cheese, cheese that has a loose-knit curd, and shredded or sliced cheese if it contains molds that are not a part of the manufacturing process. These molds can be dangerous. Foods with high moisture content can be contaminated below the surface. Shredded, sliced, or crumbled cheese can be contaminated by the cutting instrument. Moldy soft cheese can also have bacteria growing along with the mold.

- *Caution*: Never open extremely moldy cheese in the kitchen. Do not sniff the moldy item. Wrap all moldy trimmings and moldy cheeses in plastic wrap and place in a covered trash can.

WHO SHOULD AVOID EATING CERTAIN CHEESES

Pregnant women and newborns, older adults, and people with weak immune systems due to cancer treatments, AIDS, diabetes or kidney disease are at risk for becoming seriously ill from eating foods that contain Listeria monocytogenes. People in these at-risk groups should not eat feta, Brie, Camembert, blue-veined cheeses, or Mexican-style soft cheeses such as queso blanco and queso fresco unless labeled pasteurized.

WHAT IS THE BEST WAY TO MELT CHEESE

Cheese cut into small pieces or shredded promotes more even melting in a shorter amount of time. When you add cheese to any recipe, cook on low heat, stirring constantly. High heat will toughen cheese and make it stringy. When you are making a sauce with cheese in it, add cheese as the last ingredient and heat until just melted. Process cheese melts more smoothly than natural cheese.

WHAT IS THE BEST WAY TO MICROWAVE CHEESE

Remove the wrapping and place on a microwave-safe plate. Microwave at 30 percent until cheese reaches desired softness and/or temperature. Check every 10 seconds to prevent overheating. Cooking times will vary among microwave ovens. Use this method to prepare cheese nachos without making the cheese tough.

WHAT IS THE BEST TEMPERATURE FOR SERVING CHEESE

The flavor of cheese is best when eaten at room temperature, so remove from refrigerator before serving time. Soft cheeses take a shorter amount of time to come to room temperature than firm and hard cheeses. Only set out the amount of cheese you will eat to prevent the cheese from becoming dry and tough from being repeatedly warmed and chilled.

WHAT IS THE BEST WAY TO SHRED CHEESE

Cheese will shred more easily if well-chilled. It can also be placed in the freezer for 30 minutes before shredding.

SAFE HANDLING OF EGGS

SHELL EGG SAFETY

Eggs can be a part of a healthy diet. However, they are perishable just like raw meat, poultry and fish. To be safe, they must be properly stored, handled and cooked.

Concern for Egg Safety

Some unbroken fresh shell eggs may contain Salmonella enteritidis bacteria that can cause food borne illness. While the number of eggs affected is quite small, there have been some scattered outbreaks in the last few years. Currently the government, the egg industry and the scientific community are working together to solve the problem. Researchers say that if present, the Salmonella enteritidus bacteria are usually in the yolk or "yellow." But they cannot rule out the bacteria being in egg whites. So everyone is advised against eating raw or undercooked egg yolks, whites or products that contain eggs. People with health problems, the very young, the elderly and pregnant women are particularly vulnerable to Salmonella enteritidis infections. Chronic illness also weakens the immune system, making the person vulnerable to food borne illness.

STORAGE, HANDLING & COOKING OF SHELL EGGS

Proper refrigeration, cooking and handling should prevent most egg safety problems. People can enjoy eggs and dishes containing eggs if these safe handling guidelines are followed.

Don't Eat Raw Eggs

This includes "health food" milk shakes with raw eggs, Caesar salad, hollandaise sauce and any other foods like homemade mayonnaise, ice cream or eggnog made from recipes in which the raw egg ingredients are not cooked.

These egg-based recipes should be updated to start with a cooked base or so that commercially prepared pasteurized eggs or egg substitutes are used. Use a thermometer and make sure the temperature of the cooked base reaches 160 °F.

Buy Clean Eggs from a Refrigerator Display Case

Do not purchase eggs anywhere that are not refrigerated. Any bacteria present in the egg can grow quickly if stored at room temperature. At the store, choose Grade A or AA eggs with clean, uncracked shells.

Safe Storage of Eggs at Home

Take eggs straight home and store them immediately in the refrigerator at 40 °F or slightly below. Store them in the grocery carton in the coldest part of the refrigerator, not in the door. Do not wash eggs. Washing eggs could remove the protective mineral oil coating put on at the plant and could increase the potential for bacteria on the shell to enter the egg.

Use Eggs Promptly

Use raw shell eggs within three to five weeks. When fresh eggs are hard cooked, the protective coating is washed away so hard-cooked eggs should be refrigerated within two hours of cooking and used within a week. Use leftover yolks and whites within four days. If eggs crack on the way home from the store, break them into a clean container, cover tightly, and keep refrigerated for use within two days.

Freeze Eggs for Longer Storage

Eggs should not be frozen in their shells. To freeze whole eggs, beat yolks and whites together. Egg whites and yolks can also be frozen by themselves. Use frozen eggs within a year. If eggs freeze accidentally in their shells, keep them frozen until needed. Defrost them in refrigerator. Discard any with cracked shells.

Handle Eggs Safely

Wash hands, utensils, equipment and work areas with warm, soapy water before and after contact with eggs and egg-rich foods.

Serve Immediately

Don't keep out of the refrigerator more than two hours. Serve cooked eggs and egg-rich foods immediately after cooking, or place in shallow containers for quick cooling and refrigerate at once. Use within three to four days. Recipes using raw eggs should be cooked immediately or refrigerated and cooked within 24 hours.

Cooked Eggs

Hard-cooked eggs should be safe for everyone to eat. Those at risk for food borne illness should avoid eating soft-cooked or "runny" eggs. However, healthy persons may choose to eat eggs that are less than totally firm.

Use the following cooking times:

- *Fried Eggs:* Cook 2 to 3 minutes on each side; 4 minutes in a covered pan. The yolk should begin to thicken.
- *Scrambled Eggs*: Cook until firm throughout.
- *Poached Eggs*: Cook 5 minutes over boiling water.
- *Soft-Cooked Eggs*: Cook 7 minutes in the shell in boiling water.

Use Safe Egg Recipes

Egg mixtures are safe if they reach 160 °F, so homemade ice cream and eggnog can be made safely from a cooked base. Heat the egg-milk mixture gently. Use a thermometer or be sure the mixture coats a metal spoon. Dry meringue shells are safe. So are divinity candy and seven-minute frosting, made by combining hot sugar syrup with beaten egg whites. Meringue-topped pies should be safe if baked at 350 °F for about 15 minutes. Chiffon pies and fruit whips made with raw, beaten egg whites cannot be guaranteed safe. Substitute whipped cream or whipped topping. To make key lime pie safely, heat lime juice with raw egg yolks in a pan on the stove, stirring constantly, until the mixture reaches 160 °F. Combine this mixture with sweetened condensed milk and pour it into a baked piecrust. For meringue topping. For egg dishes such as quiche and casseroles, a knife inserted in the center should come out clean.

Safety Tips for Easter Eggs:

- Wash hands before dyeing the eggs.
- Use a food-safe coloring if eggs will be eaten.
- Handle eggs carefully to prevent cracking. If the shells crack, bacteria could contaminate the inside. Do not use cracked eggs for hiding.
- After hard-cooking eggs, dye them and return them to the refrigerator immediately until ready to hide.
- Hide eggs in places protected from dirt, pets and other sources of bacteria.
- The total time for hiding and hunting eggs should not exceed two hours. Discard any Easter eggs that have been cracked. The

uncracked "found" eggs should then be refrigerated until eaten.

- Eat hard-cooked eggs within one week.

Ukranian Easter Eggs

A traditional part of the Easter celebration in the Ukraine, these whole, raw eggs have their contents blown out to leave a hollow shell that is then decorated. Because some raw eggs may contain Salmonella, use caution when blowing out the contents. Use only uncracked eggs that have been kept refrigerated. To destroy bacteria that may be present on the surface of the egg, wash the egg in hot water and then rinse in a solution of one teaspoon chlorine bleach per half cup of water. After blowing out the egg, refrigerate the contents and use within two to four days; cook thoroughly before eating.

Pickled Eggs

Pickled or brined eggs are hard-cooked eggs marinated in vinegar and pickling spices, spicy cider, or juice from pickles or pickled beets. Home-pickled eggs should be kept refrigerated. Unopened containers of commercially processed pickled eggs keep for several months on the shelf. After opening, keep refrigerated.

EGG PRODUCTS

When consumers think of an egg, most picture a pristine white, or sometimes brown, oval shell containing a completely edible, versatile food. But of the 63 billion eggs consumed in 1994, more than 25 percent were in the form of egg products.

The term "egg products" refers to eggs that have been removed from their shells for processing. Basic egg products include whole eggs, whites, yolks and various blends with or without non-egg ingredients that are processed and pasteurized and may be available in liquid, frozen and dried forms. Egg products are widely used by the food service industry and as ingredients in other foods, such as prepared mayonnaise and ice cream.

Buying, Handling and Cooking Egg Products

Proper storage and handling is necessary for all egg products to prevent bacterial contamination:

- Buy only pasteurized egg products that bear the USDA inspection mark.
- Make sure containers are tightly sealed. Frozen products should show no signs of thawing. Refrigerated products should be kept at 40 °F or below. Dried egg products should not be caked or hardened.
- Store frozen egg products up to one year at 0 °F or lower. After thawing, do not re-freeze.
- Thaw frozen egg products in the refrigerator or under cold running water. Do Not Thaw On The Counter.

- If the container for liquid products bears a "use by" date, observe it. Follow the storage and handling instructions provided by the manufacturer.
- For liquid products without an expiration date, store unopened containers at 40 °F or below for up to seven days. Do not freeze opened cartons of liquid egg products.
- Unopened dried egg products and egg white solids can be stored at room temperature as long as they are kept cool and dry. After opening, store in the refrigerator.
- Reconstituted egg products must be used immediately or refrigerated and used that day.
- USDA Commodity Dried Egg Mix should be stored at less than 50 °F, preferably in the refrigerator. After opening, use within seven to 10 days. Reconstitute only the amount needed at one time and use immediately or refrigerate and use within an hour.

EGG PRODUCT SAFETY

Who Inspects Egg Products

Congress passed the Egg Products Inspection Act (EPIA) in 1970. The EPIA provides for the mandatory continuous inspection of the processing of liquid, frozen and dried egg products to ensure they are wholesome and properly labeled and packaged to protect the health and welfare of consumers. USDA's Food Safety and Inspection Service (FSIS) inspects all egg products, with the exception of those products exempted under the Act that are used by food manufacturers, food service institutions and retail markets.

The Department of Health and Human Services' Food and Drug Administration (FDA) is responsible for the inspection of egg substitutes, imitation eggs and similar products that are exempted from continuous inspection under the EPIA. Currently, only Canada is exporting egg products to the United States. The EPIA specifies that egg products may not be imported into the United States except from countries that have an egg products inspection system equivalent to that in this country.

Why are Eggs Products Useful

Food manufacturers like pasteurized egg products because of their convenience and ease in handling and storing. Institutional food service operators, such as fast food chains, restaurants, hospitals and nursing homes, use egg products to ensure a high level of food safety. Consumers are starting to see more egg products in retail food stores.

How are Egg Products Made

Egg products are processed in sanitary facilities under continuous inspection by the USDA. The initial step in making egg products is breaking the eggs and separating the yolks and whites from the shells. Eggs are processed by automated equipment that moves the eggs from flats, washes and sanitizes the shells, breaks the eggs and separates the whites and yolks, and/or makes mixtures of them. The liquid egg product is filtered, mixed, and then chilled prior to additional processing.

Why and How are Egg Products Pasteurized

The law requires that all egg products distributed for consumption be pasteurized. This means that they must be rapidly heated and held at a minimum required temperature for a specified time. This destroys Salmonella, but it does not cook the eggs or affect their color, flavor, nutritional value or use. Dried whites are pasteurized by heating in the dried form, again for a specified time and at a minimum required temperature. Since many new and different types of egg products are now being formulated, government and industry researchers are currently evaluating the effectiveness of the pasteurization processes used for these and other products. Additional research will determine if new safety measures are needed to continue to provide safe egg products for food service, industry and consumers.

Are All Egg Products Pasteurized

Certain commodities are not presently considered egg products and are exempt from this law. These commodities include freeze-dried products, imitation egg products and egg substitutes. Inspected, pasteurized egg products are used to make these commodities and companies may elect to repasteurize these products following formulation and before packaging. Officially inspected egg products will bear the USDA inspection mark. No-cholesterol frozen egg substitutes first became available to consumers in 1973. They consist of egg whites, artificial color and other non-egg additives. Specific questions about egg substitutes should be directed to the manufacturer.

What Information is Provided on Egg Product Labels

In addition to nutrition information on consumer packages, other labeling information is required for egg products.

All egg products must be labeled with:

- The common or usual name;
- The ingredients listed in the order of descending proportions;
- The name and address of the packer or distributor;
- The date of pack which may be shown as a lot number or production code number;
- The net contents; and
- The official USDA inspection mark and plant number.

Can Egg Products be Used as an Ingredient in Uncooked Foods

Egg products are pasteurized and can be substituted in recipes typically made with raw eggs that won't be cooked. For optimal safety, egg products are best used in a cooked product, especially if serving high-risk persons such as the elderly, children, the chronically ill, or those with weakened immune systems. Use a food thermometer to be sure that the internal temperature of the cooked product reaches 160 °F. Egg products can also be used in baking or cooking.

What is Dried Egg Mix

USDA Dried Egg Mix is a blend of dried whole eggs, nonfat dry milk, soybean oil and a small amount of salt. There is very little moisture in it. To reconstitute, blend 2 Tablespoons of Dried Egg Mix with ¼ cup water to make the equivalent of one large whole egg. Dried Egg Mix is packaged in 6-ounce pouches, equivalent to about six eggs each. It is distributed by USDA to food banks, Indian reservations and other needy family outlets and is also used in disaster feeding. A similar product called All-Purpose Egg Mix, containing a greater proportion of eggs, is now being manufactured for USDA. It is reconstituted by mixing one part egg mix with two parts water. All-Purpose Egg Mix is available to schools as part of the School Lunch Program. It is packaged in 10-pound bags.

SAFE HANDLING OF FISH

SELECTING THE BEST

Spotting a Safe Seafood Seller

Always purchase fish from a dealer that maintains high quality.

Based on FDA's Food Code, here are some ways of spotting a safe fish dealer:

- Employees should be in clean clothing and wearing hair coverings.
- They should not be smoking, eating or playing with their hair.
- They should not be sick or have any open wounds.
- Employees should be wearing disposable gloves when handling food and change gloves after doing nonfood tasks and after handling raw fish.
- Fish should be displayed on a thick bed of fresh — not melting — ice preferably in a case or under some type of cover. Fish should be arranged with the bellies down so that the melting ice drains away from the fish, thus reducing the chances of spoilage.

Selecting Quality Fish

Appearance is bright and shiny in quality fish, and most of the scales are intact and adhere tightly to the skin. Each species has characteristic markings and colors which fade and become less pronounced as the fish loses freshness. Eyes are bright, clear, full and often protrude. As quality goes down, the eyes often turn pink and become cloudy and sunken. This does not always apply to small-eyed fish such as salmon. Gills are red and free from slime. With time, the color fades to light pink, then gray and finally greenish or dull brown. Odor is fresh and mild. A fish just out of the water has practically no "fish" odor. The fishy odor develops with time, but should not be strong or objectionable. Flesh is firm, elastic and not separating from the bones.

Fresh Fillets and Steaks

Odor is fresh and mild. Flesh is moist, firm, elastic and has a fresh-cut appearance without traces of browning or drying around the edges. Pre-packaged steaks and fillets are tightly wrapped with no liquid and little or no air in the packages.

Safe Handling after Purchase

Whether you've purchased fish that is fresh or frozen, always keep it cold. Never leave perishable items in a hot car unless packed in ice or in a cooler; seafood products must be kept cold to ensure peak quality. It's always a good idea to keep your refrigerator temperature between 32 to 38 °F, and your freezer at 0 °F or colder.

STORAGE

Refrigeration

Store fresh fish in its original wrapper in the coldest part of the refrigerator, which is under the freezer or in the "meat-keeper" drawer. Plan to use your fish purchases within one to two days. If not, freeze them. However, do not refreeze previously frozen products because the quality will suffer.

Freezing

It is best to freeze fish in tightly wrapped package form. This takes less storage space and fits a family portion for one meal at a time. Fish freeze faster in tightly wrapped packages. Small whole fish, steaks or fillets are easy to prepare for packaged freezing. Prewrap them tightly and individually in cling wrap, forming a tight skin on the product.

Master-bag these individually wrapped items in a good, strong polyethylene bag or foil before freezing, but never more than a pound per master bag. Large fish have large surface areas exposed, and they are difficult to protect from oxidation.

The best way to handle these fish is simply to freeze them unwrapped or temporarily bag them in plastic. After freezing, dip them in water to form a protective glaze. Then you can rebag the fish and return it to the freezer. The glaze may need renewing every five to six weeks.

Label each package with the date, kind and type of fish and the weight and number of servings or pieces. A crayon or grease pencil is ideal for this purpose. Do not overload your freezer, and do not pack the unfrozen fish too tightly. Either of these practices can greatly extend the freezing time and reduce the quality. Most home-frozen fish should not be stored over six months, no more than three months for salmon..

PREPARATION

Cleanliness

Always wash hands thoroughly with hot, soapy water before preparing foods and after handling raw fish. Don't let raw fish or juices touch ready-to-go foods either in the refrigerator or during preparation. Don't put cooked foods on the same plate that held raw fish. Always wash utensils that have touched raw fish with hot, soapy water before using them for cooked foods. Wash counters, cutting boards and other surfaces raw fish have touched.

Thawing

While freezing fish quickly keeps more cell walls intact, the opposite is true for thawing. Defrost gradually so cells are disturbed less and fewer juices leak out. The best way to thaw is overnight in the refrigerator. Avoid thawing at room temperature. If you must thaw fish quickly, here are safe options: seal fish in a plastic bag and immerse in cold water for about an hour, or microwave on the "defrost" setting, stopping when fish is still icy but pliable.

Marinating

Marinate fish in the refrigerator, not on the counter. Discard the marinade after use because it contains raw juices, which may harbor bacteria. If you want to use the marinade as a dip or sauce, reserve a portion before adding raw food.

COOKING

Baking

Whole fish, whole stuffed fish, fillets, stuffed fillets, steaks and chunks of fish may be baked. Use pieces of similar size for even cooking. It's best to bake fish in a preheated, 450 °F oven following the 10-minute rule; bake uncovered, basting if desired.

Broiling

Steaks, whole fish, split whole fish and fillets lend themselves well to broiling. Place fish, 1-inch thick or less, 2 to 4 inches from the heat source. Place thicker pieces 5 to 6 inches away. Baste frequently with an oil-based marinade. Using the 10-minute rule, cook on one side for half the total cooking time, basting once or twice, then turn the fish over to continue broiling and basting.

Grilling

This technique lends itself well to thick steak fish such as salmon, halibut, swordfish, tuna and whole fish. Preheat an outdoor gas or electric grill. If using a barbecue grill, start the fire about 30 minutes before cooking. Let it burn until white-hot then spread coals out in a single layer. Adjust the grill height to 4 to 6 inches above the heat.

To grill fish, a moderately hot fire is best for cooking seafood. Always start with a well-oiled grid to prevent the delicate skin of the fish from sticking. Support more delicate pieces of fish in a hinged, fish-shaped wire basket for easier turning or handling. Frequently baste steaks and fillets while grilling to prevent them from drying out. Marinating fish an hour before grilling also helps keep it moist.

Apply the 10-minute rule for proper doneness. Use indirect heat for whole fish by banking hot coals on either side of the barbecue or preheat gas or electric grill. Oil fish well and place in an oiled fish basket. Cook fish covered, 10 to 12 minutes per inch of thickness, turning halfway through cooking time.

Microwaving

Use a shallow dish to allow maximum exposure to the microwaves. Arrange fillets with the thicker parts pointing outward and the thinner parts, separated by pieces of plastic wrap, overlapping in the center of the dish. Cover dish with plastic wrap and vent by turning back one corner. Allow 3 minutes per pound of boneless fish cooked on high as a guide. Rotate the dish halfway through the cooking time. Rolled fillets microwave more evenly and are less likely to overcook than flat fillets, which may have thin edges.

Table. Safe Handling of Fish in Cold Storage

Product	**Refrigerator (40 °F)**	**Freezer (0 °F)**
Fresh Fish	1-2 Days	2-3 Months
Cooked Fish	3-4 Days	1 Month
Frozen Fish	Use Immediately	3-6 Months
Lightly Smoked Fish (Like Salmon)	1-2 Days Recommended; After 6 Quality	Not Months Loses
Heavily Smoked Fish Kippered Cod, Smoked Whiting)	6-7 Days Recommended; After 6 Quality	Not Months Loses

Dried or Pickled	1 Week Recommended;	Not
	After 6 Quality	Months Loses
Bisques, Broth, Chowders, and Stews	1-2 Days	3-6 Months

SAFE HANDLING OF LAMB

SELECTING THE BEST

Fresh is Best

Select lamb that is pinkish red with a velvety texture. Dark red cuts generally indicate the meat is older and less tender.

Look for good marbling, and meat that is fine textured and firm:

- Look for packages that are cool to the touch and have no wear or punctures.
- Always remember to select meat just before checking out at the supermarket register.
- Make sure all meats, whether raw, pre-packaged or from the deli are refrigerated when purchased.
- Prevent "cross-contamination" by keeping fresh meats separate from other items. Put raw meat packages in a plastic bag so juices won't drip onto other foods.
- Pack raw meats in an ice chest if it will take more than an hour to get home. Keep ice chest in the passenger area of the car during warm weather.
- Take meats straight home to the refrigerator or freezer.

Product Dating

Product dating, applying "sell by" or "use by" dates, is not required by federal regulations. However, many stores and processors may voluntarily choose to date packages of raw lamb. Use or freeze products with a "sell by" date within three to five days of purchase. If the manufacturer has determined a "use by" date, observe it. It's always best to buy a product before its date expires. It's not important if a date expires after freezing lamb because all foods stay safe while properly frozen.

Product Inspection & Grading

All lamb found in retail stores is either USDA-inspected for wholesomeness or inspected by state systems which have standards equal to the federal government. Each animal and its internal organs are inspected for signs of disease. The "Passed and Inspected by USDA" seal ensures that the lamb is wholesome and free from disease. Although inspection is mandatory, its grading for quality is voluntary, and a plant pays to have its lamb graded. USDA Lamb Quality Grades are based upon palatability-indicating characteristics of the lean and carcass conformation. Conformation has no direct influence upon the eating quality. For lamb and yearling mutton the quality grades are Prime, Choice, Good and Utility.

Table. Safe Handling of Lamb in Cold Storage

Food	Refrigerator (40 ºF)	Freezer (0 ºF)
Fresh Lamb		
Roast	3-5 Days	6-9 Months
Steak/Chops	3-5 Days	6-9 Months
Ground/Stew Meat	1-2 Days	3-4 Months
Cooked Lamb		
Roast	3-4 Days	2-3 Months
Steak/Chops	3-4 Days	2-3 Months
Ground/Stew Meat	1-2 Days	2-3 Months

STORING

Refrigeration

Packaged whole cuts of fresh lamb may be refrigerated in their original wrapping in the coldest part of the refrigerator up to four or five days after purchase. Ground lamb can be stored in the refrigerator for up to two days; cooked lamb is at its best refrigerated no longer than four days.

- Use an appliance thermometer and maintain a temperature of 34 to 38 °F.
- Never leave meat in a hot car or sitting out at room temperature. Refrigerate or freeze fresh lamb Immediately afer bringing it home.
- Store uncooked lamb items together, separate from cooked foods. Make sure the raw juices do not drip onto other foods.
- Keep lamb refrigerated until you are ready to cook it.
- When transporting uncooked or cooked lamb to another dining site, place it in an insulated container or ice chest until ready to cook or eat.

Freezing

Freeze whole cuts of fresh lamb if you do not plan to cook it within four days after purchase. Wrap whole cuts of lamb separately in heavy-duty foil or moisture- and vapor-proof freezer bags or wrap before freezing. Label for ease in selecting just the right number of cuts to thaw for a single meal. Be sure to press the air out of the package before freezing. If you plan to freeze lamb in its original wrapping, overwrap the porous store plastic with freezer bag or paper. Cooked lamb cuts may be frozen in the same way as fresh, unless made with a sauce or gravy. In that case, pack the meat in a rigid container with a tight-fitting lid.

PREPARATION

Cleanliness

- Always wash hands thoroughly with hot, soapy water before preparing foods and after handling raw meat.
- Don't let raw meat or juices touch ready-to-eat foods either in the refrigerator or during preparation.
- Don't put cooked foods on the same plate that held raw lamb.
- Always wash utensils that have touched raw meat with hot, soapy water before using them for cooked meats.
- Wash counters, cutting boards and other surfaces raw meats have touched.

Thawing

Thaw uncooked lamb in the refrigerator or in cold water. Never thaw meat at room temperature. Thawing by refrigeration requires planning ahead, most likely allowing a 24-hour thawing period. After defrosting raw lamb by this method, it will be safe in the refrigerator up to five days before cooking. During this time, if you decide not to use the lamb, you can safely refreeze it without cooking it first.

To thaw lamb in cold water, leave the meat in its original wrapping or place it in a watertight plastic bag. Change the water every 30 minutes. For quick thawing of uncooked or cooked lamb, use the microwave, but plan on cooking the meat immediately after thawing because some areas of the food may become warm and begin to cook during microwaving.

Thawing time will vary according to whether you're thawing a whole roast or cuts and the number of parts frozen together. Use the Defrost or Medium-Low setting, according to the manufacturer's directions. Turn the roast and separate parts as they thaw, taking care the meat does not begin to cook. Repeat as needed. Foods defrosted by the cold water method or in the microwave should be cooked before refreezing because they may have been held at temperatures above 40 °F.

Marinating

Marinate food in the refrigerator, not on the counter. Discard the marinade after use because it contains raw juices, which may harbor bacteria. If you want to use the marinade as a dip or sauce, reserve a portion before adding raw food.

Partial Cooking or Browning

Never brown or partially cook lamb, then refrigerate and finish cooking later, because any bacteria present would not have been destroyed. It is safe to partially pre-cook or microwave lamb immediately before transferring it to the hot grill or oven to finish cooking.

COOKING

Cooking the Meat

For safety, the USDA recommends cooking ground lamb patties and other ground mixtures to 160 °F. Whole muscle meats such as chops and roasts should be cooked to 145 °F, 160 °F or 170 °F. Remember that appliances and outdoor grills can vary in heat. Use a meat thermometer to check for safe cooking and doneness of lamb.

Cooked muscle meats can be pink even when the meat has reached a safe internal temperature. If fresh lamb has reached 160 °F throughout, even though it may still be pink in the center, it should be safe. The pink color can be due to the cooking method or added ingredients. For approximate cooking times of lamb refer to Table.

Table. Approximate* Lamb Cooking Times (°F)

Cuts of Lamb	Size	Cooking Methods	Cooking Times	Internal Temperature
Lamb leg, bone in	5 to 7 lbs.	Roast 325 ºF	20 to 25 min./lb.	Medium-rare 145 °F
			25 to 30 min./lb.	Medium 160 °F
			30 to 35 min./lb.	Well-done 170 °F
Lamb leg, bone in	7 to 9 lbs.	Roast 325 ºF	15 to 20 min./lb.	Medium-rare 145 °F
			20 to 25 min./lb.	Medium 160 °F
			25 to 30 min./lb.	Well-done 170 °F
Lamb leg, boneless, rolled	4 to 7 lbs.	Roast 325 ºF	25 to 30 min./lb.	Medium-rare 145 °F
			30 to 35 min./lb.	Medium 160 °F
			35 to 40 min./lb.	Well-done 170 °F

Shoulder roast or Shank leg half	3 to 4 lbs.	Roast 325 ºF	30 to 35 min./lb. 40 to 45 min./lb.	Medium-rare 145 °F Medium160 °F
	45 to 50	Well-done 170 °F	min./lb.	
Cubes, for kabobs	1 to 1 ½″	Broil/grill	8 to 12 minutes	Medium 160 °F
Ground lamb patties	2" thick	Broil/grill	5 to 8 minutes	Medium 160 °F
Chops. rib or loin	1½″ to 1" thick	Broil/grill	7 to 11 minutes 15 to 19 minutes	Medium-rare 145 °F Medium 160 °F
Leg steaks	¾″ thick	Broil/grill 4" From heat	14 to 18 minutes	Medium-rare 145 °F Medium 160 °F
Stew meat, pieces Shanks	1 to 1½″ ¾ to 1 lb.	Cover with liquid; simmer	1½ to 2 hours	Medium 160 °F
Breast, rolled	1½ to 2 lb.	*Braise 325 ºF	1½ to 2 hours	Medium 160 °F

Notes: * Use a meat thermometer to check for proper doneness.

** Braising is roasting or simmering less-tender meat with a small amount of liquid in a tightly covered pan.

Microwaving

When microwaving unequal sizes of lamb, arrange in a dish or on a rack so thick parts are toward the outside of the dish and thin parts are in the center, and cook on medium-high or medium power. Place a roast in an oven-cooking bag or in a covered pot. Refer to the manufacturer's directions that accompany the microwave oven for suggested cooking times. Use a meat thermometer to test for doneness in several places to be sure the proper temperature.

SERVING

- Wash hands with soap and water before serving or eating food.
- Serve cooked products on clean plates with clean utensils and clean hands.
- Never put cooked foods on a dish that has held raw lamb unless the dish is washed with soap and hot water.
- Hold hot foods above 140 °F and cold foods below 40 °F.

- Never leave foods, raw or cooked, at room temperature longer than two hours. On a hot day with temperatures at 90 °F or warmer, this decreases to one hour.

LEFTOVERS

- Always use clean utensils and storage containers for safe storage.
- Divide large amounts of leftovers into small, shallow containers for quick cooling in the refrigerator and use within three or four days.
- Avoid placing large pots of stew or gravy in the refrigerator to cool since it will likely take until the next day for this amount of food to cool.
- Use stews and gravies within one to two days.
- For frozen storage, wrap meat in heavy foil, freezer wrap or place in a freezer container. For optimum taste, use meat within two to three months.
- When reheating leftovers, make sure that they have been cooked to 165 °F.
- If you may have kept the food refrigerated for too long, throw it out. Never taste food that looks or smells strange to see if you can still use it.

SAFE HANDLING OF MILK & DAIRY PRODUCTS

MILK

Grade A milk is carefully produced, processed and packaged in order to protect the safety of the consumer. Grade A milk must be pasteurized to be sold by retailers in interstate commerce. Raw milk is usually pasteurized either by low temperature pasteurization in which the milk is heated to 145 °F or higher for at least 30 minutes, or by high temperature pasteurization in which the milk is heated to 161 °F or higher for at least 15 seconds and then quickly cooled. Pasteurization destroys disease-causing bacteria and extends the shelf life of milk. However, pasteurized milk can readily spoil and could cause food borne illness if not properly protected and handled.

Maintaining the Safety of Milk

Refrigeration is the single most important factor in maintaining the safety of milk. By law, Grade A milk must be maintained at a temperature of 45 °F or below. Bacteria in milk will grow minimally below 45 °F. However, temperatures well below 40 °F are necessary to protect the milk's quality. It is critical that these temperatures be maintained through warehousing, distribution, delivery and storage. The cooler refrigerated milk is kept, the longer it lasts and the safer it is. As the product is allowed to warm, the bacteria grow more rapidly. Properly refrigerated, milk can withstand about two weeks' storage. Infants, pregnant women, the elderly and the chronically ill are most at risk from serious illness due to eating any unsafe food. These individuals and those who care for them must be especially careful to handle milk safely.

Fresh Fluid Milk

Fresh milk is categorized mainly by the amount of butterfat it contains. In November 1997, the FDA announced a new rule for milk labeling that helps consumers clarify the difference between 1- and 2-percent milk and reinforces the fact that skim milk is fat-free. Under the new rule, 2-percent milk is renamed reduced fat; 1-percent milk is renamed low-fat; and skim milk is called fat-free or nonfat, although it may contain up to 0.5 grams of fat in a one cup serving.

Buying Fresh Fluid Milk

When selecting milk at the store, make sure it is properly displayed and pay close attention to the date on the label. All fresh fluid milks should be stored at temperatures below 40 °F and should not be stacked high in the display cases. If stored above 40 °F, milk will begin to develop signs of spoilage, including sour odor, off-flavor and curdled consistency. Remember that milk should be taken from the store and quickly placed in your refrigerator at home so that the temperature does not rise above 40 °F. Once you have purchased milk and refrigerated it promptly, it should retain its fresh taste for one to five days beyond the "sell-by" date if kept at the proper temperature. If it spoils before the date expires, this indicates it was not handled properly, and it should be returned to the store for a refund.

Storing Fresh Fluid Milk

Milk should not be left out at room temperature. Pour milk to be used into a serving container and return the original container to the refrigerator. Do not return unused milk that has been sitting out to its original container where it could contaminate the remaining milk. Milk can be stored frozen at 0 °F for up to three months and will be safe to drink if it is thawed in the refrigerator, although it does not retain its smooth texture.

Buttermilk

Originally, buttermilk was made as a by-product when making butter. Lactic acid bacteria are added to fresh, fluid pasteurized skim or part-skim milk to produce the thick, tangy buttermilk. Buttermilk should be handled with the same precautions as regular fluid milk.

Flavored Milk

Chocolate and other flavors - such as maple, strawberry and coffee - may be used for flavored milks. These milks are stored and used as fresh fluid milk.

CONCENTRATED OR DRIED MILKS

Evaporated & Evaporated Skimmed Milk

This type of milk has about 60 percent of the water removed. It may be fortified with vitamins A and/ or D. Store cans of evaporated milk in a cool, dry place. It is shelf-stable, but once opened it should be treated as fresh fluid milk, kept refrigerated and used within several days.

Sweetened Condensed Milk

This is the milk that results from the evaporation of half the water and the addition of sugar in amounts sufficient for preservation. It is stored like evaporated milk.

UHT Milk

Ultra-high temperature (UHT) milk is regular fluid milk that is packed in an airtight, sterilized, cardboard container. The product is treated by flash sterilization at 290 °F. This high temperature kills all bacteria or microorganisms. The milk is then packed into sterilized containers and is shelf-stable for six months. After six months, the flavor and color begin to change and the product thickens. It is still safe, but may not produce the desired effect in a recipe. Once the package of UHT milk is opened, it is treated like fresh fluid milk and used within several days.

Nonfat Dry Milk

This dairy product is made by removing water from pasteurized, fat-free milk. Due to its low moisture content, it can be kept for long periods of time. Once reconstituted, it is handled like fresh fluid milk.

CREAM

Basic Facts

Cream has a very high fat content of between 18 and 40 percent butterfat compared to around 3.25 percent in whole milk. The rich, yellow color associated with cream comes from the carotene in the fat.

The type of cream is determined by its fat content:

- Half-and-half is a combination of milk and cream with a butterfat content of about 11 percent.
- Light cream has between 18 and 30 percent butterfat and may be called coffee or table cream.
- Light whipping cream has between 30 and 36 percent butterfat and can be whipped into solid form, although it tends to be less stable than heavy whipping cream.
- Heavy cream or whipping cream contains 36 to 40 percent butterfat.

- Pressurized whipped cream is sold in aerosol cans and is made from a mixture of cream, sugar and chemical stabilizers.
- Sour cream is made by adding a lactic acid culture to sweet cream. Sour cream usually contains between 18 and 20 percent butterfat.
- Reduced-fat sour cream has skim milk added to lower the fat content.

Storage

Store cream at 40 °F or below in its original container in the refrigerator. Do not leave cream at room temperature, and do not mix warm cream with cream that has been kept refrigerated. Use fresh, pasteurized cream within one to five days of the "sell-by" date.

NONDAIRY DESSERT TOPPINGS

Nondairy dessert toppings are made from vegetable oils but may also contain some milk products. The frozen toppings may be stored for up to one year in the freezer, or thawed and kept in the refrigerator for up to two weeks. Do not freeze dessert toppings in aerosol cans. Store the cans in the refrigerator for a maximum of two to three months.

BUTTER

Basic Facts

Butter is made from the sweet or soured cream of cow's milk by agitation or "churning." After churning, the mass of butter is washed and salted. It is worked to distribute the salt and remove extra water. To be sold in stores, butter must contain at least 80 percent milk fat. Water and milk solids make up the other 20 percent. Salt and coloring may be added if desired. Some unsalted butter is sold as sweet butter, but most people prefer the salted product. The USDA grade label on the butter carton or wrapper means the butter has been tested for quality by a government grader and has been produced under sanitary conditions. The highest possible grade is AA. Grade AA butter is delicate and sweet-flavored with a creamy texture and good spreadability. Most butter sold is grade AA or A. Because of its high fat content, butter contains many calories and therefore should be used sparingly in the diet.

Storage

Storing butter properly, lengthens the shelf life so it can be used over a longer period of time. To prevent a type of spoilage called rancidity, protect butter from heat, light and air by storing it covered in the refrigerator. Rancid butter has an unpleasant taste and smell. Butter absorbs odors from other foods rapidly. To prevent flavor changes, keep butter wrapped in moisture- and vapor-proof material or in tightly covered containers. For refrigerator storage, leave butter in its original wrapper. Opened portions of butter should be refrigerated in a covered dish. Butter can be stored for up to two weeks at refrigerator temperatures. Higher temperatures cause off-flavors and unpleasant odors to develop. Butter should not be stored in the butter keeper on the refrigerator door longer than two days. For ease in spreading, remove butter from the refrigerator 10 to 15 minutes before using it. For holding longer than two weeks, butter should be frozen. To store butter in the freezer, wrap it in moisture- and vapor-proof freezer packaging material to keep the butter from absorbing odors from other foods and to prevent freezer burn. Butter in its original carton can be overwrapped. Butter in one-pound blocks can be cut into smaller portions, repackaged and frozen for future use. If properly wrapped and held at 0 °F or lower, butter will keep well in the freezer for six to nine months. Thaw butter in the refrigerator.

YOGURT

Basic Facts

The natural sugar in milk is converted to lactic acid by means of a bacterial culture producing the creamy, pleasantly tart yogurt. Yogurt is pasteurized to destroy disease-causing microorganisms. Fat and calorie content will differ depending on whether whole, low-fat or fat-free milk is used and whether fruit or sweeteners are added. The label will give the specific information for each yogurt.

Storage

Yogurt may be kept well covered in the refrigerator for seven to 10 days past the "sell-by" date. If it is kept longer, it will develop a stronger taste. Freezing yogurt is not recommended because of the variable results in texture.

FROZEN DAIRY PRODUCTS

Basic Facts

This category includes ice cream, ice milk, sherbet and frozen yogurt:

- Ice cream has the highest milk fat and milk solids content. The milk fat content in ice cream usually ranges between 10 and 14 percent, but may be as high as 20 percent in specialty ice creams.
- Ice milk often has more sugar than ice cream, but its milk fat ranges from 2 to 7 percent.
- Sherbet also has less milk fat and milk solids than ice cream, but more sugar and usually contains fruit and fruit acid. Milk fat content of sherbet is between 1 and 2 percent.
- Frozen yogurt is made from cultured milk and has less milk fat than ice cream and less sugar than sherbet.

Storage

When purchasing ice cream and other frozen desserts at the store, make sure they are frozen solid and that the container is not sticky or frosted which indicates it has partially thawed at some point.

Table. Safe Cold Storage Times for Milk & Dairy Products

Product	How to Store	Refrigerator (35-40 °F)	Freezer (0 °F)
Pasteurized Fresh Whole or Skimmed Milk	Refrigerate immediately in original container. Keep container closed.	1 to 5 days beyond "sell-by" date	3 months. Freezing may result in change in texture. Thaw in refrigerator.
Sweetened Condensed Milk(Opened)	Refrigerate tightly covered.	1 week	Do not freeze.
Evaporated Milk (Opened)	Refrigerate tightly covered.	1 week	Do not freeze.
Cultured Buttermilk	Refrigerate immediately in original container. Keep container closed.	2 weeks	Do not freeze.
Homogenized, Reconstituted Dry Nonfat and Skimmed Milk	Keep containers tightly closed. Don't return unused milk to original containers.	1 week	Do not freeze.
Sweet and Regular Cream	Refrigerate immediately in original container. Keep container closed.	1 to 5 days beyond "sell-by" date	Do not freeze. (Change of texture, body appearance. Separation of fat emulsion.)
Non-Dairy Whipped Topping	Keep covered.	3 months in aerosol can. 3 days if prepared from mix. 2 weeks if bought frozen and then thawed.	Do not freeze aerosol cans; others may be stored in freezer up to one year.
Butter	Refrigerate immediately in original container. Keep container closed.	2 weeks	Butter made from pasteurized cream: 6 to 9 months.
Sour Cream	Refrigerate immediately in original container. Keep container closed.	2 weeks	Do not freeze.
Ice Cream	Store in original container in freezer.	Do not store here.	2-3 weeks (Opened) 2 Months (Unopened)
Yogurt	Keep covered.	7-10 days	Do not freeze.
Soft Custards, Milk Puddings, Cream and	Cool cooked dishes quickly and refrigerate	5-6 days	Do not freeze.

Request that the ice cream be placed in an insulated bag or be double bagged to reduce melting on the way home. Ice cream may be stored unopened for up to two months at 0 °F or below. However, if it will be stored longer than one month, it is best to overwrap the original container with freezer paper or wrap.

Once the container has been opened, place plastic wrap over the surface of the ice cream to minimize the development of large ice crystals and the loss of its creamy texture. Use ice cream within seven to 10 days for best quality. Each time the ice cream is removed from the freezer, and the surface begins to thaw, the ice cream loses quality. If ice cream or other frozen dairy products thaw completely, they should be discarded because of the danger of bacterial growth.

SAFE HANDLING OF PORK

SELECTING THE BEST

Fresh is Best

When buying pork, look for cuts with a relatively small amount of fat over the outside and with meat that is firm and a grayish-pink color. For best flavor and tenderness, meat should have a small amount of marbling. Look for packages that are cool to the touch and have no wear or punctures. Always remember to select meat just before checking out at the supermarket register. Make sure all meats, whether raw, pre-packaged or from the deli are refrigerated when purchased. Fresh meats may contaminate other grocery items.

The best way to prevent this "cross-contamination" is to always keep fresh meats separate from other items. Put raw meat packages in a plastic bag so juices won't drip onto other foods. Pack raw meats in an ice chest if it will take more than an hour to get home. Keep ice chest in the passenger area of the car during warm weather. Take meats straight home to the refrigerator or freezer.

STORING

Refrigeration

Keep pork below 40 °F during storage. Store uncooked pork items together, separate from cooked foods. Refrigerate or freeze fresh pork Immediately after bringing it home. Never leave meat in a hot car or sitting out at room temperature. Packaged whole cuts of fresh pork may be refrigerated in their original wrapping in the coldest part of the refrigerator up to four or five days after purchase, while ground pork can be stored in the refrigerator for up to two days. Keep pork refrigerated until you are ready to cook it. When transporting uncooked or cooked pork to another dining site, place it in an insulated container or ice chest until ready to cook or eat. Cooked pork is at its best when refrigerated no longer than four days.

Table. Safe Handling of Pork in Cold Storage

Food	Refrigerator (40 °F)	Freezer (0 °F)
Fresh Pork:		
Roast, chops or ribs	3-5 Days	4-6 Months
Ground pork, liver or variety meats	1-2 Days	3-4 Months
Ham (Uncured)	3-5 Days	4-6 Months
Ham (Cured)	5-7 Days	3-4 Months
Cooked Pork:		
Roast, chops, casseroles	3-4 Days	2-3 Months
Ground pork; store-cooked convenience meals	1-2 Days	2-3 Months
Ham (Uncured)	3-4 Days	3-4 Months
Ham (Cured)	3-5 Days	1-2 Months

Freezing

Freeze whole cuts of fresh pork if you do not plan to cook it within four days after purchase. Wrap whole cuts of pork separately in foil or freezer bags before freezing, and label for ease in selecting just the right number of cuts to thaw for a single meal. Be sure to press the air out of the package before freezing. If you plan to freeze pork in its original wrapping, overwrap the porous store plastic with freezer bag or paper. Cooked pork cuts may be frozen in the same way as fresh, unless made with a sauce or gravy. In that case, pack the meat in a rigid container with a tight-fitting lid.

PREPARATION

Cleanliness

Always wash hands thoroughly with hot, soapy water before preparing foods and after handling raw meat. Don't let raw meat or juices touch ready-to-go foods either in the refrigerator or during preparation. Don't put cooked foods on the same plate that held raw pork. Always wash utensils that have touched raw meat with hot, soapy water before using them for cooked meats. Wash counters, cutting boards and other surfaces raw meats have touched.

Thawing

Thaw uncooked pork in the refrigerator, in cold water or in the microwave oven. Never thaw meat at room temperature. Allow a 24-hour thawing period in the refrigerator. After defrosting raw pork by this method, it will be safe in the refrigerator up to five days before cooking or, if you decide not to use the pork, you can safely refreeze it without cooking it first. To thaw pork in cold water, leave the meat in its original wrapping or place it in a watertight plastic bag. Change the water every 30 minutes. To thaw pork in the microwave, plan on cooking the meat immediately after thawing because some areas of the food may become warm and begin to cook during microwaving, and any bacteria present wouldn't have been destroyed. Thawing time will vary according to whether you're thawing a whole roast or cuts and the number of parts frozen together.

Use the Defrost or Medium-Low setting, according to the manufacturer's directions. Turn the roast and separate parts as they thaw, taking care the meat does not begin to cook Foods defrosted by the cold water method or in the microwave should be cooked before refreezing because they potentially may have been held at temperatures above 40 °F. It is safe to cook frozen pork in the oven, or on the stove or grill without defrosting. Estimate one-third to one-half more cooking time depending upon the size of the meat. Broil frozen pork farther away from the heat source; preheat the skillet when pan-frying or pan-broiling. Do not cook frozen pork in a slow cooker.

Marinating

Marinate food in the refrigerator, not on the counter. Discard the marinade after use because it contains raw juices, which may harbor bacteria. If you want to use the marinade as a dip or sauce, reserve a portion before adding raw food, or boil used marinade before brushing on cooked pork.

Partial Cooking or Browning

Never brown or partially cook pork, then refrigerate and finish cooking later, because any bacteria present would not have been destroyed. It is safe to partially pre-cook or microwave pork and lamb immediately before transferring it to the hot grill or oven to finish cooking.

SAFE HANDLING OF POULTRY

SELECTING THE BEST

Fresh poultry — chicken, turkey, duck and goose — is defined by the USDA as poultry that has never been below 26 °F. When held at temperatures ranging from 26 to 40 °F, there is minimal ice crystal formation and poultry meat is still soft and pliable. There should be no detectable odor.

The surface should not be slick nor have a shiny appearance, and should not have color defects:

- Look for packages that are cool to the touch and have no tears, punctures, torn or missing labels.
- Always remember to select poultry just before checking out at the register.
- Make sure all poultry, whether raw, prepackaged or from the deli is refrigerated before and after it is purchased.
- Prevent cross-contamination by keeping fresh meats separate from

other items. Put raw poultry packages in a plastic bag so "juices" won't drip onto other foods. If raw poultry "juices" do drip on other foods, it is best to throw these other items out and immediately wash surfaces and hands.

- Pack raw poultry in an ice chest if it will take you more than an hour to get home and keep the ice chest in the passenger area of the car during warm weather.
- Take poultry straight home to the refrigerator or freezer.

Dating of Poultry Products

Product dating is not required by federal regulations. However, many stores and processors may voluntarily date packages of poultry or poultry products. If a calendar date is shown, there must be a phrase explaining the meaning of the date. Consumers should use or freeze poultry products within one or two days of purchase. If the manufacturer has determined a "use-by" date, observe it for peak quality and freshness. It 's always best to buy a product before its date expires. If a date expires after the poultry is frozen, the food can still be used. However, quality begins to deteriorate after one year of frozen storage for whole poultry and nine months of frozen storage for poultry parts.

Product Inspection & Grading

All poultry found in retail stores is either USDA-inspected for wholesomeness and safety, or inspected by state systems using standards equal to the federal government. Prior to entering the processing plant, live birds are inspected for signs of disease. Diseased birds are immediately condemned and do not enter the processing plant. In the plant, each animal and its internal organs are again inspected for signs of disease. The "Passed and Inspected by USDA" seal ensures that the poultry is wholesome and free from disease.

Inspection is mandatory, but grading for quality is voluntary. Poultry are graded according to USDA regulations and standards for meatiness, appearance and freedom from defects. Grade A chickens, the best grade, have plump, meaty bodies and clean skin, free of bruises, broken bones, feathers, cuts and discoloration.

Prestuffed Poultry

Buying retail-stuffed whole poultry is not recommended because of the highly perishable nature of a previously stuffed item. Some USDA-inspected frozen stuffed poultry MUST be cooked from the frozen state to ensure a safely cooked product. Many frozen entrées containing stuffed boneless poultry products may appear to be pre-cooked or browned, but they are NOT ready-to-eat and must be fully cooked by the consumer. If the label states "Cook and Serve," "Ready to Cook," or "Oven Ready" this indicates that the product is raw and must be fully cooked by the consumer. The safest way to cook these products is in a conventional oven. If a microwave oven is used, these poultry products should be covered to allow steam to build, and then allowed to stand for the recommended time to ensure that there are no "cold spots". Check the internal temperature in several places to make sure the product has been cooked throughout to at least 165 °F

STORAGE

Refrigeration

Packaged fresh poultry may be refrigerated in its original wrapping in the coldest part of the refrigerator for up to two days. Cooked, cut-up poultry is at its best when refrigerated no longer than two days; cooked, whole poultry may be stored for three days.

- Use an appliance thermometer to make sure refrigerator temperature is set at 34 to 38 °F. Also check the meat compartment for proper temperatures.
- Never leave poultry in a hot car or sitting out at room temperature. Refrigerate or freeze fresh poultry Immediately after bringing it home.
- Store uncooked poultry items together, separate from cooked foods. Make sure the raw juices do not drip onto other foods.
- Keep poultry refrigerated until you are ready to cook it, or in an ice chest for carry out.

Freezing

Freeze fresh poultry if you do not plan to cook it within two days after purchase. Avoid freezer burn by using heavy-duty foil, or moisture-and vapor-proof freezer bags or plastic wraps that keep out oxygen. Be sure to press the air out of the package before freezing. Wrap chicken parts separately and label for ease in selecting just the right number of parts to thaw for a single meal. Poultry may also be frozen in its original wrap if it is first overwrapped in freezer-appropriate packaging to prevent quality loss. Cooked parts may be frozen in the same way as fresh, unless made with a sauce or gravy. In that case, pack the chicken in a rigid freezer container with a tight-fitting lid.

PREPARATION

Cleanliness

Always wash hands thoroughly with hot, soapy water before preparing foods and after handling raw poultry. Don't let raw poultry or juices touch ready-to-eat foods either in the refrigerator or during preparation. Don't put cooked foods on the same plate that previously held raw poultry. Always wash utensils that have touched raw poultry with hot, soapy water before using them for the cooked poultry. Wash counters, cutting boards and other surfaces raw poultry have touched. Sanitize these surfaces with a solution of a teaspoon of chlorine bleach per quart of water before using for other foods.

Thawing

Thaw uncooked poultry in the refrigerator or in cold water. Never thaw poultry at room temperature. To thaw poultry in cold water, leave the poultry in its original wrapping or place it in a watertight plastic bag. Change the water every 30 minutes. Be sure to clean and sanitize the sink, bowl or dish used to thaw poultry. For quick thawing of uncooked or cooked poultry, use the microwave. Thawing time will vary according to whether you're thawing whole poultry or parts, and the number of parts frozen together. Use the Defrost or Medium-Low setting, according to the manufacturer's directions. Turn poultry and separate parts as they thaw; taking care the meat does not begin to cook. Repeat as needed. Cook poultry immediately after thawing in the microwave oven.

Marinating

Marinate poultry in the refrigerator, not at room temperature. Discard the marinade after use because it contains raw juices, which may harbor bacteria. Use leftover marinade as a sauce only if first brought to a rolling boil for one minute.

COOKING

Importance of Kitchen Thermometers

One of the critical factors for minimizing bacteria in food is controlling temperature. Most pathogenic microorganisms grow very slowly at low temperatures, multiply rapidly in mid-range temperatures and are killed at high temperatures. For safety, foods must be cooked thoroughly. It is essential to use a thermometer when cooking meat and poultry to prevent undercooking and food borne illness. Using a thermometer is the only reliable way to ensure safety and to determine the "doneness" of most foods. To be safe, a product must be cooked to an internal temperature high enough to destroy any harmful bacteria that may have been in the food. Color and texture changes in meat and poultry cannot be relied on to determine that foods have been safely cooked to destroy all bacteria.

All poultry and all stuffing, whether cooked alone or in the bird, must be cooked to an internal temperature of at least 165 °F. For reasons of personal taste or texture preferences, consumers may choose to cook poultry to higher temperatures. When cooking whole turkey, the thermometer should be inserted into the thickest part of the thigh, without touching the bone. For chicken, and other smaller poultry, insert the thermometer in the thickest part of the breast. If stuffed, the center of the stuffing should be checked after the thigh or breast reaches 165 °F. If cooking poultry parts, insert the thermometer into the thickest area, avoiding the bone. The thermometer may be inserted sideways if necessary.

When the food being cooked is irregularly shaped, the temperature should be checked in several places. Sometimes consumers will notice a pink color in fully-cooked poultry. Commercial marinades may have a small amount of nitrites or nitrates which gives poultry a pink color even when it is fully cooked.

Ground Chicken or Turkey

Ground meats must be cooked thoroughly to kill harmful bacteria. Unlike whole muscle meat, whose interior meat is sterile, the grinding process exposes the interior meat in ground poultry to bacteria, which may be on the surface, in the air, on equipment or on people's hands. To kill bacteria, food safety experts have one major rule of thumb: Cook ground poultry to at least 165 °F. This step, while very simple, offers the best protection that consumers can have for serving ground poultry products safely.

SERVING

Wash hands with soap and water before serving or eating food:

- Serve cooked products on clean plates with clean utensils and clean hands. Never put cooked foods on a dish that has held raw poultry unless the dish is washed with soap and hot water.
- Hold hot foods above 140 °F and cold foods below 40 °F.
- Never leave foods, raw or cooked, at room temperature longer than two hours. On a hot day with temperatures at 90 °F or warmer, this decreases to one hour.

LEFTOVERS

Always use clean utensils and storage containers for safe storage:

- Divide large amounts of leftovers into small, shallow containers for quick cooling in the refrigerator; avoid placing large pots of stuffing or gravy in the refrigerator to cool since it will likely take until the next day for this amount of food to cool.
- Remove the stuffing from whole poultry and carve the meat off the bones. Store meat and stuffing separately in the refrigerator or freezer.
- For storage in the refrigerator, wrap cooked meat and use within three days. For frozen storage, wrap meat in heavy foil, freezer wrap or place in freezer container. For optimum taste use frozen stuffing within one month and frozen turkey within two months.
- If you may have kept the food refrigerated for too long, throw it out. Never taste food that looks or smells strange to see if you can still use it.

Always use a thermometer to check proper internal temperatures to make sure poultry is thoroughly cooked. All poultry should be cooked to a minimum safe internal temperature of at least 165 °F. For reasons of personal taste or texture preferences, consumers may choose to cook poultry to higher temperatures.

SAFE HANDLING OF SAUSAGES & HOT DOGS

SELECTING THE BEST SAUSAGE

There are so many varieties of sausages! How long can you store them— and where? Are they fully cooked or not? The following background information will answer these questions and others. Use the storage chart as a guideline for proper handling.

Types of Sausages

Sausages are either ready to eat or not. They can be made from red meat, poultry or a combination. Uncooked sausages include fresh and smoked sausages. Ready-to-eat sausages are dry, semi-dry and/or cooked. Dry sausages may be smoked, unsmoked or cooked. Semi-dry sausages are usually heated in the smokehouse to fully cook the product and partially dry it.

Sausage Labeling Information

Let the label be your guide to sausage selection, handling and — if applicable — cooking. It will list the safe handling and cooking instructions, the nutrient content and the ingredients. Safe handling instructions are mandatory for all raw or partially cooked meat and poultry products. The label must say "Keep Refrigerated" if the sausage is perishable. Product dating is optional but the manufacturer may have affixed a date.

All ingredients in the product must be listed in the ingredient statement in order of predominance from the one weighing the most listed first to the one weighing the least listed last. For sausage products packaged under federal inspection, a Nutrition Facts panel is mandatory. If sausages are made and packaged in a local store, the nutrient information on the package is voluntary. The Nutrition Facts information on the label can help consumers compare products and make more informed, healthy food choices.

SAUSAGE DEFINED

Fresh Sausages

Fresh sausages are a coarse or finely ground meat food product prepared from one or more kinds of meat, or meat and meat by-products. They may contain water not exceeding 3 percent of the total ingredients in the product. They are usually seasoned, frequently cured and may contain binders and extenders.

They must be kept refrigerated and be thoroughly cooked before eating:

- *Fresh Pork Sausages*: May not contain pork by-products and no more than 50 percent fat by weight.
- *Fresh Beef Sausages*: May not include beef by-products and no more than 30 percent fat by weight.
- *Breakfast Sausages*: May contain meat and meat by-products and no more than 50 percent fat by weight.
- *Whole Hog Sausage*: Meat from swine in such proportions as are normal to a single animal and no more than 50 percent fat by weight.
- *Italian Sausage Products*: Cured or uncured sausages containing at least 85 percent meat, or a combination of meat and fat, with the total fat content constituting not more than 35 percent of the finished product. They contain salt, pepper, fennel and/or anise and no more than 3 percent water. Optional ingredients permitted in Italian sausages are spices and flavorings, red or green peppers, onions, garlic and parsley, sugar, dextrose and corn syrup.

Cooked and/or Smoked Sausages

These products are made of one or more different kinds of chopped or ground meats that have been seasoned, cooked and/or smoked. Water can be no more than 10 percent by weight. Meat by-products may be used.

Included in this category are:

- Salami
- Bratwurst
- Liverwurst
- Braunschweiger
- Hot Dogs
- Blood Sausage
- Bologna
- Jellied Beef Loaf
- Knockwurst
- Thuringer-Style

Cooked salami is made from fresh meats that are cured, stuffed into casings and cooked in a smokehouse at high temperature. It may be air-dried for a short time. It has a softer texture than dry and semi-dry sausages and must be refrigerated.

Meat Specialties

A ready-to-eat sausage product that is made from finely ground meats that are seasoned and usually cooked or baked rather than smoked. They are usually sliced and served cold.

Included in this category are:

- Chopped Ham Loaf
- Luncheon Meat

- Peppered Loaf
- Head Cheese
- Jellied Corned Beef
- Ham and Cheese Loaf
- Honey Loaf
- Old Fashioned Loaf
- Olive Loaf
- Pickle and Pimento Loaf
- Scrapple
- Souse
- Veal Loaf

Dry & Semi-Dry Sausages

Dry sausages may or may not be characterized by a bacterial fermentation. When fermented, the intentional encouragement of a lactic acid bacteria growth is useful as a meat preservative as well as producing the typical tangy flavor. The ingredients are mixed with spices and curing materials, stuffed into casings, and put through a carefully controlled, long, continuous air-drying process. Dry sausages require more production time than other types of sausage that results in a concentrated form of meat. Medium-dry sausage is about 70 percent of its "green" weight when sold. Green weight is the weight of the raw article before addition of added substances or before cooking. Less-dry and fully-dried sausages range from 80 percent to 60 percent of original weight at completion.

Dry sausages include:

- Chorizo
- Frizzes
- Pepperoni
- Lola or Lolita and Lyons sausage
- Genoa salami

Semi-dry sausages are usually heated in the smokehouse to fully cook the product and partially dry it. Semi-dry sausages are semi-soft sausages with good keeping qualities due to their lactic acid fermentation. "Summer Sausage" is the general classification for mildly seasoned, smoked, semi-dry sausages like Mortadella and Lebanon bologna.

WHO SHOULD AVOID EATING DRY SAUSAGES

Because dry sausages are not cooked, the elderly, very young children, pregnant women and those with weakened immune systems might want to avoid eating them. The bacterium E. coli O157:H7 has been found to survive the process of dry fermenting, and in 1994, some children and adults became ill after eating dry cured salami containing the bacteria. This is believed to be the first time that this product has been associated with E. coli O157:H7. These illnesses have raised some questions about the effectiveness of processes for producing dry fermented sausage free of this deadly organism. The USDA is looking at ways to identify and correct potential problems in dry sausage products, and is developing procedures for manufacturers to ensure their processing is adequate to destroy bacteria.

STORAGE OF SAUSAGE

All sausage – except dry sausage – is perishable and therefore should be brought directly home when purchased and refrigerated or frozen.

DATE ON PACKAGE OF PROCESSED MEATS

Although dating is a voluntary program and not mandated by the federal government, if a date is used it must state what the date means. Since none is a safety date, the product can be used after the date, provided it was stored safely.

Follow the guidelines, for maximum quality in sausage products:

- "Packaging" date is the date of manufacturing, processing, or final packaging."Sell-by" date is the last day a retail store may offer the food for sale. You should buy the product before the date expires, and then use according to the guidelines in the storage chart for maximum quality and safety.
- "Sell-by" date is the last day a retail store may offer the food for sale. You should buy the product before the date expires, and then use according to the guidelines in the storage chart for maximum quality and safety.
- "Best if used by" date tells when the product should be used for best flavor and quality. It is not a purchase or safety date.
- "Use-by" date is the date after which peak quality of the product begins to decrease, but the product may still be used.
- "Expiration" date marks the end of the product's useful life or the last day to be used.

SELECTING THE BEST HOT DOGS

Types of Hot Dogs

Whether you call it a frankfurter, hot dog, wiener or bologna, it's a cooked sausage and a summertime favorite. They can be made from beef, pork, turkey or chicken – the label must specify which. All ingredients in the product must be listed in the ingredient statement in order of predominance from the one weighing the most listed first to the one weighing the least listed last. And there are federal standards for their content. Smoking and curing ingredients contribute to flavor, color and preservation of the product. They come in all shapes and sizes – short, long, thin and chubby. The most popular of all categories, the skinless varieties, have been stripped of their casings after cooking. Water or ice may be used to facilitate chopping or mixing or to dissolve curing ingredients. Sausages may contain no more than 10 percent water and 30 percent fat or a combination of 40 percent fat and added water. Up to 3.5 percent nonmeat binders and extenders such as nonfat dry milk, cereal, dried whole milk or 2 percent isolated soy protein may be used, but must be shown in the ingredient statement by its common name.

By-Products, Variety Meats

Frankfurters, hot dogs, wieners or bologna "with by-products" or "with variety meats" are made according to the specifications for cooked smoked sausages except they consist of not less than 15 percent of one or more kinds of raw skeletal muscle meat with raw meat by-products. The by-products must be accompanied by the name of the species from which it was derived and must be individually named in the ingredient statement.

Species

Beef franks or pork franks are cooked, smoked sausage products made according to the specifications above, but with meat from a single species and do not include by-products. Turkey franks or chicken franks contain turkey or chicken skin and fat in natural proportions of that found on a turkey or chicken carcass.

Mechanically Separated Meat or Poultry

Carcass parts from which most of the meat has been removed still have usable meat attached. These parts are pushed under high pressure through equipment with openings so fine that a small amount of powdered bone the size of a grain of sand may pass through along with the remaining muscle meat and other soft tissue.

This is called "mechanically separated" meat, and if used in a product, the label must state it. If a serving contains 20 mg or more of calcium from the finely powdered bone, the label must give the calcium content as a percentage of the US RDAs.

Mechanically Deboned Poultry

This does not have the same requirements as mechanically separated meat and is simply listed in the ingredients statement as "chicken" or "turkey."

Handling of Hot Dogs

When you leave the grocery store with any kind of sausage, head straight home and refrigerate or freeze it immediately. If there is a date on the package, follow those guidelines for use. If there is no date, hot dogs can be safely stored unopened in the refrigerator for up to two weeks. Once opened, they are safe in the refrigerator for only one week. For maximum quality, freeze hot dogs no longer than one to two months. Never leave hot dogs at room temperature for more than two hours, or in the hot summer months when the temperature rises to 90 °F or above, for more than one hour. Finally, even though hot dogs are fully cooked, if you choose to reheat them

Table. Sausage & Hot Dog Storage Chart (for products with a "Sell-By" date or no date)

Type of Sausage	Refrigerator Storage-Unopened	Refrigerator Storage-after Opening
Fresh Sausage, uncooked	1 to 2 Days	1 to 2 Days
Fresh Sausage, after cooking by the consumer	(Not Applicable)	3 to 4 Days
Hard/Dry Sausage	Indefinitely in Refrigerator; 6 Weeks in Pantry	3 Weeks in Refrigerator, or Until It Turns Rancid
Hot Dogs and Other Cooked Sausage	2 Weeks but No Longer than 1 Week After the "Sell-by" Date	7 Days
Summer Sausage (Semi-dry)	3 Months	3 Weeks

Freeze the product if you cannot use it within the times recommended above for refrigerator storage. Once frozen, it does not matter if the date expires, because all foods kept frozen continuously are safe indefinitely. However, for best quality, use within 1 to 2 months.

SAFE HANDLING OF VEAL

WHAT IS VEAL

Veal is the meat from a calf or young beef animal. A veal calf is raised until about 16 to 18 weeks of age, weighing up to 450 pounds. Male dairy calves are used in the veal industry. Dairy cows must give birth to continue producing milk, but male dairy calves are of little or no value to the dairy farmer. A small percentage are raised to maturity and used for breeding. A calf is a young bovine of either sex that has not reached puberty and has a maximum live weight of 750 pounds. "Bob" veal is a veal calf marketed up to 3 weeks of age or at a weight of 150 pounds. "Special-Fed" veal is usually fed nutritionally balanced milk or soy based diets. These specially controlled diets contain iron and 40 other essential nutrients. The majority of veal calves are "special-fed".

SELECTING THE BEST

Choose veal in the fresh meat case that is grayish pink in color and firm to the touch. Vacuum packaged veal in the self-serve case will be more maroon in color because it has not been exposed to oxygen. Look for packages that are cool to the touch, have no wear or punctures, and little or no excess liquid. Always check the "sell-by" date. Purchase raw meats last. Make sure all meats - whether raw, pre-packaged or from the deli are kept refrigerated. Fresh meats may contaminate other grocery items. The best way to prevent this cross-contamination is to always keep fresh meats from other items. Put raw meat packages in a plastic bag so juices won't drip onto other foods. Pack raw meats in an ice chest if it will take more than an hour to get home. Keep ice chest in the passenger area of the car during warm weather. Take meats straight home to the refrigerator or freezer.

Product Dating

Product dating, applying "sell-by" or "use-by" dates, is not required by federal regulations. However, many stores and processors may voluntarily choose to date packages of raw veal or processed veal products. Use or freeze products with a "sell-by" date within three to five days of purchase. If the manufacturer has determined a "use-by" date, observe it. It's always best to buy a product before its date expires. It's not important if a date expires after freezing veal, because all foods stay safe while properly frozen.

Product Inspection & Grading

All veal found in retail stores is either USDA-inspected for wholesomeness or inspected by state systems which have standards equal to the federal government. Each animal and its internal organs are inspected for signs of disease.

The "Passed and Inspected by USDA" seal ensures that the veal is wholesome and free from disease. Although inspection is mandatory, its grading for quality is voluntary, and a plant pays to have its veal graded. Quality grade refers to the eating quality of the meat. Veal and calf carcasses are graded on a composite evaluation of two general grade factors: conformation and quality of the lean. In addition, the color of the lean carcasses is key in differentiating between veal, calf and beef carcasses. The five grades for veal are as follows: prime, choice, good, standard and utility.

Retail Cuts

There are seven basic major cuts into which veal is separated: leg, sirloin, loin, rib, shoulder, foreshank and breast. When examining a package of veal, the label can help the purchaser identify the meat in the package. For example, a label stating "veal rib chop" identifies the packaged meat as "veal", the primal or large wholesale cut from the "rib", and the name of the retail cut as "chop". This information helps consumers know what type of preparation method to use.

The most readily available cuts of veal today include rib chops, loin chops, veal for stew, cutlets, arm steak, blade steak, rib roast, breast, shanks and round steak.

STORAGE

Refrigeration

Keep veal below 40 °F during storage. Store uncooked veal items together, separate from cooked foods. Refrigerate or freeze fresh veal Immediately after bringing it home. Never leave veal in a hot car or sitting out at room temperature. Packaged whole cuts of fresh veal may be refrigerated in their original wrappings in the coldest part of the refrigerator for three to five days after purchase, while ground veal can be stored in the refrigerator for one or two days.

Keep veal refrigerated until you are ready to cook it. When transporting cooked veal to another dining site, place it in an insulated container or ice chest until ready to eat. Cooked whole cuts of veal are at their best when refrigerated no longer than two to three days. Cooked ground veal is best when refrigerated no longer than one or two days.

Freezing

Freeze whole cuts of fresh veal if you do not plan to cook it within three to five days after purchase. Freeze ground veal if you do not plan to cook it within one to two days after purchase. Wrap veal parts separately in aluminum foil or freezer paper before freezing, and label for ease in selecting just the right number of parts to thaw for a single meal. Be sure to press the air out of the package before freezing. If you plan to freeze veal in its original wrapping, overwrap with freezer bag or paper. Cooked parts may be frozen in the same way as fresh, unless made with a sauce or gravy; in that case, pack in a rigid container with a tightfitting lid.

PREPARATION

Cleanliness

Always wash hands thoroughly with hot soapy water before preparing foods and after handling raw veal. Don't let raw meat or juices touch ready-to-go foods either in the refrigerator or during preparation. Don't put cooked foods on the same plate that held raw veal. Always wash utensils that have touched raw meat with hot, soapy water before using them for cooked meats. Wash counters, cutting boards and other surfaces raw meats have touched.

Thawing

Thaw uncooked veal in the refrigerator or in cold water. Never thaw veal at room temperature. Allow a 24-hour thawing period. After defrosting raw veal by this method, it will be safe in the refrigerator for up to five days before cooking, or, if you decide not to use the veal, you can safely refreeze it without cooking it first. To thaw veal in cold water, leave the veal in its original wrapping or place it in a watertight plastic bag. Change the water every 30 minutes. For quick thawing of uncooked or cooked veal, use the microwave, but plan on cooking the meat immediately after thawing, because some areas of the food may become warm and begin to cook during microwaving. Thawing time will vary according to whether you're thawing a whole roast or cuts and the number of parts frozen together.

Use the Defrost or Medium-Low setting, according to the manufacturer's directions. Turn the roast and separate parts as they thaw, taking care the meat does not begin to cook.

Repeat as needed. Foods defrosted by the cold water method or in the microwave should be cooked before refreezing, because they may have been held at temperatures above 40 °F.

Table. Safe Handling of Veal in Cold Storage

Product	Refrigerator (40°F)	Freezer (0°F)
Raw Whole Cuts of Veal: Chops, roasts and steaks	3-5 Days	4-6 Months
Raw Ground Veal & Stew	1-2 Days	3-4 Months
Broiled, Fried, Grilled or Roasted Veal	2-3 Days	2-3 Months
Cooked Ground Veal & Gravies Made From Veal	1-2 Days	2-3 Months

It is safe to cook frozen veal in the oven, or on the stove or grill without defrosting. Estimate one-third to one-half more cooking time depending upon the size of the meat. Broil frozen veal farther away from the heat source; preheat the skillet when pan-frying or pan-broiling. Do not cook frozen veal in a slow cooker.

Marinating

Marinate food in the refrigerator, not on the counter. Boil used marinade before brushing on cooked veal. Discard any uncooked, leftover marinade after use because it contains raw juices, which may harbor bacteria.

Rinsing

There is no need to rinse raw veal before cooking. Any bacteria that might be present on the surface would be destroyed by cooking.

Partial Cooking or Browning

Never brown or partially cook veal, then refrigerate and finish cooking later, because any bacteria present would not have been destroyed. It is safe to partially precook or microwave veal IMMEDIATELY before transferring it to a hot grill or oven to finish cooking.

COOKING

Importance of Kitchen Thermometers

One of the critical factors in controlling bacteria in food is controlling temperature. Pathogenic microorganisms grow very slowly at low temperatures multiply rapidly in mid-range temperatures, and are killed at high temperatures. For safety, foods must be cooked thoroughly. It is essential to use a meat thermometer when cooking veal to prevent undercooking and, consequently, prevent food borne illness. Using a thermometer is the only reliable way to ensure safety and to determine the "doneness" of most foods. To be safe, a product must be cooked to an internal temperature high enough to destroy any harmful bacteria that may have been in the food.

Recent research has shown that color and texture indicators are not reliable. When cooking whole cuts or parts of veal, the thermometer should be inserted into the thickest part of the meat, away from the bone, fat and gristle. The thermometer may be inserted sideways if necessary. When the food being cooked is irregularly shaped, the temperature should be checked in several places.

Table. Approximate Veal Cooking Times

Types of Veal	Size	Cooking Method	Cooking Times	Internal Temperature
Rib Roast	4 to 5 lbs.	Roast 325 °F	25 to 27 min/lb. 29 to 31 min/lb.	Cook at least to an internal
Loin	3 to 4 lbs. 38 to 40 min/lb.	Roast 325 °F 145 °F with a	34 to 36 min/lb. 4 minute rest	temperature of
Loin/Rib Chops	1" thick or 8 oz.	Broil/Grill	7 min. per side 8 to 9 min per side	
Cutlets	1/8" thick ¼" thick	*Pan Fry	3 to 4 min. 5 to 6 min.	
Arm/Blade Steak	¾"thick 16 oz.	Broil/Grill	7 min per side 8 min. per side	
Cross Cut Shanks	1½" thick	Cover with liquid; simmer	1 to 1¼ hrs.	
Stew Meat	1 to 1½" cubes/pieces	Cover with liquid; simmer	45 to 60 min	
Round Steak	¼" thick ½" thick	**Braise	30 min 45 min.	

Notes: *Pan frying, which is often called "sautéing," is a quick cooking method. Meat is placed in small amount of heated oil and cooked on medium-high heat.

**Braising is roasting or simmering less tender meats with a small amount of liquid in a tightly covered pan.

Whole Muscle Meats

Cook whole cuts of meat to a minimum internal temperature of 145 °F for medium-rare, with a 4 minute rest before carving or eating or 160 °F for medium-cooked whole cuts of meat, and 170 °F for well-done cuts.

Ground Veal

Ground veal must be cooked thoroughly to kill harmful bacteria. Unlike whole muscle meat that is sterile inside, the grinding process exposes the interior meat in ground veal to bacteria that may be on the surface, in the air, on equipment or on people's hands. To kill these bacteria, food safety experts have one major rule of thumb—cook ground veal to at least 155 °F. This step, while very simple, offers the best protection that consumers have to serve ground veal safely.

Microwaving

When microwaving unequal size pieces of veal, arrange in a dish or on a rack so thick parts are toward the outside of the dish and thin parts are in the center, and cook on medium-high or medium power. Place a roast in an oven-cooking bag or in a covered pot. Refer to the manufacturer's directions that accompany the microwave oven for suggested cooking times. Use a microwave-safe thermometer inserted before cooking, or removes meat from microwave oven and use a digital meat thermometer in several places to be sure correct temperatures have been reached. Meats cooked in the microwave oven must be cooked to a minimum internal temperature of 165 °F and allowed to stand covered at least 2 minutes. Follow standing or rest times given.

5

Improvements in the Production and Marketing of Food

STRUCTURAL AID

Reference has been made in earlier chapters to Reg. 17/64 on the conditions for granting aid from the *European Agricultural Guidance and Guarantee Fund*: in setting out the requirements which a project had to meet before it qualified for structural aid, where the Community Programmes were outlined. These Programmes should have provided the sectoral and regional framework for aid but, as already indicated, they were never put in place and the derogation in Reg. 17/64, which allowed individual projects to be grant-aided for the first two years, continued throughout the lifetime of this Regulation, i.e. to the end of the 1970s. Article 11 of Reg. 17/64 set out the broad purposes for which FEOGA Guidance funds would be available.

They were:

1. The adaptation and improvement of conditions of production in agriculture;
2. The adaptation and guidance of agricultural production;
3. The adaptation and improvement of the marketing of agricultural products;
4. The development of outlets for agricultural products.

Marketing projects were limited to products which were subject to common price and market regimes but, as the range of commodities within the price policy expanded, this was no obstacle. Article 12 provided an interpretation of the four categories listed in Article 11 and it is interesting, even at such an early stage in the history of the CAP, that 'the adaptation and guidance of production' meant 'the quantitative adaptation of production to outlets' and 'improvements in the quality of the products'.

During the 1960s—and indeed for a large part of the 1970s—Reg. 17/64 provided the main source of funds for structural reform. The range of activities covered by the Regulation was very wide, encompassing production and marketing projects, and those which were a mixture of the two. Over the lifetime of the Regulation, projects to improve production structures received 53 per cent of the funding, marketing structures 41 per cent, and mixed projects 6 per cent.

Table: 17/64: Breakdown of Aid Granted by Sector, Cumulatively 1964-1979

Sector	No. of projects	Total 1964-79 ('000 ua/EUA)	Aid granted %
Land improvement and hydraulic works	2,417	683,602	32.3
Milk	709	241,227	11.4
Wine	727	245,461	11.6
Fruit and vegetables	685	137,456	6.5
Meat	775	226,176	10.7
Olives	214	45,139	2.1
Cereals	203	55,061	2.6
Forestry	227	59,790	2.8
Fisheries	475	86,210	4.1
Animal feed	124	40,174	1.9
Flowers and plants	56	15,884	0.8
Eggs and poultrymeat	110	20,362	1.0
Seeds and nurseries	87	16,009	0.8
Research and advisory services	98	24,264	1.1
Sugar	3	4,188	0.2
Miscellaneous	546	214,143	10.1
Commission 1980(*b*).	7,456	2,115,146	100.0

The Community contribution to the investment was initially very low at 25 per cent for all projects but, in 1973, this was raised to 45 per cent of eligible expenditure in projects related to production, with the beneficiary only having to provide a minimum of 20 per cent of the cost (originally a minimum of 30 per cent). Thus, right from the beginning, the Community element in structural legislation was low, unlike the price and market policy where, by the end of the 1960s, FEOGA-Guarantee was providing 100 per cent of the support. However, it should be noted that, for structural measures generally, the tendency over time has been for the Community contribution to rise, particularly in the poorer regions or in the poorer Member States.

During its lifetime, Reg. 17/64 was extremely popular and far more projects were submitted for funding each year than were ultimately aided. Table above provides a summary of the sectoral distribution of aid, 1964-1979. Three sectors —milk, wine, and meat—accounted for one-third of the aid; land improvement and hydraulic works accounted for about another third; and all other purposes the remainder.

The result was that the better-off farmers and the more prosperous farming regions were benefiting disproportionately from all aspects of the CAP. An interdepartmental group within the Commission reported *inter alia* on this issue, and its findings in relation to the regional impact of Dir. 72/159 have already been discussed.

As to the regional impact of Reg. 17/64, if it had been operating as originally intended, each Community Programme would have had specified zones of principal action within which investment aid would have been concentrated. The Commission had estimated that, as a general rule, these zones would have represented about one-third of the designated area or other appropriate measure, such as volume of production.

In reality, in Reg. 17/64, there was no provision for regional differentiation of aid, rather the funds available were allocated to the Member States according to a prearranged system of quotas. Thus, prior to Enlargement, Italy received annually an allocation of just under 34 per cent of available credits, Germany 28 per cent, France 22 per cent, and so forth. These percentages were adjusted downwards to accommodate the three new Member States after 1972.

The interdepartmental group was interested to examine how these national quotas had operated in practice and to compare them with the percentage distribution among the Member States of: (a) the agricultural labour force; (b) final agricultural production; (c) the simple average of (a) and (b), which in effect gave production weighted by the inverse of agricultural labour productivity; and (d) agricultural area. In no case did the quota exactly match any of these measures, although it came reasonably close to (c). For some countries the divergence was considerable—which was hardly surprising, as the quotas had been devised more on a basis of horse-trading than on any economic or social indicator.

Within some of the Member States, the group discovered that the quotas were apparently being divided by region, according to the size of the agricultural area. This meant that 'some of the relatively extensive and well-structured agricultural regions of the community (such as Schleswig-Holstein, Niedersachsen, Scotland, Emilia-Romagna, Toscana and Lazio) receive much higher expenditure than agricultural employment or structural criteria would suggest'. The group also commented on the considerable difference between expenditure commitments for Italy and actual payments: in 1964-72 it received about one-third of total commitments but only half that amount had been paid by 1974. Thus, even at this early stage, administrative difficulties were preventing Italy from gaining access to structural funds—a pattern that was to become familiar as the years went by.

It is of some interest to examine whether or not the perceived lack of balance between the need for structural improvement in poorer regions and the distribution of total payments from Reg. 17/64 persisted over the lifetime of the scheme. In 1989, the Commission published a cumulative regional breakdown of the aid granted. While Italy received the largest payments, and while the South and the islands received a considerable share of the total, Emilia-Romagna remained a main beneficiary, and Lazio received more than Sicily.

Germany, which received the second highest payments, still had Niedersachsen as its second highest recipient, although Schleswig-Holstein did not maintain its earlier position. In the UK, Scotland remained by far the largest recipient. In Belgium, the south is poorer than the north but received less aid, while in Ireland two regions—South-East and South-West—dominated, although the West and North-West were much poorer.

Table provides a summary by Member State of the total number of projects financed. Most were already completed by the end of 1992. About 11.5 per cent had been abandoned, for whatever reason, by far the greatest number of these were in Italy. Despite its late arrival, the UK made very good use of Reg. 17/64. Table also provides a summary by Member State of the aid granted, cumulatively to the end of 1992. This should be compared with the payments made, which forms the third part of the table. While the sources are not the same, which may have resulted in some discrepancies, in broad terms one can conclude that the account is nearly closed on this scheme. In Italy there is a considerable difference between aid granted and payments received, which presumably is a reflection of the large number of projects which were abandoned.

So the life of this extraordinary piece of legislation draws to a close. For so many years, it provided a link with the earliest days of the CAP and, in the distortions which so quickly developed in its operation, was a reminder of how soon in the life of the policy the politics of the CAP usurped the ideals of the original designers. However, some aspects of Reg. 17/64 have remained. In 1976, the interdepartmental group referred to earlier recommended that, when Reg. 17/64 ceased, its infrastructural aspects should be restricted geographically in any replacement legislation.

In a sense, this did occur with the measures which came into force in the late 1970s and early 1980s. However, it was not until the reorganization of the Structural Funds in the late 1980s that a more systematic approach to regional concentration of effort was introduced into the CAP. The aid to processing and marketing was carried forward with the enactment of Reg. 355/77.

The Establishment of Producer Groups

One of the most obvious features of agricultural production in Western Europe (and in many other parts of the world) is its organizational structure, dominated by small and medium-size independent farms. Production in such a framework comes very close to the economist's definition of a perfect market. Farmers are price-takers: they are very rarely in a position to dominate the market, even if they are organized into a commodity or special interest group. In general, they produce a homogeneous product and therefore cannot benefit from higher prices achieved through product differentiation. They are in a weak bargaining position, whether selling a product for direct consumption or for processing, and this is particularly true when the product is perishable (as with milk) or perishable and seasonal (as with fruit and vegetables).

The poor structural organization of agriculture was even more pronounced in the 1960s in the new Community than it is in the 1990s. Farming was characterized by a very large number of exceedingly small producers, each with an extensive range of products. This situation was not conducive to orderly marketing, particularly at a time when consumer demand was changing rapidly due to the marked increase in living standards.

What was required was regular supply, known and constant quality, and stable prices. It was essential that producers respond and that they took greater responsibility for the marketing of their own products. Vague references were made by the Commission as far back as the 1959 and 1960 proposals on the CAP to its intention to encourage initiatives by farmers' organizations, which would lead to better information on markets, to improve their stability, and their response to consumer demand.

The Commission reasoned that, if producers of the same commodity came together in an alliance, it would enable them collectively to improve the quality of their product by enforcing grading standards, and the continuity of supply, by having centralized storage and processing facilities. The group would market the output of its members, thereby improving their bargaining power and, as a result, obtaining a higher unit price. This in turn would help to further the aims of Art. 39.1 of the Rome Treaty, in particular as regards incomes, market stability, and supply availability.

These thoughts were carried a stage further in Reg. 26/62 on the application of certain rules of competition to production of and trade in agricultural products. Under this Regulation, farmers and their organizations were, in general, excluded from the ordinary Community rules on competition, in so far as their activities were concerned with the production and sale of agricultural products, and the use of common facilities for the storage and processing of such products.

Although, theoretically, the case for collective action is strong, in practice a recurring difficulty with any sector dominated by small-scale independent producers is to persuade them to join a group which will have power to impose standards, control prices, and even production, and once they have joined to prevent them from breaking their contractual obligations to the group, thereby undermining its collective bargaining power.

One way in which the advantages of membership of a producer group can be enhanced is to give to such groups certain formal market intervention responsibilities. Prior to the establishment of the European Community, the Netherlands provided good examples of how such a system functioned, especially in the fruit and vegetable sector. The characteristics of the Dutch system were outlined in the 1960 proposals on the CAP, and certain features of that system found an echo in some of the commodity regimes. The first example came in Reg. 159/66 *concerning additional arrangements for the common organization of the market in the fruit and vegetable sector*. This Regulation completed the arrangements for fruit and vegetables which had been hanging fire since 1962. A novel feature of this regime is the important role played by producer groups which act as the agency for internal market support.

For many commodities, provision is made in the relevant market regime for the withdrawal of produce from an oversupplied market, its storage, and disposal. These tasks are normally undertaken by an official agency or agencies established in each Member State. However, for a small number of products, market management is in the hands of the producers themselves, through producer groups which receive official recognition. Given the characteristics of fruit and vegetable production—a highly perishable product, many small-scale producers, local markets, seasonal production, volatility in supply and price-flexibility and speed of response are required if any form of market management is to be effective.

Apart from market support for certain commodities, more generally producer groups provide their members with facilities for handling and marketing the output of the relevant commodity. In their turn, the members are expected to market this total supply through the group (unless the group allows otherwise), and they must abide by the rules adopted by the group for the improvement of quality and the adaptation of supply to demand.

The involvement of FEOGA-Guidance lies in the financial encouragement it provides for the establishment of producer groups. The first example of such aid appeared in Reg. 159/66 under which Member States were given the possibility of helping producer groups to get started, by providing them with a degressive aid during the three years following their establishment. This annual aid was not allowed to exceed 3, 2, and 1 per cent respectively of the value of the production marketed by the group. The Guidance Section reimbursed 50 per cent of the Member States' eligible expenditure under this scheme. Tentative references were made in Reg. 122/67 *on the common organization of the market in eggs* and in Reg. 123/67 *on the common organization of the market in poultrymeat* to the need to encourage efforts to improve the organization of production, processing, marketing, and quality through trade groups. However, in these commodity regimes, no financial support was offered to help launch such groups.

In the light of all this piecemeal and unco-ordinated interest in producer organizations in various commodities, it is not surprising that the Commission eventually proposed the establishment of a Community framework within which Member States could encourage the formation of producer groups in any commodity. The Commission was also prompted to do so because certain Member States were already promoting these groups and there was a danger that problems would arise at Community level through the use of different criteria and objectives in the various countries concerned.

Thus, in 1967, the Commission proposed a Regulation on producer groups and their unions in COM(67)68 final, which set out common rules on the type of aid which could be given by the Member States to encourage the formation and development of these groups, and on the conditions under which they could be officially recognized.

Despite the Commission's evident interest in the creation of producer groups and despite the existing Community launching aids in the fruit and vegetable sector, the 1967 proposal did not make provision for Community aid. This was somewhat surprising and indeed was criticized by the European Parliament in its Resolution on the draft.

Although Mansholt always regarded producer groups as an extension of market organization rather than as a part of structural policy, his 1968 Plan did contain a discussion of the need to improve marketing, and one of the measures suggested to aid that process was the immediate adoption by the Council of the proposed Regulation on producer groups. The Council clearly did not heed this exhortation because, in its 1970 structural reform proposals, the Commission made a pointed reference to the thorough discussions which had taken place in the European Parliament and in the ESC on the 1967 producer group draft and stated that the Council had not even begun a discussion on it.

The 1970 reform proposals included a considerably revised draft Regulation on producer groups—the most important change being the provision of Community aid to help launch the groups. In the explanatory note to the proposals, the Commission made it clear that it regarded the improvement of market structure as primarily the responsibility of the Member States. For that reason, it proposed that the Community should refund only 30 per cent of eligible national expenditure. The logic of this position is unclear, as it will be recalled that the Community was already refunding 50 per cent of eligible expenditure on producer groups in the fruit and vegetable sector.

In 1971, when the revised structural reform package was presented to the Council, the draft Regulation on producer groups appeared again—now in a third version. The changes made were generally of a technical nature but, importantly, the Community contribution to eligible expenditure by the Member States had been reduced to 25 per cent. It was all to no avail, as the draft Regulation was not passed by the Council.

In the *Resolution* on the new orientation of the Common Agricultural Policy in 1971, the Council finally agreed in principle to the introduction of a regime to encourage the formation of producer groups but, once again, it appeared that Community aid would not be offered and that the funding would be by the Member States. Despite this, however, the Council remained unable to agree to the proposal, although discussions dragged on into 1972. The only progress which was made was under Reg. 1696/71 *on the common organization of the market in hops*.

The hops producer groups are not involved in price support operations but are intended in a more general way to assist in the centralization of supply and in the adaptation of the product to market requirements. Member States were free to grant a launching aid and FEOGA-Guidance reimbursement was limited to 25 per cent of eligible expenditure. An extra feature of this regime was the option given to Member States to aid producer groups on a temporary basis to reorganize hop gardens and to switch to more suitable varieties. The form of aid was a payment per hectare replanted or reorganized, and FEOGA-Guidance refunded 50 per cent of the eligible expenditure of participating Member States.

Discussions resumed in 1976 on the introduction of a general producer group regime and, in the following year, the Commission put forward yet another revised proposal. This was so radically different from previous drafts as to be, in effect, a completely new proposal. In the explanatory memorandum, the Commission tried to explain why such a harmless piece of legislation was causing such difficulties.

Basically the problem was that certain Member States with well-developed production and marketing structures could not see the necessity for this legislation. If anything, the differences between the Member States had grown since the original 1967 proposal.

The Commission, therefore, proposed that instead of a Regulation of universal application, there should be a measure which would apply only in those areas where the supply of agricultural produce was structurally very inadequate. Primarily this meant Italy and indeed the proposal referred solely to that country, with the provision that the Regulation could be extended to other Member States.

The Council had agreed in February 1977 that it would adopt the proposal by the end of June. It was in fact a full year later that Reg. 1360/78 *on producer groups and associations thereof* was enacted. It was almost totally unrecognizable from the draft and covered not just Italy but also Belgium, Southern France, and DOM (the French overseas departments). The commodity coverage differed by country, and in France by region. It was intended to be of assistance to farmers in regions and sectors where there were severe structural deficiencies, due to the small size of farms and poor organization. For a measure which was to last initially for five years only, at a total FEOGA cost of 24m. ua, an incredible amount of bureaucratic effort was involved. When Greece, Portugal, and Spain joined the Community, Reg. 1360/78 was extended to them, and to Ireland and the remainder of France in 1988, all for specified lists of commodities.

The only other commodity for which producer group launching aids are available is cotton under Reg. 389/82. Under the terms of Accession, when Greece joined the European Community, market support was extended to cotton and producer groups were seen as an important mechanism for the rationalization of production and the centralization of handling and marketing. For this reason, the Regulation covers not only launching aids but also investment aid to assist with structural improvements in harvesting, ginning, storage, and packaging. Producer groups in Italy and Spain are also eligible for aid under this regime.

Having sketched the rather confused history of the development of legislation on producer groups, the remainder of this Section reports on the statistical evidence of the success or failure of the various structural measures to persuade farmers to come together to improve the organization of particular commodities. Data on structural aids are available for producer groups in fruit and vegetables, hops, cotton, and miscellaneous products under Reg. 1360/78.

In 1972, Reg. 159/66 was replaced by Reg. 1035/72, which consolidated all the existing Community legislation on fruit and vegetables. Arrangements for launching aids for producer groups were retained unchanged. The pattern which is so familiar from other structural aids is present here also: aid is concentrated in a very small group of countries and it is not necessarily related to the size of the sector.

For instance, the very small number of producer groups set up under this legislation in Belgium and the Netherlands is indicative of the strength of the previously long-established marketing structures based largely on the cooperative movement.

Therefore, there was little incentive or need to seek launching aids. In contrast, the relatively large number of launching aids in the UK is an indication of the previous absence of joint ventures by farmers rather than an indication of the size of the horticultural sector. The size of producer groups varies considerably from one Member State to another, as evidenced by the absence of any relationship between the number of groups and the level of investment.

Hops provide a real contrast to fruit and vegetables. This is a very small sector, highly localized in traditional areas of production where, of course, it can be quite a significant crop. Much of the output is grown on contract. The schemes of aid came to an end some years ago and 1985 was the last year for which data were available. The situation with regard to cotton is quite different. Greece is the largest producer and so far (at the time of writing) was the only Member State to have made use of the launching and investment aids, although the Commission anticipated that Spain, which is the only other significant producer, might well begin to show an interest in this measure.

In 1991, the Commission reported to the Council on the operation of Reg. 1360/78. By the end of 1990, the Member States had granted recognition to 560 groups. The discrepancy is explained by 'the slowness of the Member States' administrations in drawing up implementing rules and requesting refunds'.

Despite the fact that Belgium was included in the scheme right from the start, no groups in the relevant production sectors (cereals, cattle, pigs, and

Lucerne) had applied for recognition, even though the requirements had been made easier.

Indeed, the Commission stated that the Belgian authorities had reported 'that those concerned are uninterested in the very idea of producer groups and that, in the present circumstances; this is unlikely to change in the future'. For that reason, the Commission proposed that, when the life of the Regulation was prolonged, Belgium should be excluded. This was rejected!

Certain Commodity Sectors

Throughout the lifetime of the CAP, there have been certain commodities which have been the source of constant concern, not only because of the level of production in relation to demand but also because of the organizational structure of the sector, the quality of the product, and the location of production. This Section is devoted to a discussion of structural schemes which have been put in place to try to change some of these features.

The commodities are milk, citrus, orchard fruit, and wine. The last three of these commodities all have characteristics in common: they are produced in locationally well-defined areas, often where there are few alternatives; being permanent crops, there is a long commitment to their production. Thus, changes within the same sector or shifts out of the sector to another crop are difficult to achieve and carry with them considerable income risks. They are often the product of small or medium-size farms. Milk, too, has many of these characteristics although its production is much more widespread.

Structural legislation aimed to facilitate adjustment in specific commodities has three distinct (though often related) purposes. It is intended to enable farmers:

1. To switch to another product;
2. To upgrade the quality of the existing product; and
3. To improve marketing and processing by the producers.

The first of these aims has been associated most notably with milk and wine; the second with citrus and wine; and the third with the promotion of producer groups for fruit and vegetables.

Schemes to improve quality, and marketing and processing run the risk that modernization not only improves productivity and, hopefully, income but also increases production. If a citrus grove or a vineyard is grubbed up and replanted with new varieties, almost inevitably they will be of higher yield. If an obsolete processing plant is modernized, it is very likely that the new machinery has a greater capacity, necessitating a higher throughput if the plant is to be commercially viable.

The potential for conflict between the farmers' welfare and macro-policy objectives is very real. Sometimes they can be reconciled: the demand for citrus and quality wine is more buoyant than for most food products, but for milk and table wine there is a fundamental clash, as total demand is falling over time.

Milk

In the discussion of the original proposals on the CAP, reference was made to the fact that milk was already a problem commodity. This basic situation was made considerably worse by the introduction of a common target price in 1968 which was well above the level which would have achieved market clearance.

The error of this initial position was then compounded by the reluctance of any of the main institutional forces—Commission, Council of Ministers, European Parliament—to accept that market support prices needed to be controlled far more rigorously than they were. On the supply side, reliance was placed on mechanisms such as production levies and quotas to curb output, while on the demand side, schemes were devised to stimulate consumption and to subsidize sales to unlikely groups, such as the military. Apart from quotas, which have at least kept production from getting completely out of hand, none of these schemes was of any lasting use. The unpalatable truth still is that there are too many dairy cows, yielding too much milk, and too many farmers dependent on dairying for their livelihood.

The structural schemes outlined here were intended to tackle that unpalatable truth. Farmers should be persuaded to give up milk production and turn to another enterprise, or to utilize the milk on the farm and not to market it, or to retire. The first structural scheme was adopted as long ago as 1969: Reg. 1975/69 *instituting a system of premiums for the slaughter of cows and for the nonmarketing of milk and milk products*.

This legislation arose out of the Mansholt Plan where the situation in the milk sector was described as 'alarming'. The Commission suggested various measures on the price and market front to control the immediate situation and it also recommended the slaughter of 250,000 cows each year In 1969 and 1970 (additional to normal culling), and the granting of aid in the same two years for the production of beef. The Commission further suggested that dairy farmers who were willing to retire should receive additional aid over and above that being offered under the normal retirement scheme. Dairy farmers setting up one of the new Production Units (PUs) should receive additional aid if they switched from milk to beef fattening.

The draft Regulation on cow slaughter and beef promotion appeared in COM(68) 1000(c). By the time Reg. 1975/69 was passed in October 1969, the beef promotion aspect had been dropped and had been replaced with the non-marketing of milk premium—which indirectly could achieve the same results, by encouraging farmers to feed whole milk to calves reared for beef. The cow slaughter premium was less generous than in the original proposal and a ceiling had been placed on the amount of aid which any one beneficiary could receive, which effectively limited compensation to 10 cows. FEOGA-Guidance reimbursed 50 per cent of the cost of the premiums. The scheme ran until

1974, during which time nearly 234,000 cows were slaughtered on 54,000 farms. Considering that the original intention was to cull over twice that number of cows, and in no more than two years, it must be assumed that this scheme would have had very little impact in a Community with a dairy herd at that time of about 22m.

The second measure intended to curb milk production was Reg. 1353/73. Under this scheme a premium was paid on condition that the producer gave up, for four years, all sales of milk and milk products from the holding in question and simultaneously kept a specified number of adult cattle on the same holding. The level of the premium was based on the quantity of milk supplied by the producer in the twelve-month period preceding the reference date. As an alternative to this scheme, Member States could in certain circumstances grant a development premium for the specialized raising of cattle for meat production. The whole scheme was scheduled to cost 60m. ua and to be completed by the end of 1974, although in fact it was extended. FEOGA Guidance contributed 50 per cent of the eligible expenditure.

In 1974, the Commission published a very detailed report on the operation of the scheme, in which it indicated that the cows for which the premium was granted represented just over 1 per cent of the dairy herd and milk yield. The report provided a regional breakdown of the impact of the scheme and, not surprisingly, in many Member States, it was in the regions with larger farms that the scheme was most popular. For small producers, to abandon dairying, with its regular income, in favour of rearing cattle, for which the return is lower and paid once only, is a considerable risk. In some of the Member States, the recipients tended to be in the 50-60 year age-group, which suggests that the shift to beef production was the first step to retirement.

Practically all the farmers who participated in this scheme had done so by 1976 but the reimbursements by FEOGA to the Member States were only completed in 1983. This slow pace of reimbursement is a feature of structural schemes and is partly due to the slow pace at which the Member States complete their own accounts and requests for payment. It does not necessarily mean that the individual beneficiary does not get paid promptly (though this may happen) but it does mean that Member States may be less than enthusiastic in publicizing the existence of schemes, because for some years they have to finance the total cost.

Thus, Germany had the largest number of beneficiaries but the quantity of milk which qualified for the premium only averaged 571 hl. Per farm, whereas in the UK, with the second highest number of beneficiaries, the average quantity was 1,464 hl. This is a good illustration of the difference in the structure of the industry in the two countries and explains why over half the total reimbursements from FEOGA went to the UK.

In its 1974 report on the scheme, the Commission concluded that it had been a success in slowing down the expansion of milk production. However, its optimism was misplaced and, in 1976, the Commission issued its Action Programme for the progressive achievement of balance in the milk market. By the mid-1970s, the dairy sector was very different from what it had been in the early 1960s. Although the number of dairy cows had remained fairly static over time and, if anything was tending downwards, milk production had risen by about 1.7 per cent per year from 1960 to 1975. The average milk yield per cow in 1960 was 3,083 kg. And 3,637 kg. In 1975, with the best regions having an average of more than 4,600 kg.

Another change was that far fewer farmers were feeding fresh milk to calves on the farm but instead were sending all the milk for processing. A major cause of these organizational changes was undoubtedly the price incentive. As the Commission described it: 'The behaviour of producers and dairies has been influenced mainly by the substantial increase in milk prices and the high level of the guarantee which together ensure them an unlimited market'. However, there was no suggestion in the Action Programme that the market imbalance was to be tackled head-on by a decline in the money support price. Instead, the Commission announced a package of measures which included a new scheme for the non-marketing of milk and the conversion to beef cattle or sheep. It also proposed the suspension of national and Community-supported aid to the dairy sector, and the introduction of a co-responsibility levy.

At first glance it may seem irrational that, at a time when there were schemes to reduce the number of dairy cows and to lower the amount of milk going for processing, there should still have been investment aid for the modernization of milk production and processing. However, it could be argued that a slimmed down dairy sector would still need to be modern and efficient and, if the provision of cheap capital would help to achieve that goal, it was a good long-term investment.

The real problem was much more profound: the various elements of the milk policy were sending confused and contradictory signals to the farmers, and the weight given to each element of policy did not correspond to the stated objective of restoring market balance. Thus, the imposition of a co-responsibility levy (rather than a cut in the money support level) did not represent a serious attempt to dampen down supply. Investment aid far outweighed the structural schemes being discussed here. Thus the farmers who were likely to leave dairying were often the elderly and those with very small herds. But these were not the categories of dairy farmers who were responsible for the surplus in the first place.

The Commission tried to inject a sense of urgency into the discussions on milk production controls but the Council of Ministers did not respond with matching speed on any aspect of the Commission's recommendations—reference was made to the length of time it took to get the principle of co-responsibility accepted, and its inadequacy when finally put in place. Things were no better with the structural scheme. Two draft proposals in succession on the introduction of a scheme for the non-marketing of milk, and conversion of dairy cow herds to other livestock enterprises were put forward in 1976. The second was radically different from the first and, by the time the Council finally accepted the scheme in 1977, major changes had once more taken place.

Reg. 1078/77 provided farmers with a choice: either a premium to compensate for agreeing to cease dairying or a premium to convert to the production of beef cattle or sheep. Unusually, this scheme was funded in part from FEOGA-Guarantee as well as from the Guidance Section. In its comments on the proposed scheme, the European Parliament drew attention to the danger that such a measure might well solve one problem by creating another: 'a conversion policy is likely to have favourable results . . . only if the beef and veal market, which in many ways is just as sensitive as the milk market, is not to be disrupted as a result'. This was a very real issue at the time, as the beef sector had been displaying increasing signs of instability since the early 1970s.

Applications for aid under Reg. 1078/77 were made from mid- 1977 to mid1981. During that time, the Commission issued five reports on the progress of the scheme. In total, about 123,000 applications for premiums were approved by the end of 1981, representing over 6 per cent of dairy farmers and 6.7 per cent of the Community dairy herd. This was equivalent to the whole dairy herd of Belgium and Denmark. Germany was by far the largest recipient of the non-marketing premiums in terms of total applicants but the average size of herd was by far the smallest. As with the 1973 scheme, the large herd size in the UK is very much in evidence: only 5 per cent of the applicants but 16 per cent of the cows.

As to the conversion scheme, applications were dominated by France and Germany, although in terms of the number of cows kept, France and the UK accounted for about two-thirds of the total. The significant differences between the size of herd in the two premiums is quite striking: converting to beef or sheep production is unrealistic for a small dairy farmer.

In the final report on the scheme, the Commission expressed its disappointment at the results. Although the withdrawal of nearly 1.7m cows from milk production exceeded the original target of 1.3m., the net impact was very modest. Between 1977 and 1981, milk deliveries to dairies rose by about 10m tones, while the scheme only removed 6m tones. It was an expensive scheme, with eligible expenditure being fully funded by the two sections of FEOGA. The average cost per cow was about 700 ECU and the scheme was expected to cost 1,200m ECU. It was confirmed by the Commission in 1987 that the scheme had caused problems on the beef market and it recommended that the scheme should not be reintroduced.

In 1987, the Commission issued a discussion document on the implementation of stabilizers in the milk sector, which was mostly concerned with the operation of the quota system. Although the sector had changed appreciably since the early 1970s, it was clear it had not changed sufficiently. In 1973, 43 per cent of all farms produced milk; by 1983 this had fallen to 31 per cent. However, as a proportion of Gross Agricultural Product (GAP), milk had become more important, rising from 17.3 per cent in 1973 to 19.2 per cent in 1985.

Not surprisingly, milk was one of the most costly sectors in the Community's Budget: 38 per cent of FEOGA-Guarantee expenditure in 1973 and nearly 30 per cent in 1985, and the latter figure was expected to rise. Full self-sufficiency had been reached in 1974, and between then and 1983 milk deliveries had increased by an annual average of 2.6 per cent, while consumption rose by about 0.5 per cent each year.

When the milk quotas were introduced in 1984, all Member States except Denmark and Greece established national schemes to facilitate producers who wished to discontinue milk production. In return for the surrender of their quota, they received compensation. Approximately 100,000 producers took part in this scheme. In 1986, the Council agreed to a reduction in the quotas by 2 per cent in 1987, and a further 1 per cent in 1988. In order to facilitate these reductions, a Community cessation scheme was introduced under which producers who gave up milk production permanently received annual compensation for a period of seven years.

The initial response to this scheme by producers varied considerably from one Member State to another, with some countries being well below expectations. The Commission suggested that this was due to three factors: the earlier national schemes had removed many of the potential out goers; in some regions, the absence of adequate alternatives to milk production; and the level of the premium was too low to persuade farmers to abandon dairying.

There can be no doubt that the size and shape of the dairy sector has changed significantly over the lifetime of the CAP, and yet problems remain. The tendency towards overproduction has been curbed but not eliminated. The various structural schemes must have eased many producers out of the sector relatively painlessly but, having removed many marginal producers; it may actually be more difficult to achieve change in the future. Neville-Rolfe commented:

It is sometimes said that the disappearance of tens, or even hundreds, of thousands of . . . small operators would *ipso facto* solve the problem of the milk surplus. It would be unlikely to do so. The larger the herd, the greater the probability . . . that its operator will be adopting the feeding and breeding practices needed to increase milk yields per cow. In this respect structural reform, unless accompanied by measures to restrict output, is liable to increase total output.

It was precisely for these reasons that quotas became inevitable. However, ominously, in 1987 the Commission pointed out:

The introduction of the quota system has not prevented but rather encouraged rationalization and improved management at farm and dairy level to the present and future advantage of producers and consumers. Technical and biological development has continued since 1983 with the result that an important production potential is still remaining untapped within the sector.

The Commission made the above statement in the context of the expected termination of the quota system in 1989 and it added that if the quotas were abolished without any other action being taken it would result 'in an unparalleled explosion in milk deliveries. History would then record that the five-year experiment of the quota system had failed to resolve any of the fundamental problems of market imbalance but had only postponed the collapse of the common market organisation under the financial burden of ever-increasing stock levels'. In fact, the quota system was retained but the comments quoted remain valid. The underlying tendency to overproduction is being kept in check—but that is all. The removal of the quota system would present the Union with a very tricky situation, which would have to be managed with great care. Otherwise, all the efforts made to change the structure of the sector, carried out at considerable expense, could well be negated.

Citrus and Orchard Fruit

Two of the oldest schemes to improve the structure of production were concerned with citrus fruit, and apples, pears, and peaches. The reasons for the measures were not the same. In the case of citrus, there was a low level of self-sufficiency in the Community and a rising demand but the producers found they could not exploit this situation, as their competitive position on the internal market was poor. The deficiencies were at every stage of the market: production of varieties with little consumer appeal, and poor handling and processing of the fruit. For apples, pears, and peaches there were also problems with the varieties being grown but this was in an already oversupplied market, so that the solution lay in encouraging growers to leave the sector rather than attempting some improvement in production and marketing.

Reg. 2511/69 laying down special measures for improving the production and marketing of Community citrus fruit provided aid to assist growers of oranges and mandarins to replace existing varieties of trees with others more suited to consumer demand, and to encourage better handling, storage, and processing of citrus. Growers who replanted were eligible for an additional income aid to help tide them over the reorganization period. This aid was payable in five annual instalments and was based on the extent of the area replanted. FEOGA-Guidance reimbursed 50 per cent of the expenditure incurred by the Member States on the grubbing and marketing aids, and the whole of the additional income aid. The Member States were required to draw up improvement plans and these were approved by the Commission in 1973.

Thus, even with a highly targeted scheme such as this, the administrative delays were considerable.

Table provides cumulative information on the operation of this scheme up to the end of 1988. The table is unusual in that the Commission has provided data on the extent to which the various aspects of the scheme have been carried out. Some have been reasonably successful—market reorganization in Italy, replanting in France, and restructuring in Greece but otherwise, given the length of time the scheme has been in operation, its results are very disappointing.

In 1989, the Commission published a report on the implementation of this scheme. One of the problems of the scheme is that growers are unwilling to grub up and replant their groves with better varieties, because of the expense involved and the loss of income while the new trees are reaching maturity. This, of course, is what the income aid was intended to provide for, but obviously it has failed in its purpose.

The analysis of supply of all the main commodity sectors in the proposals on the CAP in 1960. Fruit and vegetables were identified as presenting particular problems of data interpretation but, even allowing for the uncertainties, a number of products were identified as being in surplus. Among these were apples, pears, and peaches. The original aid scheme was Reg. 2517/69 laying down certain measures for reorganising Community fruit production. The aid provided was for the grubbing up of apple, pear, and peach trees. The recipient had to undertake not to replant with similar fruit for five years. The aid was in the form of a payment per hectare grubbed, payable in two instalments. The Guidance Section refunded 50 per cent of the grubbing premiums, and the Member States were forbidden to encourage in any way, directly or indirectly, the planting or replanting of fruit trees of the types concerned.

In 1972, when the Commission proposed certain amendments to Reg. 2517/69 (which, in the event, were not accepted by the Council), the ESC took the opportunity to make some wide-ranging comments about this scheme. Among a number of critical observations was one to the effect that the measure was not sufficiently well targeted. Varieties of fruit which were in demand were being grubbed up, along with the less desirable varieties. This particular point was addressed in Reg. 794/76 laying down further measures for reorganizing Community fruit production.

It re-enforced Reg. 2517/69 and made provision for the granting of a premium for grubbing named varieties of apple and pear trees, the actual level of the premium to be fixed in relation to the state of growth of the trees, with a maximum amount of aid per hectare grubbed. The estimated total cost of the measure was put at 8.55m. ua and the Guidance Section of FEOGA reimbursed 50 per cent of Member State eligible expenditure.

The major beneficiary was Germany, although the area grubbed per grower was much smaller than the average in France and Italy. The second part of the table relates to Reg. 794/76, which was a much smaller scheme with only 8,500 participants and less than 12,000 ha. grubbed. It was very largely confined to France and Italy, although the actual area grubbed per grower was very similar right across the Community.

In 1979, the Commission issued a report on the operation of the 1976 scheme which stated that the original target had been the removal of 15,500 ha. of orchards. On the basis of the removal of about 12,000 ha., the Commission estimated that the scheme would reduce the production of apples by about 186,000 tones and pears by 48,000 tones. Given that the area represented about 4-5 per cent of the total area of apple and pear orchards, the impact of this scheme in improving market equilibrium must have been negligible. Over the same winter that this scheme was operating, an additional 7,000 ha. were grubbed without receipt of the premium.

The Commission suggested that these were varieties which did not qualify for aid, or were on plots below the minimum accepted for the payment of the premium, 'or possibly because the producers did not wish to commit themselves to not replanting apple trees, pear trees or peach trees on the plots grubbed'. This is another example of a scheme which may well be helpful to the individual producer who is thinking of leaving the sector to do so in a less painful manner, by the provision of an income cushion, but it achieves little else.

The problem of overproduction of apples, pears, and peaches still remains: in 1994, in its review of the future of the fruit and vegetable sector, the Commission provided estimates of production and use in 2000 compared with 1990-2. All three fruits were expected to remain in surplus. It was clear that the deterrents to overproduction in the fruit and vegetable sector generally, applied since the late 1980s, were not functioning as intended. The growers were content to produce not for the market but for withdrawal.

The Commission was contemplating the need for considerable changes to the system of market support and to the role of producer groups, as well as to the system of grubbing up. The Commission stated that it was 'not convinced that large-scale subsidized grubbing up is sufficient in itself to solve the problems of structural surpluses. At all events, to be effective, a grubbing-up scheme must be accompanied by rules on planting rights, with appropriate monitoring measures'. At the time of writing, the reform of the fruit and vegetable sector was still under discussion.

Wine

Wine was already identified as a problem commodity at the time of the 1960 price and market proposals, when the Commission recognized that long-term market equilibrium might require structural changes to involve the grubbing-up of vines, and changes in the varieties of grapes. However, despite this early identification as a problem sector, it was not until 1976 that a scheme was adopted to facilitate the grubbing-up of vineyards. This measure was introduced at a time of considerable crisis in the wine sector, involving very heavy expenditure for market withdrawals and the compulsory distillation of un-saleable surpluses.

Wine must be the least homogeneous of all agricultural commodities but, in the broadest terms, its production is divided into table wine and quality wine psr (produced in specified regions). The market is dominated by table wine and it is this part of the sector which causes the problems on the supply side. Production of table wine is declining slowly but not at a sufficient pace to match the decline in consumption.

In the early 1970s, when new plantings of quality vines began to exceed new plantings of table wine varieties, re-plantings were still heavily dominated by the latter. By the second half of the 1970s, re-plantings were also dominated by quality vines.

Over the lifetime of the CAP, the disequilibrium in the wine sector has proved to be more intractable than even that of milk, although the latter has received much more publicity. Milk has been a high-profile commodity firstly, because of the very high expenditure on its market support and secondly, because it is a Community-wide commodity, dominated by northern producers. Wine is a regional commodity, mostly in the south—Italy mainly and southern France, until the Enlargements of the 1980s. The addition of Greece, Portugal, and above all Spain, has made the production and marketing difficulties very much worse but, because of the tendency of commentators to ignore southern-type commodities, the scale of the problem is not appreciated outside the Institutions of the Union.

There are, however, many similarities between the wine and the milk sectors: the existence of many small producers, often with few viable alternatives, and production in both LFAs and in lowland areas with lower costs. There are also similar experiences with modernization: the elimination of the small producers with low yields and their replacement with higher yielding, more intensive, and specialized units. One major difference between wine and milk is the unpredictability of output of wine from one year to another, which makes the kind of control mechanisms used for milk totally inappropriate for the control of the supply of wine.

As mentioned above, the chronic imbalance in the wine sector was first seriously addressed in the mid-1970s. In 1977, the Commission warned that, if anything, the situation was going to deteriorate further:

There is an ever-increasing tendency to plant vines on more fertile land which permits higher yields; furthermore there is a spread in modern know-how concerning fertilizers, irrigation and plant health, and this will inevitably bring yields closer to the maximum levels which are theoretically possible. . . . It is possible that the average yield throughout the Community within a few years may be the same as those at present found only in certain wine-growing regions, and this would mean, if the area under vines remained stable, that supply would be much higher than the present level of consumption.

It was in the light of considerations such as these that, in 1976, a temporary ban on new plantings was imposed but the Commission was clear that such a step could not provide a solution to overproduction. Indeed, there was a danger that the ban might itself prompt growers to try to raise the yields of their existing vines through better management techniques. The Community faced a real dilemma: in hill areas yields tend to be lower than in the plains, so from a narrow point of view, economic logic might suggest that production should move to the more fertile sites on the plain.

However, lowland areas have many more options in terms of possible crops than hill areas. In addition, the cultivation of vines and the making of wine are labour-intensive, unless carried out in very large undertakings. In hill areas, where employment opportunities are not good, wine is an important user of labour.

Finally, because wine is not homogeneous the varieties suited to high-yielding mechanized production on the plains are more likely to be the ones for table wine rather than quality wine. These thoughts were very much in the minds of policy-makers in the late 1970s, in the context of the recent introduction of Dir. 75/268 on LFAs.

In 1978, the Commission put forward an Action Programme for wine. Production of table wine was increasing by 1 per cent annually over the long term, while consumption was virtually static. The area planted was practically constant but yields were rising due to replanting with high-yielding varieties, and new plantings on the plain. The Commission proposed a programme which included market management and structural measures. An important aim was to reduce the area under vines by progressively removing from cultivation regions which had no natural advantages for vine growing.

In addition, naturally suitable areas should be replanted with quality varieties. Despite the seriousness and urgency of the situation on the wine market, the Council displayed its usual tardiness in strengthening the structural reform measures. It was not until 1980 that a new package of structural schemes came into force. Prior to that, in the 1970s, three measures had been introduced, two of which applied only in France.

The first structural measure was Reg. 1163/76 on the granting of a conversion premium in the wine sector. It covered the three years 1976/ 77-1978/79 and consisted of a payment per hectare of vines grubbed, the actual level of payment depending on the type and condition of the vine. FEOGA Guidance reimbursed 50 per cent of Member States' eligible expenditure. The total FEOGA cost of the measure was estimated to be 78m. ua. One interesting comment on this measure is to be found in the Resolution of the European Parliament on the proposal.

While agreeing in principle with the proposal, the Parliament was clearly sceptical about its effectiveness. In particular it recalled 'that previous Community measures for the grubbing-up of fruit trees and the voluntary slaughter of cattle did not produce satisfactory results and made very little impact'. It regarded as 'purely theoretical' the Commission's estimate that the grubbing aid would affect as much as 120,000 ha. of vines. In this it was to be proved absolutely correct. Not surprisingly, the final FEOGA cost was also much lower than the original estimate.

The second measure—Dir. 78/627 *on the programme to accelerate the restructuring and conversion of vineyards in certain Mediterranean regions of France* —was part of the Mediterranean package. The intention was twofold: to improve those areas where quality wine could be produced, and to encourage growers in other areas to change to other products. Effort was concentrated mainly on Languedoc-Roussillon, with lesser amounts available in the departments of Ardeche, Bouches-du-Rhône, Var, and Vaucluse. The results of this scheme are given: 3 1,000 ha were restructured and 19,000 ha converted. Based on statistics published in 1986, this out-turn was considerably less than originally intended namely, 66,000 ha restructured and 33,000 ha converted.

The third reorganization scheme set up in the 1970s was for the conversion of vineyards in the Charentes departments in France. This was quite a different measure from the other vineyard schemes, as it was intended to reduce the area devoted to the production of cognac, demand for which had fallen due to the recession of the early 1970s. As there was a surplus of white table wine, the French wished to discourage the diversion of wine from cognac production to the general white wine market. The plan was to grub up 5,000 ha and, this was overachieved.

By the time these three schemes had come to an end, something in excess of 100,000 ha. been removed from wine production. However, in a sector which, at that time, had about 2m ha in production, of which almost two-thirds were for table wine, these measures would have had an insignificant effect. Clearly more needed to be done. In 1978, at the same time as the Commission made its proposals on the Charentes and the Mediterranean areas of France (outlined above), it presented a major package of wine measures to the Council. It was not until 1980 that the structural elements of the package were accepted by the Council.

There were three linked measures; the first—Reg. 456/80 on the granting of temporary and permanent abandonment premiums in respect of certain area under vines and of premiums for the renunciation of replanting followed on from Reg. 1163/76. However, it was broader in scope, in that it provided not only for temporary abandonment of wine production as previously but also an incentive to those who had received the temporary abandonment premium under the earlier legislation to make that permanent.

The second measure—Reg. 457/80 establishing a system of premiums for the cessation of wine-growing in France and Italy—was intended to encourage elderly wine-growers to leave the sector. It provided an enhanced payment to growers who were receiving the permanent abandonment premium under Reg. 456/80, or the conversion aid under Dir. 78/627 in the Mediterranean regions of France. This incentive was in addition to any retirement pension which they might be receiving under Dir. 72/160. As far as can be ascertained, no payments were ever made, for which over 11m. EUA had been allocated.

The third measure was Reg. 458/80 *on collective projects for the restructuring of vineyards*. This was intended to apply in any wine-growing region, naturally suited to wine production, which was not included in any other structural adjustment scheme for wine. It was designed to assist groups of growers to undertake restructuring of vineyards collectively and included not only aid to improve the vineyards but also to assist with related works such as road improvement.

Under Reg. 456/80, about the same number of producers participated in the temporary and permanent abandonment schemes, a little over 50,000 in each category with 70,000-76,000 ha. Reg. 458/80 attracted 249 growers with 28,000 ha of vines. A ceiling had been placed in this latter Regulation on the total area eligible for FEOGA reimbursement of 223,800 ha which was actually subsequently increased. Based on the 1988 data, there seemed little likelihood it would be reached—let alone exceeded.

The oversupply in the wine sector had continued to deteriorate: in the words of the Commission—'the measures relating to structures adopted by the Council since 1976 . . . had not really succeeded, by 1984, in prompting a qualitative and quantitative reform of Community wine production'. It was in this context that Reg. 777/85 was enacted.

It was targeted predominantly at the producers of table wine but included also table grapes, grapes for drying, and wine for cognac in the Charentes because, to some extent, these categories are interchangeable with table wine. It also included aid for the cultivators of vine root-stock. The aim was to reduce the total area devoted to table wine production by about 180,000 ha.

By the end of 1988, 28,000 had been abandoned but only in two Member States—France and Greece. The life of this Regulation was cut short at the end of the 1987/88 wine year by the introduction of a new scheme covering all areas under vines—table wine and quality wine. This new measure was prompted by the introduction for wine of production stabilizers, i.e. the budgetary controls on expenditure from FEOGA-Guarantee.

The series of structural schemes enacted in the 1970s and 1980s to reorganize and reduce the area devoted to wine production give the impression of frenetic and increasingly desperate activity in a sector which was out of control. In 1986, the Commission commented that 'the future must be viewed with great concern'. No end to overproduction was in sight and, as if the situation was not bad enough, Enlargement of the Community in 1986 increased the area under vines by 80 per cent! Although yields are low in Spain, it is a major producer (the area under vines is greater than in France or Italy), and it is in structural surplus. As a result, the overproduction of EC-12 was bound to get worse.

Little had changed by the early 1990s: the area under vines continued to decline but not at the same rate as the decline in consumption. The structural surplus remained; the market support mechanism had become too complex and was still allowing growers to realise an adequate return on wine destined for industrial distillation, thereby encouraging producers to regard this as a normal outlet. The response to the grubbing up schemes had resulted in environmental damage in hill areas and had created patches of waste ground in the countryside.

The structural schemes reduced area by about 50,000 ha. per year but 'the premiums granted seem more to accompany than to foster a natural decline in areas under vines'. This is a situation already observed for other problem commodities. Put bluntly, if nothing was done, the surplus by the end of the century would be twice its 1986/87-1990/91 level. The removal of surplus wine through distillation is no solution as it merely transfers the problem, at considerable budgetary cost, to the industrial alcohol sector—a parallel disruption to that experienced in the beef sector by the encouragement given to dairy farmers to reduce milk deliveries and move to beef production.

The 1993 discussion document put forward a bewildering range of ideas to try to achieve the Commission's stated objective of market balance by the end of the century, without increasing overall budgetary expenditure. This document is no different from earlier discussion documents on wine in its failure to emphasize that the real problem in the wine sector has been that distillation of surpluses has been carried out at too high a price, i.e. the price received by the producer is sufficiently attractive so that it does not act as a deterrent. Unless this fundamental aspect of pricing is adequately addressed, no structural programme and no reorganization of the market regime can succeed in achieving market equilibrium. At the time of writing, the new arrangements for wine were still being discussed and it is not possible to be confident that equilibrium can be achieved in the few wine years remaining before the turn of the century.

A footnote to the structural measures for wine: as from the beginning of 1990, funding for the measures still in place—Regs. was transferred from FEOGA-Guidance to Guarantee. This recognition of the link between structural measures intended to improve the performance of the market, and the market support regime itself goes right back to the original proposals on FEOGA in Reg. 26/62, before the Fund was divided into two sections.

Originally, FEOGA had three tasks: to provide refunds on exports, to intervene on the internal market, and to support 'structural changes necessitated by the development of the common market'. The achievement of a common market in a particular commodity, through the operation of a market regime and structural measures directly linked to that regime, was an idea which very quickly disappeared in the early struggle to launch the CAP. Nothing more was heard of it after 1963. Yet it is ironic that, nearly thirty years later, such a link was recreated by putting market support and market reorganization under the same heading in the Fund.

Improvements in Processing and Marketing

In the first Section of this chapter, reference was made to the fact that the processing and marketing support activities of Reg. 17/64 were continued in Reg. 355/77 on common measures to improve the conditions under which agricultural products are processed and marketed. This Regulation was a long time in coming. The life of Reg. 17/64 was limited following the introduction of the financial Regulation 729/70, which laid down the basis for future assistance of a structural nature. If for no other reason than that of legal necessity, consideration had to be given to the replacement of Reg. 17/64 by some other measure in the sphere of marketing and processing.

More than that, however, there has always been a tendency to concentrate aid to agriculture in that sector of the industry which lies on the farm and to neglect the need to improve the handling of the products once they leave the farm. For many years, Reg. 17/64 was the only Community measure of any importance providing such post-farm aid, despite the fact that it was recognized that the agricultural sector was weak in the handling of produce.

In setting the new guidelines for the CAP in 1971, the Council had invited the Commission to continue to study the problems of marketing and processing, and to submit a proposal on their alleviation. In 1973, in the *Improvement* memorandum, the Commission announced its intention to make such a proposal but it was not until mid-1975 that it finally managed to submit this proposal to the Council in COM(75)431. The Commission reasoned that a more efficient processing and marketing sector would be in a position to pay better prices to producers, to diversify output, thereby stimulating demand, to concentrate more on exports, and (rather obscurely) to 'better handle products from remote areas of the Common Market'.

The proposal was for the establishment of multi-annual programmes, each of which would cover one or more agricultural products. Within these programmes the Community would provide aid for suitable projects intended to promote the rationalization and expansion of processing and marketing. Assistance was to take the form of a capital subvention of not more than 25 per cent of the value of the investment, with the beneficiary providing at least 50 per cent and the Member State participating in the funding as well. The estimated cost of the scheme was 400m. ua over a five-year period.

While largely in agreement with the intentions of the Commission, the ESC had a number of reservations. For one, the Committee was of the opinion that the proposed Regulation was 'of direct concern to consumers, farm workers, and workers in the food industry and the distributive trade' but that insufficient regard was being paid to the interests of these parties. The ESC also believed that the effectiveness of the measure could be improved by the formation of producer groups and urged the Council to adopt the long out standing draft Regulation on such groups. This point was echoed by the European Parliament.

Another point on which the two bodies agreed was their scepticism concerning the Community's ability to control the new measure in a manner which would avoid exacerbating the surplus problem. Both Parliament and ESC considered the proposed scheme as financially inadequate. The Parliament stated that 'the Commission's proposal represents a limited step which will result in a decrease in the total real amount of Community aid to be granted for the improvement of marketing and mixed production/ marketing structures, and which will make no substantial contribution to reducing agricultural surpluses and limiting the need for intervention'.

The ESC commented that '80 million units of account per year is not enough to solve all the problems of improvement of agricultural product marketing and processing facilities, especially as costs will continue to be pushed up by inflation'. It was not until 1977 that a modified version of this proposal was passed by the Council and it is hard to believe that either the Parliament or the ESC would have regarded the changes as beneficial.

The programmes 'to develop or rationalize the treatment, processing or marketing of one or more agricultural products' had to be drawn up by each Member State and agreed by the Commission before applications for the funding of individual projects could be considered. These projects could be for a wide range of activities: the development of new outlets for agricultural products; lightening the burden on intervention by improvements to the structure of a market; assistance to regions having difficulty adjusting to some aspect of the CAP; improvement of marketing channels or rationalization of the processing of an agricultural product; improvement of quality or presentation . . . While the contribution from FEOGA-Guidance to eligible expenditure was fixed at 25 per cent, in later years this was modified in various countries and regions, e.g. in the Mediterranean, and the West of Ireland. Strange little schemes were added on from time to time as, for instance, a special measure to rationalize and improve slaughterhouses in Belgium.

6

Food Tourism and Catering Services

INTRODUCTION

Hospitality is probably the most diverse but specialized industry in the world. It is certainly one of the largest, employing millions of people in a bewildering array of jobs around the globe.

Sectors range from the glamourous five-star resort to the less fashionable, but arguably more specialised, institutional areas such as hospitals, industrial outfits, schools and colleges. Yet of these many different sectors, catering has to be the most challenging. Whatever the size of the catering operation, the variety of opportunities available is endless. "The sky is the limit with catering".

CATERING INDUSTRY

The food service industry encompasses those places, institutions and companies that provide meals eaten away from home. This industry includes restaurants, schools and hospital cafeterias, catering operations, and many other formats, including 'on-premises' and 'off-premises' caterings. Catering is a multifaceted segment of the food service industry. There is a niche for all types of catering businesses within the segment of catering.

The food service industry is divided into three general classifications: commercial segment, noncommercial segment, and military segment. Catering management may be defined as the task of planning, organizing, controlling a n d executing. Each activity influences the preparation and delivery of food, beverage, and related services at a competitive, yet profitable price. These activities work together to meet and exceed the customer's perception of value for his money.

CATERING SEGMENTS

Catering management is executed in many diverse ways within each of the four segments. The first, commercial segment, traditionally considered the profit generating operation, includes the independent caterer, the restaurant caterer, and the home-based caterer.

The food service catering industry is segmented. The non-commercial segment, or the 'not-forprofit' operations, consists of the following types of catering activities: business/industry accounts, school, college and university catering, health care facilities, recreational food service catering, social organizations and transportation food service catering. The military segment encompasses all catering activities involved in association with the armed forces and/or diplomatic events.

KINDS OF CATERING

There are two main types of catering on-premises and offpremises catering that may be a concern to a large and small caterer. On-premise catering for any function—banquet, reception, or event—that is held on the physical premises of the establishment or facility that is organizing/sponsoring the function.

On-premise catering differs from off-premise catering, whereby the function takes place in a remote location, such as a client's home, a park, an art gallery, or even a parking lot, and the staff, food, and decor must be transported to that location.

Off-premise catering often involves producing food at a central kitchen, with delivery to and service provided at the client's location. Part or all of the production of food may be executed or finished at the location of the event. Catering can also be classified as social catering and corporate catering. Social catering includes such events as weddings, bar and mitzwahs, high school reunions, birthday parties, and charity events.

Business catering includes such events as association conventions and meetings, civic meetings, corporate sales or stockholder meetings, recognition banquets, product launches, educational training sessions, seller-buyer meets, service awards banquets, and entertaining in hospitality suites.

ON-PREMISE CATERING

All of the required functions and services that the caterers execute are done exclusively at their own facility. For instance, a caterer within a hotel or banquet hall will prepare and cater all of the requirements without taking any service or food outside the facility. Many restaurants have specialized rooms on-premise to cater to the private-party niche.

A restaurant may have a layout strategically designed with three separate dining rooms attached to a centralized commercial food production kitchen. These separate dining rooms are available at the same time to support the restaurant's operation and for reservation and overflow seating.

In addition, any of the three dining rooms may be contracted out for private-event celebrations and may require their own specialized service and menu options.

Other examples of on-premise catering include hospital catering, school, University/college catering.

OFF-PREMISE CATERING

Off-premise catering is serving food at a location away from the caterer's food production facility. One example of a food production facility is a freestanding commissary, which is a kitchen facility used exclusively for the preparation of foods to be served at other locations.

Other examples of production facilities include, but are not limited to, hotel, restaurant, and club kitchens. In most cases there is no existing kitchen facility at the location where the food is served. Caterers provide single-event foodservice, but not all caterers are created equal. They generally fall into one of three categories:

Party Food Caterers

Party food caterers supply only the food for an event. They drop off cold foods and leave any last-minute preparation, plus service and cleanup, to others.

Hot Buffet Caterers

Hot buffet caterers provide hot foods that are delivered from their commissaries in insulated containers. They sometimes provide serving personnel at an additional charge.

Full-Service Caterers

Full-service caterers not only provide food, but frequently cook it to order on-site. They also provide service personnel at the event, plus all the necessary food-related equipment- china, glassware, flatware, cutleries, tables and chairs, tents, and so forth.

They can arrange for other services, like décor and music, as well. In short, a full-service caterer can plan and execute an entire event, not just the food for it.

TYPES OF CATERING ESTABLISHMENTS

Various catering establishments are categorised by the nature of the demands they meet. The following are some of the catering establishements.

RESTAURANT

A restaurant is an establishment that serves the customers with prepared food and beverages to order, to be consumed on the premises. The term covers a multiplicity of venues and a diversity of styles of cuisine.

Restaurants are sometimes also a feature of a larger complex, typically a hotel, where the dining amenities are provided for the convenience of the residents and for the hotel to maximize their potential revenue. Such restaurants are often open to non-residents also.

TRANSPORT CATERING

The provision of food and beverages to passengers, before, during and after a journey on trains, aircraft and ships and in buses or private vehicles is termed as transport catering. These services may also be utilised by the general public, who are in the vicinity of a transport catering unit. The major forms of modern day transport catering are airline-catering, railways catering, ship catering and surface catering in coaches or buses which operate on long distance routes.

Airline Catering

Catering to airline passengers on board the air craft, as well as at restaurants situated at airport terminals is termed as airline catering. Modern airports have a variety of food and beverage outlets to cater to the increasing number of air passengers. Catering to passengers en route i s normally contracted out to a flight catering unit of a reputed hotel or to a catering contractor or to the catering unit operated by the airline itself as an independent entity.

Railway Catering

Catering to railway passengers both during the journey as well as during halts at different railway stations is called railway catering. Travelling by train for long distances can be very tiring; hence a constant supply of a variety of refreshment choices helps to make the journey less tedious. On-board meal services are also provided on long distance trains.

Ship Catering

Ship catering is catering to cargo crew and passenger ship passengers. Ships have kitchens and restaurants on board. The quality of service and facilities offered depends on the class of the ship and the price the passengers are willing to pay. There are cruises to suit every pocket. They range from room service and cocktail bars to speciality dining restaurants.

Surface Catering

Catering to passengers traveling by surface transport such as buses and private vehicles is called surface catering. These eating establishments are normally located around a bus terminus or on highways. They may be either government run restaurants, or privately owned establishments. Of late there has been a growing popularity of Punjabi style eateries called dhabas on the highways.

OUTDOOR CATERING

This catering includes the provision of food and drink away from home base and suppliers. The venue is left to the peoples' choice. Hotels, restaurants and catering contractors meet this growing demand. The type of food and set up depends entirely on the price agreed upon. Outdoor catering includes catering for functions such as marriages, parties and conventions.

RETAIL STORE CATERING

Some retail stores, apart from carrying on their primary activity of retailing their own wares, provide catering as an additional facility. This type of catering evolved when large departmental stores wished to provide food and beverages to their customers as a part of their retailing concept.

It is inconvenient and time consuming for customers to take a break from shopping, to have some refreshments at a different location. Thus arouse the need for some sort of a dining facility in the retail store itself. This style of catering is becoming more popular and varied nowadays.

CLUB CATERING

Club catering refers to the provision of food and beverages to a restricted member clientele. Some examples of clubs for people with similar interests are turf clubs, golf clubs, cricket clubs etc.

The service and food in these clubs tend to be of a fairly good standard and are economically priced. Night clubs are usually situated in large cities that have an affluent urban population. They offer entertainment with good food and expensive drinks.

WELFARE CATERING

The provision of food and beverages to people to fulfil a social obligation, determined by a recognised authority, is known as welfare catering. This grew out of the welfare state concept, prevalent in western countries. It includes catering in hospitals, schools, colleges, the armed forces and prisons.

INDUSTRIAL CATERING

The provision of food and beverages to 'people at work,' in industries and factories at highly subsidised rates is called industrial catering. It is based on the assumption that better fed employees at concessional rates are happy and more productive.

Catering for a large workforce may be undertaken by the management itself, or may be contracted out to professional caterers. Depending on the choice of the menu suggested by the management, catering contractors undertake to feed the workforce for a fixed period of time at a predetermined price.

LEISURE-LINKED CATERING

This type of catering refers to the provision of food and beverages to people engaged in 'rest and recreation' activities. This includes sale of food and beverages through different stalls and kiosks at exhibitions, theme parks, galleries and theatres. The increase in the availability of leisure time and a large disposable income for leisure activities has made it a very profitable form of catering.

RELATIONSHIP BETWEEN CATERING INDUSTRY AND ALL OTHER INDUSTRIES

Food is the sustainer of life regardless of whether they belong to animal kingdom or plant kingdom. All living beings consume food as they come in nature. Subsequently they may convert the raw natural food into usable form on their own. This transformation never involves the art and science of coking, which is a speciality of human beings alone. Importance of food for the human beings is amply, accurately and appropriately stated in the following age old sayings: "hungry man is an angry man" and "even the army marches on stomach" where stomach implies food Employment of largest number of people in the world in general terms and in commercial terms is in food preparation and servicing. Roughly half the world population is actively engaged in the art and science of food production and then alone comes reproduction.

Food production, simply stated, is the transformation of raw food material into palatable, appetizing and easily palatable tasty food. Unlike all other living organisms, man has to "buy" food by paying money. Where does the money come from? It comes only from industries. Any industry in the world has the primary objective of making money. Money so generated by the industrial activity is shared between the employer and the employee, however disproportionate it may be. Money so shared is used to take care of the three important objectives: food, clothing and residence.

Whatever left after meeting these primary objectives may go towards acquiring wealth. Food is the very basis of existence or survival. To buy food, man needs money. The money comes or must come from industries, all of which have the primary objective of making money and share with those who help generate it. Since the raw food needs to be transformed into palatable food fit for consumption which is achieved, as already stated, through general cooking or commercial cooking.

Therefore, there is no industry in the world which is not directly or indirectly, one way or the other, related to the food industry. Commercial food industry or the catering industry is the only industry that provides food, at a price, away from home. Various types of catering services available would include general or speciality services such as transport catering, welfare catering, industrial catering, etc.

CATERING AND CUSTOMER

CATERING TO DIVERGENT

It sounds rather crass, but when they die, in the next 10-15 years, all of their money-some $10 trillion dollars-is going to another group of people, most of whom don't like banks. They would rather go to Fidelity, play the market, not having lived through a downturn. One of the challenges as we go forward is how the banking industry is going to transform itself, move from the current group who provides the bulk of our earnings, to a second group who will assume society's wealth, and who does not realty like us.

Who likes banks? Those 55 years and older plus those who have lower incomes and less education, according to a 1997 ABA survey-valued customers, but not a group we can solely survive on. Also customer satisfaction is slipping somewhat for banks.

You need to know when you should allocate resources from the group giving you the bulk of your earnings now, to the group that does not like you. You will also get a boost from the federal government's change to electronic benefits transfer on January 1, 1999. Most states will have an EBT environment by the end of 1998.

The people who now get a Social Security check will have to become accustomed to an electronic transaction, and that's in your favour. A lot of the back-office work, you can change through electronic transactions. EBT will provide a large infusion of the infrastructure required for electronic commerce, by increasing the number of point-of-sale terminals.

The ABA asked the Federal Reserve and the Treasury to review the regulations surrounding transaction accounts, because the existing regulations are all in the realm of paper-based accounts. We would really like to get rid of the periodic statement under Regulation E because a purely electronic account will not have any outstanding items so you don't realty need a statement.

Banks will have to do some new things, though-electronic benefits transactions on automated teller machines, and maybe statements on demand. What can you do today on the Internet? You can do consumer education; you can have interactive advertising; you can distribute forms and applications; you can provide account information. You can do some internal transactions, some bill payment and, perhaps, some electronic commerce for the more daring. Electronic commerce, a broader term than electronic banking, better describes what ultimately we might want to do. What customers want today is not necessarily what they are going to want next year. You have to continually reassess.

Reliability on Tomorrow's Systems

Today, most of you keep your real stuff on a mainframe, a rather secure system. On the Internet, how are you going to let people like me hack around in your computer? You are going to be doing the same kinds of things on the Internet that you do today to render service and security to your customers. You will have a lot of the same, concerns. You could have a saboteur on the inside.

You could have a huge virus or software that fails. The new one is the hackers, but then you've got people who forge checks, too; they just attack in a different way. Whatever system you have must be reliable, sound, and secure. What kinds of things will give you these qualities? Well, you have technical standards; you have best practices, and the regulators providing guidance to the industry.

You are going to a much more efficient system and you should have greater margins as you implement it, but meanwhile, many larger institutions have proprietary systems that work very well. Probably nobody here has had a customer question, in the past 50 years, whether her check is going to clear. You are coming off of that kind of reliability. Bankers have systems that, perhaps, can be expanded to an Internet environment.

Determining who has the best products to help you is part of creating a plan. You want, perhaps, to start small, with, say, electronic bill payment, see how secure it is, how your customers accept it, and then go forward. You may lose money, but you are going to do it because your customers want it. There are threats to banks' dominance of the payments system, one of the biggest of which is the post office. You may say that will never happen because it is not an insured depository, but I would submit, for example, that the largest financial institution in Japan is the post office. Financial modernization, after 30 years, seems finally to be coming. Companies with unlimited capital, such as, say, General Electric Corp., will be able to compete very effectively, not for the little old ladies' $50,000 CDs but for their kids' money.

That's why ABA is very concerned. With direct deposit, a customer need never walk into a branch. A customer in Alaska can directly deposit funds into a bank in Alabama and write checks or use his debit card all day long in Alaska. All across the country, community bankers are saying to themselves "Aha!

Maybe I have an opportunity here." This stuff is coming. How are you going to respond? You are concerned about how your customers perceive you. Are you stodgy-as one of ABA's new industry ads shows -or are you out there on roller-blades? Now, you have to be concerned about customer perception beyond the community where you do business.

The Growth of Service Activities

Service sector economics now constitutes a major branch of economic studies although it is a field which no more than a decade ago was variously referred to as the 'poor relation' and the 'Cinderella of academics and politicians alike'.

The explanation of the interest recently evinced in the economics of the service sector is to be found in the extent to which service industries have expanded relative to other economic activities. Whilst the tendency for the tertiary sector to grow in comparison to primary and secondary activities has been identified and commented on for many decades special factors, such as the potential for services to generate new jobs, have helped thrust the sector to the forefront of economic analysis in the last few years.

The relative growth of services in the British economy since 1971, quantified on the basis of official statistics, could well stand as on outline of events in most developed economies during this period. Between 1971 and 1986 the output of the service sector increased by 2.5 per cent a year, or more than twice the rate, 1.1 per cent, achieved by other economic activities. Within the sector commercial services-distribution, catering, financial, business, recreational and personal services-expanded faster than other services, 3.1 per cent compared with 1.7 per cent a year, whilst specific commercial services grew very rapidly indeed-banking and business services by as much as 5.1 per cent per annum.

As a result, by 1985, service activities in Britain accounted for three-fifths of GDP and commercial services themselves were responsible for a third of total output. The importance of service activities is no less when judged by labour force size. On the basis of both numbers of employees, and by numbers of employees plus the self-employed, by 1985 services accounted for 66 per cent of Britain's labour force compared with 53 per cent in 1971. Commercial services alone provided jobs for 37 per cent of all employees in 1985.

The Need for New Measures

At a time when the bases, compilation, accuracy and usefulness of a range of official economic statistics have come under close scrutiny, the measurement of service outputs has not escaped attention. Recently there has been some shift away from a simple acknowledgement that service output measures may be subject to a degree of unreliability towards an apprehension that any errors they contain might lead to a downward bias in the measure of service output, and therefore, GDP growth rates.

It has in fact been suggested that output increases in services may have been underestimated in recent years by as much as 2-1/2 per cent a year implying that annual growth of GDP itself should have been substantially higher. For both conceptual and practical reasons the outputs of many service activities are notoriously difficult to quantify both absolutely and in terms of change over time.

Yet because of their size and growth it is especially important that a reasonable degree of accuracy must attach to service output measures which should reflect current best practice given the data and resources available. If this is not the case then, because of the weight of service activities in the total economy, the accuracy of the registred change in GDP and national productivity, the relative contribution to growth of service and non-service activities, the pattern of structural change within the service sector and the policies to which these various phenomena have given rise, must all be called in question. This assembles some of the principal results which have emerged from a study of alternative output measures for British service industries.

The study reviews the methods currently used by the CSO to measure real output changes in specified services and seeks to devise, develop and implement new measures for these activities. For this purpose an empirical approach has been adopted. Whilst basic conceptual considerations are taken fully into account in that the alternative measures which are compiled can be integrated into the national accounting framework, it is felt that the theoretical complexities associated with service output measurement have received due attention elsewhere whilst very little has been done at the practical level.

When compiling new service output measures the two principal uses for which they are employed must be borne in mind. The original raison d'etre for measuring service sector output is for use, in conjunction with output indicators for industrial activities, to yield a measure of real growth in total GDP. This is the primary role for which the CSO devises and compiles output measures for service sector activities. Increasingly, however, as the weight of services in the economy has grown service output indicators are now used extensively, in conjunction with labour force and other relevant economic series, for the analysis of long-term developments in individual service industries.

Their employment in the latter context accentuates the requirement that they fulfill minimum reliability criteria: it is possible that offsetting errors in individual service industry output measures may modulate their impact on the reliability of overall GDP measurement but this does not apply when attention is focused on the analysis of developments in a specific service industry. The results obtained in the present exercise suggest that official measures of GDP growth may well have been marginally understated as a result of the methods used to track service output changes. Even more significantly, perhaps, the alternative measures which have been compiled portray patterns of development for some individual commercial service industries which are very different from those yielded by official output measures.

When considering alternative output measures attention has been directed first at the strengths and weaknesses of official practice as a prelude to an attempt to improve the rationale and reliability of the resulting output indicators. However in some cases it is necessary to regard the new measure simply as an alternative to the official index: an alternative with a different, rather than superior, base and/or derived from quite separate data sources.

Another feature of the search for alternative indicators is that it has been conducted with an eye to the improved reliability of service output measurement in the future. To some extent this means that data series which are available only for recent years have been drawn upon. Nevertheless a major objective of the study has been to assess the extent to which the official picture of past service sector developments is changed if alternative output measures are used.

The alternative measures have therefore been carried backwards in some cases to 1971, in others to 1973 and for a large number to 1978, using 1985 as the base year. There are three reasons for the latter choice. First data limitations mean that all series cannot be uniformly taken back to a common early date so that a recent year must be adopted as the base. Secondly at the time when the research was initiated 1985 was the latest year for which data-whether values, 'quantities' or 'weights'-were generally available.

Thirdly, the CSO was then in the process of re-basing its output indicators using 1985 GDP weights. The new output measures draw much more extensively on unofficial data sources than do those compiled by the CSO. Broadly such sources can be divided into two types: those which yield data series covering an industry-wide set of activities; and those which contain data relating to individual service industry organisations and firms. Typically the assistance of the latter was enlisted to provide weights with which industry-wide quantity series for different kinds of output can be combined to produce a single output measure for the service sector in question. It is to the credit of the CSO that there has been a continuous attempt to modify service output measures in the light of methodological developments and the emergence of alternative data sources.

Whilst this has had the desired result of improving the reliability of service output measurement inevitably it also introduces inconsistencies and breaks in the time series where-either on practical or other grounds-the new methods have not been carried back to earlier years. A feature of the new measures postulated below is that every effort has been made to ensure temporal consistency in the series which they yield. It has not proved possible to devote to 'quality' aspects of service output the attention they properly merit.

In part this reflects the fact that the incorporation of quality changes in output measures may be even more difficult in services than in goods-producing industries where frequently its assessment is equally neglected. This in turn is due to the consideration that the quality of a given service varies greatly and in many cases is highly subjective. Nevertheless the results do have implications for this aspect of service output measurement, especially in the case of the catering trades. Were quality aspects taken into account more fully, further consideration would need to be given to the relative merits of measures based on deflated value series and service output units.

Coverage of the Measures

The search for alternative output measures has been restricted to the commercial service industries, essentially distribution, catering, financial, business and personal services, for which suggests that output has risen especially rapidly. Within this group of commercial services the CSO distinguishes for output measurement purposes as many as 37 service industries, output changes in which are currently assessed by a total of 114 indicators. These services accounted for some 30 per cent of total GDP in 1985 and about a third of people employed in Great Britain. Given the vast range of service activities which must be covered by official output measures it is natural that the CSO makes use of readily available, relevant, series to yield the required indicators, series which themselves are normally official in the sense that they are compiled by other government departments.

Since the quest for new measures has entailed a search for and detailed examination of, alternative data, involving the identification, location and perusal of non-official sources and also the co-operation of individual firms and organisations it proved necessary to regard the full range of commercial service activities as no more than a frame from which individual service industries could be selected for intensive analysis.

When choosing industries from this list for which alternative measures of output change are identified and implemented, several criteria have been applied. A principal consideration has been to direct efforts to services where, on the face of it, current practice appears to be weak. At one end of the scale this principle tends to divert attention away from activities such as retailing, where the measures are generally regarded as being relatively sound, towards such services as advertising where the official output indicator is based on an employment series.

Secondly some priority was given to activities for which at first blush-sometimes deceptive-alternative measures appeared feasible. Thirdly an attempt has been made to cover the larger service industries such as banking and insurance, and ceteris paribus, attention was focused on service activities which, a priori, are thought to be rapidly expanding, a criterion which points to the inclusion of, especially, financial and business services. Since a systematic attempt has been made to base alternative output measures on numbers of service units produced, such service industries as estate agents, stockbroking and legal services where official output measurement is already founded on numbers of service units-of property transfers, transactions, and court proceedings-have not been considered as candidates for alternative measures. The service industries for which new measures were ultimately compiled fall neatly into three groups.

First, there are ten selected financial and business services: banking, building societies, finance leasing, hire-purchase, insurance, accountants, architects, advertising, computer services and construction plant hire. Secondly eight recreational services have been covered: broadcasting, theatres, libraries, museums, professional sports, participatory sports, local authority leisure centres and betting and gaming. Thirdly, the five catering trades-restaurants, public houses, clubs, catering contractors and hotels-have also been included.

Alternative Output Measures

Continuous CSO action to modify and improve service output measures means that they have developed from year to year in an essentially ad hoc manner with considerable diversity in their conceptual underpinning. Output measures for the commercial service sector rely heavily on deflated value and employment indicators and whilst output measurement for some service activities is based on counting numbers of service units, such practice applies to only a fraction of the output of the commercial service sector.

In fact it has emerged that the use of this type of measure can be extended to a considerable number of commercial services and an attempt has therefore been made to generalise and implement this approach, especially in the case of the financial and recreational services. This method can be summarised as the compilation of [sigma]poqo where q represents the industry's output quantities of the industry's output prices and 0 and 1 refer to the years compared.

This is 'the traditional [measure] used for multi-product industries wherein an index of production is constructed from a weighted sum of various outputs produced by the industry'. Such a deflated value approach to output measurement will yield the required result-as measured by the traditional direct method based on weighted quantities-only if the deflator, the price index, relates specifically to the products or services in question. This condition is not fulfilled in the case of many service output measures where for practical reasons some form of general price index is used.

It is partly to remedy this weakness in service output measurement that, wherever possible, alternative measures have been based in this exercise on the traditional direct methodology using numbers of service output units. A fundamental requirement for the use of this 'traditional' or 'direct' approach is that, for purposes of practical measurement, the outputs of the industry or service in question should be relatively homogeneous.

No economic activity yields a single, identical, product or service so that in practice it is sufficient if the bulk of an industry's activity is represented by a limited range of output types. It is their supposed inability to fulfill this criterion which has discouraged the application of the traditional, direct, measurement methodology to service activities.

Generally it has been assumed that there exists, virtually, an infinite variety and range of outputs in the case of most, especially financial, services: that no two life insurances, mortgages, bank accounts, and the output activities associated with them, are the same. It is argued that this view is based largely on a misconception, associated with what, for want of a better term, we shall call the 'digit illusion', and that in fact many service industries-including betting and gaming-fulfil the basic criterion for the application of the traditional, direct measurement methodology in that the bulk of their output is accounted for by a limited range of essentially homogeneous activities.

For the impression of enormous diversity in the output of most financial services derives from the fact that the values associated with a specific activity-the sums assured by a life company, sizes of mortgages provided by a building society, the amounts loaned under hire-purchase agreements by a finance house, the values of cheques cleared by a commercial bank, the car insurance premiums charged by an insurer etc-do have an infinitely large range. It has been assumed in the search for new output measures that such differences can be essentially ignored. In the case of mortgages, for example, the output associated with writing 500,000 pounds sterling in a deed is, with some relatively minor qualifications, little different from that associated with inscribing 50,000 pounds sterling or even 5,000 pounds sterling; differences in the numbers of digits required in this and other financial instruments-cheques, insurance policies, hire-purchase agreements, betting slips-have relatively little bearing on the amount of output involved.

In brief for a given type of financial activity it is normally legitimate, when measuring output, to ignore the 'digit illusion'. This has the effect of rendering homogeneous a wide range of financial activities, making them amenable, in principle, to the traditional direct, measurement methodology. It means, by way of illustration, that output changes for the life insurance industry can be based on changes in numbers of policies. It must be stressed however that a distinction must be drawn, and numbers counted, for each major type of service/activity provided by the service industry in question where value added per service unit varies significantly between activity types.

This means, for instance, in the case of the life insurance industry, that numbers of policies must be counted separately for ordinary life insurance, industrial life, annuities and personal pensions. It also means that attention needs to be drawn to a feature of this approach which is peculiar to financial service industries: the distinction between stocks and flows. Clearly, the resources devoted to, and therefore the amount of output associated with, the annual 'maintenance' of pre-existing mortgage will be substantially less than required when initiating a new mortgage.

In principle, and where practical, it is as important therefore to draw a distinction when measuring output between numbers of existing mortgages issued in a given year and the numbers of existing mortgages as it is to count separately the numbers of, say, different kinds of policy issued by life insurance companies. Indeed the same distinction needs to be drawn in the case of life insurance-between new policies and policies in force-and in principle at any rate in many other financial service industries: between new and existing contracts for hire-purchase and finance leases for instance.

The practicability of extending the traditional measurement methodology to commercial services thus hinges, in the case of each activity, on the availability of two kinds of data: industry-wide series of numbers of each type of principal product, the series q; and appropriate weights with which these various product series can be combined to yield an aggregate output measure for the service industry in question. To a degree inadequacies in the measurement of service output changes simply reflect the relative lack of interest with which they were regarded in the past and a consequent failure to devote sufficient resources to the collection of basic output data.

Also, it is to some extent, due to the 'insubstantiality' of most services, the fact that they 'pass away' in the moment of production, that a systematic effort has not been made to base their output measurement to a much larger extent on numbers of service units produced. In fact regardless of whether or not a service has any kind of physical embodiment, in the vast majority of cases there exists a physical record or token that a particular service has been performed. The outputs of all kinds of commercial service industries are very well 'documented'-by the ticket required for entrance to Wimbledon, the bill for a meal, the contract which records the finance leasing of a fleet of aircraft-in a form which in principle allows the numbers of each type of service to be recorded.

In this sense, and at this level, the output of service activities is registered at least as well as the products of industrial pursuits. The nig universal existence, at the 'grass roots' level, of this detailed record of service sector outputs, to an ever increasing extent in computerised form, augurs well for the future extension and development of the kind of direct output measurement advocated here. This comprehensive data base has not yet been properly exploited to yield aggregate series of the numbers of each type of service produced on an industry-wide basis. However research and enquiry have revealed that representative bodies of various kinds at the industry level-especially trade associations-have come to regard the compilation of aggregate numbers of each kind of service produced, using these data bases, as one of their primary tasks, and such sources have been widely drawn upon. That they may not be based on series for numbers of service units which are fully comprehensive for the industry in question should not be regarded as a major weakness of the alternative output measures.

Usually only the major 'products' are counted and in this respect the circumstances are no different from those which exist when the method is applied to industrial activities. For both industrial and service activities so measured the implicit assumption is the same: that real changes in the non-covered outputs parallel the aggregate change measured for the covered operations. Unfortunately, with few exceptions, service industry organisations, do not collect, process or publish, the kind of data which are needed to obtain the 'weights' required for aggregating these various output series into a single measure for the industry in question. In these circumstances it has proved necessary to have recourse inter alia to the goodwill of individual firms in order to derive suitable weights which must be accepted as typical for the service industry in which they operate.

Wherever possible alternative measures have been derived from an application of the traditional, direct methodology based on numbers of service output units. However even when allowance is made for the 'digit illusion' some service industries-such as architecture and accountancy-remain in that class where output units are, in essence, infinitely variable in nature. In these cases an attempt has nevertheless been made to upgrade the output measure, usually by identifying and compiling a more appropriate price deflator. This presents the results of the search for new output measures for the selected commercial activities. Initially the new output series are presented separately for the three major service complexes-financial and business services, recreational services and the catering trades-which have been covered and compared with the official measures. The part concludes with a consideration of the implications of the results for future developments in the measurement of service output.

Financial and Business Services

In 1985 the ten financial and business services for which new output measures have been compiled contributed, in total, about 35 pound sterling billion to GDP and employed approximately a million people. In the case of banking, the largest of the services in this sector, it proved possible to base the new measure wholly on numbers of service units-numbers of accounts, clearings, cash and credit card transactions. This contrasts with official practice in which indicators derived from deflated series for deposits and loans, as well as employment, carry the bulk of the weight.

In life insurance, also, numbers of policies of various types, distinguishing between new policies and policies in force, replace the official series comprising deflated consumer expenditure. Similarly the new building society measure is founded wholly on numbers of service units-shareholders, existing borrowers and new loans-instead of, as is the case with the official measure, a combination of deflated liabilities, employment and numbers of advances. For general insurance, a measure reflecting broadly the stock of insurable assets has been substituted for the official indicator based on deflated premiums.

In the case of two services, architects and advertising, a deflated value series places officla measures based on employment. The primary feature of the new measures used for accountants, computer services and hire-purchase, is the use of deflators which have been specially constructed to reflect more closely than those officially employed developments in the activities in question. The official practice for both construction plant hire and finance leasing has been to base indicators on output developments in user industries. Instead of this approach the new measures are derived from gross output in the case of construction plant hire and the value of assets newly leased and of the stock of leased assets in the case of finance leasing, each deflated by price indices specifically compiled for the activities in question. The new measures for the covered financial and business services are set alongside the official indicators.

The basic date series from which these were derived are such that not all of them cover the full span of years, 1971 to 1986, so that it is convenient to combine them into three groups: five industries-building societies, hire-purchase, insurance, advertising and construction plant hire-for which growth rates are available for the whole period 1971-86; six industries where the information is shown for 1973-86; and all ten covered financial services, architects, finance leasing and computer services-for which alternative and official growth rates can be compared for the period 1978-86.

In the case of the first group, for which measures extend over the full period 1971-86, whilst there are some very significant differences between alternative and official growth rates-for building societies the former is appreciably higher than the latter whilst the opposite is true for hire-purchase-the arithmetic average growth rate for all five services, at 4.1 per cent per annum, is identical for both alternative and official measures. The same generalisation applies to the group of six industries over the period 1973-86: for hire-purchase, advertising, construction plant hire and banking the two measures yield quite different results but these contrasts offset each other so that the average alternative growth rate is identical with the average official growth rate.

Results for the group of ten industries, relating to the period 1978-86, paint a very similar picture; of individual industry diversity but overall similarity. In this case only for building societies, insurance, advertising and accountants do alternative and official methods yield rates of output change that are at all akin. Yet, overall, the average alternative growth rate, 7.4 per cent per annum, is not much greater than the 7.0 per cent registered officially. The official measure for finance leasing is constructed to minimise distortion in GDP measurement whilst the alternative measure has been compiled in such a way as to enhance the reliability of the industry's growth indicator *per se*. If this service industry is left out of account, the average alternative growth rate, at 6.6 per cent, is below the average official rate, 7.6 per cent.

This set of results contains a further point of interest. Whilst, as pointed out, there are substantial differences in the case of most industries between the alternative and official measures, the inter-industry growth patterns are remarkably similar whether gauged by alternative or official indicators: again leaving out finance leasing the correlation coefficient for the remaining nine pairs of, alternative and official, growth rates is +0.95. Although comparisons of unweighted average growth rates can be quite instructive more attention should be focused on differences between alternative and official measures revealed by weighted aggregate indices of the kind. These output indices, derived from the alternative and official measures for individual industries and relating to the same groups of industries and periods specified have been obtained from an aggregation procedure which is based on 1985 contributions to GDP.

The results contained are summarised in the form of average annual rates of growth that also contains growth rates obtained from weights derived from 1980 industry contributions to GDP and 1985 industry employment levels, to test the sensitivity of the results to alternative weighting systems. In the case of the five industries for which there is full coverage over the period 1971 to

1986 the alternative growth rate is 4.4 per cent and the official one 4.8 per cent on the basis of 1985 GDP weights.

A discrepancy of no more than a tenth between the two versions is also suggested by 1980 GDP weights. This group of five industries accounted for only 20 per cent of the contribution to GDP and an estimated 27 per cent of employment of all financial and business services in 1985. In contrast the group of six was responsible for 56 per cent of output and an estimated 42 per cent of employment and the group of ten for as much as 74 per cent of output and 56 per cent of employment. Greater significance should therefore be attached to the results obtained for these latter two groups. All three weighting systems show that for the group of six industries, over the years 1973 to 1986, the official measure understated growth by about a fifth when compared with the aggregate alternative measure; much the same picture emerges for the group of ten industries during the period 1978 to 1986 where, on the basis of both 1985 and 1980 GDP weights, the official measure, compared with the alternative, under estimates growth by about a fifth.

When considering this disparity two industries merit special attention: banking which is by some way the largest of the ten industries; and finance leasing on account of the fundamental difference in the methods underlying the alternative and official measures. In fact if banking-with alternative and official growth rates of respectively 8.2 and 6.5 per cent per annum for the period 1978 to 1986-is left out of account the picture hardly changes at all: the alternative aggregate growth rate for the remaining nine industries over the period 1978 to 1986 emerges as 8.0 per cent per annum compared with an official growth rate of 6.0 per cent.

This is in sharp contrast to the effect of excluding finance leasing. In this case the alternative growth measure for the nine remaining industries falls to 7.5 per cent whilst the official measure rises to 7.2 per cent so that most of the differential disappears.

Recreational Services

In 1985, recreational services, SIC class 97, contributed almost 6 billion pounds sterling to GDP and provided employment for 430,000 people. Apart from cinemas, for which the official output indicator is based on numbers of attendances, the measures used by the CSO rely for the most part on deflated series of turnover or consumers' expenditure on the service in question. In the case of local authority libraries, however, employment-based indicators are used. In the search for alternative measures it has proved possible, for these services, to base the new indicators largely on numbers of service units. Thus the output index for 'group' 974, broadcasting and theatres, reflects changes in numbers of radio and television hours transmitted and of attendances at theatres etc, whilst that for libraries and museums has been founded on numbers of books issued and numbers of visitors. The new measures for sport, 'group' 979, an activity that accounts for almost half of the output of recreational services, has been derived from a variety of indicators which reflect, inter alia, changes in numbers of attendances at paying spectator sports, sports hours transmitted by television and radio, membership of participatory sports clubs and measures which trace changes in numbers of betting slips and football coupons.

Only in the case of local authority leisure facilities was recourse made to conventional deflated value series. The output series set out for cinemas and for authors and artists are those used officially: that for cinemas being already based on numbers of service units whilst no alternative measure could be readily identified for 'group' 976. For comparison with the overall official measure for recreational services the five component output measures have been combined into a single output index using weights based on 1985 contributions to GDP. The official measure suggests that the output of this service industry complex grew, between 1973 and 1988, at an average annual rate of 2.9 per cent; the alternative points to a significantly slower rate of increase of 2.0 per cent.

One factor which may go some way towards explaining this discrepancy is that whilst in principle the alternative measure includes local authority libraries and leisure facilities throughout the period, the official indicator embraces these activities only since their transfer to class 97 of the 1980 SIC. Yet it can be seen that even in recent years the official measure has registered a significantly higher rate of growth for this industry than that shown by the alternative measure.

THE CATERING TRADES

In 1985 the catering trades' contribution to GDP totalled 7-1/2 pounds sterling billion and the industry employed more than a million people. Output measures for these trades are summarised, in terms of average annual growth rates. In the early years of the period covered the official indicator was based on turnover data supplied by a voluntary panel of catering organisations deflated by price indices specific to each of the catering trades.

From the beginning of the 1980s the official measure has been derived from changes in the margins of the individual catering trades as recorded in the DTI's annual catering trades' enquiry, again deflated by specific price indices. Although in principle it should be possible to measure output in the catering trades on the basis of numbers of service units-hotel bed occupancy, numbers of bar transactions etc-attempts to use this approach proved, for practical reasons, to be fruitless. Therefore to test the sensitivity of the official measure alternative output series were constructed using the price indices officially compiled but applying them throughout to turnover data yielded by the catering trades inquiries, interpolating results for early years where no such inquiries were conducted.

It is clear that these alternative measures alter the picture quite significantly for some trades. Whilst for restaurants, clubs and catering contractors changes in output are not greatly different whether measured on the official or alternative bases, sharply contrasting developments emerge for public houses and the hotel trade: the substantial growth recorded for public houses by the official measure virtually disappears with the alternative, whilst the opposite occurs in the case of hotels. These quite significant modifications to the subsectoral picture, in effect, cancel out: on both official and alternative methods catering output increased over this period by about 1 per cent a year.

The reliability of catering output changes cannot, however, be allowed to rest there. For when these changes are compared with labour force developments there would seem to have been substantial long-term declines in labour productivity: taking the official output measure in conjunction with changes in the number of employees in catering, labour productivity appears to have fallen by as much as 1.7 per cent a year between 1971 and 1986. To help determine whether these results reflect real developments in this service industry or whether they arose from statistical series which are sufficiently unreliable as to produce a misleading picture of events, alternative, more sophisticated, full-time equivalent labour force series have been constructed.

Since both part-time working and self-employment are important features of the catering trades' labour force, allowance for developments in both these aspects has been made in the FTE series shown. Whilst the introduction of FTE labour force series improves the productivity picture there nevertheless remains an apparently substantial fall in catering productivity: an annual average decline of 1.7 per cent a year using numbers of employees is modified to a deterioration of 1.2 per cent on an FTE basis. Of the individual trades only catering contractors emerge with enhanced FTE productivity, displaying an improvement of 1.7 per cent a year.

The other four trades register deteriorations: restaurants by 2.1 per cent a year, public houses 0.1 per cent, clubs 3.6 per cent and hotels 1.2 per cent. It is theoretically feasible, on the basis of most formulations of the production function, that in certain circumstances output in any economic activity might increase over the long term at a rate below that registered for labour inputs.

This could arise in particular if there were a fall in capital intensity but such a development does not appear to have been a feature of catering during this period. A measure compiled for the industry suggests that between 1971 and 1986 the stock of equipment grew at an annual average rate of 3.6 per cent a year which, in conjunction with an annual rise of 2.3 per cent in the FTE labour force, points to a 1.4 per cent annual increase in capital intensity.

In these circumstances it is difficult to accept that either the official or alternative output measures presented adequately reflect output growth in the catering trades. A probable explanation of this deficiency is that the measures fail to take sufficient account of developments, in some general sense, in the quality of catering output, be it a reflection of changes in the range of services offered, the milieu in which they are provided, the nature of the food and drink supplied or the standards of customer service. It is relevant that following comparatively little change in its size during the 1950s and 1960s the catering industry's labour force has grown substantially over the last two decades, especially during the early 1970s.

These developments have generally been explained by contrasts in the nature of the labour market between, on the one hand, the earlier decades and on the other the 1970s and 1980s. The earlier prevalence of full employment meant that because catering work was notoriously unattractive and ill-paid the industry was able to adjust its labour force towards its basic manning requirements. This kind of effect was reinforced by the impact of the selective employment tax which led to a significant fall in catering employment when it was implemented during the later years of the 1960s and a rapid increase in the early years of the 1970s after its abandonment. This thesis is also supported by case studies of the impact on the industry of technological innovations.

A recent survey of organisations operating in the catering trades revealed that rather than causing redundancies 'the time saved by new technology and improved productivity was being used wherever possible to enhance customer service'. A stagnant productivity performance in catering is equally difficult to reconcile with the rapid growth of both take-away food facilities and self-catering accommodation. In the event it has been decided to use labour inputs, to be precise the FTE measure shown, as a surrogate output measure for this industry.

It is felt that whilst far from ideal it provides a less unsatisfactory output measure, over the period in question. On this basis an annual average growth rate of 2.3 per cent emerges for catering output, hardly an unreasonable achievement for what is largely a leisure industry during a period when GDP increased, on average, by 1.7 per cent a year. Furthermore when applied to the individual catering trades this labour force based method yields results, for changes in real output over these years, which are intuitively much more plausible than those derived from either the official or alternative methods. It suggests that between 1971 and 1986 output in all five trades increased substantially: in restaurants by 2.4 per cent a year, in public houses by 2.5 per cent, in clubs by 3.1 per cent, in catering contractors by 2.8 per cent and in hotels by 1.6 per cent.

Measure for All Covered Services

The alternative output measures compiled for financial services, recreational services and the catering trades are combined and compared with their official counterparts. Group 1, for which the series relate to the full period 1971-86, comprises five financial services and the catering trades. Group 2 covering the period 1973-86 includes in addition banking and recreational services. Whilst group 3, for which the output indicators are available for the period 1978-86, embraces all the service industries for which alternative measures have been compiled. These aggregate output indices, both official and alternative, are derived from those presented in the relevant tables using as weights the 1985 contribution of each activity to GDP. The results are summarised in the form of average annual rates of change. To check the sensitivity of these final results alternative and official measures of growth are also compared using as weights the services' 1985 employment levels and 1980 contributions to GDP.

The picture which emerges is one in which the alternative measure consistently points towards a higher growth rate than that indicated by its corresponding official index. Moreover the size of the differential varies comparatively little regardless of the group, period or weighting system to which attention is directed. If most attention is attached-in view of the size of their coverage-to the results for groups 2 and 3, it appears that compared with the alternative methods the official indicators have understated growth by between 13 and 18 per cent.

Given that in most cases the alternative measurement methods differ radically from those officially employed it is perhaps remarkable that, overall, the discrepancy should be no greater than this. To what extent, as it stands, would the official measure of GDP growth be changed if the alternative measure is substituted for the official indicator? The answer is: very little. Basing this adjustment on the alternative/official differential revealed for group 2 the annual average GDP growth rate for 1973-86 is unchanged at 1.3 per cent per annum, and using the group 3 results the annual growth rate for 1978-86 rises from 1.6 per cent to 1.7 per cent. If the disparity between official and alternative growth rates depicted held for the commercial services excluded from this exercise then the official GDP growth rate of 1.3 per cent registered for the period 1973-86 is boosted to 1.5 per cent per annum and the GDP growth rate of 1.6 per cent for the years 1978-86 is raised to 1.9 per cent a year.

There are good reasons for supposing that these upward revisions to the GDP growth rate will understate rather than overstate the actual shortfall. In the first place output measures which lean towards numbers of service units will to some extent be biased downwards compared with those derived from deflated sales or turnover values because the data sources in question tend to cover any new services in the latter but not the former.

Secondly whilst official output measures which rely on employment series usually incorporate some productivity improvement, this has not been applied to the FTE based measure compiled for catering so that it may well underestimate actual output growth in this activity. Thirdly salary indices which have been used as surrogate price deflators in the case of accountancy and computer services will tend to overestimate actual output price increases-and therefore bias downwards the resulting output measure-since no allowance is made for the impact on unit labour costs of any productivity improvements in these services. While the implications for GDP measurement of the substitution of alternative aggregate service output indicators may not be unduly significant it is clear that they are more substantial for the commercial service sector as a whole. They are even more significant for individual service complexes. Although the new measure for financial and business services differs relatively little from the official measure, especially if account is taken of the contrasting conceptual treatment of finance leasing in the respective approaches, the alternative obtained for recreational services points to a significantly lower growth rate and that compiled for catering is about twice the official growth rate. Contrasts between alternative and official measures are even more pronounced for individual service industries.

Service Output Measurement

Substitution of the new output measures for those officially compiled would have made little difference to GDP growth rates in recent years. In effect discrepancies which emerged between alternative and official output measures for individual service industries have tended to offset each other. There is no guarantee that this condition would hold in the future and for this reason alone the search for alternative, improved, measures of service output change should be pursued. In contrast significantly large differences between alternative and official output measures have emerged for particular services and these have very important implications for the analysis of economic developments in individual service industries.

The validity of the economic analyses to which these activities are now widely subjected depends crucially on the accuracy of the output and productivity measures that are employed to map their development over time. For this reason, especially, new and improved service output measures are required.

The research which lies behind the results is that new service output measures can be further developed both extensively and intensively. Whilst the service industries examined were chosen as systematically as possible on the basis of specific criteria, only limitations imposed by time and resources prevented other service activities being subjected to a similar kind of scrutiny. Moreover in many of those service industries which have been surveyed scope for further measurement improvements remain. In this connection attention needs to be drawn to the results obtained for building societies and the catering trades. In the case of the former serious doubts attach to the alternative measure which, although it yields a growth rate higher than the official one, nevertheless implies, as it stands, a long-term fall in labour productivity in this service industry. Also it is clear that the search for improved catering output measures needs to be continued: the labour force indicator adopted for the purpose of this exercise must be regarded as no more than a stop-gap strategem though on the basis of existing statistical sources there is at present little immediate prospect of new measures being based on numbers of service output units.

None the less the data deficiencies are essentially practical, not conceptual, in nature and with appropriate statistical arrangements could no doubt be remedied eventually: already there is some experience of collecting data relating to hotel room utilisation which some time in the future might form the basis of a service unit-based measure. Generally there seems to exist a large reservoir of data relating to both output indicators and weights, collected by a variety of service industry organisations, which lies outside the purview of official sources.

It is difficult to avoid the impression that the current exercise has barely scratched the surface of this fund of material and that, in particular, much is available at the firm level which has yet to be systematically collated in a way that it can be used to measure developments for whole industries. Certainly it is clear that within the firms in question most service outputs are documented in detail, increasingly in computerised records, so that alternative measures based on numbers of output units should become progressively more practicable. There appear to be two basic options for tapping into this kind of data base. One would comprise an official periodic survey of each of the main service industries in which, as in the case of some industrial censuses, questionnaires would seek information about numbers and values of those output units which are best measured for each service. The inquiries into the distributive, catering and service trades periodically conducted by the Business Statistics Office might be developed in this direction.

The alternative is to adopt the approach followed, in the main, in this exercise and base new output measures on the information which is collected by trade associations and other industry organisations. This option is less attractive than the systematic collection of the requisite data, on a comprehensive and consistent basis, by means of an official census.

IMPORTANCE AND USAGE OF DRESS CODES

A survey was conducted to investigate the nature and use of employee dress codes of organizations that market professional services. The study sample consisted of personnel administrators employed in selected service organizations that are members of the American Society of Personnel Administrators; the total sample included 1000 administrators. The analysis of responses revealed that dress is important in marketing services and that compliance to a dress code is a criterion for employee performance evaluation.

While most administrators agreed that dress is a significant factor in their companies' success, few organizations had formal written dress codes; dress codes are most often communicated orally. Traditions in the professions, the expectations of customers, Chief Executive Officers of the organizations, and past experiences were the factors that dominate the development of dress codes. On the question of dress code requirements for male vs. female employees, the study revealed that more service organizations specify dress for males than for females.

For traditional business attire, comparing the dress codes of the different service organizations revealed several significant relationships. In recent years much emphasis has been placed on the importance of dress and appearance for professional success. Often organizations make an effort to manage dress and appearance so as to communicate to the client/customer in the most effective manner. Such controls have traditionally been manifested in policies called "dress codes." The responsibility for the administration of dress codes has conventionally been treated as a personal function. "Proper" business dress has long been a part of the norms of professional services practitioners such as bankers, accountants, stock brokers and management consultants. However, it is interesting to note that in the marketing literature there is little attention devoted to dress as it relates to the marketing of professional services.

This is particularly interesting when one considers the growth of professional service industries as a part of the U.S. economy and the broadscale increases in attention focused on services marketing by practitioners and academicians. The marketing literature does, however, address the issue of personal appearance as it relates to the personal sales interview.

It is well documented from a behavioural standpoint that dress has a significant impact upon perception and image formation as a part of the interpersonal communication process. Peak discovered that when personality traits are correlated with clothing styles, persons who wear conservative clothing are perceived as being more intelligent, mature, generous, sincere, trustful, understanding and dependable than those wearing more "daring" styles. Premeaux and Mondy, dress establishes a level of respect and authority. This is often necessary to get the work done.

In a study on occupation and grooming it was found that less positive characteristics are attributed to those who were groomed "poorly" than to those well groomed. There is an essential difference between the professional salesperson and the professional service practitioner which underlies the justification of this study.

Sales personnel are designated as the "front-line" customer contact persons for an organization which markets goods. Management, as well as salespersons themselves, are not only aware of the role of personal appearance and dress in interpersonal communication, but have employed the resources necessary to incorporate dress codes into promotion and marketing strategies. On the other hand, it is argued that professional service practitioners see themselves as "doers" rather than, sellers". Therefore, it is felt by some that these employees do not focus the necessary attention on those behavioural factors important in selling or marketing as would designated marketing personnel.

As Denny states: One of the fundamental misconceptions many accountants have about marketing is that...someone else can bring in the new clients and then they can take over and do the work. Unfortunately they are wrong...It takes an accountant to sell accounting services. The literature dealing with services marketing ends support to the premise that the dress behaviour of employees could be a salient attribute of the buyer when involved in the purchase process of a professional service.

Two commonly cited characteristics of services, intangibility and inseparability, give credence to this postulate. Because services are intangible in nature, perceptual and communication problems exist during the exchange process which make the true quality of the service difficult to evaluate and distinguish. Pricing and valuation problems result, leading the buyer to feel uncertainty.

With complex technical services such as legal, financial or consulting research, the problem is magnified because of the lack of knowledge of the buyer. It can be argued that because the buyer cannot see the true quality of the service for evaluation that he might use surrogate criteria such as the behaviour of the practitioner, the physical appearance of the facility or other tangible cues. Dress behaviour, then, can become a tangible evaluative criteria for the buyer, regardless of the relationship dress has to the skills of the practitioner or quality of the service performed.

Another theoretical argument offered which distinguishes services from goods is that of inseparability. Often production and consumption of services cannot be separated temporally or spatially. Consequently, personal contact exists between the producer and consumer, allowing the buyer to have the perceptual exposure necessary to observe behavioural and physical characteristics of the seller.

The premise set forth as the rationale for this study is that through their behaviour, each practitioner in a service organization which has customer/client contact plays a role in marketing that organization's service. Since dress is an important aspect of that behaviour which plays a role in the communication process during this interaction, dress behaviour can be a salient factor in the exchange process.

If this premise is accepted, and dress is perceived to be important in marketing of professional services, then the question of management or control of employee dress arises. One would assume that organizations would make an effort to manage appearance so as to communicate to the client/customer in the most effective manner.

The purposes of this study were to identify the nature and extent of usage of dress codes among selected service organizations and to determine the importance of dress in the marketing of professional services as reflected in the attitudes and opinions of personnel administrators and in the policies of their organizations.

The study sample consisted of personnel administrators employed in selected service organizations that are members of the American Society of Personnel Administrators; the total sample included 1000 administrators. The study involved a questionnaire designed to secure information about the perceived importance of dress codes among selected service organizations. Questions concerned the importance of employee appearance for service organizations, the factors used in developing dress codes, the requirements of dress codes, the effect of dress codes on employee performance evaluations, and the dress code requirements for male and female employees. Questionnaires were returned by 304 personnel administrators, a 30.4 per cent return. Data was analysed using frequency distributions, and cid-squares were computed to determine statistical significance. The number of respondents from various types of service industries which were used in this study: Type of Service Organization Number in Sample Management/Marketing Consultants 51 Health Care and Human Services 47 Hotel/Restaurant/ Entertainment 40 Financial 39 Employment Agencies 39 Other 35 Engineering and/or Computer Services 30 Legal 13- Total 304 The personnel administrators responding to the questionnaire clearly indicated that appearance of professional employees was a significant factor when a potential client or customer evaluated their company's services. Most of the respondents indicated that personal appearance was a "very important" factor in this evaluation process.

Of the 304 responding personnel administrators, 73% indicated that a dress code, either formally or informally communicated, had been established for their service organizations. Among those respondents whose organizations employed any type of dress code, 67% noted that individual employee compliance to the code was a criterion for employee performance evaluation. Eighty-five per cent of the respondents indicated that compliance to a dress code was either absolutely necessary or very important when employers underwent performance evaluation.

The employment of an established dress code varied little by type of services, ranging from 66 per cent for management consultants to 83 per cent for employment placement services. But the differences in the formalization and use of compliance varied more dramatically. While only 19 per cent of management consulting firms had established written dress codes, 60 per cent of the hotel/restaurant/entertainment groups used written codes.

The data revealed that differences in the use of written codes existed between types of services, and that these were statistically significant at the.05 level. Only 42 per cent of management consulting firms considered dress code compliance in evaluation of their employees, while 80 per cent of employment placement/personnel services considered dress compliance as a factor in performance reviews. The respondents were asked to rank the level of importance of eleven factors when developing a dress code. The scale ranged from "very important," "fairly important," "of little importance," to "no importance," with each given numerical weights of 1, 2, 3, and 4 in corresponding order. Mean scores and the percentages responding to each level of importance are reported. Customer expectations, tradition/convention in the profession, and the opinion of the organization's C.E.O. were the three most important factors listed by the respondents in the development of dress codes.

Among those respondents whose organizations employed any type of dress code, chi-square analysis was performed to compare the classifications of the companies to the formality of the dress codes. Though not statistically significant, the study revealed that more of the local/independent service organizations used formal written dress codes, while more of the multi-located firms utilized dress codes which were informally communicated. Over one-third of the respondents indicated that their dress codes had been established within the last 20 years.

Many of the companies had made changes in their dress codes within the last 10 years. Though not statistically significant, it was found that the firms with revised dress codes were more relaxed in requiring a traditional business look. The differences in the degree of requirement for wearing a "traditional business suit" by type of business organization. Of all types of services in the sample, financial services most required business suits, and engineering/computer least. Those organizations classified as personnel services expected the wearing of suits with skirts more often than others, and again the engineering/computer services required the traditional suit with skirt to the least degree.

Most of the respondents indicated that dress is important in marketing services and that compliance to a dress code is a criterion for employee performance evaluation. While most administrators agreed that dress is a significant factor in their companies' success, few organizations had formal written dress codes; dress codes are more often communicated orally. The results of this study lend support to the premise that dress and appearance of employees could be a salient attribute of the buyer when involved in the purchase process of a professional service. Although the usage of dress codes differed among service organizations, many administrators agreed that dress and appearance are particularly important in making an initial impression and in progressing in a business career. More needs to be known about the actual impact of dress and appearance on the communication process with clients and customers in professional service organizations.

QUALITY IN SMALL- AND MEDIUM-SIZED HOTELS

Total Quality Management can be defined as a satisfaction of social shareholders via implementing effective planning, programmes, policies, and strategies, as well as using human and other assets efficiently and continually within an organization.

This approach will continue to be one of the hot topics among practitioners, academics, and professionals in the new millennium. This presents how a new TQM readiness model can be utilized for providing social shareholders' satisfaction and continuous improvement in small- and medium-sized hotel organizations.

Five-star hotel staffs appear to have better organizational strengths than four-star hotel staffs in North Cyprus. Four-star hotel employees indicate substantial differences in their perceptions concerning TQM readiness elements. An extensive literature review has been conducted.

Issues examined include the following:

- Where to start?
- Is it valuable to bring such a total system?
- Should some parts be imported instead of the whole? and
- Is there any cheap way to bring TQM to small- or medium-sized organizations?

Oakland, the first decision of where to begin can be daunting, referred to as the Total Quality Paralysis problem in quality-management literature. This has been confirmed by other experts and academics who state that small- and medium-sized enterprises generally are less comfortable in bringing TQM into their organizations than large companies are due to limited managerial knowledge, skill, ability, incentives, resources, and time. Only a few studies have been developed on TQM readiness assessment criteria in small- and medium-sized firms. Scholars and others have a common understanding that the more clearly the TQM readiness factors are assessed, the healthier a transition can be achieved to the TQM process. The TQM literature states, "Organizations, which are ready for change in climate, have more opportunity to achieve a successful implementation in a shorter period of time". A common point endorsed in the literature is that there must be a readiness survey before designing, developing, and implementing a TQM programme. This may help to determine TQM factors within an organization and to identify potential problems that may create resistance to TQM and will help to develop a database for future comparisons. Walker and Salameth have stated that only a small percentage of hotels have heard "the siren call of TQM implementations" even in the U.S. It is interesting to note that after 10 years, the literature regarding hotels is still sparse.

Although some viable hotels in limited geographical areas have reported that their TQM performance resulted in profit increased, employee satisfaction, and better usage of economic resources, only a few case studies have been published. As Bloomquist and Breiter indicate, "While those case studies are important in elaboration on the theme of quality management, there remain no reliable statistical data on industry-wide performance credited to quality management."

CHALLENGE FOR HOTEL ORGANIZATIONS

Cyprus is the third-largest island in the Mediterranean. Cyprus has a great historical heritage, conserved environment beauties, and a good climate, and after the war in 1974, the island was divided into north and south parts. No study has been conducted on how TQM can be applied in small- and medium-sized hotel organizations in North Cyprus, which is a major deficiency since tourism is the leading sector. North Cyprus is certainly not the only country where tourism is the most important business sector. The World Tourism

Organization statistics, tourism in the world is expected to reach a volume of $US 4 trillion after 2000. This will mean that one out of nine people in the world will be employed in tourism industry in 2010.

The aim of this analysis is to provide a better understanding of how different groups of managers, chiefs, and employees perceive their readiness towards the TQM philosophy in North Cyprus four and five-star hotels. In June 1999, a preliminary investigation was carried out through one-on-one interviews with several assistant general managers, department managers, chiefs, and other lower-level employees from the four- and five-star hotels of North Cyprus. The aim was to design a more realistic TQM readiness model, as well as to prepare a better quantitative questionnaire for the targeted hotels.

The hypotheses of this study are as follows: There is no difference between small-and medium-sized hospitality organizations' hierarchical levels concerning their TQM readiness. There is a difference between small-and medium-sized hospitality organizations' hierarchical levels concerning their TQM readiness. A new model with its first selected eight factors of TQM culture was identified.

These factors are leadership, participation, teamwork, employee satisfaction, empowerment, influence, change, and training. It is important to mention that the assessment factors may not represent all the TQM readiness culture factors. In time, other related factors may be added to this group.

THE ASSUMPTIONS UNDERLYING THE MODEL

The assumptions underlying this model include the following:

- The readiness model factors are iterative; in other words, every organization may use several different preassessment factors, and the rank of these factors also may be different.
- TQM is not a completely new strategic system but rather is a process of developing the current system, opening its way to continuous improvement.
- The readiness model will decrease the total cost, time, and energy of an organization in transforming it into a new TQM culture.

The model involves two important stages. The first stage is to understand and to monitor the present organizational system, especially when dealing with the factors of TQM philosophy and its soft components such as leadership, teamwork, participation, influence, empowerment, and employee satisfaction.

The second stage is the process of examining the gap between upper, middle, and lower layers of personnel in order to prevent possible resistance from different layers at the time of transitioning to a new TQM culture, as well as preparing a database for future assessments. This database may serve as a benchmark where yearly data can be compared with the previous year, necessary precautions can be taken against weaknesses, and the organization can open its way to a continuous improvement process.

Of course, if the necessary proactive precautions can be taken successfully every year, the actual gap among the layers of staff will be narrowed in terms of employee resistance and inefficient use of time, money, and energy. As a result of successful TQM applications, the social shareholders will be more satisfied, and effects of internal challenges will be minimized for the organization.

The data in this study were obtained from four- and five-star hotels. In these hotels, the general manager, usually the owner or a relative who has a very close relationship to the investors, has overall responsibility for all activities. The department managers work under the control of the general managers and report directly to them.

Department chiefs largely serve the role of supervisors, reporting to the department manager. The rationale for selecting four- and five-star hotels is because they attract the majority of tourists in North Cyprus. A total of seven out of 10 hotels were included in the study. There are two hotels that are identified as five-star hotels; the remaining five are four-star hotels. All seven of these five- and four-star hotels were sampled, which provide an overall 100 per cent sampling ratio among five-star hotels and 87 per cent sampling ratio among four-star hotels. This stratified-sampling ratio is very high, and therefore the research is designed to be representative. Stratified sampling has been used in determining the number of employees of four- and five-star hotels. The stratified sampling technique "separates the population into relative homogenous groups".

The hotels employed approximately 550 permanent staff according to statistics gathered from the tourism ministry at the time of the research. The average return rate from the quantitative survey collected from the managers, chiefs, and employees was 73 per cent, 85 per cent, and 39 per cent respectively. Among the 500 questionnaires distributed, 267 were returned, 10 were not completely answered, and 13 were considered biased. Consequently, 23 responses were deleted from the analyses.

The net return rate of 43.8 per cent was quite adequate for the set of questions. A perception survey, a self-administered questionnaire addressed to all managers, chiefs, and employees of the targeted hotels, was prepared in order to collect the necessary readiness data from a more comprehensive perspective.

Respondents were asked to indicate their degree of agreement with each statement on a five-point Likert scale: 1=strongly agree, 2=agree, 3=somewhat agree/disagree, 4=disagree, and 5=strongly disagree. Furthermore, three questions were asked about the ranking of the hotel, type of ownership, and the job position. Items for each subscale were subjected to a reliability assessment. The Cronbach coefficient alpha value for the total scale was 9602, and the subscales were 9092, .8425, .8812, .7177, .6993, .7164, .6976, and.7744 for leadership, team, influence, empowerment, participation, training, change, and satisfaction.

Usually, a reliability coefficient above 0.50 is considered to be a sufficiently high reliability. A factor analysis of the TQM readiness questions in the survey was performed. In order to identify the actual factors in the survey, all questions that did not load cleanly on one factor were dropped from further analysis, which left 61 questions. The frequency and one-way analysis of variance were calculated as a second statistictical technique. Levin and Rubin, ANOVA tests are used for determining the significance of the differences among more than two sample means.

The critical mean scores of the TQM readiness survey for the four- and five-star hotel mangers, chiefs, and staff. A one-way ANOVA analysis is used to explore whether there is a significant difference in the perceptions among upper-, middle-, and lower-level employees of the hotels. In terms of highest and lowest scores, it has been observed that there is little consistency in perceptions among the three staff levels. Results for five-star hotels indicate that employees have significantly higher scores on seven items: teamwork, leadership, and influence.

For those seven items, employees had the highest mean scores. Considering all 61 questions, four-star hotel employees are less positive than five-star hotel employees. They have significantly higher scores on 32 items. For those 32 items, all staff has different scores on each item. Interestingly, the managers have higher mean scores than chiefs and employees on eight items, which are mainly dealt with through satisfaction, empowerment, participation, and leadership.

The chiefs gave negative scores to change, empowerment, teamwork, and participation factors through six questions. Four-star hotels had aggregate means for the 61 items indicated by managers, chiefs, and employees. Both managers and chiefs expressed a moderate level of TQM readiness, while employees exhibited a low level of TQM readiness. However, in five-star hotels, the aggregate means for the same items were managers, chiefs and staff, where all expressed a moderate level of TQM readiness.

Therefore, the null hypothesis was rejected, and the alternative hypothesis was accepted. North Cyprus is a suitable island for tourism because of its undeveloped industry, rich historical and cultural heritage, natural beauty, and relatively unspoiled environment. The various governments that have come to power all have stated that tourism is the primary sector in achieving economic development. The aim of this research was to find out how different groups of managers, chiefs, and employees of four- and five-star hotels in North Cyprus perceive their readiness towards the TQM philosophy With this study it is possible to point out to the owners arid managers the weak and strong aspects of the TQM soft side components they are practicing, and it also provides an opportunity to remove the resistance and conflicts that arise because of perception differences about this philosophy Some researchers point out that in many cases, TQM has been applied without any readiness research and has thus resulted in failure.

As Weeks, "The perceptions of managers, chiefs, and employees are crucial because individuals act as if their beliefs or perceptions are real." Social shareholders are defined by the author as interested or chain parties who are in the same business arena and are a part of the same business life in a free market economic system such as customers, owners, employees, suppliers, government, municipality, and so forth. Two of the five-star hotels are in the same complex and therefore are considered as one hotel. Two hotels have been excluded from the research due to extraordinary reasons.

COMPETITIVE ADVANTAGE

This offers an in-depth treatment of conversion franchising, where new franchisees are added to a franchised system by recruiting existing independent entrepreneurs or competitors' franchisees. The first part of the paper examines conversion franchising as a source of competitive advantage. This discussion leads to the articulation off our propositions. The second part of the paper looks at the empirical results of our study of 72 North American franchisors.

Seventy-two per cent of these firms use conversion franchising in their domestic markets, and 26 per cent use conversions in international locales. The propositions relating to a franchisor's decision to use conversions based on increased levels of experience, economic resources, and to a lesser extent skills! knowledge, all were supported. These results lend support to the literature indicating that resources and skills serve as sources of competitive advantage. Implications for research and practice are discussed. Franchising is emerging as a preferred method of doing business throughout the global economy.

A recent study by the International Franchise Association estimated that, by early in the new millennium, nearly 50 per cent of every U.S. consumer dollar would have been spent in franchised locations. Business franchising has spread rapidly to most continents during the past decade. Given the widespread use of franchising, how can firms leverage better this method of doing business? Some firms have gained increased advantage by adding mobility to their franchised operation by bringing their products/services to the customer where and when they demand them.

But increasingly, firms are turning to conversion franchising as a way of enhancing growth and of gaining competitive advantage in multiple markets. Conversion franchising occurs when a franchisor adds new franchisees to the system by recruiting existing independent businesses or competitors' franchisees.

The purpose of this chapter is to examine closely this emerging phenomenon by drawing on relevant literature and by reporting the results of an exploratory study of conversion franchising. Before discussing some of the competitive advantages that can accrue from employing conversion franchising, it first is instructive to review some of the advantages of traditional franchising. Franchising's longevity and success also may be due to the fact that, organizationally, it represents a collaborative alliance.

The alliance depends on the cooperation of two entrepreneurs in order to be successful. Further, these partners depend on cooperation among a network of entrepreneurs to advance common methods and goals, like the sharing of information on innovations that potentially could benefit all franchise partners.

Franchising traditionally has offered many competitive advantages over independently formed and operated businesses. The franchisor has access to capital at lower risk; cost sharing with the franchisee; rapid market penetration at a relatively lower cost than establishing one's own distribution system; economies of scale; a motivated workforce of indigenous entrepreneurs; and reduced monitoring and control costs. The franchisee gets an opportunity to enter a business at less cost with a proven product or service and brand name. Additionally, the franchisee frequently receives management assistance in the areas of business location, facilities design, operating procedures, purchasing, and marketing.

These advantages have been born out by a superior survival rate for franchising over independent ventures. Next, we turn to a discussion of conversion franchising and its competitive advantages. Conversion franchising occurs when a franchisor adds new franchisees to the system by recruiting independent businesses, chains, and/or franchisees from other franchised systems. Conversion franchising offers additional advantages to those discussed under traditional franchising. The use of conversion franchising appears to be expanding in recent years, as several industries have experienced changing environmental conditions that often have combined to favour this form of franchising.

The environmental conditions fostering conversions include economic, market, competitive, and technological changes. A contracting economy can mean tight credit policies, making it difficult to raise funds for new projects. During one such period, 3.7 per cent of the domestic hotels converted to a new brand affiliation. A restricted real estate market has led many fast food franchisors to convert existing urban locations to their system rather than to devel op new sites. Saturated markets and increased competition coupled with the growing consumer demand for rejuvenated brand names have generated conversions in the real estate and hospitality industries.

Independents have converted to ReMax and ERA, while Holiday Inn has converted some Ramada Inns and vice versa. Keeping abreast of changing technology has forced firms to seek conversions with systems on the cutting edge of technology, such as Century 21 and Coldwell Banker in Real Estate or Marriott's reservation system in the lodging industry. Resource-based models of organization indicate that established know-how serves as a basis for competitive advantage. Experienced franchisors have developed such managerial capabilities.

Moreover, experienced firms often operate in more competitive arenas, in turn forcing them to try innovative strategies such as conversions. Experienced franchisors have learned to share their know-how with franchisees and have established a record of strong performance, in part because they have taken the time to build brand equity and economies of scale in purchasing, advertising, and distribution, all of which are attractive to independent businesses. Thus, we suggest the following proposition: Proposition 1: The decision to use conversion franchising is associated positively with the experience of the franchisor.

Once a business has converted to a new franchise, is the conversion likely to lead to sustainable competitive advantage? Possible answers to this question are examined in the ensuing discussion. Using the framework of competitive advantage from the field of strategic management is consistent with the view expressed by Castrogiovanni and Justis that researchers need to consider findings from outside the franchising field to assess their generalizability to franchisors.

Competitive advantage is concerned with developing a value-creating strategy by uniquely combining bundles of valuable firm resources and skills to yield positional advantages that result in positive outcomes. Firm resources include both tangible and intangible assets. Firm skills include organizational, technical, and market knowledge, among others.

Aaker argues that a retail location superior to the competition's can act as a key asset, leading to competitive advantage. Barney suggests that a valuable location can act as an imperfectly imitable physical capital resource for the firm, while Day and Wensley see location as a tangible resource that can enable a firm to exercise its capabilities, leading to positional advantage. An existing location may be the only space available on a crowded playing field. This is particularly true in the restaurant, retail, and hotel industries, where location is a key element. Franchisors can acquire location resources in tight real estate markets by converting independents or chains that possess strategic locations.

A strong brand name may be regarded as a superior resource or as a key asset, leading to competitive advantage for today's firms. Consumers in every industry are increasingly brand conscious. At the core of the franchising concept is the bundling of a brand or a trade name with a good or service to sell to entrepreneurs in return for fees or royalties. The need to maintain brand equity motivates franchisors to grow their systems in order to develop promotion economies and, therefore, to spread promotion costs over more units. Converting independents to a franchise system allows for rapid growth and increased name recognition.

For example, in the hotel industry converting members of other chains has been shown to lead to increased occupancy rates. Thus, conversions permit firms to reposition themselves under a new brand to enhance their competitive position. Human resources are critical to the proper execution of any strategy

Franchising taps into entrepreneurs who sign on as franchisees to manage individual business units. Sen provides an extended discussion of the franchisee as a source of managerial talent. While entrepreneurs may be motivated to do well, they often are inexperienced and require considerable training on the part of the franchisor.

Using inexperienced franchisees poses a risk of adverse selection, that is, the franchisee misrepresents his/her abilities to the franchisor. Conversion franchising enables the franchisor to bring in experienced franchisees who already have managed a similar business in the industry, either as an independent or as a franchisee for a competitor, thereby reducing the risk of adverse selection. Experienced managers are more likely to enhance a repositioned unit's performance than one with less industry experience. Furthermore, such an experienced franchisee requires less training support. An existing customer base is a major resource that independents and members of other chains possess that can be internalized by the franchisor upon conversion. Since converts can resume business rapidly with existing customers, royalty streams also can begin flowing quickly to the franchisor.

Of course, an additional benefit is that a competitor now has been co-opted into the system instead of working against it. We suggest the following: Proposition 2: The franchisor's decision to use conversion franchising is associated with the potential resource advantages provided by conversions. It has just been argued that conversion franchising brings together key resources of the franchisor and franchisee that have a high potential for improving the competitive positioning of each alliance member.

We now will examine important skills that can play a role in creating competitive advantage. As a cooperative alliance, conversion franchising facilitates the sharing and enhancement of skills to improve the competitive position of both the convert and the franchisor in expanding markets. Skills or capabilities are those attributes that enable the firm to coordinate and to exploit its resources. At the core of the firm's capabilities are its knowledge base from which the skills originate. Thus, we now examine the role knowledge of markets, technology, and organization plays as key sources of competitive advantage provided by a firm's skills.

When a franchisor enters a new market, he or she does so with a limited knowledge of local market conditions and consumer preferences. Since cultures, consumer behaviour, and marketing methods are often different in various markets, franchised systems may need to be adapted to fit local requirements better.

Feltenstein argues that firms need to think globally but to act locally and that much of the variability in sales, service, costs, and margins is determined by local market knowledge. Experience in growing the business provides enhanced knowledge for franchisors in areas such as market and site selection. Acquiring experienced converts helps leverage the advantage of such experience. Moreover, converting independents or other chain members who have been operating in the local market for some time allows the franchisor to internalize these skills into the franchise system. Newly allied members also can aid the franchisor in maneuvering around local rules and regulations that otherwise could slow down or could block a venture. Since conversions typically are of firms operating in the same type or in closely related businesses, converts bring their technical knowledge and expertise to the partnership.

Two general types of technical knowledge are especially relevant in the case of conversions: industry and franchising knowledge. Knowledge relevant to the industry in terms of competitors, substitutes, methods of distribution, and general industry practices are critical to determining competitive advantage. A convert brings new perspective on industry knowledge to the franchisor, broadening the latter's knowledge base and vice versa.

Experience in a particular type of franchising is critical to a system's competitive advantage. The franchise concept is developed on what is believed to be a successful set of practices, and then knowledge bundles are replicated for franchisees. Independents who convert may obtain the immediate advantages of competing with a proven franchise concept. Converts who are previous franchisees presumably have switched because they perceive the new franchisor to have a superior franchise concept.

Such franchise-experienced converts, however, also may provide additional knowledge from their prior franchising experience to enhance the concept of their new franchisor, thereby providing advantages for the entire system. Converts' technical skills are enhanced by the franchisor through extensive training of new members through operating manuals and procedures, and through technical guidance and support. For example, PIP Printing, a leader in the quick-printing industry, offers its franchisees training workshops. The technical skills of the franchisee are enhanced further by the introduction of sophisticated computer systems. In real estate, 20 per cent of the firms in the U.S. are organized as a franchise. New franchisees in this industry gain access to nationwide databases of existing housing stock. Franchising enables a firm to harness the efforts of entrepreneurs while reducing the costs of monitoring a large multiunit organization. Thus, organizational skills revolve around monitoring to prevent franchisees who either may under invest in their units or may shirk on product quality because these actions affect the entire franchise system.

The scale or size of the system contributes to improved organizational coordination. Increased size of the firm enhances monitoring capabilities of the franchisor by reducing the lower per unit costs of monitoring. Conversions enable a franchisor to expand more quickly, thereby strengthening the organizational monitoring skills of the franchisor. Another way to control opportunism is through the payment of fees to the franchisor; this provides financial incentive not to behave opportunistically because the franchisor risks forfeiting the fee if the franchisor suspends the relationship.

Monitoring capability also can be enhanced by learning how best to control the franchisee's behaviour over time. Thus, the longer the franchisor has been offering franchises, the greater the likelihood of improved monitoring skills. Independents can gain other improved organizational efficiencies, such as increased purchasing power, joint or pooled advertising, and other benefits of similar economies of scale, by joining a franchise system. We offer the following proposition: Proposition 3: The franchisor's decision to use conversion franchising is associated with the potential skill advantages provided by conversions.

The literature on competitive advantages stresses those factors that facilitate the development of competitive advantage. However, traditional strategic management theory also notes that the acquisition of skills and resources may also be seen as threats or as challenges confronting the firm when undertaking a new strategy. Anecdotal evidence from franchise experience suggests that certain problems may be encountered when making conversions. Some of the resource-related challenges posed by conversions include the added time it takes to implement a programme or to socialize or to retrain converts. Newly acquired entrepreneurs may be experienced but may be unwilling to work as part of a team or to readily adopt new business methods, thus diluting the advantages of a conversion.

Market, technical, and organizational capabilities may be threatened because of the need to adopt new rules or methods to accommodate a new local market or to attract a convert to join. In short, the franchise concept and standard contract may be changed for opportunistic rather than strategic reasons in order to attract and retain new converts. The reality of the existence of such threats or barriers suggests the following: Proposition 4: The franchisor's decision to use conversion franchising will he associated negatively with the perceived existence of threats posed by the conversion.

The purpose of this empirical part is to provide a description of the current nature and extent of the use of conversion franchising among North American franchisors; and to provide an initial examination of the propositions relating to the factors behind the decision to use conversion franchising by franchisors. A random sample stratified by size and industry of 250 North American franchisors were selected for the study from the Franchise Annual. The top manager of each firm was sent a cover letter and a two-page questionnaire concerning their use of conversion franchising; one follow-up mailing was sent three weeks later.

Seventy-eight firms responded. Six decided not to participate because of mergers, company policy, etc.; 72 firms returned useable questionnaires for a 29 per cent response rate. This compares favourably with other surveys of franchise companies that have reported similar return rates. The profile of franchisors in our sample reveals a good distribution of firms across eight broad industry sectors. The firms are large, averaging 746 total units and having an average of 23 years experience in franchising. The majority of responding managers hold sufficiently high level positions in their organizations to be considered knowledgeable about their firm's franchise strategies. A comparison of respondent firms to a random sample of 40 non respondents in terms of industry, size, and age revealed no significant differences. This should reduce concerns of response bias in our sample. The survey instrument consisted of 10 questions. After defining conversion franchising, the first question asked the respondents to indicate their agreement concerning 18 characteristics of conversion franchising.

These characteristics represented the advantages and barriers of conversion franchising. Responses were made on a Likert-type scale ranging from 1 = not at all to 5 = highly descriptive of your experience. Other questions asked whether the firm used conversion franchising and explored the extent and reasons for doing so. The last three questions explored the use of conversions in international markets. We describe the variables used to explore the four propositions. The decision to convert was assessed by the following survey question: Has your firm used conversion franchising now or in the past?

A simple yes/no response was recorded. This is the categorical dependent variable for investigating the propositions. The remaining variables serve as the independent variables. Franchisor experience was expressed as the number of years the firm had been in business. These were combined further into two factors using principle components analysis with varimax rotation; these factors explain 50 per cent of the variance in conversion advantages. One factor represents "market/location skills" and is comprised of 4 items and has an eigenvalue of 1.58 and a reliability of =.60. The second factor represents "economic resources" and is comprised of five items and has an eigen-value of 2.87 and a reliability of varies =.73.

Two items did not load on any factor. A third item was dropped from the market factor due to reliability problems. These latter three items were not included in any tests of the propositions. Other sources of competitive advantages based on skills were drawn from the Franchise Annual. Technical advantages included seven dummy variables representing eight industry sectors. Franchising knowledge was assessed by the number of years the firm had been franchising. The organizational skills assessed were monitored through scale and financial bonding. Scale was measured by the number of franchised units possessed and financial bonding was measured using the initial franchising fee charged by the franchisor. Competitive barriers/threats were assessed strictly with subjective measures drawn from the eighteen conversion franchising characteristics described earlier. Seven of the items represented potential barriers or threats.

These were reduced to two factors using principle components analysis. The factors explain 49 per cent of the variance in conversion barriers. One factor was labeled "changes" because of the adjustments to existing procedures required by conv ersions. This factor was comprised of three items and has an eigenvalue of 1.52 and a reliability of infinity =.50. The second barrier was labeled "effort" because of the extra effort required by the franchisor to make conversions and was comprised of four items and possesses and eigenvalue of 1.89 and a reliability of infinity =.60 The nature and extent of conversion franchising is described using descriptive statistics. The exploration of the propositions was analysed using discriminant analysis.

The decision to convert represents a nominal dependent variable. The analysis derives a linear combination of independent variables that will discriminate best between the firms that use conversion franchising and the nonusers. The analysis determines whether the competitive advantages and barriers posed by conversion franchising account for a significant variance in the decision to convert. In addition, this method of analysis determines both the predictive accuracy of the independent variables and their relative importance in explaining the decision to convert.

Seventy-two per cent of the firms surveyed use conversion franchising in their domestic markets. Almost half began using conversions prior to 1987; the remaining firms have started using conversions since that time. Among the firms using conversions, an average of 26 per cent of their units are conversions. In responding to an openended question as to why businesses converted to their franchise, our respondents identified eight major reasons. The most frequently cited reasons were to acquire a brand name, which represents one of the major competitive resources conversions can provide businesses.

Awareness, identity, and recognition on a national or global level were cited as the chief benefits of branding. Franchisor characteristics and operating results were tied for second as the most frequently cited reasons for conversion. Key franchisor characteristics included proprietary products and quality of operation and system. Operating performance benefits of conversions included better pricing, leading to increased sales and profitability.

Support services such as technology and research and development, as well as training, each were tied for third in importance for conversions. These represent technological and organizational skills frequently mentioned as advantages of joining a good franchise system. Cost savings and other marketing benefits represented the fourth and fifth major reasons why franchisors believe that businesses convert to their system.

These reasons appear to be congruent with the expected competitive advantages of conversion franchising discussed previously. One of the difficulties in using conversions is that franchisors may have to make adjustments to their normal franchise plans in order to attract well-run businesses to convert. However, less than 25 per cent of the franchisors using conversions needed to make any changes to their normal conversion franchise plan.

Most changes made to attract converts included reduced fees; added training; reduced royalties; covered remodeling costs; additional capital;

longer contracts; and other. Thus, a variety of changes are made by a minority of franchisors in order to attract businesses to convert to their system. The majority of franchisors who are currently using conversions to grow plan to continue using them in the future. Thirty-one per cent plan to increase their use of conversions; 25 per cent plan to use them at the same rate as in the past. Only two per cent of the franchisors plan to decrease their use of conversions in their domestic markets. These intentions indicate that franchisors are satisfied that conversion franchising delivers distinct advantages over other forms of doing business. The survey also briefly explored the franchisors' use of conversions in international markets.

Twenty-six per cent of the respondents use conversion franchising in international markets. Half of these franchisors began using conversions internationally in 1990 or after, and currently an average 5.8 per cent of their overseas units are conversions. The country markets in which they have the largest number of conversions include Canada, Germany, France, and the U.K.. Importantly, of the franchisors using conversions internationally, 61 per cent intend to increase their future use of conversions internationally.

By way of summary, the descriptive data reveal that a substantial proportion of North American franchisors are using conversion franchising. Businesses were attracted to convert because of numerous competitive advantages associated with conversion franchises. The future of conversions appears to be quite promising, especially in international markets, as the domestic market becomes more saturated.

All four propositions advanced regarding the factors associated with a franchisor's decision to use conversion franchising were examined using discriminant analysis. Since there were only two categories for the dependent variable, a single discriminant function was derived. The function, using competitive advantages and barriers to predict the decision to convert, is meaningful. The function accounts for 55 per cent of the variance in the decision to convert.

The validity of the function is ascertained by how well it predicts the classification of firms between those that use conversion franchises and those who do not. The derived function correctly classified 93 per cent of the firms. This is almost a 33 per cent improvement over chance alone. A statistically significant and valid function also may be interpreted. For interpretation, we use the discriminant loadings from the structure matrix. These loadings are simple correlations between each independent variable and the discriminant function. The loadings can be interpreted similar to factor loadin gs to assess the relative contribution of each independent variable.

The analysis of the discriminant loadings and their ability to discriminate between franchisors who convert and those who do not reveals five variables that significantly explain the decision to convert. Proposition 1, the decision to convert is associated with franchisor experience. Only experienced franchisors with an established reputation and system can use conversions meaningfully. Proposition 1 is supported as "experience," has a relatively high, positive loading, and is also a significant discriminator between franchisors who use conversions and those who do not.

Proposition 2, concerning the resource advantages associated with conversion franchising, is supported. "Economic resources" has a high positive loading, and its mean is also significantly different between the two groups of franchisors. Firms that use conversions perceive that they derive greater competitive resource advantages than firms who do not u se conversions. Proposition 3 concerning the association of "skill/knowledge" advantages of conversion partially is supported. Franchise skills market skills, and industry knowledge all are associated with the decision to convert.

Franchise and market skills have the two highest, positive loadings and are significant discriminators as indicated by tests of mean differences. The retail industry sector has a moderate but negative loading. The negative loading suggests that nonretail industry experience is more relevant in the decision to convert; other industry categories did not have high loadings, however.

The ability of this variable to discriminate between the two groups is marginal. Organizational monitoring skills achieved through scale and bondings had relatively weaker loadings and were not significantly different among the two groups of franchisors, contrary to our proposition. Finally, competitive barriers did not add significant discriminating information to the decision to convert, contrary to Proposition 4. Neither effort nor changes had strong loadings, nor were their means significantly different between the two groups of franchisors. However, the negative sign of the loadings for effort was in the predicted direction.

Overall, our implicit model of franchisor experience and the competitive resources and skill advantages provided by conversion franchising appear to be significant predictors of the decision to use conversions. Although competitive barriers appear to exist, they do not appear to contribute significantly to the decision to convert, at least among this sample of franchisors. Although conversion franchising appears to have been used for some time, its use has accelerated recently. Over half of the firms have started using conversion franchising since 1987.

While conversions appear to be more prevalent in domestic rather than international markets, a greater proportion of firms intend to increase their use of conversions in international versus domestic markets. The descriptive data also seem to support the franchising and strategy literature regarding why firms convert to a franchise system. Resources such as brand identity, franchisor support, and training were among the most frequently cited reasons.

Three of four propositions concerning the factors affecting the decision to use conversion franchising were supported in whole or in part. The most significant discriminant variables explained 69 per cent of the variance accounted for by the discriminant function. Our results confirm that firm experience, economic resources, market skills, franchising knowledge, and selected industry experience all contribute significantly in explaining why franchisors use conversion franchising as part of their growth strategy.

These results support the strategy and marketing literature, indicating that resources and skills serve as sources of competitive advantage. The results also support the franchising literature regarding the various benefits of this form of business organization. Competitive barriers were related negatively to the decision to use conversions but did not have strong loadings, nor did the means of the barriers differ significantly between those firms that use conversions and those that do not. It seems reasonable to assume that franchisors tend to focus more on the advantages rather than on the threats when considering whether or not to use conversion franchising.

The results of this study should be examined in the light of its potential limitations. The sample size may be considered somewhat small, especially when analysing the propositions due to missing data. The results are pertinent only to North American franchisors. However, North American franchisors are the most mature and therefore are the most likely to consider conversions.

Our data reveal that business experience is a significant factor in the decision. Our respondent companies had similar profiles to nonrespondents, minimizing response bias. Our measures of competitive advantages and barriers were drawn mostly from the field rather than the literature; this may reduce their explanatory power. However, both subjective and objective measures of competitive advantages were used to reduce same-source bias.

Slightly more than half of the variance in the decision to convert was accounted for by the variables examined in this study. Thus, these results provide a partial but not a complete picture of the factors affecting a firm's decision to use conversion franchising. With the limitations in mind, we offer some implications for practice and research. North American franchisors considering the use of conversions should possess significant experience in their business to develop both their business concept and a strong identity for their brand.

Having done so, franchisors then have something to offer to businesses seeking to join their franchise system. When investigating potential businesses to convert, franchisors must evaluate carefully the resources needed to attract technically qualified businesses with a good track record in order to gain resource advantages. Conversions may enhance the franchisor's market skills if the new franchisees are located in more distant markets and possess a prime business location. Conversions appear to be more attractive in nonretail sectors such as business and personal services and lodging. However, additional research is warranted to confirm these results. North American businesses seeking to convert to a new or different franchise system are advised to seek a franchise with a proven concept and a strong brand identity in the markets in which they want to expand.

Successful business converts should have a proven track record of financial performance. These potential converts should demonstrate that their management team is well experienced and qualified in their industry; however, they may lack some key resource or skill that the franchisor can provide. This has demonstrated the relevance of employing theories of competitive advantage to guide systematic studies of conversion franchising. Future studies should develop more robust measures of competitive advantages and threats.

Larger samples from other parts of the world also should be included to determine if the factors affecting the decision to use conversion franchising are the same in other national or regional markets. A particularly fruitful avenue for future research suggested by our data is the use of conversion franchising for international expansion.

While a minority of the North American firms currently are using international conversions, the majority of these firms intend to increase the use of conversions for international growth. Studies examining the factors affecting the international conversion decision also would be a valuable addition to the franchising knowledge base.

CATERING AND FOOD SERVICE

Catering is the business of providing food service at a remote site. Mobile catering is the business of selling prepared food from some sort of vehicle. It is a feature of urban culture in many countries. The food service generally encompasses those places, institutions, and companies responsible for any meal eaten away from home. This industry includes restaurants, school and hospital cafeterias, catering operations, and many other formats. The companies that supply foodservice operators are called foodservice distributors. Foodservice hard goods like ovens and refrigerators are often sold by large buying groups.

Some companies manufacture products in both consumer and foodservice versions. The consumer version usually comes in individual-sized packages with elaborate label design for retail sale. The foodservice version is packaged in a much larger industrial size and often lacks the colourful label designs of the consumer version.

Foodservice sales to restaurants and institutions are estimated to be approximately $400 Billion, about equal with consumer sales of foods through grocery outlets. A food cart is a motorless trailer that can be hauled by automobile, bicycle, or hand to the point of sale, often a public sidewalk or park. Carts typically have an onboard heating or refrigeration system to keep the food ready for consumption.

Foods and beverages often served from carts include:

- Halal food such as lamb or chicken over rice, or in a gyro
- Ice cream and other frozen treats
- Coffee, bagels, donuts, Egg sandwichs and other breakfast items

Food Truck is a mobile kitchen, known colliqually in some regions as a "X" Truck, is a mobile venue that sells food. Some, including ice cream trucks, sell mostly frozen or prepackaged food; others are more like restaurants-on-wheels.

Food trucks make frequent appearances at carnivals, construction sites, and other temporary venues where large numbers of people gather. Some college campuses and surrounding areas boast many food trucks with loyal followings; for example, visitors to Harvard University or MIT in Cambridge, Massachusetts or the campus of the University of Pennsylvania in Philadelphia may see some very popular trucks parked outside the main entrances to buildings at lunchtime. At Rutgers University, the Grease Trucks serve "fat sandwiches" that contain an ensemble of ingredients such as steak, cheese, chicken fingers, french fries, mozzarella sticks, jalapeño poppers, and more. In the United Kingdom, these are known as burger vans and can be found on nearly all major trunk roads at the side of the road selling their food. A 1/4lb burger can be purchased for about £2.

Many people prefer to stop at one of these Burger vans when travelling due to the cheap price, rather than stop at a motorway service station where prices can be extremely high. Sometimes also called "maggot wagon," "roach coach," or "gut truck," these rolling restaurants can frequently be found at or near construction sites. An early version of the food truck was the US Army's mobile canteen and before that the old West's chuckwagon.

A mobile kitchen is a modified van with a built-in grill, deep fryer, or other cooking equipment. It offers more flexibility in the menu since the vendor can prepare food to order. A vendor can choose to park the van in one place, as with a cart, or to broaden the business's reach by driving the van to several customer locations. Examples of mobile kitchens include taco trucks on the west coast of the United States, especially Southern California, and fish and chips vans in the United Kingdom.

A concession trailer has preparation equipment like a mobile kitchen, but it cannot move on its own. As such it is suited for events lasting several days, such as funfairs. In addition to being operated as private businesses, mobile catering vehicles are also used after natural disasters to feed people in areas with damaged infrastructure. The Salvation Army has several mobile kitchens that it uses for this purpose. An event caterer serves food with waiting staff at dining tables or sets up a self-serve buffet.

The food may be prepared on site, made completely at the event, or the caterer may choose to bring prepared food and put the finishing touches on once they arrive. The event caterer staff isn't responsible for preparing the food but often help set up the dining area. This service is typically provided at banquets, conventions, and weddings. Any event where all the attenders are provided with food and drinks or sometimes only hors d'oeuvres is often called a catered event. A catering company or specialist is expected to know not just food preparation, but how to make it attractive. Many events require working with the entire theme or colour scheme. Catering companies have moved towards full-service taking charge of not only food preparation but also decorations, such as table settings or lighting.

It's not that food is no longer a focal point, but rather that it is part of a broader mission. Many suggest that catering is about satisfying all the senses. A caterer and his or her staff should be friendly and coorperative because, after all, they are in the food service industry and should follow the motto "the customer is always right". Catering is typically sold on a per-person basis, where adding additional people is a flat price per person.

Keeping the cost of the food and supplies below this is required to make a profit on the catering. With the correct atmosphere, professional event caterers experience can bring clients satisfaction of all the senses in a way that makes an event special and memorable. Of course, beautifully prepared food can appeal to your sense of taste, smell and sight—perhaps even touch, but the decorations and ambiance should play a significant part in the clients enjoyment as well. Industrial catering includes providing food for airline passengers, schools, prisons and other institutional settings. It can include contract management of client foodservice facilities.

Airlines often have divisions or hire third parties to provide food for passengers. Catering is covered by two different groups. "Independent caterers and companies with a catering business on the side" is a phrase that could be combined with the previous sentence.

CATERING TIPS AND TRICKS

CHOOSINGRIGHT CATERING SERVICE

Food is an integral part of any party so one must choose a catering service wisely. But how does one choose the right caterer for an event? It is important to do a lot of research, check references, and often request a sampling to make your final decision. List your catering needs In order for a caterer to provide an accurate estimate for your party or event, you must communicate your needs clearly. Do you have a location for your party/event reserved and is there a kitchen on site? How many guests are coming to your event?

Find out if the potential caterer has a minimum guest requirement. Take into consideration that some of your guests may have special dietary needs and be certain to communicate this with your caterer. A great caterer will be ready for any surprise that may surface, but at what cost to you? Discuss your budget with your caterer and what options are available. Ask yourself, do you prefer a buffet style or a silver-service sit down dinner for your guests?

Be clear about your proposed menu, do you have a theme or style at the event that will be reflected in the cuisine? Your budget may or may not determine how flexible your caterer is to meet your needs. Keep in mind; it is the type of food that often determines the bulk price of the catering job. Find out, and possibly request, if the caterer will provide a detailed contract of service and outline what the payment terms will be. Does the caterer use fresh or frozen food for recipes? Is the produce grown locally? Is it organic? Will any of the dishes be pre-made and then frozen until the party/event? Does anything come from a can?

Does the potential caterer supply decorations, linens, tables and chairs? Very often there will be a brochure catering services supply with examples of past event and table decorations. It is important to be very clear in what your event needs and what the caterer will be supplying. Is a menu board provided for the guests that describes the ingredients of the dishes being served?

Will the catering company provide a wait-staff? What is their required dress code? What is the ratio of servers to guests? A rule of thumb is one server for every 10 guests. Be certain to ask your potential caterer if taxes and gratuities are included in the final bid. What happens to the leftovers? Often, upon request, a catering service will compile a food basket at no additional charge for the host or hostess of the event. Remember, it is critical that you communicate with your potential caterer exactly you want; the result, you get what you want and the caterer can provide an accurate bid for the job as well as the exceptional service your event deserves.

SERVING ALCOHOL AT YOUR EVENT

When one commits to planning an event or party, one must decide whether or not to serve alcohol to the guests. There are a few considerations to keep in mind and discuss with your caterer. Where will your event or party be taking place? It is important to confirm that your event or party site will allow alcohol on its premises. Once you have made certain that you can serve alcohol at your chosen site, ask your caterer if he or she holds a liquor license.

He or she must have a valid liquor license. If he or she does not hold a liquor license, then you must contact a liquor-licensed dealer. Prepare to provide a guest estimate for your caterer to work with. The caterer in turn will supply you with a quote for the number of bartenders that must attend bar and the quantity of ice, glasses, and mixers necessary.

The amount of bartenders depends on the number of guests. Your caterer or licensed liquor dealer will be responsible for setting up the bar. You must now determine what you wish to be served from the bar as well as if you require your guests to pay for alcohol themselves. A cash bar requires the guest to pay for their drinks. Guests tend to consume less alcohol when it isn't free. This is a basic bar with all the works and at no charge to the guests. The open bar includes hard liquor for mixing drinks, wine, beer, and soft drinks.

A limited bar will set boundaries on what will be served and in what moderation. An example of a limited bar is an event in which beer and wine is offered to the guests at no charge and hard liquor is offered at a pre-determined price. Whatever you decide in regards to serving alcohol at your event or party is up to you.

WEDDING CATERING

After watching the happy couple exchange vows and begin their married life together, your guests will be hungry. Many of the guests may have scaled back on eating in order to look good for pictures or just because they were so busy during the day. When you're putting together such a large assortment of people, there are bound to be those that have certain ways or preferences of eating. You may find that there are vegetarians or those that can not eat dairy.

You might have a diabetic in the crowd or some other health restriction. You should certainly try to have options for any sort of eating arrangement. In the case of those that don't eat meat, you might want to have a cheese lasagne available or other pasta dish. This is becoming widely popular to have two options anyways, so why not offer them?

Another way to cope with varied needs is to serve dinner in a buffet style. This allows each person to pick only what they want or what they can eat. A lot of wedding caterers rely on word of mouth to get their services recognized. If you can, talk to other people that have gotten married in your town to see who they recommend. Of course, you will still want to see them for yourself, but this list can be a great starting point. Another way to find good catering is to talk to the reception hall coordinators.

Many times they will either require the use of a particular caterer or they have a list of those that they recommend. Of course, you will want to schedule an appointment with all of the catering candidates in order to do a taste test of their menu options. At that point, you can pick what you think your guests will enjoy. A good meal is a great way to send your thanks to your guests for coming to your wedding. This is the part that shouldn't be skimped on for any reason.

Of course, that doesn't mean that you can't find moderately priced options. Try your favourite restaurant, for example. If they're able to cater, then you may be able to get a better deal because you're buying food in bulk. Having a friend who is a cook is even better-so long as they don't mind working through the wedding. So you've tasted the offerings of the caterer and you've selected your main menu options. What about drinks? Much like selecting the menu options, you will need to factor in what kinds of drinks everyone would like to drink. The easiest way to take care of this is to offer a full service bar.

In this way, guests can have mixed drinks of all varieties or they can stick to wine and beer. You want to plan this option out carefully as you may end up paying more than you would like. Check with the provider as to how many drinks each guest can have, or can expect from the supply that will be brought. In most cases, there is no limit. A word of advice: Don't ever have a cash bar. Making your guests pay for their drinks when they may also have paid for their outfits and transportation is just a lot to ask.

In terms of wine and beer, tastes and varieties are enormous-how does someone choose? The best advice is to select four to five different kinds of beer with each one having enough to fill everyone's glass. This may surprise you, but sometimes all of your guests will like the same thing and you may want to make sure that they can have it. As for wine, you may want to have at least one of each a red varietal and a white varietal.

This ensures a milder and more acidic selection. A way to make sure that everyone is happy is to find blends of each of these wines. By blends, this means to find a red that includes a merlot, syrah, and pinot noir, while the white might include a chardonnay, reisling, and zinfandel. These can be tricky to find, but they are crowd pleasers. Toasts are just not toasts without a little glass of champagne. It's common sense to make sure that the new couple and their wedding party have the very finest in champagne, while the rest of the guests have another variety.

In many reception halls or catering services, the champagne for the wedding party is provided. Of course, there will also be designated drivers at the wedding, so you will also want to have water, sodas, coffee, and juices available as well. When you're planned it thoroughly, everyone will be well-watered throughout the evening.

HOW TO START A CATERING BUSINESS

The catering industry in the United States is estimated to be worth $5 billion a year. Caterers are hired to perform an assorted number of jobs-everything from cooking to serving, mixing drinks, and whipping up delicious desserts. Functions range from dinner parties that serve a handful of guests to enormous events that serve thousands of guests. Normally a caterer will define their niche, meaning a caterer will choose what type of functions to specialize in as well as their job description.

For example, you may offer the best fondue table for up to 100 guests, perhaps you would rather prepare meals for business catering parties that are held within banker's hours. There really are no limits in regards to catering styles. Once you have arrived to the idea stage it is great to begin a business catering plan. Be meticulous when you detail how the catering business will be operated, managed and capitalized.

The following checklist can help you organize your ideas into the beginning of a business catering plan:

- What services will your catering business offer? Will you run a full service catering business, corporate catering service, custom event catering service, or a scheduled events catering business?
- Research necessary permits and requirements your local government imposes on a catering business.
- Determine your start up costs of your catering business. Remember to include everything-permit fees, catering equipment, marketing, uniforms, catering supplies etc.

- Construct a budget, forecast and projection.
- How will you finance the start up of your catering business?
- Research liability insurance needed to protect your catering business.
- Where will you house your catering business office and how will you manage your business? Prepare to think about cancellations, payment policies, consultations, menu-planning as well as samples, contracts and the transportation of food.
- What food suppliers do you intend to work with?
- Will your catering service rent equipment for special requests?
- What will you name your catering business?

  Owning a catering service not only includes cooking but also be prepared to wear many hats such as: accountant, manager, marketer, sales representative, and bill collector. Additional questions to consider when constructing your catering business plan:
  - Is my business idea practical and is it in demand?
  - What is my competition?
  - What is my advantage over existing services?
  - Can I deliver a better quality service?
  - Can I create a demand for my business?
  - What will be my legal structure?
  - How will I compensate myself?

Your answers to these questions will help you create a focused, well-researched catering business plan that can serve as a blueprint for your new catering service.

Whatever you choose to specialize in, running a catering business offers creativity, flexibility, and growing opportunities. Maybe you've got the details of the actual wedding ceremony worked out, but what about the reception?

One of the major costs of the wedding reception will definitely be the food, so you'll want to make sure you'll have enough food for everyone without spending too much money. Here are some top ways to cut on your catering bill that will ensure that your guests enjoy your reception-and you save money. Most couples want to order an extra tray or two of hors d'oeuvres in case extra guests show up.

This is fine but you should still make sure that you're not order more appetizers than you actually need; use your discretion based on the guest list. For instance, if you know a number of your guests are vegetarian, you may not need to order as many appetizers with meat. Also, ordering two or three types of hors d'oeuvres will help to reduce your catering bill. If you buy more of the same dish, you can usually save money with most catering companies-different kinds of foods will increase the bill, so it's important to keep it classy but simple at the wedding-even when it comes to food. Caterers will also try to encourage you to spend more than you may need to on the actual meal as well.

You may not need a five course meal if you've already purchased three types of appetizers and a salad, or three extra desserts if you already have a pretty large wedding cake. The time of day that you hold your wedding will give you a good indication of how much food to serve; if you're having the ceremony in the afternoon or early evening, you may want to serve more food.

There are some foods that are always going to be expensive, even if you only order small amounts. So, since you have to order a considerable amount of food, ordering dishes that aren't so costly will help you to keep your catering bill reasonable. Certain seafood, like shrimp, lobster and salmon will definitely make your catering bill higher, so if you have to have them, try to use them as only one of the course choices for dinner, or purchase these fo1ods as appetizers to save on costs. Food stations are a unique way to serve a variety of foods at your wedding reception, and you can be sure that everyone will find something they like to eat. This way, you won't have to worry about people changing their minds about their meal choices once they arrive at the reception. A food station with different types of pasta is usually a hit with most guests, and can be very economical.

You can also include food stations with other types of the ethnic foods, such as Mexican or Indian fare, to celebrate the cultures of the people who will be attending your wedding, or to acknowledge your backgrounds. You may also be able to cut your catering bill by not requesting an elaborate setup for your food stations and tables. Using a single colour for tablecloths, usually white, will cut down on labour costs.

Index